MANAGEMENT'S CHALLENGE:

THE PEOPLE PROBLEM

MANAGEMENT'S CHALLENGE:

THE PEOPLE PROBLEM

by Samuel Feinberg

Fairchild Publications, Inc.
New York

Library of Congress Catalog Card Number: 75–21952
Standard Book Number: 87005–141–5

Printed in the United States of America

Preface

Most persons, whether in business, government, medicine or education, have average or unexceptional abilities. They live lives of quiet or loud desperation, trying to bluff and/or bluster their way through without being discovered.

During the 1960's, this stratagem was relatively easy. Booming business resulted in shortages of management talent and consequent promotion of many persons to ever higher posts which they were able to fill just so long as products and services virtually sold themselves. However, the slowdown in the economy during the 1970's has tended to show up a substantial number of executives as products of the "Peter Principle": employees advance through jobs until they are promoted beyond their level of competence. The camouflage of a vigorous business climate is dissipated as more average persons come face to face with inescapable and, for them, insoluble problems.

In business firms, certainly in the giant publicly-owned companies, the corporate organization has often replaced individual authority. Men at the top have become coordinators more than commanders. Not infrequently, powers of the chief executive are more fiction than fact. More than ever before, authority as well as responsibility are being delegated, and lower-to-upper-level executives are being permitted to make mistakes—up to a point. There are many senior executives who serve mainly as parental figures, who give encouragement, approval and, sometimes, advice that may or may not be followed.

The wave of the future is participative management—parts played by many people in the decision-making processes that are vital to self-development. Thus, self-development becomes the key to greater volume and profit for the company and promotion for the individual.

The gnawing question still remains: how many subordinates will come through as independent thinkers and how many will need the security of being told what to do and how and when to do it?

Essential to this are managers who listen—the least practiced factor of human relations—who make certain their people are treated as individuals, not as cogs in a wheel, numbers on time-cards, faceless creatures in an automated society. Management can expect only nominal improvement in results unless it demonstrates on a day-to-day basis it truly cares about employees.

Primary responsibility for efficient, effective employer-employee relations, as for customer relations, is up to the supervisory staffs. They have to provide a psychological setting that stimulates people, an environment that lifts morale by providing adequate incentives for initiative, judgment and enthusiasm, an atmosphere of continuing communication and follow-through, and an authority that builds respect, perhaps even regard—certainly not fear.

There is only one way to build a team—by knowing the strengths and weaknesses of all co-workers. On the one hand, there is the minority of men and women who thrive on tough assignments, who are restless achievers, who may well reach the top. On the other hand, there is the majority who must always perform low-to-middle-rank staff and line functions under constant, close supervision.

Current conditions demonstrate that the real leaders, who can move and shake people to better-than-average achievement, are few and far between. Assuming they are more than ordinarily competent themselves—a big assumption—most supervisors at all levels have to compromise, to do the best they can with the best they have at their disposal. The best, unfortunately, may be none too good, but that's life. We can't expect miracles when it comes to human beings; yet we can still hope. Otherwise, who needs psychiatrists or, for that matter, managers?

This book, like "How Do You Manage?," published in 1965, is a distillation and updating of "From Where I Sit" columns in *Women's Wear Daily.* The contents, reflecting changes as well as ongoing trends, cover the spectrum of management and leadership—from communication to the generational gap, from improved productivity to physical and emotional health, from the status of blacks and women to social awareness and responsibility in general. Reflecting the times, it is appropriately titled *Management's Challenge: The People Problem.*

All the material is relevant to the functions of executives in general, to top decision-makers as well as to others at all levels in every business and industrial firm and in every service organization.

The closing paragraph of the 1965 preface bears repetition: "To the victors belong tomorrow's leadership, the spoils of the ever-intensifying competitive race for high individual and mass productivity, for the best sales-and-profit-making brains of the future."

In short, the more things change, the more they stay the same!

Samuel Feinberg

Contents

Chapter 10 EMOTIONAL HEALTH 221

The Enigma That Is the Human Being • Individual Mental Health—Greater Corporate Effectiveness • "Legacy of Neglect": Industrial Mental Health • On-Job Conflicts: Effects on Individual Performance • Taking out Guesswork of Costs of Problem Employees • Boredom Hits Both Executives and Workers • Executive Tension Marks the Man, Not the Job • Four Types of Rigid Executives Have Anxiety Problems • Well-Rounded Man Is a Management Myth

Chapter 11 STRESS AND DISTRESS 243

Each Man Has His Own Breaking Point • One Man's Stress Is Another's Stimulus • Do Executives Take Enough Vacation? • Stress, Anxiety May Be Okay but Watch Out for Panic • Raising Questions Is 50 Percent of Management's Battle • World of Difference between Occupational Stress, Distress • "Strategy of Living" with Anxiety, Fear, Ambition, Envy

Chapter 12 THE MIDLIFE CRISIS 259

Middle Life: Challenge or End of the Line? • Youth Worship in American Society— Its Pros and Cons • "Outplacement"—Help for Person, Saving for Firm • Where Does Early Retiring Leave Off and Firing Begin? • Emotional Problems of Men in Retirement

Chapter 13 HARD CORE PROBLEMS 281

Bernie P.— A Compulsive Gambler Who Kicked the Habit • Problem-Drinking: Industry's Billion-Dollar Hangover • Causes of Drug Problems More Vexing Than Symptoms • Corporate Guide for Employment of Ex-Drug Addicts, Ex-Convicts

Chapter 14 HELP FROM THE EXPERTS 305

What Can Be Done about the Parent, Adult, Child in Us All? • TM: Personalized Technique to Relieve Harmful Stress • Assertiveness Training: "Don't Say Yes When You Want to Say No" • Is Primal Therapy Panacea for Emotional, Physical Ills? • Harvard Class of '49 Turns to Mastering Business of Sex Partnerships • Effect of Sex, Marriage Problems on Job Performance • "Shared Participation": Key to Riddle of Human Behavior?

1

TAKE IT FROM THE TOP

Penney's Strategies

J.C. Penney Co., the nation's No. 2 chain, represents the most remarkable metamorphosis of any retail company.

From a largely cash-and-carry, popular-price dry goods chain in smaller western and midwestern towns in 1958, the company has expanded into hard lines, credit and mail-order selling, separate divisions of discount, drug and supermarket stores, auto accessories and servicing and all forms of insurance by mail. It has entered the Belgian, Italian, and Japanese markets and is working on a joint venture in Canada. All told, Penney has more than two thousand retail units.

Father of Penney's transformation is William M. Batten, who retired as chairman and chief executive officer in 1974 but is still a director. Batten, who started at the company as a part-time salesman, became a vice-president in 1953 and a director in 1955. In 1957, he submitted to the board a memorandum of suggestions that became the basis of the present organization. The board authorized a continuing study to determine strategies. Batten was elected president and chief executive officer the following year to execute his concept. He was promoted to chairman in 1964.

Outwardly serious, Batten has a sense of humor that often reveals itself in a quick, warm smile or hearty chuckle. As is generally true of all Penney executives, Batten is without airs. Retired president Cecil L. Wright traces this down-to-earth trait to the fact that "so many of us came up from scrubbing floors."

Batten responded to the following questions:

Q. How did you follow up on whether you had effective communications up and down the line of command?

A. Despite efforts considerably more comprehensive than a few years ago, communications is one of the biggest areas still needing improvement. We're not satisfied that people are listening and understanding. Problems of keeping people tuned in, and how they fit in, are a monumental task. I don't think we'll ever reach the optimum where everybody will know everything he wants to know—or should know.

Q. How did you assure yourself of managers motivated to increase their competence, and that of their subordinates, rather than to guard their spheres of influence and thwart others' ambitions, initiative, and nonconformity?

A. There is no complete answer. Imperfections of human nature are always at work. The superior who always finds people mediocre tells us we've got a problem in *him,* in his ability to train, keep, and furnish us with people for promotion. A store manager who's always losing people is a parasite and suspect as a manager.

Q. What are the qualities you look for in potential top managers?

A. No. 1 on the list: the fundamental virtues of truthfulness and integrity. Without these, there is no point in talking about anything else. I have also looked for management skills of analysis. Are people willing to sacrifice the long-term, healthy growth of the company for a quick sales gain three months from now? I look for poise, inner toughness, staying power, the ability to relate the present to the future and not give in to pressures of today and perhaps destroy something of real value.

Q. Do you believe organizational loyalty is dead, that talented employees feel freer to look elsewhere for greater immediate opportunity than they did in the past?

A. I would quarrel with this statement, just as I would with any other generalizations. In technical areas such as data processing, people are more loyal to their profession in a sense than to a particular company. But I don't feel this is true in merchandising.

True, people will not stay too long on any job if they think they're promotable. Failure to use human resources and potential is the greatest failure any company can have. I have tried to make certain that persons with higher-career objectives achieve these in our company, or elsewhere if need be. If there's some other company or some other industry that's best for somebody at Penney, we tell him, "good luck; you've got one life." If we have a place for them, we'll take back people who feel they've made mistakes in leaving us, who have found out the grass elsewhere was not as green as they thought it would be. They may be better people than when they left us.

Lack of technological or merchandising knowledge caused us to bring in new people for such areas as credit, data processing, systems engineering, operations research, furniture, major appliances, and automotive service stations. We had no "faculty." But we now have capable teachers among our own people, have set up our own training centers, and are compelled less and less to hire anybody from the outside.

We now have many more opportunities within our company. We have much greater dimensions—everything is open. But everybody doesn't want to be president or chairman; a person may like the area he's in and doesn't aspire to the pressures of higher positions.

Q. What is the greatest challenge facing senior management?

A. To try to build the kind of total environment that motivates our 200,000 associates [Penney doesn't use the word "employees"] to do their best. More self-starters—people at all levels whose bosses make them feel they're more than Social Security numbers. It's terribly important, too, that people have fun doing their jobs. If they don't have fun, they're not doing their jobs or there's something wrong with them or with the company. Every organization has so much potential power, pent up within its people, that it has not yet been able to unleash. We're still trying to unlock the key to this enigma.

Q. What about consumerism and other facets of the social scene?

A. I have sought to help increase the awareness of our people of the role of our company in terms of its contribution to society. We can no more stand aside from a social revolution than from an economic revolution. We can no more have a healthy business in a sick society than we can in a depression. Penney cannot pursue its own gain independently of the larger social gain. There are things we, as a company, can and must do to make a unique contribution to the quality of life in this country.

Characteristically, Batten responded with a self-deprecating laugh to the question: "What do you conceive was your special contribution to Penney as its chief executive officer?" His reply, after some reflection: "I hope that, by the way I operated, I set an example for some of the things that are important. What I said was not as influential as what I did. The speeches I made or conversations I had with my officers were not as effective as setting an example for the organization in fulfilling my duties in the longer-term, longer-range direction, the overall strategies, and representation of the company in outside affairs."

Now at the Penney helm are Donald V. Seibert, Batten's successor, and Walter J. Neppl, president and head of day-to-day operations since April,

1976. Seibert, who was born August 17, 1923, began at Penney as a shoe clerk in 1947 and, prior to assuming the top post, was vice-president and director of corporate planning and development. He made his real reputation building the catalog division from small beginnings. Neppl was born June 15, 1922 and rose through the Penney ranks to executive vice-president in 1972 before becoming president.

The all-important roles of Penney associates were underlined in the 1974 management conferences in Florida and California. The theme was "The Penney Difference"—which to Seibert "comes through as the vision and spirit of our people." About forty-five hundred associates, representing all phases of the chain's domestic and international operations, plus wives or husbands, attended one of the two gatherings. The conferences, in a tradition set by James Cash Penney, who founded the company in Kemmerer, Wyo., in 1902, used to be held every two years. Now, they are quadrennial.

The 1974 conferences were the first in which Penney's managers played major roles in discussions. In the past, these gatherings were largely confined to the top command's speeches which, of course, remain a must. Seibert credits Jack B. Jackson, Neppl's predecessor as president, with the change to "participation by our people. The more they participate, the more they take back with them."

Federated's Top Successors in Wings

Chairman Ralph Lazarus and president Harold Krensky, the two top executives of Federated Department Stores, plan to retire by 1980.

Lazarus, who is also chief executive officer, says the giant chain hopes to be under "successor management" by 1980.

The Federated chain, with 1974 volume of about $3,300,000,000, is the top-ranking traditional department-store organization. In 1974, too, its 4.6 percent profit made it the outstanding performer in that respect among both conventional and general merchandise chains.

Lazarus' retirement schedule is a year later than the outside date he had set for himself several years ago when he said: "I plan to retire when I see it's better for the business—but definitely by 65" to pursue "a second career—it could be in higher education or urban problems." By that reckoning, Lazarus, who joined the Lazarus store in 1935, became president in 1957, chief executive officer in 1960 and chairman in 1967 and who was 62 on Jan. 30, 1976, would retire on or before the same day of 1979.

Now, he says: "If I can retire properly before the mandatory date (an age-65 retirement schedule becomes effective in February, 1976), I will. If I can't, I won't. If the corporation is not in shape, the board may want to keep us on."

Krensky remarks: "What Ralph has said applies exactly to me."

Lazarus discloses he and Krensky do not plan to phase out together. Apparently, the latter would retire earlier, as he is 20 months older than Lazarus. However, the chairman warns, "Don't take anything for granted. Exact dates are very imprecise. Conditions could change. Harold or I could be hit by a streetcar tomorrow."

In any event, the end of the two-generation reign of "the Lazari"— Ralph's father was Fred Lazarus Jr., a founder of the chain—looms by the end of this decade. For the first time in almost half a century, a non-Lazarus will be at Federated's helm.

Asked to name their probable successors, Lazarus shies away from being any more specific than: "We're pretty much on schedule as to who our successors are likely to be. There are half a dozen identifiable candidates, more or less. The number and the individuals are fluid. We have the best harvest of possible successors since 1952, when I became executive vice-president." There's a trace of a smile as he says this.

"No, I won't tell you who they are. The organization structure could be different at the time a new chairman and president are elected. Outside directors are involved in this with us."

Krensky, who began his Federated career at a Filene's subsidiary in 1943 and rose to group president in 1969, vice-chairman in 1971 and president in 1973, interpolates: "Anyone who comes up with a good track record can put his hat into the ring. It could be a person who is now a virtual unknown."

Lazarus and Krensky are asked whether the committee members of the Vista program provide the most likely, not to say most visible, line of succession to Federated's throne room at this juncture. Lazarus describes Vista, his brainchild, as "a bottom-to-top and top-to-bottom review and analysis of customers, employees, buildings and businesses—of what we are doing, what we should be doing in the future and how we should go about it. The only requirement is to challenge anything and everything without regard to tradition or assumptions that might have governed our thinking in the past."

(More on Vista later.)

The chairman agrees, "Some of our ablest people are among the committee members. But some others, not on the committees, are breaking into new jobs and have not yet been asked to join one or more of the committees. We don't want to take them away at this time from their regular duties." Krensky adds: "New committees may be formed and present committees changed or dropped. They'll never be static. We'll rotate people. Names of members could change within three months."

Lazarus and Krensky make no bones about admitting these men are bright stars in the Federated firmament, but caution against any interpretation that they have thereby been necessarily tapped as their successors.

Aside from the status of leadership among the First Families of Federated, the monetary rewards for the chairman and president are among the half-dozen highest in retailing. Under three-year contracts given them at the 1974 annual board meeting, Lazarus' pay was set at $300,000 plus lifetime annual retirement allowances of $90,000; Krensky's at $285,000 and $65,000 respectively.

However, Lazarus sees a difference between leadership and power: "Leadership is the ability to allow people to do their jobs in a constantly improved way on their own—in other words, to have the leader work himself out of a job. There are people who have power but not leadership."

To reports of lack of sufficient able middle-management in some divisions, the chairman comments: "There's always a scarcity of middle-management. But our middle-management is now stronger than in many a year. By and large, we take fewer people from the outside." Krensky adds, "The lifeblood of any business is to have people come up through the ranks, to have a very strong bench. We develop more of our own than most stores. Yes, we've played the checkerboard game, but the keystone of a successful, well-managed business is to have successors ready to step up when people leave or pass on."

Questioned on the absence of female presidents in Federated divisions and in retailing in general, Lazarus replies: "There is no reason why a woman should not be president of one of our department stores at the right place at the right time. When that will happen, I can't predict." Krensky: "There are women in our organization who, with further development, could become a president."

At this time, they say, the chain has "quite a few" women in important positions. The corporation reports that 44.5 percent of its store officials and managers are females. On the corporate front, Phyllis Sewell, vice-president for marketing research, is the top woman in the Cincinnati home office, and Jenna Lou Tonner is operating vice-president for executive search in Federated's New York corporate office.

On equal employment opportunity, Federated has increased the number of its minority employees from 15.8 to 16.4 percent of its total employee population of 86,000.

Lazarus on social responsibility: "We encourage young people to engage in social programs in the conviction that we're as much a community organization as a corporate organization. I don't know what tests leadership more than to give our people lessons in leadership where they're not getting a paycheck signed by our company." All levels of management at the nineteen store divisions and corporate headquarters of Federated Department Stores have embarked on a program of introspective evaluation, called "Vista."

Lazarus calls this program "the most comprehensive, most searching self-examination" Federated has undergone in its almost half-century history.

He emphasizes that a greater number of management people than in the past will be directly involved in expanding business in existing divisions and locations and in entering new markets in "our stepped-up program for seeking a maximum share of volume and profit in our trading areas." Of primary significance, Lazarus adds, is Vista's aim to nurture and unearth executive talent for Federated's leadership in the 1980s in succession to the current top corporate and divisional command.

Lazarus' capsule view of Vista's destination: "1) To help keep us flexible and more responsive to our customers. 2) To broaden and develop our future management. 3) To intensify our profit opportunities."

Vista was broached as a permanent management tool by Lazarus at the conclusion of an annual meeting of store principals in March 1974. At that time, the chairman suggested the groundwork for the undertaking: "We've got our house pretty much in order but we ought to take a good look at our problems and opportunities. What should we do to 'own' more customers? How should each of our businesses be organized to get the best people to run these organizations? How should we better explore the uses of the computer?

"Let's start this program from scratch with no sacred cows. We can't adapt from someone else because, then, it would be only a top-down program that couldn't ensure people development. Each division should work with all its bright people in taking a new look at where the divisions and the corporation will be five, ten and more years from now. Let's refine divisional and corporate concepts and develop papers in a collective critique that will give the corporation and its divisions greater professionalism.

"No matter how well we may have coped with change, the people who run our stores are understandably wary of the future and the even greater change it promises. Population growth is slowing. The explosive suburban expansion of the '60s is largely behind us. Life styles continue to proliferate as America learns to enjoy its new diversity. But what else may lie ahead is not altogether clear. Each division is now conducting a bottoms-up review and analysis of its business: where it is now, where it would like to go, how it might get there, what it knows and what it needs to know."

Lazarus adds: "We're trying to challenge the basic principles of organization that have been part of our mentality since the 1920s and see whether these apply to tomorrow's business. We think it is of utmost importance to make increased use of the talents of hundreds of our people at all management levels in this in-depth program and build more understanding between them and corporate leadership. We want to involve divisional managers more in corporate affairs and have more young people participate in the direction of their stores. I doubt that we have listened enough to them in the past. We will do so in the future."

Seven subcommittees of store principals are engaged in long-range business and people planning, total management information, organization planning, new business and market opportunities, customer payment and credit practices, study of executive compensation and study of corporate services as these apply to store divisions.

In-store and special-study groups have been formed and talented young people have joined top management in drawing a new roadmap to Federated's future. The 19 divisional plans are being analyzed by men and women from division and corporate levels both for action and for exploratory research that may be required by some divisions into unsolved problems.

"Each roadmap," according to Lazarus, "is separate and distinct as it has always been in Federated's successful philosophy of autonomy. We ask only that each division keep itself young and fresh with common principles and objectives."

The Krensky Style

Is Harold Krensky too good to be true?

Ask a dozen former associates, manufacturers and other longtime observers of the president of Federated Department Stores what makes him tick, why and how he rose in three decades to the No. 2 post in the hierarchy of the No. 1 conventional department store chain. You are deluged in a plethora of encomiums that add up to a stereotype of a peerless, flawless Horatio Alger hero.

Of whom else would it be said he is all of these things: charming, sincere, warm, bright, perceptive, intuitive, modest, relaxed, brilliant, exciting, humane?

The mind reels at the thought there isn't a chink in his armor.

What else to do, then, than to confront Superman and seek to uncover the person behind the legend?

Conceding "the skills needed to merchandise goods are highly important," Krensky is nevertheless convinced "the skills of a professional manager in building an organization are one of the most significant ingredients in the growth of a retail business. I like people, I like working with people, and I hope I am developing people."

Krensky-watchers think merchandising of people, personal creativity, and motivating others are his greatest strengths, although they're not belittling his ability with figures. Krensky's comment: "To be people-oriented is to be profit-oriented."

When he was a merchandise manager at Bloomingdale's, Krensky suggested it was his job to shape, mold, and, in a sense, serve as a father-confessor, as a friend, rather than a boss or one who second-guesses buyers. The influence he wielded over his people at Bloomingdale's was clearly reflected in the enthusiasm a buyer expressed about Krensky's return from Filene's: "When I had a problem, he was the kind of man who always lent a sympathetic ear." When a buyer was through explaining her dilemma—business or personal—he gave her a box of paper tissues he kept in the bottom drawer of his desk so she could blow her nose or wipe away her tears.

How does he hope to translate best divisional merchandising and operating achievements into better performance chainwide?

"What you're really asking me is: 'What the hell is your job?' My contribution is to help people motivate themselves, to work with the divisions to develop the concepts of the business for continued growth, to play a highly supportive role in this development. 'Supportive' is the key word."

The extreme delicacy of the task is understandable when it is considered that Krensky has to deal with the chief executive officers, whose titles may be chairman or president, of nineteen divisions.

Obviously talking about something to which he has devoted a lot of thought, the Federated executive remarks:
"There are three forms of merchandising: merchandising people, merchandising merchandise, and merchandising figures. Usually, one individual cannot do all three. If he can, he's a rare gem. You're trying to effect a marriage of creativity and technical skills, of a Picasso and an Einstein, a combination you seldom meet. So, you take a guy with major skills and try to surround him with others of different skills and you compose a team. That's what retailing is all about. It shouldn't and can't be a one-man business.

"The objective of personal communication, as I see it, is to convert corporate goals into satisfactory results, the only feedback that means anything. It is just as important for me to hear what our people are saying as for them to hear what I'm saying. If you listen, you don't necessarily hear; and, if you look, you don't necessarily see. I know people who walk through stores and hear and see very little."

What are the characteristics he looks for in potential top managers?

"All the normal skills of professional management. To try to find and develop creativity in people and, most important, to determine what motivates the individual so you may employ the necessary techniques to motivate that person to do a superior job. Motivation is probably one of the most unsung, most important elements in the retail business. In a business that is so dependent on proper management of so many people, motivation of those with the proper skills must be continuous. You must study the individual, what makes him tick. As a manager, you must ask yourself: What the hell will motivate this guy—is it status, is it security, is it money? Or is it fulfillment and achievement. This takes a pretty mature person.

"You're talking about taking average people—and most of us are average —and getting them to perform in a better than average manner. This is where most stores can do a better job."

May's Way of Life

"If we two were not here running the company today, we believe that Management by Objectives would still continue as a management style. Of course, it would be changed every year as it has until now."

The speaker, David E. Babcock, was looking at Stanley J. Goodman. Babcock was then president and chief administrative officer, and Goodman chairman and chief executive officer of the May Department Stores Co., No. 2 conventional chain. They were being interviewed on the chain's seven-year progress with MBO.

Montreal-born Goodman, who was sixty-five in March, 1975, relinquished the board chairmanship three months later to Babcock, born in 1914, but remained as chief executive officer. David C. Farrell succeeded Babcock as president at 42. Farrell was previously president of the Kaufmann's division, the chain's top performer in profit-to-sales ratio. He moved to May's St. Louis headquarters in the spring of 1975. Goodman continued as chairman of the executive committee until the spring of 1976. At that time, Babcock became chief executive officer.

MBO, as May's vehicle for professional, participative management and organization development, includes:

- Written job descriptions and clarified lines of authority and responsibility.
- Work-progress reviews at frequent intervals throughout the year.
- Frank interchange of information and ideas between executives and their superiors to facilitate feedbacks on employee attitudes at all management levels and dissipate command authority.
- Appraising individual and divisional results against objectives, and corporate results against objectives and against the results of other companies.
- Thorough self-appraisal, a greater voice for lower-to-middle management people in reviewing their own results against established objectives.

Goodman and Babcock believe "every man and woman can improve their performance on the job through self-development, and this can be accelerated by providing a climate that will encourage each person to give total personal involvement and commitment." In furthering personal goals through attainment of corporate objectives, May's top team is convinced MBO is "the only means to produce long-range quality profit."

At Babcock's suggestion, Goodman and divisional presidents attended chief-executive courses at American Management Associations. Then, in-company and college sessions were held successively for executives reporting to store presidents and for those reporting to vice-presidents. These were followed by meetings of buyers and assistant buyers.

Babcock prepared a store president's position description and performance standards, "the base line from which excellence begins," in a thirty-nine-page manual for in-company consumption.

Major Functions of Store President. To provide leadership that will result in:

1. Achievement of store's annual objectives and long-range plans.
2. Constant building of store's reputation for value, fashion, quality, and service.
3. Development of an organization which permits store and company to achieve long-range plans, and every person to achieve his full potential.

Specific Duty and Responsibility. Responsible for development of:

1. Long-range plans optimizing store's opportunities for growth.
2. Annual goals and objectives consistent with long-range plans.
3. Plans for facilities adequate to achieve store's long-range plans.
4. Strategies permitting store to take advantage of opportunities for new and enlarged business.
5. A plan of organization satisfying needs of store and company.
6. Information systems that measure performance, permit executives at all levels to control their operations, and foster decision-making at the lowest possible level.
7. High morale and feeling of participation at all levels in management of the company.
8. Appraisal systems that measure performance and show clearly the organizational strength of store in relation to needs.
9. Store philosophy and policy, and communication of these to personnel responsible for their implementation.

Within four years, all the companies had carried MBO down through the middle-management level. However, the key word at all levels has remained "implementation."

Goodman started the conversation:

"I was not raised in MBO and am not a lifelong MBOer, as Dave is. But I can say it's been a great success in constantly training executives. Much of our achievement of the past seven years can be associated with the thrust of MBO in the business. In our business, we need things that are working for us all the time—automatically. Much of the fun we get out of our unulcerated business lives is because MBO has reduced a hell of a lot of tension, lack of self-confidence, uncertainty, insecurity, back-biting, and confusion—all the factors that limit people's effectiveness. We believe our general level of effectiveness is one of the best in retailing.

"We have gone through a development process in the company. Our eleven department store operating companies are managed with a certain amount of autonomy, and we don't dictate centrally what they should do or nag them. Each has moved in its own way.

"In everything in life, there's content and form. Content involves how to achieve earnings and growth through actual objectives and job descriptions. Form is the professionalism brought to running a business—this may be compared with the form you bring to playing golf or tennis.

"Why is the human-relations approach to management made much better through MBO? Because the relationship of an executive with his boss has to include times when the boss wants him to do things he's not doing to improve his performance. Without MBO, the boss is in a position where he has to sound critical. Then, you get the defensive human reaction of a man when he's being criticized. Instead, we ask for a regular updating when he tells us himself how he's doing."

Goodman pointed out: "As a nation, we must integrate social and economic goals and, as business managers; we must be judged not for the quantity but the quality of profits. High profits for the most efficient should never be thought of as going counter to the social needs of our society, because it is precisely the companies good enough to achieve high profits in a competitive environment that will be good enough to get results on social problems."

May's chairman terms social responsibility "a good example where MBO is helpful. Social responsibility is in the written objectives in every one of our companies, for me, for the president, and for each of the company principals. This is the perfect example of the value of MBO because, if you didn't put it in the form of a written objective reviewed periodically, social responsibility would amount only to periodic nagging by the boss."

Babcock picked up the discussion:

"MBO makes people more adult in that they learn how to be self-critical. Many people are brilliant but cannot see themselves as wrong about anything, certainly not in overall judgment. It's very difficult for a man to tell his boss or his wife how he's doing. An annual review, as such, is traditionally a moment of truth. A man goes in with trepidation when he's asked to give an objective report of himself. But under MBO, as we seek to practice it, people are trained to understand they can give us their performance ratings on specific objectives and admit their inadequacy in certain respects. A response beyond 'great' to the question 'How are you doing?', a meaningful dialog, are encouraged only in an atmosphere in which corporate and divisional management say to their respective subordinates: 'It's your session, start talking.' Executives reporting to us know that if they are properly self-critical, we will be properly supportive of them and help with particular objectives that may require strengthening. Similarly with divisional executives, most of whom are reviewed by their company heads at least four times a year, we've learned that the guy who is really self-critical of his results and frank in his self-appraisal has the mark of a great executive."

At this stage of MBO development, subsidiary presidents have each year sent the chairman updated self-appraisals of their own performance. Goodman or Babcock have then sat down with each man and talked it over.

Goodman and Babcock have spent the full month of March each year on annual reviews. Each company spends a month on the same task. Goodman said "the time is the price of admission. You can't do MBO unless you devote that much time to it."

Goodman: "Dave and I would be the last persons in the world to tell you the formal MBO program has gone down into the salesperson level. Naturally, the mere fact that all the supervisors are in MBO must be reflected in some application of it at the sales level. In many cases, our companies work with salespeople on productivity objectives, and that is in the MBO picture."

Babcock: "There has to be a rub-off on salespeople, but you can't look for the formal content of having salespeople with, say, eight objectives. As you narrow the list of responsibilities, it's much more difficult to set objectives."

Goodman stressed that "size of itself is not our objective. It's the quality of earnings that matters to us." Babcock remarked: "The only thing that counts is the quality of earnings. After all, you could cut expenses to the bone or not spend capital budgets and improve earnings. But that's not quality of earnings. We're making progress in that respect through professional management."

Babcock went on: "Basically, we have not deviated, even when our figures were down, from what we said in 1967 we would do. We have changed our MBO procedures somewhat by emphasizing the human relations part of management. We have gone further down the road with a self-appraisal approach, begun about 1968, and have procedurized the hell out of it to make it simpler."

Goodman: "We have always taken the long view of objectives, not flash-in-the-pan results."

Goodman summed up: "We don't for a moment want anyone to think our MBO program is *it*, that we hold it up as a model for everybody. All we can report is that we in May's top management have embraced it, each of our companies sees the value of playing the game, and it's worked out very well for us. But we don't want to give the impression we're the greatest or that this is the only way to manage. What we're saying is: If you want to win the game, you should have the natural aptitude plus the best possible form. MBO, we think, is the best possible form. But the quality of the people is even more important than the form. Again, we want to emphasize, we haven't invented anything. [Peter Drucker coined the MBO phrase in 1957.] We've simply brought aspects of behavioral sciences from industry into retailing."

Babcock interjected: "We have found—and not to our surprise—that strong people can be taught to manage and that good managers can be made better."

Babcock is convinced that, "if, by their management style, you can tell who the chief executive officer is, then you can't have a really good tandem team. In day-to-day operations of the president and the chairman, it should become apparent they're a tandem—not one the boss, and the other the subordinate."

"The ideal tandem," Babcock feels, "is a man who has a strong administrative background and another man who has a strong merchandising background."

He was obviously referring to Goodman and himself as well as other top management teams of major subsidiary companies in the May organization. Goodman's background, since he joined May twenty-seven years ago, is almost entirely in merchandising. Babcock has been in personnel work in his twenty-nine years in retailing, seven at May Co.

Out of Carter's Steel-Trap Mind

What in others might be deemed pomposity and vanity comes out of the steel-trap mind of Edward William Carter as an objective presentation of the brilliant results of his vision and boldness through the years. Carter is chairman of Carter Hawley Hale Stores, renamed in 1974 from Broadway-Hale Stores.

In the thirty years since he joined the then three-unit, $40 million-volume Broadway Department Store in Los Angeles, the company has grown into a chain of department and specialty stores which went over the $1.2 billion mark in 1974.

In his particularly soft-spoken manner, Carter replies to a number of questions:

"For many years, I have sought to spend one-third of my time on outside activities—educational and cultural matters and a number of diversified directorates. There have always been three facets in my life—art and music, business, and education. These have broadened me and made me a better merchant.

"Operation of major retail businesses is as intricate a process as any in the business spectrum. Professional management—applying scientific business principles—has more and more replaced the entrepreneurs who founded and carried on family businesses.

"Only when the student has been prepared with a first-class liberal arts education should he be taught business administration.

"At the undergraduate level, students have better use for their time than studying business. They should be dealing with liberal arts rather than vocational things. They are then ill-prepared to grasp concepts of business management except to obtain a working knowledge of the tools of such subjects as accounting and statistics. These should be a relatively small part of the curriculum. Increasingly, executives of major businesses—retail, financial, and manufacturing—must be broad-gauged human beings.

"At our company, we take some graduates from liberal arts, some from graduate school. Certainly, there's a place for all kinds of people—high school graduates, too. But I think the opportunities for success at the executive level are much more limited for those who have not had the advantage of a college education." Carter smilingly concedes "a good number" of CHH executives have had graduate or mid-career training at Harvard Business School, his alma mater.

"The well-educated young man," Carter continues, "has tended to do very well here. But we are careful not to take more people than we can absorb. The best ones want to assume responsibility as early as possible, and we must bear this in mind consistent with their abilities."

Asked what he looks for in potential executives, Carter ticks off "character, health, intelligence, breadth of vision, an intangible ability to get on well with people, motivation, strong leadership ability, and technical competence."

For best corporate results, Carter concludes, "divisional chiefs must relate to headquarters executives because such rapport will make divisional functions more efficient. However, corporate executives must be wise enough not to interfere in areas that can be adequately managed locally. Above all, they should avoid taking credit for decisions or implementation of decisions at the local level that may turn out to be more effective."

Philip M. Hawley, joined Broadway-Hale in 1958 and became president in 1972 at forty-six. He is Carter's heir-apparent; the chairman has described him as "the foremost young executive in America today and my natural successor when I retire."

Equally as soft-spoken as Carter, Hawley asserts that "the role of management at the corporate level should be to stimulate thinking but not usurp decision-making. Local autonomy becomes more important as a business grows larger. Satisfied and challenged people are a key to success. I try to inspire my management team. I try to lead my people and be their partner. I set the standards. But I don't attempt to do the job for them. You really don't know how good your people are unless you give them responsibility. I don't hand them a roadmap and then try to drive, too. If they start heading the wrong way, I stop them."

Macioce's Concern About People
As Well As Sales

"I'm not enough of an expert to be able to buy for a store, but I am a merchant in the sense that I know enough to manage a retail chain intelligently."

Thomas M. Macioce, president and chief executive officer, heads Allied Stores Corp., third largest in volume among traditional department store chains.

While his background gives him strengths in financial areas and in management control, he also believes in having "an awareness of the sensitivities and concerns of the people with whom you come in contact."

His rise within the chain, since joining it in 1960, reflects the Horatio Alger aspects of his life.

Macioce, an earnest advocate of the American system that permits a boy to rise from an East Harlem birthplace in 1919 to the top post in a major corporation, says: "I have always followed one basic philosophy in my lifestyle and business career: You meet the same guys on the way down that you meet on the way up. So you had better pave your road to success with integrity, honesty, solid friendship."

He claims he has always been a "people" man, largely due to the influence of his father, a self-educated barber who came here from Italy, and to his associates at Columbia College and Columbia Law school where he was a scholarship student.

The Allied chief is "convinced that the only way to build a great organization is not to ask a man his statistical age but to allow him the autonomy and latitude to perform the best job of which he is capable, not what you predetermine to be his potential. A chief executive's job, and the degree to which a chief executive is able to remain in control of his job, depends on surrounding himself with executives willing to assume responsibility, with people who come to him with problems for whose solutions they are ready to make recommendations.

"The job of the chief executive is to evaluate strengths and weaknesses of recommendations made without fear and then to make the ultimate decision. If you operate a business where all executives bring you their problems without encouraging them to develop their own analytical ability, if you do not have the ability to listen, you are only molding people into your own rigid thinking. You tend to lose young people by an autocratic, strong-willed approach."

Macioce, who started as a lawyer, agrees that "offering opportunities to general management people such as me, as well as to those with buying and merchandising background, to rise to the head of a company is a healthy thing. To select one area of experience arbitrarily over another is to swing the pendulum too far in either direction. As time goes on, merchants will also need expertise in finance, credit, real estate, and consumerism."

When Macioce guided the interviewer on a tour of Allied headquarters, he put out lights in a number of unoccupied offices. Without any embarrassment, he observed: "I watch expenses in a minute sense as an example to others. The fastest way to earn a dollar is to start with saving pennies."

Macioce's base salary in 1974 was $175,000, an increase of $25,000 over the previous year. A subsequent four-year contract calls for maximum aggregate base salary and other compensation of $325,000 in 1975, $350,000 in 1976, $375,000 in 1977, and $400,000 in 1978.

As a final thought, Macioce ventures: "There's nothing like success to make you feel great."

Behind One of Retailing's Greatest Success Stories

Ultimate strength and lasting qualities of any organization are dependent on a four-pronged doctrine of management.

This is the advice of Harry B. Cunningham, honorary chairman, S.S. Kresge Co.

Cunningham is the father of Kresge's K mart discount department store division—one of the greatest success stories in retail history. K mart is number one among discount department store chains, and its parent is number three (after Sears, Roebuck and J.C. Penney) among the general merchandise chains.

Cunningham spells out the four tenets of Kresge's management philosophy:

1. There must be primary concentration on the organization's strengths. The chief executive should be acquainted with his associates' weaknesses as well as their strengths, but he should focus on capabilities.

"I am convinced," Cunningham explains, "that failure to build on strength is the most common management weakness. There is a natural tendency in every large organization to concentrate on weakness because personnel appraisal forms and supervisors' reports normally stress areas needing improvement. But, if this necessary reporting is not offset by emphasis on the positive, the result can be deleterious. Supervisory people may think the best way to improve their status with their superiors is to find as much fault as possible with their subordinates. It becomes obvious that the sharp guys are those who never overlook a weakness. So everybody criticizes, and the entire organization becomes dispirited."

The tragic consequence of this kind of executive orientation, Cunningham continues, is loss of confidence by top management. The chief executive sees mostly unfavorable performance reports and, inevitably, deteriorating operation figures. He then becomes defensive and may concentrate on expense reduction, which results in worsening morale. He may try to fall back on the "tried and true" principles responsible for the company's success in "the good old days." But he hesitates to innovate because he has really lost faith.

"The effective manager," according to Cunningham, "is always intelligently optimistic. He knows he doesn't have a company full of superior people. But he also knows that superior work can be performed by ordinary individuals, even in an unfamiliar area, if they are sufficiently challenged —and if top management demonstrates beyond any doubt it has complete confidence in the capacity of its people to handle the new assignment.

"So, when the chief executive decides to steer his company in a new direction or try a different business for which the organization seems ill-prepared, he doesn't wait until experts in the new field can be hired. He goes ahead with what he has."

2. The exciting and social aspects of the corporation's business should be emphasized. "In addition to the opportunities for advancement provided by the tenfold increase in our sales and profits, being part of the world's fastest growing major retailing company has been a heady experience for everybody at Kresge."

3. Effective management must be participative. The most powerful stimulus to progress by an organization is its morale. Without esprit de corps, the best management plan is doomed to failure. A strong executive may produce a short-term coup without giving primary consideration to employee attitudes, but there is no business corporation with a consistent growth pattern that doesn't have extraordinary morale. Developing and maintaining this spirit requires much more than monetary recognition, but financial compensation, based on achievement, is a good place to start. That's why all Kresge executives (including every store manager) have incentive contracts. The company also has an attractive stock purchase plan for over twenty-five thousand key employees. But the most essential factor in morale is a sense of contribution at all levels of the organization.

The chief executive should keep open all pipelines of upward communication and encourage well-reasoned dissent. And he must be willing to reverse his own decision when it is obvious a policy needs changing. It is not enough to say he welcomes constructive suggestions—he must show he depends on the counsel of his immediate subordinates and that he expects them to maintain this same relationship with their staffs. There is a fine line here. Carried too far, participative management can result in chaos. And there are times when the boss is a minority of one—when he must have the courage to make lonely decisions if he is convinced his course is right, or even if he just thinks the percentages are with him. But unwillingness to listen to contrary opinions is a sure indication of weakness.

4. The chief executive and the entire organization must be constantly receptive to change. New ideas are almost always disruptive, and it is natural for affected people to oppose them. Moreover, a majority of new theories are unworkable—perhaps even dangerous—and it is easy for the boss to become irritated by having time and money seemingly wasted on them. But, if he lets that attitude show, he does a terrible disservice to the future of his company.

Cunningham concludes by quoting Sir Hugh Walpole, English novelist-critic: "Don't play for safety. It's the most dangerous game in the world."

Filling The Management Succession Pipeline

Rawleigh Warner, Jr., spends "a great deal of time wondering and worrying" how to assure a management-succession pipeline filled with well-trained, strongly motivated, high-potential individuals "to take on the larger and more demanding problems and positions of the 1970s and 1980s."

Warner has been chairman and chief executive officer of Mobil Oil Corp. since July 29, 1969. Born in Chicago February 13, 1921, he went into the investment business in his native city and then joined Continental Oil Co. where he rose to assistant to the president. With Mobil since 1953, he started as assistant to the financial director of Socony-Vacuum Overseas Supply Co., name of a former subsidiary and, after eight promotions, became president of the parent corporation in 1965.

A cross-section of economists and financial analysts rates Mobil the best managed of the major oil companies. By coincidence or not, Mobil is the only one of the five largest oil companies to have a bachelor of arts (Princeton) as chairman and a bachelor of business administration (St. John's University) as president (William P. Tavoulareas). The top executives of the other four concerns are all engineers.

"The thing you spend most time on, the single most important thing, is people," Warner observes. "One of the nice things about coming up on the financial side is that you're exposed to all kinds of problems. The name of the game is profits. And profits happen only through people."

Questions put to Warner on early identification and development of management talent for the long-range success of the corporation and his replies:

Q. How do you follow up on whether you have effective communication and feedback up and down the line of command?

A. This is done largely by setting Management by Objectives both for division and individuals. I sit down with all fellows who report directly to me, and we go over each one's goals for the past year, as written down by him, and what he has accomplished. Each person and I can check in December what was actually said in January, not what we thought was said then. The subordinate can't think I wasn't being fair to him if his performance fails to measure up to written objectives, and I can't think the job wasn't done properly if it does measure up. We seek to have a climate rather than a structured environment. This is done by making it possible for all employees to say what they feel, not what they think I want to hear. Our people must be perfectly free to demonstrate their creativity and initiative. If something results from this independent thinking, we want to be sure they get individual credit for it. What we do at meetings of the executive committee of the eight inside directors, who meet twice a week with managers whose activities are being considered, is repeated at all other levels.

Q. To what extent do you delegate authority as well as responsibility?

A. Since 1959, the organization has been restructured by decentralizing authority, decision-making, and responsibility within the various divisions, and by centralizing only planning and programming. Each year, we have been refining this procedure of getting managers to make the gutsy decisions to achieve what they want to achieve, of giving each division a certain amount of money to spend as well as they can. Any manager who has an involvement of more than $5 million must come to the executive committee for approval. Above $2 million and up to $5 million, the chairman or the president can approve. Capital expenditures up to $2 million fall under four executive vice-presidents.

Q. What do you do about people who have stayed too long on one job, have lost interest in it, and are not working at full potential?

A. An awful lot of people rise to certain jobs and then level off. We keep them there so long as they are making a contribution and have an open mind about developing people to the utmost, about not blocking their advancement. The thing that's most difficult to evaluate in precise terms is ability to develop people. There really is nothing more important. Almost the hardest task of an existing management is the quality of the people that it leaves behind to carry on the job. People who have stopped making a contribution must be phased out of the system. Early retirement at fifty-five is bound to penalize to a degree, but if you take it actuarily for ten years, it would be a package that makes it quite attractive to retire early. You've got to do it in a way that doesn't mean too much financial sacrifice for people, that doesn't destroy them emotionally. From my experience, I know that more people are relieved when the suggestion for early retirement is made under proper circumstances than you'd imagine.

Then, we're able to promote the younger people, from twenty-five to close to forty, that much faster. We can give them wide exposure to many demanding line and staff jobs as they begin to stick their heads above the crowd, and see how they react. When they show the balanced judgment we're looking for, we can groom them for substantially more exacting jobs. What we're trying to do is to merge the abilities and requirements of the older folks with the demands of the organization and the development of the younger people coming along to fill the top three hundred to four hundred jobs in the company.

Q. What other characteristics, besides "balanced judgment," do you see in potential top managers?

A. The basic fundamental is integrity. Without this, you can't build anything. The horrendous Watergate developments were a reminder that the need for integrity has never been greater. Even in as large an organization as Mobil, people tend to take their cue from the top—for good or for ill. Leaders in large organizations need not only personal probity but must work, quite consciously, to generate openness and honesty in the organization.

Every man must have ambition in the right amount; overweening ambition will ruin a fellow. He must have motivation, drive, and determination. He must be good with people, sensitive to others' views, wishes, desires. He must have leadership qualities. A leader leads by example; he persuades, he doesn't push. You can drive a lot of people for a short period of time, but sooner or later you can't do anymore. You can get all kinds of experts, people who concentrate on their technology—and we need lots of them—but it's a difficult, nebulous thing to develop leaders.

Q. How does the company answer the demand of young people that they be placed in challenging jobs as quickly as possible?

A. As soon as we get a feeling about a young fellow, we begin to probe on what kind of job we can give him that will be challenging. With the youngsters just out of college, you can't promise them the moon in the recruiting stage and then not give it to them. You can bet your last dollar this will gravitate back to campus. In recent years, we have been getting and keeping our fair share of the graduates. Of course, there's bound to be some attrition. Some people aren't fit for large organizations, and we hope they find this out early enough. We and they ought to know within twelve to fifteen months whether they have the abilities and temperament to thrive in a large organization.

Q. How far ahead does the company plan its reservoir of talent for the top corporate posts of the future?

A. I can't tell at this point in history which two fellows, after I reach sixty-five, will be chairman and president of the company. But I can say it is entirely conceivable the two top positions will be filled from a present group of twenty to thirty fellows at different age categories. At lower management levels, I know from written reports what has happened in the past year to move men from fair to superior ratings.

The Toughest Job at Xerox

Head of a $3 billion-volume multinational company whose name, fame, and fortune are based on photocopy machines and photographic papers, C. Peter McColough, chairman and chief executive officer, Xerox Corp., concedes that "direct communication is the most satisfactory way" to talk to people.

With forty-six thousand employees in the United States and ninety-six thousand worldwide, "communications is the toughest job in the company," the pleasant, outgoing man who presides over Xerox's destinies admits. This, he points out, is despite management letters and company newspapers "to get information to them before they become aware of it from someone else."

McColough holds monthly luncheon and dinner meetings with top and middle managers. His general practice is to talk for ten minutes, then answer questions for from one to two hours. McColough flies in one of the company's three small leased planes for informal sessions with sales and service managers in some thirty facilities.

However, the Xerox chief observes, "We're still not getting enough feedback; you never get enough. It's difficult to get people to open up their minds. You never do the job in communications you should do, or would like to do."

In a rapidly growing company such as Xerox, McColough explains, managers must themselves grow rapidly. "The manager, who last year may have had twenty people in a less complex situation, may this year have seventy; next year, even more. Not everyone can handle that many people."

The company's worldwide growth, profits, and stock market appreciation during the 1960s constitute one of American industry's most spectacular success stories. Xerox is involved in such nonxerographic operations as education, aerospace work, military technology, medical diagnostics, and mainframe computers.

McColough is responsible for creation of autonomous, regionalized divisions to replace the functional organization under which only he or the corporate president (Archie R. McCardell) could make a major business decision.

The chairman says he has "a very real belief that creativity should be general and not specialized. It is not enough for creativity or innovation to be only in research and development, important as these are. Technological progress alone could not make the company as successful as it has been. We try to get people to be receptive to creativity in all functions. As we get bigger, the tendency is to become less innovative. We're trying to build a general climate of listening to all sorts of ideas, no matter how nutty they may seem. We want to be damned sure to give an audience to everybody so that we don't take the risk of missing out on another Chester F. Carlson." This was the man who invented xerography, the copying process that is the foundation of Xerox.

The company's "people development" program is built around executives—the top one hundred people in the organization. Constantly looking ten years ahead, Xerox plays the spotlight on these persons at least once a year and, after evaluation, some leave the list, others go on.

McColough volunteers that this roster has "been accused of being a Crown Prince group," but he feels "we must continue the practice aboveboard." The one hundred most promising people below the top one hundred are also appraised. The company tells them not to be afraid to take risks and make mistakes. McColough points out that, "if a guy gets cracked hard for one mistake, it will get known through the company and nobody will ever try to make a mistake. I have personally made many mistakes. We think it's pretty well understood throughout the organization how we stand on this for all our people."

McColough looks for these characteristics in potential top managers:

1. creativity and innovation in all phases of the business, not just in research and development;
2. drive, to a very high degree;
3. good judgment;
4. ability to work with and motivate people;
5. willingness to take risks to realize production, volume, profit, and executive development targets.

Xerox sends executives for as long as four months to advanced management courses to various colleges. The company also pays part of the cost for people who, for purposes of self-development, study at night school or, in some cases, get time off during the day.

A one-million-square-foot International Center for Training and Management Development is operating in Leesburg, Va. In its first half year, more than six thousand Xerox sales and service people, computer scientists, and managers from all over the world were scheduled to study at the center—up to one thousand at a time.

In 1971, Xerox instituted a Social Service Leave Program under which, each year, twenty or more employees are given up to a year's leave of absence at full pay to enroll in a nonprofit social service program of their own choice. Participants are selected by a seven-member evaluation committee, only one of whom is a company officer, from applicants—from managers to floor sweepers—with three or more years of service. The annual cost for retaining those on sabbatical on the payroll is over $500,000.

In 1973, the program was made more flexible by permitting employees, reluctant about staying away from their jobs for a full year, to go on leaves of six months or less. Nineteen employees took part. In 1974, there were thirty-four employees in the program; in 1975, 28. The program has been expanded to Rank Xerox in Europe where eight employees were granted time off for such assignments. Under a revised plan, major operating units of the company are now responsible for their own Social Service Leave Programs. Each of the programs has its own employee committee which selects those who will be granted leaves.

Among assignments for nonprofit organizations unconnected with partisan politics: developing and implementing training programs to prevent drug abuse, developing a curriculum and teaching science at an experimental school, counseling Puerto Rican college students on summer employment, helping minority groups build business skills, assisting lower-income families to own their homes, developing a literacy program, teaching basic education skills in a prison, helping ex-convicts find employment, work with the mentally retarded, administration of a floating medical center on the S.S. Hope in Brazil, and salvage of flood-damaged art and monuments in Venice.

Any outside pay for these jobs is supplemented by Xerox up to the level of the employee's normal income.

A Xerox technician, who spent a year combating illiteracy in Arkansas, reports: "I am more independent today than I have been at any other time in my life." He believes that company structure severely restricts a manager's options in decision-making. "During my leave of absence," he says, "I actually made original decisions—some of them bad, but decisions that were mine." Now back repairing and vacuuming out Xerox copiers, he is unsatisfied with his lot. "I'm plagued with frustration. . . . I don't get the intellectual activity on my job that I got on my leave."

A Xerox physicist, back from leave, reports he now has different attitudes. "Vague rumors and impressions I used to think were important don't bother me anymore. I see my role in the company more clearly defined."

James M. Wainger, Xerox vice-president, personnel and organization, related the program to the manifold problems and possibilities of retirement: "Our social service program was not originally conceived in terms of its applicability to retirement. Still, if we are thinking about preparing for retirement from the time we first hire a person, this certainly is germane. We have said to all our employees that if they'd like to take up to a year off to work for a social service agency anywhere in the world, they should make contact with the agency of their choice and come back to us with an application. Applications are screened anonymously by a committee of average employees whose decision is final."

According to McColough, "The company has always felt a deep responsibility to help solve significant social problems. In addition to financial support, there is a critical need for people of talent, dedication, imagination, determination, and competence." Acknowledging self-interest, he expects more dedicated young people will be attracted to Xerox. "Many of our best people," he explains, "would not be here today if Xerox stood only for profits. We've encouraged our people to be involved. We are determined to put something back into society."

Among other companies sponsoring such undertakings are IBM, Cummins Engine, and Prudential Insurance.

Xerox's practice is to have top people relieved of "pressure" jobs, while they are in their late fifties or early sixties, and stay on in a consulting, advisory capacity until retirement at about sixty-five. Retirement is mandatory at sixty-five unless special exemption is granted by the board.

McColough has said that "no chief executive should serve more than ten years." This indicates he plans to retire at fifty-six in 1978.

Clogged Communications—Sterile Surroundings

"It made everyone seem so human, as if we all had interests in common."

"Maybe we should have meetings more often."

These spontaneous remarks were expressed following a mid-1972 meeting attended by some eighteen hundred of the twenty-five hundred New York-based employees of Standard Oil Co. (New Jersey). The first comment came from a rank-and-file employee; the second, from an executive.

The session was held to inform Jersey Standard's people that, before the end of that year, the corporate name would be changed to Exxon Corp. and the names of brands would undergo a similar change.

It was apparent that the significance of the name change took second place to the excitement generated merely by the convocation of the clan, by the opportunity to meet other employees, not to mention the privilege of seeing and hearing the corporate top command.

What should have been an unremarkable fact of a co-workers' gathering became remarkable because this was the first of its kind in the nation's largest oil company. With 1974 sales and revenues of over $45 billion, Exxon has superseded General Motors as the No. 1 industrial company in the world. Until about 1968, management–employee discussions of various issues were scheduled each spring and fall. However, these have been discontinued presumably because the company had no important news to impart.

It is unfortunate that giant and even smaller corporations often eliminate employee gatherings under company sponsorship as too much of a bother and expense. Management may have to pay the penalty in clogged communications and sterile surroundings. In the case of ninety-year-old Exxon, the difficulty of keeping unfounded, sometimes demoralizing, rumors in check is compounded when about 140,000 employes in dozens of widely scattered installations are involved.

All of which is not to indicate that Exxon isn't trying to act as much like a small company in its employee relations as possible.

In 1969, a few months before J. Kenneth Jamieson was promoted from president to chairman and Milo M. Brisco from executive vice-president to president, the latter and Robert E. Acker, then manager of executive development, now corporate secretary, replied to these questions:

Q. How do you follow up on whether you have effective communication up and down the line of command?

A. Inspection trips, on-the-job observation, discussions with managements of affiliates, internal review procedure which requires all managements to come in and report progress in achieving stated objectives. Each manager is charged with dual, equal responsibility for running the plant and development of people. We get our answer in performance along the policy lines laid down.

Q. How do you check on people who have stayed too long on one job, lost interest in it, and are not working at full potential?

A. Every manager has to have at least a five-year plan for his top jobs, to try to be in a position to choose from among quality replacements. We pick the man not only for a particular post but one with the most potential beyond that job. Of course, we always have people who find the level at which they want to work, and we want them too.

Q. How does the company answer the demand of young people entering the organization that they be placed in challenging jobs as quickly as possible?

A. This is an evaluation that has been going on for a number of years to an increasing degree and is uppermost in our minds. We know we must place young people in challenging or meaningful jobs or we'll lose them. We can't stockpile them, can't give them dull, routine clerical-type jobs. We talk to young employees who are one or two years out of school to encourage them in their objectives.

Q. Does the company have a formal development program that includes risk-taking and other real problems that will be faced by future managers?

A. Yes. There are not many businesses more risky than looking for oil. We would die on the vine if we didn't find oil. We also take risks in the management development field. We press our managers to tell us who are their most profitable people among those who've been with them less than five years.

Q. What are the characteristics you seek in potential top managers?

A. Managerial competence, leadership qualities, highest of integrity, good analytical ability.

Michael L. Haider, Jamieson's predecessor as chairman, looked for the following criteria in advancing executives and pinpointing potential top managers:

1. Does the man take a proprietary interest in the business, or does he act like a "paid hand"? Is he trying to come up with answers he thinks "they" want or will agree with, or does he try to arrive at decisions he would make if he were the owner of the business? Does he think for himself? Does he have the courage of his convictions, or is he merely a "corporation man," one who just follows the book?

2. How broad are his interests? Is he interested only in the phase of the business he is in, or does he think in terms of the interrelationship of what he is doing with other functions of the business? Does he think in terms of the business as a whole? Is he aware of the relationship of the business to the community? Is he interested in things outside his business, such as community affairs, politics, and governmental affairs, literature, music, and the business community as a whole?

3. Does he have sound judgment, not only with respect to business matters, but also with respect to people and things outside his functional activity? In other words, does he have "horse sense"? Does he seem to have the natural ability to apply his own judgment in evaluating situations, or does he merely apply the book?

4. Does he have the ability to plan, arrange, and think ahead? Does he anticipate situations and events? Does he think logically and analytically?

5. Does he have the ability to lead people, or does he drive them? Does he get people to do things by persuasion, or does he have to rely on his authority to get things done in his organization?

6. Is he tolerant of other people's opinions? Is he willing to consider viewpoints other than his own? Does he seek advice of others, and yet is he able to make up his own mind? Does he work effectively with other people?

7. Does he have constancy of purpose? Does he have goals and objectives he works toward, or does he drift with the currents?

8. Does he have ambition, a desire for self-development, a desire to excel, and does he control these or do they control him? Does he seek and accept

authority and responsibility because of a desire to make a contribution or because of a desire for power?

9. Is he willing to pay the price of success? Many men with ability to advance are not willing to accept the interference in their social life, the many necessary activities outside working hours, the traveling, and other personal inconveniences that go with success. No matter how much potential a man may have, he is not going to advance far if he is not willing to pay the price.

Rise in Grace

Integrity and entrepreneurial ability are the principal characteristics J. Peter Grace seeks in potential top managers.

"Quite often," explains the president and chief executive officer of W.R. Grace & Co., wide-ranging industrial and consumer products organization, "people with the most ability don't have the integrity. For whatever reason, they're not forthright, they cover up when they don't want to spill their guts to me. It's very difficult in a company of our size (over $3 billion sales and revenues, 74,500 employees) to make sure there is adequate communication. The bigger the company, the harder it is to know what's cooking when the top man has to rely on the integrity of subordinates to give him the right story."

On entrepreneurial ability, Grace has this to say:

"We are looking for generalists, who may have had a scientific background, with the potential to become heads of our various groups and divisions. But we're looking for entrepreneurs, more than for generalists, for people who smell money, who just naturally are money-makers. We assume these executives would pick only the same kind of people to work with them. We're allergic to any others."

To the heads of operating units who meet these requirements for future top management, Grace reports, he has no hesitancy in delegating authority as well as responsibility. "They're supposed to act as the president for their particular business," he points out, "and the more they do it, the more I like it. I want as little as possible to do with day-to-day operations." Felix E. Larkin is chairman and chief operating officer.

The pleasant-mannered chief of a worldwide empire encompassing chemicals, consumer foods and services, natural resources and other products and services, indicates he has enough to do "planning our moves, making deals, motivating people, promoting young persons of ability, devising new ways to compensate them and give them a piece of the action, keeping the board of directors happy, keeping the investment community reasonably understanding of what's happening, and helping our image in different parts of the world." He's "on the road" for a time equivalent of three to four months a year.

The following questions were put to him:

Q. How do you follow up on whether you have effective communication up and down the line of command?

A. The only way is to have people as group executives who think the way you do. You need such people because they are handling certain numbers of employees you don't yourself ordinarily see. I go out in the field as much as I can. Periodically, I go to Europe, where we have twenty-six thousand employees, for meetings.

Q. How do you check on whether executive potential is being properly assessed, and executive performance properly appraised?

A. We have a management development committee which goes over organization charts and has replacements with immediate, two-year, five-year, and longer-range needs in mind. The committee may decide to shift people sideways to other divisions if they're being blocked in promotion. We believe in moving executives into unrelated areas of responsibility as the only way to bring them along for top management but know we don't do as much of this as we should. We have put three thousand people in middle-to-top management on the computer and can immediately fill any demand for special skills.

Q. How does the company answer the demand of young people entering the organization that they be placed in challenging jobs as quickly as possible?

A. We try to put people in their early thirties in big spots as soon as possible. We have at least five people with MBAs who have come to us in the last few years and are now holding management positions in the United States and various European countries. Generally, we have no feeling one way or the other for liberal arts versus technical graduates except for chemicals where we prefer people with technical degrees. A higher percentage of liberal arts people are generalists, but many scientific school graduates are very good generalists.

Q. Do you believe organizational loyalty is dead, that talented employees feel freer to look elsewhere for greater immediate opportunity than they did in the past?

A. Yes, but we think we're doing as well as, or better than, any other company with young college graduates. However, a disturbing number are trained by us and grabbed off by other companies who don't train people. Our former location might have been a factor in our losing people to Wall Street. [The company has since moved from the downtown financial area to midtown Manhattan.] At the upper middle to top levels of management, we have very little turnover.

Q. What do you do to encourage creativity on the part of employees?

A. We promote and reward people who are worthy. We ask our people stimulating questions and, if they're not creative, put them in branches of our business where creative instinct is not essential. Of course, there's a greater or lesser degree of creativity in all business.

A Furious-Paced Son of a Fabled Father

Edgar F. Kaiser arrived punctually at his New York office on Park Avenue for the 8:30 A.M. interview that would begin his typically tight schedule for the day.

Directly after lunch he flew to Venezuela to look at a dam four hundred miles west of Caracas, "where we're having some problem," for a 1 1/2-day visit. He then returned to Oakland, Calif., headquarters of Kaiser Industries Corp., parent of the one hundred-company, worldwide organization, with 1974 assets of more than $3.6 billion and sales and revenues of over $2.6 billion. A day later, he went to West Germany for two days, Paris one day, London one day.

Kaiser is chairman of Kaiser Industries, head of all operating divisions of the parent concern, and chairman of a number of affiliated companies.

Like Henry J. Kaiser, his father who died in 1967 at eighty-five, Edgar Fosburgh Kaiser is compulsive about keeping busy. Unproductive time is anathema to him. Always on the go as he is, he sets a vigorous pace for associates much younger than himself.

Through the years, Edgar has participated in, among other things, pioneering programs of enlightened labor-management relations. The particular project of "good human relations" that has given him greatest personal satisfaction is the Kaiser Foundation Hospitals and Health Plan, whose genesis was a small medical facility on a Mojave Desert construction site. Working together with independent groups of doctors, the Kaiser management devised a way to provide medical care at a reasonable price. A self-sustaining plan, based on monthly prepayments, was developed for both hospital treatment and out-patient preventive care. The program has been opened to the public as well as to Kaiser's 52,000 employees, about 3,200 of them in Oakland. Some 2 1/2 million people are served.

This medical program exemplifies Edgar's conviction that the primary challenge to business is "not the building of structures but the building of human beings." In the same spirit, he holds: "Our returns must be in terms of people, their aspirations, their hopes and ideals, as much as on the balance sheets."

The Kaiser Foundation, which dispenses grants for medical research and hospitals, controls 32 percent of Kaiser Industries through stock bequeathed by members of the family.

The Kaiser chairman says he is following his father's example in always wanting to talk with men all the way down to the lowest levels to obtain points of view on specific problems. He fully endorses Henry J.'s philosophy that "labor relations are no more than human relations. Man wants to be treated like a human being. He is jealous of his dignity and self-respect. He resents either being exploited or neglected. He wants to be heard on issues that affect his well being. He wants to earn his way and to enjoy the fruits of labor. He wants some say as to the conditions and terms under which he may live and work."

Edgar observes: "Any success I have had has been dependent on people who have taken the load off my shoulders and helped me build a strong organization."

The chairman has little use for "the older fellow who almost automatically claims something can't be done. I am all for the young fellow who wants to know why it can't be done. Of course, when a business expands as ours has, it isn't realistic to say it can be done the same way as in the past."

After ten years with the Kaiser companies, certain men are picked to go to such universities as Harvard and Stanford for courses in preparation for higher jobs. "One of the most important things about this formal development program is the fresh look they get in association with people from other companies and other industries."

Each of the companies and divisions has a specific five-to-ten year plan for a reservoir of talent for the top posts of the future.

Edgar's requirements of his executives: integrity and devotion to and enthusiasm about the business.

His concept of his own special contribution to the company: "To inspire my people and make them feel they're part of this ball club; to be available when they need me." In addition to his preoccupation with people, he cites his roles in getting new business and as a trouble-shooter.

The chairman, whose family's control of more than 40 percent of Kaiser Industries' common shares punctuates his continued power, would "love it" if a Kaiser succeeded William R. Roesch as C.E.O. and president some day. Blunt, informal Roesch, who rose through the Jones & Laughlin ranks, asserts that, "if the heirs to Kaiser want professional management, they've got to compete with professionals for the job." There are bets that Edgar Kaiser, Jr., will go up the corporate ladder when Roesch succeeds the elder Kaiser.

Asked about his retirement, the chairman, who was sixty-seven on July 29, 1975, is only definite that "I am not going to stay around as chairman until I'm eighty-five [as his father did] just because my name is Kaiser."

Piloting a Quality Airline

You can't have a quality organization unless you have quality at the controls.

Or, as Albert Vincent Casey puts it: "The common thread of management that identifies quality of leadership is motivation of people toward individual and group achievement of mutually agreed-upon goals."

Casey ought to know. He's chairman and president of American Airlines and was previously president of the Times Mirror Co., the publishing complex.

When he joined the airline in early 1974, revenues, profit, morale and public acceptance were at a low ebb. This was particularly humiliating for an airline that for years cherished a reputation for being number one in quality of effort and performance. In the first year of his regime, all four mainstays of a sound structure were substantially strengthened. In 1975, the sluggish economy and rising fuel costs impaired revenues and profits. However, company spirit and public approval have remained at high levels. In a generally declining use of air travel and freight, AA's share of the market has continued to improve.

A new slogan, "We're American Airlines doing what we do best," was adopted. Casey says, "This reflects the fact the company is a 'people' business. Our people are proud to be Americans." Get it?

Casey was born in Boston in 1920, worked his way through Harvard in the class of 1943 and, following four years as an officer in the Army Signal Corps, graduated from the Harvard Business School in 1948. He joined Southern Pacific Co., where he rose to assistant vice-president and assistant treasurer and left in 1961 to become vice-president and treasurer of REA Express.

In 1963, he joined the Times Mirror as vice-president for finance. The next year, he was named executive vice-president and a director and, two years later, was elected president and a member of the executive committee. He was in charge of two dozen subsidiaries, comprising magazines, book publishing and forest products. His compensation and bonus amounted to $300,000.

But he wasn't satisfied. "Franklin D. Murphy, the chairman, was the boss, and I wanted to run my own show, to be the boss man. However, Otis Chandler ran the newspapers and Norman Chandler, the owner, had told me his son would be the head man in six years."

After eight years as Times Mirror president, Casey decided he had to move to a spot where there would be less division of authority. He grasped the opportunity to join American Airlines as president and chief executive officer in February, 1974. He has remained a Times Mirror director. Otis Chandler is vice-chairman and publisher of the Los Angeles Times.

Two months after Casey joined American as president and chief executive officer, he added the chairmanship in succession to C.R. Smith, the air-line's legendary leader, who had returned to the airline from retirement in the fall of 1973 to succeed George A. Spater and, at 75, returned to retirement in Washington.

Casey made it clear it was the chance and challenge to be top man that drew him to American. His straight salary was set at an annual figure of $220,000, about twenty-five percent less than he had previously made. He received the same pay in 1975—"I was the only man in our top management who didn't get a raise that year. But how much can you keep? I could have earned a ten percent bonus if the airline were profitable. But that's a fictional figure—there was no profit then." Most important to him is that his admitted "supreme ego about my own capabilities" is getting full play at the company.

The four senior vice-presidents, who meet with Casey for an hour every Monday morning, are Gene E. Overbeck, 46, administration; Robert J. Norris, 50, finance; Donald J. Lloyd-Jones, 43, operations; and Robert L. Crandall, 39, marketing.

Casey points out that four of the five top-team members were financial vice-presidents of large corporations, the only exception being lawyer Over-beck. Casey and Lloyd-Jones are the only top-team members on the board.

Casey reports Overbeck "runs the president's office. Anytime, old Casey (he sometimes refers to himself by that name, "Old Case" or "Old Dad") is away, Overbeck is in charge. He acts as a conduit." Asked if that made Overbeck the logical man to fill the presidency, Casey demurs: "If I were hit by a bus, he would not automatically be the next president. No, I won't tell you who is most likely to succeed me in that position. At our next annual meeting in May, 1976, the board will discuss the possibility of adopting a program leading to the eventual selection of a president. I hope my successor will be one of the members of the management team."

Casey cites four principal functions of any top management team: 1) manufacturing a product or providing a service; 2) designing and selling the product or service; 3) the job of the scorekeeper (controller); 4) the "people" function. In the case of American, Casey explains, the respective management components are flight maintenance, marketing, finance and "the boss and leader—me."

His style of management is "to have very few people report to me. I charge each of my four top managers with clear-cut representations of goals. After they have parceled out responsibilities to their department heads, prog-ress is measured constantly. If they do not carry out what they told me they would do, they will be replaced." That, he stresses with typically disarming frankness, "is my style."

What are the characteristics Casey looks for in potential top managers? "A conscientious worker. He takes his job seriously. He dedicates a major part of his time to accomplishing his assignment. I like a man who develops his team. I like a person with an abundance of common sense and an understanding of the priorities of a situation. I want a person who really knows the technical side as well as the 'people' side of his job. I don't know the technical side."

Reviewing his company's changing fortunes, Casey observes: "For many years, AA was the quality airline in every direction—people, terminals, food. The only reason why we strayed from this leadership was a pilot slowdown beginning in December, 1972, and continuing into the following spring. Pilots flew by the book. This resulted in deteriorated service and quality to the public. I knew—I was a customer at the time. The morale of everybody in the company was affected. The feeling was, 'Why bother, the pilots would screw it up anyway'. The slowdown was settled in April, 1973.

"But, shortly afterward, Spater, then chairman, admitted he had made an illegal gift to CREEP (Committee for the Re-election of the President), another punch in the stomach for AA. However, Spater voluntarily acknowledged corporate political contributions before any other chief executive did so."

Spater, a lawyer who became American's general counsel in 1960, was intelligent but too easy-going and indecisive. Certainly, he was far removed from the gregarious, yet hard-driving manner of Smith—or of a Casey.

In common with most of his opposite numbers at other major airlines, Casey is on the horns of a dilemma posed by a listless economy, a static passenger and freight market, and skyrocketing costs.

The only avenue out of this labyrinth of revenue-profit problems for each airline, Casey points out, is to carve out a larger share of the available pie of air traffic—"we must take business away from the others."

The road out of this murky tunnel, he continues in his ebullient manner, must be lighted by a management team, competent both on the people and technical sides. It is up to this top-echelon command—in AA's case, it's a president's office of four senior vice-presidents and the big boss—to show the way by quality of performance at corporate headquarters to quality of day-to-day, front-line service by some 35,000 subordinate managers and rank and file employees.

As the government regulates prices, routes and other procedural matters, distinctions among airlines are likely to assume a fuzzy look. The fact is that quality at every level and in every function is all that an airline has to sell. How well any one airline surpasses its competitors in this respect, impresses its superiority upon current and potential customers, and holds and gains their continuous patronage—ay, there's the rub.

One morale-booster under Casey is a Human Resources System "to provide an intense experience in self-learning by identifying and amplifying selective strengths, weaknesses and developmental needs as professional managers." Casey has also introduced a program of "rap sessions with our troops all over."

Casey is heartened by quarterly inflight surveys and by letters indicating that passenger opinion of AA is at the highest point in six years of measurement. Flight attendants continue to receive the highest "excellent" percentages of nineteen rated categories, among these reservations, ticketing, boarding, on-time performance, schedule convenience and cocktail service.

Among AA subsidiaries are Flagships International, which owns and operates Sky Chefs, Americana Hotels and Management in Maintenance. The hotel chain is the only loser of this group. Casey wants all subsidiaries "to make money on their own and not ride on AA's back."

The AA chief executive's number one goal is not so much to push up its approximately $1 1/2 billion revenues as to restore its profitable basis. He explains: "Revenues aren't everything; profit is. Only with profit will we have job stability and security. Only profitable companies can attract capital to our labor-and-capital-intensive business. Very few other businesses have both of these characteristics. We're being inundated with soaring fuel prices—far and away our number one problem today."

His biggest job? "To keep every phase of quality at our present high level and hold on to the extra piece of the market pie into which we have bitten. This job is going to be tough."

Spring Mills' Philosophy of Management

Managers must help recruit, develop, and identify strong people and place them on the faster "career track" that will produce executives capable of guiding the company's future growth.

This is one of the precepts of "Corporate Philosophy of Management," first written statement of the goals and objectives of the top management of Spring Mills, textiles and frozen foods. A booklet containing this thinking has been distributed to the 2,100 salaried employees.

President Peter G. Scotese, who conceived the booklet and is responsible for much of its content, explains that "our goals and objectives have changed significantly in the past fifteen years when the company was a smaller, paternalistic, southern-based manufacturer. It was functionally organized, with production and marketing on about the same level leaning toward production. Now, it is divisionalized into profit centers with marketing running the show. All divisional presidents have marketing backgrounds, and they are in charge of both marketing and production."

Scotese senses that transmission of basic management principles by frequent, meaningful, face-to-face meetings had become increasingly difficult in a steadily expanding, ever more complex organization. Scotese and H. W. Close, chairman, emphasize that the written statement supplements—but does not supplant—personal contact between corporate management and their subordinates at all levels throughout the company.

The booklet—dedicated to the science of professional management—espouses the causes of both Management by Objectives and Management by Exception. The former system requires extensive and frequent measurement and evaluation of results and "appropriate action to stay on plan or get back on plan. Management by Exception permits delegation of decision-making far down the line. So long as the manager generally adheres to accepted basic principles and achieves planned results, he will be left alone. The company focuses attention on the exceptions—the areas not performing as planned and expected."

Other nuggets from "Corporate Philosophy of Management":

• Quality of earnings is important to us. Size or volume alone is not our goal.
• Any manager's No. 2 man or woman should be interchangeable with his superior.
• We have found that bringing together people with different areas of specialized knowledge, as characterized by our corporate management committee, produces valuable synergism and a clear understanding of broad objectives and strategies.
• We expect every manager at every level to think about return on investment constantly. It is the single most important fundamental he and his associates must consider.

The corporate heads sum up:

"We are a professionally managed, market-oriented company with specific earnings growth objectives and a firm commitment to integrity. We know where we are going, and we are counting on highly motivated people, a commitment to long-range planning, a lean, loose organization and a thorough knowledge of our operating environment to get us there. A management team, strongly unified by an understanding of corporate objectives and principles, is essential to our success. We are determined to have all of this, but we will never 'arrive' because 'success is a journey, not a destination.' "

Scotese's professional management philosophy stems from a background encompassing retailing as well as the textile industry.

Prior to joining Springs in his present post in 1969—he was elected the first nonfamily president in the firm's eighty-five-year history—Scotese was chairman of the Milwaukee Boston Store division of Federated Department Stores for six years. Before that he was with Indian Head Mills for sixteen years, rising from territory salesman to corporate vice-president.

Convinced most people can be motivated to produce above-average results, Springs has developed a system of goals and rewards recognizing that highly capable people need the opportunity to demonstrate their ability and compensating superior performers "beyond normal salary levels."

How does he follow up on whether he has effective communications up and down the line of command?

"In a relatively new undertaking, we are conducting attitude surveys among our employees. We're spending a lot of time on the job enrichment potential of hourly employees. We are experimenting with prescreening of first-line supervisors to see if they're fit for the job."

The company applies three basic management rules to all operations:

"In the near term, avoid catastrophe; in the intermediate term, maintain the operation; for the long term, improve the operation."

Since 1969, Springs has had a corporate management committee of five persons—the chairman, president, and three executive vice-presidents. Each has different areas of experience and talents.

"It's fundamental," Scotese explains, "not to get too many people oriented the same way."

What are the characteristics Scotese looks for in potential top executives?

"No. 1 by far is a high degree of integrity. After this comes intelligence —good common sense and judgment; ambition and desire to succeed, which translates itself into putting in whatever time and efforts are necessary to get results; imagination, some sensitivity to creativity, and ability to withstand and overcome frustration."

Q. How do you assure yourself of managers who are motivated to increase their competence, and that of their subordinates, rather than to guard their spheres of influence, and thwart their people's ambitions and initiative?

A. We have a key management inventory review where our corporate management committee insists on an individual annual review of the key personnel of each of our divisions by the division presidents. This includes "comers"—potential key managers. They must identify candidates for every key position and summarize by divisions who will be replaced when, whether they'll be replaced in a year or five, whether they're promotable or not. We must create the climate that makes this possible. We can't issue an edict. Internal candidates are being compared with external candidates for key jobs. We look internally first but will frequently compare with external candidates if there's any doubt at all.

Q. How does the company answer the demand of young people entering the organization that they be placed in challenging jobs as quickly as possible?

A. We have an administrative trainee program which has been cut back to one year instead of two to give newcomers exposure to management jobs faster. We have many young people in responsible positions—they're doing extremely well.

Q. Does the company have a policy of moving executives into other areas of responsibility in order to bring them along for top management?

A. We have an interchange of executives between divisions and between corporate staffs and divisions. The president of the knit goods division was formerly marketing head of the apparel fabrics division. A young attorney from our general counsel's office was made general manager of our Indonesian textile operations.

Q. Do you feel organizational loyalty is dead, that talented employees feel freer to look elsewhere for greater immediate opportunity than they did in the past? If so, why?

A. I think we have loyalty to the extent that it's possible and desirable. I don't think it's something we insist on. We can't insist that people be loyal; we have to earn it. I think a lot of young people don't feel the need to have loyalty. It's a new way of life, and they don't feel married to the corporation. It's a fact of life and we'll live with it.

Q. How does the chief executive follow through on the effectiveness of his people?

A. Through the establishment of individual goals and objectives and the frequent measurement of progress toward those goals and objectives.

Q. What does the chief executive officer conceive to be his special contribution to the company?

A. The important thing required of me is a basic leadership role. This has to do with instilling a sense of direction and getting planned results through other people.

In 1972, Springs instituted a retirement plan at age sixty for operating heads. Scotese, fifty-five (1975) says: "This does not necessarily mean they leave the company; they may be retained as consultants. Two divisional presidents have retired and have stayed on under this arrangement." As for himself, he does not intend to be president beyond sixty. "In a profit-and-loss kind of responsibility," he explains, "demands are just too enervating to expect people over sixty to carry on."

Nine Ingredients in Recipe
for Company Growth

Do you really hear what your subordinates tell you? Listening is practically a lost art. Make sure you talk the same language as every one of your employees, whether he be research man or janitor, that you allow the right individuals full rein for their creativity, and you're well on the way to success.

So says Rudolph Hurwich, chairman, Dymo Industries, a diversified company with headquarters in Berkeley, Calif., who gives his employees their full share of credit for the organization's rapid growth from shoestring beginnings. The firm started in 1958 as a manufacturer of hand-operated embossing gadgets that punch out identification tapes. Initial working capital was $67,000; fixed assets, $100,000. Eight acquisitions have been made in four areas of activity—marking, labeling, and information-transfer systems; business equipment and supplies; professional cleaning and laundry; and portable classrooms. In 1974 the company, listed on the New York Stock Exchange, has foreign subsidiaries and is in the $100 million sales category, up from $2.35 million in 1960.

Now in his mid-fifties, Hurwich is a graduate of Massachusetts Institute of Technology with a degree in mechanical engineering. Before he came to the San Francisco Bay area in 1949, he was for several years a general building contractor in Chicago.

Nine ingredients in the Hurwich recipe for successful growth:

- The cornerstone of effective management controls is an effective communications program. Common understanding must be established among the entire work force so that the two-way flow of information is useful to all concerned.
- The most important ability a manager can perfect is that of interacting and communicating with other people within their frame of reference.
- Practice the nearly lost art of listening. Translate company goals and directives so that you, your associates, and your subordinates are talking the same language.
- Nothing beats person-to-person contact. To really understand just how a man thinks and reacts under different situations, to have an appreciation of his values, deal with him on a face-to-face, one-to-one basis, rather than through memos or department meetings.
- "Monitor" your dialog. Be sensitive to the person's background and viewpoints, and focus your communications accordingly so that you get your point across.
- Define the boundaries of allowable experimentation and then encourage your people to use their imagination and intuition to the fullest.
- Develop "goal-oriented" rather than "task-oriented" employees. The task-oriented are people who shun feedback and personal responsibility and lack initiative.
- Use the "profit center" instead of the "budget center" approach which seems to encourage people to worry more about an arbitrary budget than to think creatively about improving profits. Quite often, profit center managers shy away from long-range planning in favor of short-term gains on the mistaken assumption that the former method may be an unnecessary diversion. They must be encouraged to see the direct relationship between today's profitability and long-term growth.

- The individual and the organization both have a strategy for survival and growth, Hurwich points out. Thought must be given by managers to proper balance of personal and corporate goals, he concludes.

Cary Grant: Starring on the Business Stage

Want to get along well with Cary Grant? Treat him as a businessman rather than as an actor.

He's been a director of Faberge since 1968, a director of Metro-Goldwyn-Mayer since July, 1975, and a director "emeritus" of Western Airlines. For about ten years of his stardom, he made his own productions and realized a large share of the after-tax profits.

At the outset of an interview, businessman Grant peered intently at his visitor's face. The reporter was nonplussed until Grant explained: "I wanted to see if your eyebrows show any white. They do." With this comment, he chortled in characteristic Cary Grant manner. Calling attention to his own whitening eyebrows, he commented in his distinctive voice pattern and timbre: "There's nothing that ages a man more than white eyebrows." At his suggestion, Faberge's principals have assigned a chemist to investigate the possibilities of a permanent dye.

As for his still abundant head of white hair, "I'm not interested in dyeing it." With a chuckle, he related the story of his then 89-year-old mother (she died at 95), who urged him to dye his hair "because your gray hair makes me look too old."

Asked what he thinks about being 71 or thereabouts, the nonchalant, suave charmer rejoined: "What else can I be? I'd prefer to be younger and know what I know today and be able to apply it to life in every aspect. I'm reminded of what someone said: 'If I had known I was going to live this long, I'd have taken better care of myself.' "

The hotel where he makes his New York home is directly across the street from Burlington House, Faberge's headquarters. He conducts his business in the apartment just as he does in his Beverly Hills home and Las Vegas apartment.

Assessing his contribution to Faberge, Grant ventured: "People recognize me and possibly associate me with the company." He suggested that George or Richard Barrie (president and executive vice-president, respectively) be asked for an opinion.

Richard Barrie said, "Cary has done a lot for us in super-classy publicity over the past seven years. He has appeared at company sales meetings in this country and in London and Paris. He has product ideas.

"He makes a positive contribution to our board. He's made many appearances for us at charity balls. He is the master of ceremonies at the annual Straw Hat Awards, sponsored by us, in which we honor contributions by members of the theatrical profession to the summer theater. Without Cary, the company would not have gone as far as it has."

During his Faberge connection, Grant has generally adhered to a personal policy of never visiting a store to the accompaniment of advance publicity. "I don't like to do it because it stops department business, and it's lost revenue for the store."

When he does go to a store, it's to talk to executives and perhaps to visit them in their homes. He recalled being "caught" once in the cosmetics department of Filene's in Boston. "Never again." He knows "lots of actors and others who go to department stores to plug a book or whatever, but that's not for me."

As a further mark of the Grant sense of dignity and privacy, he has not appeared on any TV program for Faberge or any other company. Nor has he ever been on an interview, talk or game show. "I'm not the right man for this. Whatever aura surrounds my name is better in the movies than in half-minute television ads. Faberge's tieups with Joe Namath, Pele, Jimmy Connors, Muhammed Ali, Larry Csonka, Margaux Hemingway and Lola Falana are good moves. They'll achieve the objective of drawing public attention to Faberge products."

Richard Barrie reported Grant is paid "a small fee" as a consultant and director. The pay is understood to be $25,000, with directors' fees added.

Grant views Faberge's foray into the motion picture industry in this light: "Here was a great chance for Faberge, which spends many millions in advertising, to get a great deal of publicity mileage from movies whose titles would carry the message: 'Brut Productions Presents.' Gulf & Western owns Paramount, but it can't persuade viewers of its films to say, 'Give me a bottle of G & W.'

"Motion pictures have a possible life of 30 years or more—a period of continuous advertising value. This is gained at relatively limited expense when it is considered that a single 30-second TV spot commercial on prime time of a hit show may cost more than $60,000. If a Brut production makes a great profit, as 'A Touch of Class' did, the extra advertising cost to Faberge is very little."

Grant stressed it would be "a conflict of interests for me to be associated directly with the casting or physical production of either Brut or MGM films." He has "kept hands off because I don't want people coming to me and saying, 'I have a cousin-in-law who would make a great star.' "

Archibald Alexander Leach (Grant's real name) has been an entertainer since he was 14. He was a singer, dancer and juggler in a troupe that traveled through the British provinces and appeared in London vaudeville houses. He came to the United States at 16. Between engagements in a vaudeville act, he was a stiltwalker at Coney Island. After appearing in several operettas on Broadway, he was signed in 1931 to a five-year contract by Paramount, which changed his name. He appeared in 72 films.

He became a millionaire many times over as a producer in partnership with others. "Where else," he asked, "can you make $1 million in ten weeks?" In 1942, he changed his name legally, and became an American citizen.

Soon after the birth of daughter Jennifer in 1966, Grant retired from the screen. "My daughter's birth," he remarked in typical underplaying style, "was my last production. Filmmaking required too much of the time I was willing to devote to it. I wanted to be near my daughter. Wherever I am in the world, I make sure to get to California for my visitation rights."

Since his voluntary retirement from films, he has had "no regular hours with any company with which I have been associated."

With a worldwide image for 40 years as the quintessence of glamor, virility and polish, how does Grant view himself? After a moment's hesitation, he came up with "I suppose one is being oneself when one is relaxed, not hypocritical, not putting on a facade."

2

THE ART
OF LEADERSHIP

Top Executives: Heroes One Year,
Bums the Next

Pity the poor top executive whose sharp drop in annual compensation has changed him from a peerless leader one year to just another faulty human being the next year.

Consider the pay of the four chief executives of General Motors for 1973 and 1974. In the former year, Thomas A. Murphy made $832,997; in the latter, $272,500. Elliott M. Estes went from $758,976 to $236,250; Oscar A. Lundin from the same figure to $228,750, and Richard L. Terrell from $722,993 to $228,750. The chairman and president of Ford Motor Co. suffered similar fates. Henry Ford 2nd and Lee A. Iacocca dropped from $865,000 each to $291,667. Chrysler's chairman Lynn Townsend and other top officials also took sharp income losses.

These hot-shots of the auto industry were the victims of a steep profit decline that washed away the cash and stock bonuses responsible for their record earnings in good years.

For executives who draw anything under $225,000 even in their best years, it's hard to shed bitter tears over the financial misfortunes of men who ordinarily do so much better than themselves.

However, to complicate matters, the ill winds of economic climate that bedeviled the auto titans turned into golden sunshine for the oil moguls. Four of the 10 highest-paid U.S. executives in 1974 were oil men. J. Kenneth Jamieson, chairman, Exxon, received $677,000 compared to $597,000 in 1973; Rawleigh Warner Jr., chairman, Mobil Oil Corp., made $596,000 versus $499,667; Maurice F. Granville, chairman, Texaco, $579,000 versus $536,000, and Bob R. Dorsey, chairman, Gulf Oil Corp., $544,264 compared to $490,000.

It is scarcely conceivable that any of the oil men were greater geniuses in 1974 than in 1973, any more than the auto company heads became (n)incom(e)poops over night.

It's all a reflection of changing fortunes that make the lives of the elite of business and industry both enviable and forbidding. Top executives of publicly-owned corporations are constantly exposed to the cold light of external as well as internal scrutiny. Lives that are enviable in good times become forbidding when things turn sour. The same man may be a hero one year, a bum the next.

Of course, salaries and bonuses—up or down—don't tell the whole story. In bad times as in good, the members of the Six-Figure Club often retain perquisites that ease the stresses and strains of carrying on in the face of adversity. Tax-free perks in all fields add substantially to base pay and bonuses. For example, an allotment of $20,000 worth of legitimate perks to a top executive in the 50 percent bracket, without creating imputed income, is the equivalent of $40,000 or more of extra salary. As for the corporations with a tax rate of 52 percent, an earnings charge of only $9,600 is incurred for the $20,000 package.

This assumes that heads don't roll because of poor corporate and individual performance or for policy differences or personality conflicts. The casualties in the executive suites of retailing and related industries—dog-eat-dog occupations of long standing—are at least as volatile as those in any other business.

More mobility among middle-to-top management in industry in general is illustrated by changes at Chrysler Corp. This company was hit by recession the hardest of the Big Four auto producers. Lynn A. Townsend resigned as chairman and chief executive officer to be succeeded by John J. Riccardo, former president, who in turn was succeeded by Eugene A. Cafiero, former senior executive vice-president. Townsend said he was retiring voluntarily—"no pressure from anyone but myself"—to make way for "an early and orderly management transition to our younger executives in a new era requiring substantial change."

Annual meetings are virtually the only opportunity shareholders have to vent their disappointment in not getting a higher return on their investment. Chrysler's Townsend was noticeably discomfited by stockholders' pointed complaints at the 1975 annual meeting.

At TWA, which sustained huge losses in 1974, F. C. Wiser resigned as president and Blaine Cook left as marketing senior vice-president. The board decided Wiser was not the right man to step up to the chairmanship in succession to Charles C. Tillinghast Jr., who was due to retire in January, 1975. In early 1975, Wiser joined Pan Am as president and chief operating officer.

Robert W. Sarnoff, RCA Corp.'s chairman and chief executive officer, was summarily dismissed by the board at the completion of his five-year contract at the end of 1975. He has been replaced by Anthony L. Conrad, previously second in command.

Donald P. Kircher has been replaced as chairman and president of Singer Co. by Joseph P. Flavin, recruited from Xerox Corp. where he was executive vice-president for international operations.

Management Exorcist Urged for Every Firm's Survival

"More than ever before, any business that wants to survive needs an exorcist in the management suite."

This is the advice of Dominick B. Maimone, executive partner for client services and development, J.K. Lasser & Co., international certified public accounting firm.

The management exorcist, according to Maimone, must be "a cost-conscious, result-oriented and no-nonsense disciplinarian, a determined, practical and hard-nosed executive who can and will make the hard decisions that have to be made and implemented."

Maimone describes the exorcist's huge responsibility:

"It is the management exorcist's job to cast out, to rid the company and all of its people of, the demons that have taken over. I'm talking about the demons of inefficiency, of sloppy work habits, of waste, of absenteeism and of a head-in-the-sand posture. I'm talking about the demons in people who don't put in a day's work for a day's pay, or managers who don't manage—and of a 'what-the-hell, it's only company money' attitude.

"Even if we are still successful, it is the management exorcist's job to keep us from being prisoners of our own past or present successes. It is his or her job to open our eyes to the fact that the swift and radical changes occurring in the marketplace require swift, new and radical approaches on our part. We must learn that change devalues not only tradition but also experience. It is the exorcist's voice that must constantly remind us the immutable law of nature applies not only to life but also to business. That law is 'ADAPT'—adapt to change, or perish.

"Therefore, it is the management exorcist's job to eliminate any smug satisfaction with the status quo. He must make each of us rethink every single facet of our business, of our planning and of our strategy in light of the current situation."

Other facets of the exorcist's job:

- He must make management re-examine many of the things it has always accepted as gospel. It isn't always what management doesn't know that gets it into trouble. Too often, it's what management does know. But what it knows may simply be no longer so and "does it in."
- The job requires elimination of fuzzy thinking. The management exorcist will make executives redefine and redirect their efforts and expenditures. Executives must change as markets and customers change, as suppliers and capital sources change in a changing environment.
- It is the exorcist's job to see that the business is liquid, that the organization is lean and competitive and kept that way. He will insist that the product be marketed more aggressively, more efficiently and more selectively. It's a case of working smarter as well as harder.
- The exorcist will require managers to use and tighten up all internal controls. He will reinstate efficiency and cost-saving in every department—in manufacturing, in purchasing, in marketing and, most important, in managing.
- He will compel management to control inventories better. With more and more scarce materials coming into full supply, with consumer resistance building on certain items, companies must keep only enough stock to supply their normal demands. Stocks must be kept balanced—and moving.
- The exorcist will insist that managers identify not only immediate problem areas and specific problems but also those they see coming. Solutions must be developed and implemented swiftly. "We can't wait. We must do it now. It's better to be early than late. If we are early, then we're only early. But, if we are late, then we may be too late."
- Blocks to internal communication must be eliminated. The exorcist must see that managers explain to their people not only the seriousness of the situation, not only the fact that they—like the company—are in a fight for survival, but also exactly what contributions each is expected to make.
- It is the exorcist's job to see that all the people in the organization take pride in their work. "He must help them rediscover the self-fulfillment in the work ethic, the professionalism in a job well done, and the satisfaction in a customer well served."

The management exorcist, Maimone continues, "must eliminate the enervating permissiveness, the wishy-washy management direction too often disguised or mislabeled as 'motivation' or 'job enrichment'. He must eliminate thoughtless assumptions at every level. He must teach everyone that, when we assume something—indeed, when we assume anything, it means we are taking that thing for granted. Every assumption, even the most fundamental, must be questioned.

"The days are gone, long gone, when any of us can take our suppliers, our customers or our capital sources for granted. That's a sure way to lose them. And, in this economic environment, we can't take our jobs for granted either. All of us—management and employees alike, not only have to earn our jobs, we also have to earn the right to keep them. None of us 'has it made.' Not now. Not ever again. No one has paid up his or her dues for life in this fight for survival. There are no paid-up members. There can't be. We all have to continue to pay our dues, and we have to pay them every day.

"This means we must insist on and get punctuality and performance by every single individual every single day. All this, in turn, will result in increased productivity and increased profits. And that's exactly what it's all about. Productivity and profits is not only the name of the game, it IS the game."

Maimone concedes to anyone who may be elected or appointed or who volunteers to be "the tough but sensitive" management exorcist in a company that the things they must do are obvious. Recalling the old statement, "Genius is the statement of the obvious," he adds: "Genius is also the understanding of the obvious. And the facts of life prove that survival is the application of the obvious."

Management and Leadership Are Two Different Qualities

Management and leadership may or may not be present in the same person. Chances are, they're not.

Management is the science of getting things done through people; leadership, the subtle art of getting people to do things. These definitions are not one and the same. Appointment of a man or woman by superiors as a manager does not automatically carry with it the privileges and responsibilities of a leader who cannot be named from above, who is the choice of the group being led and about whom the others rally.

The distinguishing styles that mark a manager and a leader and the earmarks of maximum effectiveness in either capacity are the basis of management development and sales training programs and seminars sponsored by Richard Stern Associates and Teren Co., Stern's subsidiary.

These consultative services are conducted for all types of companies and organizations in both industry and government, manufacturing and retailing, on both Wall Street and Madison Avenue. The selfsame approach, the identical terminology, is used whether the client is Metropolitan Life Insurance, Consolidated Edison, Capital Cities Broadcasting Corp., Associated Merchandising Corp., Frederick Atkins, or Alexander's. The principles are universal.

Richard B. H. Stern, president of the Stern organization, and L. Renshaw Fortier, Teren's co-founder and president, had these thoughts on management versus leadership, the manager's or leader's behavior as it affects the managed or led, and management team building.

What makes an effective manager from the view of the managed?

Results, organization, knowledge, intelligence, skill, discipline, efficiency, success of the enterprise—all things that those who are being managed can perceive. If, as a result of the manager's behavior, each man has his assigned task and understands the rules of conformity and procedures, everybody recognizes the manager is managing.

What makes an effective leader from the view of the led?

A sense of success, fulfillment, enthusiasm for the project, courage, honesty, fair play, dedication, recognition, warmth—all things that those who are being led can feel.

What, then, is the difference between leadership and management? Both are communication processes. However, the former deals in feelings, the latter in intellect; the former in emotional relationships, the latter in conscious, professional relationships. The first is an art, the ultimate art of communications; the second a science, the product of knowledge and disciplines. Both are projections of behavior and, as such, studies of attitude. But each differs substantially from the other.

A manager's approach to his function is either "task oriented" or "human resources oriented." The manager's orientation or attitude falls into various sectors of commitment to task or to people, and these variations may be temporarily in evidence in the same persons at different times. There are no implications that any one segment has any inherent superiority in managerial capacity, intellectual ability, or technical competency over any others.

Individual styles of leaderships are reflected in degree of emotional capacity, sensitivity to the feelings of others, full and free expression of feelings, and combinations thereof.

No "Ideal" Leadership Style: It's an Art, Not a Science

Laurence Peter, author of *The Peter Principle,* finds three basic rules of conduct for the creative executives: 1) When in charge, ponder. 2) When in trouble, delegate. 3) When in doubt, mumble.

Obviously, Peter has his tongue planted firmly in cheek in this instance. Otherwise, any attempt to boil down the lore of creative executive conduct to three rules would be insufferable gall. Such gall is evident in the pontificating and prating of television psychologist Dr. Joyce Brothers and newspaper columnist Abigail Van Buren, who provide instant analysis of individual problems on the basis of necessarily sketchy, subjective information.

Consider, on the other hand, the mature, reasoned approach to a discussion of leadership styles by James Owens, a management professor and acting dean of American University's School of Business Administration and a business and government consultant.

Refreshingly candid, Owens concedes:

"Leadership is a mysterious and only vaguely understood ingredient that cannot be easily entered into a neat column. It is an ever-elusive riddle to those who must master it. The successful manager must master this phenomenon in practice, if not in theory and understanding, because his very survival as a career manager depends on it. Leadership must be created and sustained daily by a manager. With it, other managerial skills and resources come to life, and work. Without it, managerial skills and group talents become paralyzed—and work results grind to a halt."

Early studies, Owens points out, make leadership synonymous with such built-in traits as aggressiveness, self-control, independence, friendliness, religious orientation and optimism. Presumably, lack of leadership means these traits are absent. However, Owens notes, a mass of social science research adds up to very ambiguous results: sometimes, effective leaders possess some or all of the positive characteristics, but often none or few of these.

Over the past several years, this expert on management and organizational behavior has asked "several thousand" executives to comment on the validity of his concept that "there is an influential relationship between a manager's total personality and his success as a manager on the job." Virtually all agree with him.

Most of these managers, Owens explains, are of one mind that "a manager who is naturally low in his ability to trust others has little chance to succeed. Despite his best efforts, he will be unable to delegate properly and thus becomes a bottleneck as work piles up on his desk, and a source of frustration to people who want a chance to get involved and grow. A manager who requires a high degree of security in his life is unable to take any risks and thus fails. A manager who struggles within himself with a poor self-image and an inherent low level of self-confidence avoids decisions and radiates, as a kind of self-fulfilling prophecy, certain failure. Other examples include the effect on managerial success of personality characteristics such as racial prejudice, intolerance for unfamiliar ideas, and dislike or distrust of the young."

It is clear to Owens that "the personality of a man is his inner life—background, life experiences, beliefs, attitudes, prejudices, self-image, fears, loves, hates, hopes, and philosophy of life. In this sense, a man is like an iceberg. Only a small fraction of what he is appears above the surface (his observable behavior, what he does); the rest is his inner life, the seven-eighths of the iceberg that lie, unobservable, below the surface. However, the manager's inner personality spills over into his behavior which, in turn, affects others with whom he works, eliciting from them either cooperative or resistance reactions. Quite independently of his personality, what makes a leader effective is simply what he does."

Owens describes five leadership styles—autocratic, bureaucratic, diplomatic, participative, and free-rein. The managers with whom he has been in contact deny there is an "ideal" style, insisting instead that the "best" style depends on a) the individual personality of the manager himself; b) the individual followers—the kind of people they are, and the kind of work they do; and c) the particular situation and circumstances on any given day or hour.

The managers reject any "cook-book or formulized recipe" for effective leadership. They believe a manager can grow in his career only if he grows as a total personality, which he is long before he begins to function as a manager. What this means is that personal growth as a human being underlies and becomes, to a great extent, the real foundation upon which managerial and career growth can develop. Managerial success is not a peripheral set of "techniques"; it is a working out of one's essential being in the form of action.

Owens' conclusion:

"Leadership is still an art despite the efforts of social science researchers to make it a science. The summaries of essential leadership theory and managerial opinion, based on experience, have been presented only as a help to, not a substitute for, the final individual judgment of the manager as he lives with his particular people in his particular situation."

However, every such manager must operate by some leadership style or styles. And Owens hopes that the ideas he has set forth will aid the manager in his analysis, evaluation and development of his own personal leadership style. If the manager finds that some of his personality characteristics are liabilities, he must begin to change, if he can or wishes to. If he can't change, he must, as a person with mature judgment, assess himself carefully and seek the kind of job that fits his personality.

What Do Managers Think of Participative Leadership?

Participative leadership and management effectiveness are by no means synonymous.

This is indicated by responses of 318 executives to a questionnaire, containing 39 leadership characteristics, administered while they were attending management education programs at the Harvard Business School.

Over 50 percent of the respondents are in general management positions. The remainder are in such functional jobs as finance (17 percent) and marketing (11 percent). More than 50 percent of these managers are over age thirty-five, with 18 percent having more than twenty years in business, 15 percent with less than five years of experience.

Larry E. Greiner, associate professor of organizational behavior, Harvard Business School, at the time of the study, is now professor of organizational behavior, Graduate School of Business Administration, University of Southern California.

The 318 managers were divided into approximately two groups. One group was asked to rate each characteristic of participative leadership. The second group was told to check the five characteristics they found most effective in handling managerial situations and the same number they found least effective.

The ten highest participation characteristics:

1. gives subordinates a share in decision-making
2. keeps subordinates informed of the true situation, good or bad, under all circumstances
3. stays aware of the state of the organization's morale and does everything possible to make it high
4. is easily approachable
5. counsels, trains, and develops subordinates
6. communicates effectively with subordinates
7. shows thoughtfulness and consideration of others
8. is willing to make changes in ways of doing things
9. is willing to support subordinates even when they make mistakes
10. expresses appreciation when a subordinate does a good job

The ten most effective leadership characteristics:

1. counsels, trains and develops subordinates
2. communicates effectively with subordinates
3. lets the members of the organization know what is expected of them

4. sets high standards of performance
5. knows subordinates and their capabilities
6. gives subordinates a share in decision-making
7. stays aware of the state of the organization's morale and does everything possible to make it high
8. keeps subordinates informed of the true situation, good or bad, under all circumstances
9. is willing to make changes in ways of doing things
10. expresses appreciation when a subordinate does a good job

Seven of the top ten characteristics appear in both lists of characteristics. Significantly, however, the first four items on the effectiveness list are completely different from the first four items on the participation list. Moreover, the four highest-rated effectiveness characteristics rank only five, six, twenty, and twenty-six, respectively, in a complete ranking of the participation items by the first group of managers.

Of the entire list of leadership characteristics, the item with the highest effectiveness rating is concerned with training and developing subordinates (which challenges a stereotype that managers are preoccupied only with daily decision-making). These managers place considerably more value on the role of manager as teacher than as decision-maker.

Advocates of the participative style fall into what Greiner calls the "actor" school of thinking:

"Their key assumption is that managers are like sensitive players in a drama, relatively flexible and able to alter their behavioral styles, even in the later years of life. They see managers as able to exercise conscious, rational control over their own behavior and to adapt continuously to new cues and role demands placed on them by their organizations. With this model of a highly receptive leader in mind, members of the actor school emphasize the use of management education to convert executives to a participative style. As a result of their influence, thousands of managers have been exposed to company and university programs stressing both the humane and the productive aspects of participative leadership. Some of those programs have focused on team decision-making, others on joint goal-setting, and still others on listening skills for two-way communication."

Opposed to the actor school is the "born-leader" school. Its members take the position that a leader's style is deeply rooted in personality which, in turn, is a complex product of genetic inheritance and the maturation process. They see each manager's style as representing a highly individualistic, often unconscious, pattern of acting out ingrained values, conflicts, and attitudes acquired over many years. And they express strong doubts that managers, as they become older, can easily adopt new forms of behavior.

Younger managers in the study tend to emphasize work priorities, proving their technical competence, and backing up subordinates. This more aggressive orientation is understandable, Greiner points out, if one views younger managers as full of energy and enthusiasm, yet possessing doubts about their own competence. In addition, these managers are usually in lower-level or specialist positions where they must visibly demonstrate their talents while also coping with heavy workloads and intense pressure for results.

Managers between thirty and forty are mainly in middle-management jobs where they must deal with eager subordinates as well as complex tasks that require numerous "trade-offs." Hence, they favor (a) taking a more personalized approach to others, (b) relating to subordinates, and (c) making group decisions. Psychologically, the middle manager is often exploring his ability to handle heavier responsibility while taking greater risks, so he understandably turns to others for consultation and support.

Managers in the over-forty group display a shift toward fatherly concerns. These older executives, who are usually in top management, seem strongly preoccupied with counseling, developing, and training subordinates. They are also concerned with the broad issue of communications.

Greiner suggests that companies learn all three age groups contribute differently to the organization. He urges that this variance be more sensitively accounted for in manpower planning and performance-assessment decisions.

The Give and Take of Effective Delegation

Every manager has responsibilities delegated to him by his superiors and delegates certain tasks to his subordinates. This is scarcely the same thing as saying that every manager provides effective delegation.

On the contrary, there is a great deal of grumbling on practically every management ship about just that lack. Such complaints are voiced, more or less under the breath, as "he doesn't tell me enough," "he thinks I'm dumb and spells everything out in triplicate," "I can't understand him," "he cuts me up when I ask questions," "he's too bossy," and "he's too wishy-washy."

For all those involved, knowingly or otherwise, in this dilemma, Gerald G. Fisch submits five rules that he assures have stood effective delegators in good stead over the years. Fisch, a senior partner of Kates, Peat, Marwick & Co., management consultants, Province of Quebec, Canada, has spelled out these five axioms. Fisch's formula:

1. Since you are at the receiving end as well as the giving end of delegation, delegate to your subordinates as you would like matters to be delegated to you. This is a rule that is most frequently disregarded. We are all too ready

to tell our superiors how they should delegate to us but, when it is our turn, we forget all the things we would like our chiefs to do with us and add a few mistakes of our own.

2. Don't take communications or understanding for granted. Try a simple experiment. Take a person with whom you are working and have him record the tasks you have delegated to him and his impressions of what is really expected. Next, write down your expectations and interpretation of your requirements. In comparing the two statements, you will be amazed to find substantial discrepancies between what you think you have communicated and what has in fact been understood.

3. All men are not created equal in terms of ability and behavior. Many of us are not sufficiently sensitive to, or aware of, the real strengths and weaknesses of others. This is not surprising since our tools for measuring effectiveness and ability are quite poor. Thus, we often delegate a task to a man who is capable of doing perhaps much more, or we may delegate a really tough assignment to a man who does not have the least comprehension of how to execute the assignment.

4. It's not what you say, but how you say it. Many an act of delegation, whether in written or oral form, goes awry because the spirit or the emotional climate between the two persons involved is less than ideal. Human beings are emotional even in management, and when the spirit of delegation is one of understanding and sympathy, there is greater effectiveness than if the climate between the two people is cold or hostile.

5. Don't forget environmental constraints. In every business enterprise, there are constraints in delegation. These begin with formal legal constraints, go a step further to social and cultural constraints, and still further to specific organizational constraints and peculiar styles indigenous to given corporations, partnerships, or government departments.

Fisch makes it clear he favors "a flexible management style. Effective managers must be flexible in style, autocratic in some instances, democratic in others, participative in the third. For example, it is inappropriate to be participative with a group of people who cry out for leadership. On the other hand, it is equally unreasonable to be excessively autocratic with a group of highly trained intellectuals on issues where the corporation is paying good money to obtain the benefit of their resources. In dealing with equals, autocracy can do a great deal of harm. When a superior wants solutions, not problems, one needs to be incisive and positive."

3

THE SCIENCE
OF MANAGEMENT

Two Retail Worlds of Ownership and
Professional Management Merging

Family lines have continued in command of retail companies longer than in business in general. The reason is that the world of store chains is closer to its beginnings as big business than are the industrial giants. After all, professional management in retailing dates back only to 1906 when Sears, Roebuck pioneered the sale of public securities.

The retirement of Bruce A. Gimbel as chairman of Gimbel Bros. in August, 1975 at 62 marks the departure of the fourth generation of Gimbels (the fifth generation, represented by Robert, Bruce's son, left the firm several years ago in favor of Wall Street). Thus, the Gimbels have reached the end of the line in retailing. The chain, which includes Saks Fifth Avenue, has been controlled since 1973 by Brown & Williamson Industries, American subsidiary of British-American Tobacco Co.

Ralph Lazarus is due to relinquish his Federated chairmanship within the next few years, after which only a handful of Lazari of the fourth and fifth generations will continue to occupy corporate or divisional posts. At R.H. Macy & Co., fifth-generation Kenneth H. Straus is a senior vice-president. At Rich's, fourth-generation Michael P. Rich is a senior vice-president.

Of course, professional management—the power of performance over pull—need not be confined to outsiders. It can be and has been exercised by family members. However, in the past, poorly prepared men, bolstered by sizable family stockholdings, have often been perpetuated along with those who fill high-echelon positions strictly on merit. Increasingly, for competitive reasons, the family has had to seek an orderly transition at the helm regardless of ancestry.

Among the steadily declining number of family members remaining as chairmen of department store chains are G. Stockton Strawbridge, Strawbridge & Clothier; William B. Thalhimer Jr., Thalhimer Bros.; Kenneth N. Dayton, Dayton-Hudson; Joseph L. Hudson Jr., Dayton-Hudson's J.L. Hudson division; Albert D. Hutzler Jr., Hutzler Bros.; J. Arthur Baer, Associated Dry Goods Corp.'s Stix Baer & Fuller division, and George M. Ivey, J.B. Ivey. Bernard and Robert T. Sakowitz are, respectively, chairman and president of Sakowitz. Stanley Marcus is chairman of Neiman-Marcus's executive committee, while his son Richard C. is president.

In August, 1975, Robert Sakowitz moved up from vice-president of Sakowitz, the Houston-based, privately-owned specialty store chain, to president, and his father Bernard assumed the new post of chairman as well as chief executive. Bernard says this should assure family ownership for at least another generation. He believes "it's a tragedy when a guy like Stanley Marcus, a guy like Andrew Goodman or a guy like Grover Magnin sells a company. As stores get absorbed by big groups, they say they'll not change, but there's got to be a change. You're responsible to a whole new group. The only people I have to please are Ann (his wife), myself, Bob and my daughter."

The elder Sakowitz is referring to mergers of Neiman-Marcus and Bergdorf Goodman into Carter Hawley Hale within the past half dozen years. In the case of Grover Magnin, Sakowitz's long memory takes him back to Bullock's purchase of I. Magnin & Co. in 1944 and the merger of Bullock's-Magnin in 1964 into Federated which later separated that division into two subsidiaries.

Asked for comment on Sakowitz's statement, Stanley Marcus responds: "I don't want to get involved in any controversy. This is a free country." Having said which, he adds: "Under the ownership of 'C double H,' we do better planning than before and have improved our net profit substantially. No, I won't tell you what our net is, and I have no idea what Sakowitz' is. If I were doing it over again, I would have done it five years earlier.

The elder Marcus reports that, as executive vice-president of CHH, he usually spends four or five hours a day three days a week at Neiman's and one or two days a month at Bergdorf's and Holt Renfrew, the parent company's Canadian specialty store chain.

The 70-year-old Marcus (1975) is "in fine health" and plans to retain his Neiman and CHH posts for the foreseeable future.

Andrew Goodman decided to sell Bergdorf's following the resignation as vice-president of his son Edwin to work, first, for the Bedford-Stuyvesant Development and Service Corp. and, then, for WBAI, a listener-supported, New Left radio station, of which he is general manager. Two sons-in-law of Andrew also opted for non-retail careers after occupying Bergdorf posts for a number of years.

In early 1975, Andrew Goodman, then 68, was succeeded as president and chief executive officer by Ira Neimark, previously executive vice-president at B. Altman. Goodman now serves as chairman. Leonard J. Hankin continued as executive vice-president for store management.

The two worlds of retailing—management by a member of the founding or controlling clan and non-family management, are slowly but surely merging into one world of professionals, whether family or outsiders.

Are Managers Born or Can They Be Made?

Lawrence A. Appley is convinced the fundamental principles of professional management can be taught, that men and women "need not be born to be managers, they can be made."

As the longtime president, then chairman of American Management Associations who retired in 1974, Appley speaks from many years of close observation of the thousands of executives who have attended AMA management and presidents' courses. Appley's background also includes vice-presidencies of Montgomery Ward and Richardson-Merrell, drug manufacturer.

The core concept of management is getting things done through other people—any activity that involves leading any group of people toward the attainment of common objectives in any walk of life. Management is *not* the direction of things; it *is* the development of people. Management is taking people as they are, with the knowledge, training, experience, and background they have accumulated, and developing those people by increasing their knowledge, improving their skills, and correcting their habits and attitudes. Managers should not be interested in the development of perfect standards of performance just for the sake of attaining perfection in that medium. What is important is the process of applying the technique—the process of bringing a supervisor and a subordinate closer together in their mental images of what is to be done and how well it is to be done.

He who does things himself is an individual producer and not a manager.

He is not getting things done; he is doing them. The manner in which one gets things done through others differs in every respect from the way in which one does things himself. He who is expert in attaining high individual productivity is not necessarily effective in attaining high individual productivity from others, nor is there any basic requirement that he be one in order to do the other.

Management knowledge is more important than technical knowledge. It is expected that a manager will select competent specialists and that his talent will be based upon his ability to coordinate their efforts. He does not have to be a specialist to manage specialists.

Assuming that both the mediocre and the inspired leader have the basic requirements that any manager would have to remain on the payroll—honesty, industry, technical capability, loyalty—there are at least five basic characteristics that separate excellence from mediocrity:

1. has a record ' ' attainment
2. has a purpose in life that is aimed at helping other people rather than exploiting them
3. practices consultative supervision (participative management)
4. is intellectually mature
5. is emotionally stable

Managers Cast Fishy Eye on Own Training and Effectiveness

Analysis of managerial effectiveness as a whole has been left to teachers and other professional observers of management development. How managers view their own training and development has not been subjected to the searchlight. That is, until now.

Robert F. Pearse, professor of behavioral sciences, Boston University School of Management, has filled the gap with a survey for American Management Associations. He has held his university post for the past ten years and has also had management development and other personnel experience in the automotive, drug, and food industries. His report, "Manager to Manager: What Managers Think of Management Development," is designed to provide managers with the opportunity to share with their peers how they spend their time developing and applying administrative and technical skills, their evaluations of their own effectiveness, and what kinds of additional training they should be receiving to make them better managers.

A total of 2,026 of the 7,000 managers in AMA's general management division participated in the questionnaire.

Sixty-four percent of the respondents are in top management, with those from ages forty to fifty-nine comprising about three-quarters of the total in that group. Twenty-five percent of the total number of respondents are in middle-management, with those from thirty to forty-nine also comprising about three-quarters of its group. The remainder of the respondents are divided into lower management/supervisory, professional/technical, and self-employed/proprietor classifications.

Highlights of the findings:

Managers at both top and middle levels spend about twice as much time in relationships with their subordinates as they do with superiors.

Respondents' estimates of the order of importance to them of managerial functions: planning, motivating, coordinating. Their ranking of managerial activities, in the same order: interpersonal, administrative, personal, technical.

Managers consider in-house, out-of-house, and university-based training substantially less significant than actual on-the-job training and self-development. Evaluating the relative worth of training courses they have taken, managers say courses in interpersonal relationship skills are twice as beneficial as courses in improved personal effectiveness. Courses in administrative skills and technical problem-solving are also considered less helpful than interpersonal skills training.

About 85 percent of the respondents would like to take more short management training courses aimed at developing a single skill. They want more short courses in communication, improving the effectiveness of individual subordinates, and improving work group or departmental effectiveness.

About 20 percent of the participants have taken sensitivity training and related interpersonal skills courses during the past three years. One out of five say this training has led to a major improvement in interpersonal effectiveness on the job.

Among other findings:

About two-thirds of the top and middle managers feel that a young person can reach supervisory or lower management level without a formal management education. However, only 20 percent of top managers and 13 percent of middle-managers believe today's young person can go all the way to the top on his own training initiatives.

The executives with MBA degrees contend behavioral science and business policy courses were most useful to them in the real world of management; courses in real estate, least useful. Eighty-two middle-echelon managers view behavioral science courses as of the greatest value; forty-six, production and operations management studies.

Managers see several reasons why management programs are relatively ineffective:

1. Many decision-makers believe managerial effectiveness is inherent; hence, it cannot be acquired through skills training courses,

2. Many authoritarian managers at top levels don't really want highly developed, skillful, creative subordinates. Instead, they want technically competent people who will carry out orders without expecting much in the way of opportunities to demonstrate real initiative.

3. Large bureaucratic systems demand manager conformity. As one manager puts it: "Either you feed the system what it wants or you don't eat."

4. Top management does not view utilization and development of investments in human resources in the same way it looks at capital investments. Human resources are mobile. They leave, become ill, or function below par. Since an organization can never "own" its human resources, a modest human resources investment is about all a company really ought to make.

Pearse sees top policy-making decisions about management development and human resources investments limited by these other key factors:

1. Smaller and middle-size organizations, particularly those founded and operated by entrepreneurs, do not have time or money to spend in developing a complete management education program.

2. Without a philosophy of professional management, expenditures are largely wasted, and the waste isn't recognized and dealt with.

A crucial question: can managerial skills be effectively taught in formal training programs? Pearse's answer: much of formal management education being offered today is simply not adequate to train practicing managers to do their jobs well. A new curriculum, based on the best currently available concepts of educators, is badly needed.

Pearse insists "there is a case for a more sophisticated approach to management development as a human resources investment. Management practitioners will have to have far more managerial skills training through formal education programs than they have received in the past and more than most of them are getting today."

Pearse predicts three components of the effective management development program of the next decade:

1. Human resources accounting to measure cost-benefits aspects more precisely than ever before.

2. Training related more specifically to actual manager needs and tied to career development.

3. A shift away from people-using organization and toward people-building organizations.

What's Your Score in Professional Management?

Today's professional manager differs substantially in individual skills, organizational abilities, and value systems from yesterday's owner-manager.

Profiles of each type are portrayed by H. Igor Ansoff, dean of the Graduate School of Management, Vanderbilt University.

In a period of transition, he places each type in a passing "mass-production era" or in a current stage of "management by technocracy." The mass-production era witnessed accelerating abdication of strategic control by top management, a step in the loss of owners' direction of their firms' fortunes. In management by technocracy, "the role of top management in large firms has become increasingly ambiguous and less powerful; corporate staff have become the symbol of 'lean,' efficient corporate management; and goal setting for major strategic thrusts has been progressively delegated to lower management levels. Top management limits its scope to budgeting review, public relations, and management development. When this occurs, a coalition of technocrats takes over the decisions and leaves top management to 'rubber stamp' their consensus."

Ansoff characterizes the manager who, for his time, effectively dealt with the challenges of the mass-production era:

In a smoothly growing world, past experience was a reliable guide to the future. The problems encountered at any managerial level were likely to be a repetition on a large scale of problems experienced earlier. The overall character of the manager's problem world throughout his career was built on a stable technological base, known customers, a familial internal organizational structure, and a familiar if dynamic competition. The problems and surprises, the risks and the opportunities, that challenged him came from changes in known variables—sales, inventory, costs, competition—and not from structural changes such as a major influx of foreign competition or drastic obsolescence of technology.

On the other hand, the manager had little exposure to the political, societal, and cultural influences that affect business decisions. He was a skillful crisis manager so long as the options available to him included familiar solutions. He had only limited skills in solving novel problems that had no precedent in his previous experience. Nor was he skilled in leading the organization on major departures from historical organizational development.

The entrepreneurial manager, Ansoff continues, is distinctive from his mass-production counterparts in the following respects:

1. He is globally profit-minded both in time and space. His concern is both with immediate and long-term profitability. He has no emotional attachment to the traditional business of the firm. All opportunities are to be weighed against the overall profitability of the enterprise. He applies Alfred P. Sloan's creed: "The strategic aim of the enterprise is to produce a satisfactory return on the resources invested in it. If the return is not satisfactory, either the deficiency must be corrected or resources allocated elsewhere."

2. He tempers his devotion to profitability with social effectiveness. He is a responsible citizen who does not believe that what is good for business is good for the country. Still, he is clear-minded about protecting the primary wealth-generation purpose of the firm from erosion by unacceptable constraints or by diversionary or depressing activities.

3. He finds his satisfaction, not only in the extrinsic rewards of money and power but also in the intrinsic satisfaction of creative managerial work.

4. His familiarity with his business firm is less on terms of what it has done and more in terms of what it can do based upon its resources, strengths, and weaknesses, and the constraints on its behavior. He has a continuing interest in, and broad knowledge of, opportunities outside the traditional business of the firm.

5. His problem-solving perspective is broad: technological, competitive, economic, political, cultural, sociological. He is a man of many talents— entrepreneur, planner, administrator, systems architect, politician, and statesman. The difficulties of breeding this paragon of all virtues are formidable; perhaps group management is the only possible way to bring all these talents together.

6. He is a creative problem-solver. He continually searches for new alternatives; he is a habitual learner, quick to assimilate new information and isolate the controlling variables and devise novel solution procedures.

7. He is a skillful leader of group and organizational problem-solving. Where he lacks personal expertise, he is skilled in the art of using experts.

8. His risk propensities are not biased in favor of the familiar, nor is he a habitual gambler on the unknown. He attempts to develop a balanced portfolio of risks commensurate with possible gain.

9. His leadership skills lie in inducing the organization to take bold departures from tradition.

Such a man, Ansoff points out, can operate only within a complementary organizational development, some of whose features are:

1. Authority based not on power but on knowledge, in which work is designed to the dual criteria of task effectiveness and intrinsic motivation of the individual.

2. An organizational structure that accommodates both the stability of an efficiency-seeking bureaucracy and the fluidity of individual innovative behavior.

3. A surveillance system that scans the environment beyond limits of current business for major trends, projects these into the future, translates them into threats and opportunities for the firm, and injects this information into appropriate action points. A forecasting system that does not assume the future to be an extrapolation of the past but explores structural changes underlying current trends. An information system that communicates up and down as well as sideways to link people according to common tasks.
4. A reward and motivation system that recognizes both current profitability and imaginative investment in future profitability, is tolerant of risk-taking behavior and meaningful failure, builds rewards into the content of jobs, and is sympathetic to the changed personal values of both workers and managers.

Incompetence, Overdependence: Management's Achilles Heel

One-man, authoritarian rule is supposedly an anachronism. At the very top of major corporations, it is increasingly giving way to the corporate executive or president's office—three or more men who wield group influence on final decisions. Command authority in general appears to be going by the boards because subordinates won't have it. A voice in major decision-making is sometimes being granted at the lowest management and even rank-and-file echelons. The claimed purpose: everyone should experience his primary life goal of self-realization, with minimum interference from superiors.

That's the message spouted with varying degrees of rejoicing and regret, of honesty and hypocrisy, at one management meeting after another.

But it ain't necessarily so if you take the word of Robert N. McMurry, industrial psychologist and head of The McMurry Co., thirty-year-old management consulting organization based in Chicago.

"Tens of thousands of persons," he explains, "are available to fill safe, secure, well-structured positions, while probably only one in a hundred can cope with the risks and demands of a relatively unstructured high-level assignment. Fortunately, most businesses require relatively few true decision-makers because most positions, including many of those in middle management, are comprehensively structured. Hence, authority, with its decision-making responsibilities, tends to be centralized in a few hands. Despite this, there is a chronic shortage of genuinely qualified managers—those who can cope with truly major decisions."

As McMurry views the scene, probably 10 to 20 percent of all employees have the self-confidence and levels of expectations to make the decisions and take the risks required in higher management positions. However, he continues, the vast majority of people will spend their entire working lives as employees, most in structured jobs in lower or middle management.

"The majority of these persons will spend practically all their lives in work and off-the-job environments in which they will be called upon to make only occasional and negligibly risk-taking decisions. Furthermore, the majority of these middle-managers (below the rank of vice-president) voluntarily or involuntarily spend all their lives in a posture of relatively docile submission to authoritarian leadership, whether on the job, in the military, in the church, or in dealing with such government agencies as IRS. When they are given authority with its attendant risks, many abdicate it without delay. Authority is difficult to delegate permanently to middle management; it is constantly being bucked upwards."

The "Achilles Heel" of the substantial proportion of incompetents in middle and top management positions, according to McMurry, is overdependance with consequent anxiety and indecisiveness, and is usually not related to technical ability, intelligence, integrity and dedication.

The authoritarian style of leadership remains universal, McMurry goes on, primarily because "it best suits the needs of most people for structure, guidance, and freedom from the need to accept responsibility and make decisions." In their form of government, in the armed services, in political and religious groups, as well as in business and industry in general, he contends, the majority seek only enough democracy and self-determination to save face. He insists the predominantly autocratic style of leadership has endured for hundreds of years because it is most acceptable to those who want to be relieved of the necessity for making other than minor or technical decisions, and because it is most efficient from a production point of view.

Why are many persons throughout most enterprises so acutely dependent? McMurry notes a contradiction in the case of "the man in the street" who pictures himself as strong, decisive, and unneedful of guidance and support, yet is simultaneously often passive, dependent, and submissive. The answer, the psychologist says, is simple:

"Although anxiety is endemic in America, any overt admission of dependence, anxiety, and the need for support and guidance is equated with weakness. In the prevailing culture, to be called weak is intolerable to the majority of males and, more recently, to many women as well. Everyone wears a mask to conceal the individual's underlying anxieties and insecurities not only from others but from himself as well."

Many of industry's most notable overstrivers, McMurry further argues, overcompensate with masculinity, or machismo, by becoming authorities on all topics, boastful, and outwardly excessively sure of themselves. In practice, they are very daring and self-assured until the crunch comes. At this point, their compensation breaks down, and they are often subject to a total psychic collapse.

McMurry cites three steps management can take to identify victims of "the overdependency syndrome":

1. Management must first evaluate each supervisory or managerial and executive position to ascertain its decision demands.
2. Management must next inventory its present supervisory and executive staff to identify those who may now be over their heads.
3. In selecting candidates for initial employment or for promotion, care must be taken to examine by a combination of appraisals, tests, and interviews all candidates to make certain they do not give evidence of overdependence where they are.

McMurry concludes that "only management and its staff are in a position to take prophylactic action to avoid the tragedy that is almost inevitable" when an employee is over his head on the job with consequent psycho-physiological damage to himself, not to mention costliness to his employer.

No Mystery in Management if You Honor People's Values

A cartoon caption in *The New Yorker* magazine reads: "Angeline, guess what! I've chucked the chairmanship of the board and taken a job as a piano player in a bordello."

A company head, stricken with a heart attack, received a wire from a union with which his firm has a contract: "Wish you complete recovery. This resolution was passed by vote of 13 to 12."

Needless to say, serious management problems underlie these examples of grim, even gallows, humor.

Henry M. Boettinger, AT&T's director of corporate planning, has some pertinent thoughts on the subject:

"We have encrusted the art, craft and science of management over the years with so many professional mysteries that the hard kernel of its nucleus has become obscured." He suggests there are only three ways anyone in charge of a number of people can improve individual and group performance and the organization's operations and results:

1. Improve their training. It is the quickest way to get better results. But human limits and the learning curve soon reach diminishing returns if that is the only method embraced.
2. Let the group discover latent talents in themselves and turn unused capacity into realized ability. Among the forms such efforts can take: securing a

sharing of common goals by inspiring oratory and bulletins, goading the reluctant, encouraging the timid, rewarding accomplishment and recognizing creative contributions. Acquiring these new levels of confidence takes longer than training but less time than the third method.

3. Invention, development or copying of new tools, techniques and methods that can cause great leaps forward but need the most careful preparation and the longest time to show results. But such hardware and software cause organizational stress and destroy many informal communication systems.

"Every effective manager," according to Boettinger, "uses all three of these methods, with emphasis and selection geared to his specific problems at certain times. Yet, none can be used in isolation for long. Every staff man and consultant must have some expertise in each of them, even though he may specialize predominantly in one of the three fields."

Albert W. Mankoff, vice-president, Lexicon, Inc., Raleigh, N.C.-based consulting firm, contends values, not attitudes, are the real key to motivation.

Mankoff notes that "one increasingly popular way of determining the reasons for lack of motivation is the attitude survey. But efforts to use the attitude survey as a basis for determining the direction of change quite often come to grief. There are three basic reasons for this failure:

1. Management may refuse to accept the findings.
2. Management, although "accepting," may refuse to deal openly and honestly with the data—leaving the reports to gather dust in the desk of someone whose eminence, position or ego might be threatened by the publication of the results.
3. Most insidious is that attitude surveys do not always measure the appropriate thing in the first place.

Mankoff, whose firm specializes in organizational and management development, emphasizes the difference between attitudes and values. Attitudes are beliefs predisposing one to respond in some preferential manner. Attitude measurement is so ambiguous as to be of limited use. By seeking to put the spotlight on the generalities of attitudes, the research dollar and the necessary focus on the specifics of values—how a person's attitudes are formed and shaped—is misdirected. Attitudes may be changed in a very short time when the discrepancies in an individual's values can be shown to him.

While an adult may have hundreds of thousands of beliefs and thousands of attitudes, that person will possess only a few dozen basic values. These values are enduring modes of conduct and criteria for guiding action. Values may not be measurable, but they can at least be compared. It is the basic value system to which a person subscribes that ultimately determines how he relates to himself, his family, other people, his job, his boss.

Discussing the quandary of people within a business organization who are subjected to, or involved in, making choices that conflict with what they know to be right, Mankoff continues:

"Our free-enterprise system, for all its positive qualities, sometimes engenders values that are seen by many as materialistic, competitive, separative and selfish. Young people write off the system as characterized by greed, and novelists and filmmakers depict it as infected with bitter ruthlessness. All too often, these images are confirmed by the reality of court actions and congressional investigations. If those at the policy level of business view the world and their mission in purely selfish terms, and translate these values into appropriate action to gain their ends, these values—reflected in managerial style—form the model for behavior throughout the organization."

How Managers Can Communicate Better

Ask any executive—or anyone else, for that matter—what his principal problem is. Regardless of how didactic, diffuse, ponderous, flowery, or sincere the reply may be, it all comes down to insufficiences in the elements of communication.

Glenn A. Bassett, personnel development consultant at General Electric's corporate headquarters in Fairfield, Conn., seeks to provide some insights. He tackles the question, "What Is Communication and How Can I Do It Better?"

Bassett suggests the answer falls into one of three categories:

1. Probably most prevalent is the type of manager that responds: "You bet your——I communicate well; I spell everything out in spades so there's nothing left to doubt."
2. The second type reacts with surprise and asks you: "What do you mean, 'How well do I communicate?' I don't think about communicating, I just do it."
3. The third type reflects on your question thoughtfully before saying something like, "How can you ever know how well you get your ideas across to another person? All I can tell you is I work more hours trying to communicate than I can count, and it still doesn't work some of the time."

Each, in his own way, is "correct," according to the GE consultant. Communication, he emphasizes, "is many things. In order to use it well, it is first necessary to know what it consists of. Communication has at least five major facets: verbalizing, definitions, control, body or silent language, and sharing experiences."

Bassett elaborates on each of these facets:

Verbalizing. We should not underestimate the mystique and power of words; neither should we allow ourselves to be taken in by fast or fancy talk. A common approach to foolish or superficial use of words is to employ largely meaningless abstractions and back them up with the trappings of authority. If everyone expects a particular executive to have the answer, and cannot question the answer he gives, he doesn't have to admit to embarrassing ignorance; he need simply verbalize a bit of impressive nonsense. A subordinate or colleague who wants to defend himself against this practice must insist (to himself) that, if the words don't make sense in terms of his own experience, he should challenge their meaning if he can, or suspend acceptance. The alert communicator will not be intimidated by high-sounding words.

It is well to be skeptical about your own words as well as those of others. If you must verbalize an unusual message, for instance, have it restated to you by someone with whom you otherwise have good communication. Get feedback from those the message will be aimed at. Expect and look for error. And get help from experienced wordsmiths—a good secretary, an experienced writer, a friend with good verbal skills.

Definitions. With words and language, meaning is normally etched into the nervous system by experience. But, because people's experiences differ, it is often useful to specify the kind of experience or event included in the definition of a word.

Whenever you are faced with gaining acceptance of a group that has a lengthy history of jargon behind it, it is important to be alert to words, phrases, or expressions used in an unusual way—with jargonized communication. Admit your confusion to those who can help dispel it.

Control. Most business organizations are at least partially modeled after the military so far as internal "command communications" are concerned—although there is perhaps less emphasis on training and more on rewards or penalties for effective or ineffective response. In industry, control communication has no doubt been overused; yet, some form of it is always necessary. For example, the manager who has convinced his subordinates he has a firm sense of market changes finds ready acceptance to his order to schedule overtime to meet sudden heavy product demand.

The important consideration is that consistent response is ultimately based on willingness to follow proven leadership.

Body or silent language. Bodily motions, eye contact, and nonverbal sounds are all important forms of communication. Employees learn to cue on the nonverbal communications of the boss. His facial expression or lightness of gait in the morning may determine whether the bad news can be communicated today or not. Employees learn to choose their words based on whether the boss leans forward toward them or rocks back from them in his chair.

The most important step a manager may ever take toward being a more effective communicator could well be that of mastering his own body language. If his words say one thing while his body says another, the body communication will probably get precedence in credibility. If your feelings are reacting against what you have to say, ask yourself, "What am I doing now that I don't normally do when I feel good about saying something?"

Sharing experiences. Communication that leads to sharing/cross-verifying/filling out experiences is perhaps the most artful and satisfying kind there is. The more similar the backgrounds of two people, the easier communicative contact will be. When specific experiences are not shared by communicator and audience, other experiences that are shared will have to become the starting point. In society as a whole, the theater, films, and literature are commonly used tools to simulate unshared experiences for the benefit of others.

By the time a person becomes a manager, according to Bassett, "he has usually learned how to turn off his hearing to those without the authority to make him listen. He now needs to begin to hear his subordinates, but too often is out of the habit of listening to people in a status below his own. He must resensitize himself—train himself to hear and notice the details of his subordinates' communicative inputs." The new manager must obtain information—his key resource—from former fellow workers, new colleagues at the same level, and higher management, all of whom may choose with care the confidences they wish to share with him. This may lead, at the outset, to "management by cronyism."

But, as the manager moves up the ladder, he must himself validate information inputs—become sensitive to minor discrepancies and minute ambiguities.

Every Manager Is Pygmalion

Instance after instance of the communication gap continue to accumulate. Dr. J. Sterling Livingston, president of Sterling Institute, management consultants, and former Harvard Business School professor, linked it to Robert Burns' "The gift of God, the gift he'd gie us, to see ourselves as ithers see us."

In a study of ten department store managers in two medium-sized organizations, he found that store managers do not always see their managerial styles in the same way that the central staff executives view them. For example, the store manager who was unanimously considered by the executives of one of the companies to be their most directive, autocratic manager, identified his style as *consultive*—controlling with a loose rein.

Livingston also reported that store managers who were unanimously ranked as the most effective at both retail organizations identified their managerial styles in exactly the same way as these were identified by the central staff executives. On the other hand, the least effective managers saw their styles in almost opposite terms from the way in which the executives saw them.

This suggests that "effective managers may have one unique characteristic—they are more objective about themselves and are better able to see themselves as others see them than are less effective managers who are likely to have trusting, tolerant, and other consultive-type styles."

Livingston says that similar, tentative conclusions have been drawn from studies of managerial styles in other highly competitive industries.

Of the opinion that the *interactive* style of management—objective, analytical, flexible—is most likely to contain "the priceless ingredient" in managerial effectiveness, Livingston highlights important features:

First, managers with this style are objective in seeing themselves and in appraising the capabilities, expectations, and motivation of other people. They recognize that each individual is different, that persons do not pursue their own self-interest with equal determination. They know that men with equal potential vary considerably in their personal development, initiative, and willingness to take responsibility. They know that some men are self-motivated and can direct and control their own activities, but that others are "followers" or "leaners" who need guidance, stimulation, and development.

They know that individuals respond differently to pressure, incentives, and personal attention. Since they seek to improve the performance of each individual in their organization, they adapt their pattern of behavior to the man rather than expect all men to fit a mold created by a particular concept of management. Since their flexible type of leadership enables them to match the pattern of management to the individual's expectations, capabilities, and motivation, they find relatively few "unmanageable" men.

Second, these highly effective managers are catalysts who initiate the action needed to achieve high levels of performance. The significance of this characteristic can be seen in the managerial problems listed by ineffective managers as their most difficult. The most interactive managers, contrary to those who are least interactive, are not troubled by lack of initiative on the part of subordinates.

Third, interactive managers use a problem-solving approach that not only facilitates determination of what needs to be done but also develops the capacity of subordinates. Instead of telling subordinates what to do and how to do it, interactive managers typically ask them to identify the problems or obstacles that must be overcome in order to reach desired levels of performance. Their objective is to get each individual to identify what he must do to improve his performance, and then to devise his own plan to achieve the desired results.

These managers do not "take over." They stop short of telling their subordinates what to do or how to do it, unless the urgency of the situation demands it. Their action is guided by the desire to develop the capacity of subordinates, to get them to take responsibility for the consequences of their actions, and to give them the full sense of satisfaction that comes with achievement.

Finally, interactive managers stimulate their subordinates to achieve high levels of performance by asking them to commit themselves to the attainment of their planned objectives. These commitments are often obtained in group meetings, and progress is reviewed in similar meetings. This process insures the full involvement of the subordinate in the achievement of the desired results and creates a powerful motivation to perform effectively.

What are *You*—a directive, consultive, or interactive manager? Think it over! Livingston likens managers, particularly those who manage young men and women at the lower rungs of the career ladder, to George Bernard Shaw's Pygmalion—the story of the transformation of a flower girl to a lady.

Some managers, he explains, "always treat their subordinates in a way that leads to superior performance. But most managers, like Professor Higgins, unintentionally treat their subordinates in a way that leads to lower performance than they are capable of achieving."

On the basis of a number of case studies and other scientific research, Livingston believes:

- What a manager expects of his subordinates and the way he treats them largely determine their performance and career progress.
- A unique characteristic of superior managers is their ability to create high performance expectations that subordinates fulfill.
- Less effective managers fail to develop similar expectations and, as a consequence, the productivity of their subordinates suffers.
- Subordinates, more often than not, appear to do what they believe they are expected to do.

According to Livingston, "managers cannot avoid the depressing cycle of events that flow from low expectations merely by hiding their feelings from subordinates. Indeed, a manager often communicates most when he believes he is communicating least. For instance, when he says nothing, when he becomes 'cold' and 'uncommunicative,' it usually is a sign that he is displeased by a subordinate or believes the latter is 'hopeless.' The silent treatment communicates negative feelings even more effectively at times than a tongue-lashing does. It usually is astonishingly difficult for managers to recognize the clarity with which they transmit negative feelings to subordinates."

The consultant asserts that "the power of positive thinking or generalized confidence in one's fellow man" is not sufficient. Subordinates, he explains, will not be motivated to reach high levels of productivity unless they consider the boss's high expectations realistic and achievable. If they are encouraged to strive for unattainable goals, they eventually give up trying and settle for results that are lower than they are capable of achieving. It is therefore not surprising that failure of subordinates to meet the unrealistically high expectations of their managers leads to high rates of attrition, voluntary or otherwise.

Managerial expectations, Livingston continues, "have their most magical influence on young men. As subordinates mature and gain experience, their self-image gradually hardens and they begin to see themselves as their career records imply. Their own aspirations, and the expectations of their superiors, become increasingly controlled by the 'reality' of their past performance. It becomes more and more difficult for them and their managers to generate mutually high expectations unless they have outstanding records. If a young man has high aspirations, he will leave in hope of finding a better opportunity. If, on the other hand, his manager helps him achieve his maximum potential, he will build the foundation for a successful career."

4

EVERYBODY IS SOMEONE'S SUBORDINATE

Subordinatemanship

If you're someone's subordinate—and almost everybody is—your idea of the job may be entirely different from that of your associates. More likely, though, you don't veer materially from anyone else in the way you conceive and execute your duties and responsibilities.

Dr. Barry T. Jensen, director, Behavioral Sciences Division, General Systems Industries, Torrance, Calif., discusses the differences. Dr. Jensen received his Ph.D. in psychology from Ohio State University and has held a variety of management, personnel, and research positions. His company develops educational training programs and information systems programs for computer use.

Regardless of his level, a good subordinate, according to Dr. Jensen, can lead his boss—not in the Machiavellian sense of control and manipulation but as an active, influential member of the management team.

This would be at odds with a dictionary meaning of "subordinate": "subservient" or "submissive." That is, when the boss speaks, the typical subordinate manager jumps; until the boss speaks, he waits for directions. On the other hand, a minority follow the definition of "subordinate" as "placed lower in power and authority." It is only the uncommon subordinate who is aggressive.

Jensen provides an example of how subordinates lead an organization in getting things done:

Employees of a division, separated geographically from the parent company, had very low morale. Lower-echelon managers were complaining: "Top management isn't doing its part; we need some direction." The division director's attitude was: "I can't tell them how to solve the problem because I don't know—that's why they were hired." The many problems of that organization included poor communication—top management had not clarified its expectations of the subordinate managers. Six months later, morale was high. When asked what had happened, several lower-echelon managers replied: "Top management wouldn't tell us what to do, so we made our own decisions."

Jensen continues: "With some managers most of the time, and with most managers some of the time, one needs to force a decision. This kind of action is risky but sometimes advisable. Assuming that force is desirable and possible, and with an acceptable calculated risk, a subordinate can do many things. He can initiate a low-key activity in advance of seeking approval. The purpose is to create a *fait accompli* on the ground that the boss will find it easier to go along with the status quo than to change direction. He can inform his boss of the proposed date of initiation of an activity and then wait for negative instructions."

Subordinatemanship is begging for trouble when the underling goes counter to his boss' order (without the latter's knowledge) and doesn't come up with the hoped-for success. Even with a success, the subordinate may place his boss in an embarrassing position with *his* boss and peers. The boss might overlook the infraction, but will remember it, and may take positive action after two or three such occurrences. A good axiom for the subordinate in this regard: "Never let your boss be surprised; maintain open communication with him."

The subordinate's boss has easier access, to higher management and, therefore, is the one who should be able to sell the intermediate manager's program. Getting the boss involved as a working partner makes him a better salesman. The boss likes to think of himself as still having technical ability; being asked to consult is flattering, providing the subordinate doesn't ask for details the boss has long since forgotten.

This psychologist outlines nine characteristics of a good subordinate:

1. Loyalty. The employee supports his superior's decisions, does what he can to make his boss and the organization look good.
2. Problem-solver. The man who stands high with his boss solves problems without creating new and more difficult ones.

3. Informant. The good subordinate serves as his boss's ears so that the superior is not caught unaware by *his* superiors.
4. Creative. The subordinate's plans for doing things differently must be workable.
5. Protector. The subordinate must keep his boss out of trouble.
6. Openness. The boss should know when trouble is brewing or schedules are slipping.
7. Empathy. The subordinate should "sit behind the boss's eyeglasses" for a few minutes.
8. Responsive. A good subordinate responds adequately to a situation. Sometimes the boss really doesn't want a certain action taken even if he thinks or says he does.
9. Organizationally directed. The good subordinate thinks and acts in terms of the whole organization, not simply his specific job assignment.

Lots of luck, Mr. or Ms. Subordinate!

Value Systems of Managers and Subordinates

What happens if a conformist supervises highly tribalistic people? Or if a sociocentric is in charge of an egocentric? Is your firm run by or with one of these value systems or is it subject to manipulative or existential systems?

These were some of the questions discussed at a seminar, "Profiting from Changes in Values for Working," conducted by psychologists Charles L. Hughes and Vincent S. Flowers. Basic aim of the gathering was to help the middle-management participants understand and better deal with such problems as alienation and marginal productivity as earmarks of job dissatisfaction and turnover among both white-collar and blue-collar workers.

Hughes and Flowers credit Dr. Clare W. Graves, professor of psychology, Union College, Schenectady, N.Y., for developing, over a twenty-year period, the theory of six value systems of psychological existence. However, they claim they have translated this theory into practical terms.

Definitions of these value systems:

Tribalistic. The job best suited to this employee is one that promises easy work, friendly people, fair play, and, above all, a good boss. He likes a boss who tells him exactly what to do, how to do it, and encourages him by doing it with him.

Egocentric. The two major requirements of a job for this employee are that it pay well and keep people off his back. He doesn't like any kind of work that ties him down but will do it if he has to in order to get some money. Because of the raw, rugged value system and aggressive individualism of this employee, he needs a boss who is tough but allows him to be tough too.

Conformist. A traditionalist, this employee likes a job that is secure, where the rules are followed, and no favoritism is shown. He feels he has worked hard for what he has and thinks he deserves some good breaks. He likes a boss who calls the shots, isn't always changing his mind, and sees to it everyone follows the rules.

Manipulative. The ideal job for this employee is one that is full of variety, allows some free wheeling and dealing, and where pay and bonus are based on results. He feels he is responsible for his own success and is constantly on the lookout for new opportunities. He is loyal to the dollar. A good boss to this employee is one who understands the politics of getting the job done, knows how to bargain, and is firm but fair.

Sociocentric. A job that allows for the development of friendly relationships with supervisors and others in the work group appeals to this employee. Working with people toward a common goal is more important than getting caught up in the materialistic rat race. He likes a boss who gets people working in close harmony by being more of a friendly person than a boss. He doesn't usually rise to middle and higher management.

Existential. This employee likes a job where the goals and problems are more important than the money, prestige, or how the work should be done. He prefers work that offers continuing challenge and requires imagination and initiative. To him, a good boss is one who gives him access to the information he needs and lets him do the job his own way.

Hughes was with Texas Instruments in industrial relations and organizational development for ten years. He was also with IBM in management development for five years. He is now in private practice, based in Dallas, working for corporate clients. He also conducts public seminars, some with Flowers, as a phase of management training carried out by the Professional Development Institute, College of Business Administration, North Texas State University, Denton.

Flowers, a C.P.A. (he began his career with Price Waterhouse) as well as Ph.D., is director of planning and assistant to the dean of the business school at the Texas university, and is a consultant on organization psychology. He was associated with Hughes at Texas Instruments for seven years.

Hughes amplified their views on the various value systems:

"We have been essentially in a manipulative socioeconomic system ever since the founding fathers. Only in the last three or four years have we seen a great rise in existential and sociocentric values and a corresponding decline in conformity. The concept of loyalty has shifted—it isn't automatically 'my country, or my company, right or wrong.' Education has had a tremendous impact on values, more than any other factor with the possible exception of sex role training as a child.

"Of one hundred people in general, the primary value of thirty is conformist; twenty-five, tribalistic; ten to fifteen, manipulative; ten, egocentric; ten, sociocentric; ten, existential. In the case of managers from department heads to chief executive officers, about 35 percent are manipulative; 25 percent, conformist; 15 to 20 percent, existentialist; 10 percent, tribalistic; and 5 percent, egocentric. The conformity pattern is decreasing and the sociocentric and existential patterns are increasing at about the same rate. Between the third and fourth levels of organizations from the top, the value systems shift; the pattern changes to more conformity."

Of presidents surveyed, those in the age group from forty to sixty are likely to be stronger in conformity; younger managers, more manipulative and existential; those over sixty, sociocentric. As a whole, most sociocentric people are under thirty, with more well-educated females than males with sketchy education represented.

Tribalism, sociocentrics, egocentrics, and conformists are much more the characteristics of hourly paid employees than of managers. Salaried people are more likely to be manipulative and existential. Women who rise to higher management are existential and manipulative, having adopted the value systems and patterns of men. But 60 percent of women as a whole are otherdirected, another term for tribalism. On the other hand, 60 percent of men are inner-directed—manipulative, existential, or egocentric.

The Two Hats of Subordinate and Boss

"Openness" is part of the climate in a growing number—but still small minority—of firms engaged in organization motivation. The basic goals of the changed climate required for an effective human organization were put in the form of some "personal questions" by John Paul Jones, late corporate vice-president for organization development, Federated Department Stores.

Jones observed that most executives wear two hats—that of a subordinate and that of a boss.

First, he suggested, they put on the subordinate's hat and ask themselves:

1. What would be the effect on you if your bosses decided that unity of purpose was more important than unity of command? What would happen to your sense of dignity and self-worth if you were a full participant in the decision-making processes that affect you?
2. What would happen to you if your bosses decided to increase your sense

of autonomy and substitute interdependence *with* them for subordination *to* them?

3. What would be the effect on you if your bosses abandoned authority as a way of commanding your efforts and substituted a sharing of problems with you in an atmosphere of open communication, mutual trust, and confidence?

4. What would be the effect on you if you could honestly feel your errors would be treated supportively as part of the learning process?

5. How would you feel if everyone around you in the organization was honestly dedicated to your growth—not to the idea of controlling or manipulating you?

6. What would happen if the conflicts you have in your organization could be worked through without any win-lose consequences to you?

7. What would happen if your boss and his associates made you a full partner in their face-to-face group—sharing their problems and talents with you and contributing their support to solving your problems?

8. How would you feel if the only decisions you implemented were those to which you had become fully committed?

Okay, Jones said, now put your boss's hat on. And ask yourself:

How do you think your subordinates would operate under such arrangements? Are they really that different from you? Why don't you do something about it?

As a pioneer in industrial organization development, Jones had a philosophy based on the works of behavioral scientists Rensis Likert, Mason Haire, and Douglas McGregor. He was particularly devoted to the late Professor McGregor's idea that men exercise self-direction in objectives to which they are committed, and not only accept but seek responsibility. Potential is only partly explored, and the trouble lies with organizations, not people. This concept is at odds with the prevailing traditional authoritarianism that assumes the average man inherently dislikes work and must be coerced into it by threats of one kind or another.

Organization development, Jones noted, draws its fuel from relevant research findings in the behavioral sciences, and its energy from a growing number of people in business, industry, and academic circles. They are applying these findings and learning with others that they can produce a more rewarding work life. They have also learned that, at present at least, these basic principles are the only answer to a work environment that has moved in a generation from "hands" to "brains," in which specialization of knowledge has become so great, the problems of large and small organizations so complex, that we are in danger of being swallowed by our own technology.

Dwelling on the experimental approach he endorses, versus the one of rigidity he abhors, Jones added:

"Behavior is the most believable communication of climate. Behavior of managers is the most critical feature and is based on their assumptions about the integrity, motivation, and ability of those whose efforts they manage. As McGregor pointed out, such assumptions may be contradictory and nonexplicit, buried in our subconscious minds, but they do govern the ways in which we manage people. Furthermore, assumptions and their consequent managerial behavior are perpetuated by the construction of organizational and managerial hierarchies which are pretty standard for all firms."

It is safe to say, he continued, that most business organizations are characterized by a low degree of openness in the climate. Information is segregated on a "need to know" basis, and "need to know" is always defined by the original possessor of the information—never by the potential receiver. Why? Because the possessor never questions his own integrity, motivation, or commitment to the goals of the organization, but he's not so sure about his subordinates—nor, indeed, about his colleagues and organizational peers.

All human relationships have mutuality. If I behave toward you in ways that demonstrate hate, fear, or contempt, you will behave toward me in a similar manner—and we will conduct our organizational business in an atmosphere of mistrust, secrecy, misinformation, manipulation, and revenge. It is a safe bet that everyone has—or has had—at least one such relationship in his business life.

Jones didn't suggest that all such relationships can be eliminated. But he did suggest that their improvement, and the improvement of work environment, begins with and depends upon *you,* not the other guy.

"Interpersonal competence," from Jones' experience, "is not the only variable of organization change. This is affected by a number of variables that have nothing to do with the feelings, value systems, biases, emotions, opinions, or interpersonal skills of people involved. These variables include existing organization structure, technology, workload, layout of machines or processes, allocation of tasks, physical conditions, and requirements of work. By the same token, however, most of you have had the feeling of futility that comes about when organization change is approached primarily from the standpoint of those variables only to find that what we have done is to shuffle the problems, rather than solve them, because we have not considered and dealt with the feelings of the people affected by these kinds of changes."

From all this, Jones drew the conclusion that "many of us are still trapped in the concept of the purely rational manager, the nonexistent machine-like executive who makes all decisions based purely on fact and logic and the equally nonexistent and machine-like subordinate who accepts these decisions in the same way. The observed reality of the matter is that, in the face of strong feelings or sentiment, logic and fact are often ignored because they aren't congruent with the values, sentiments, or feelings of the people to whom they're presented. Furthermore, we have no consistent set of values to which

all humans subscribe, and this means we are always dealing in any change
situation with other people whose values may be quite different from our own."

"Your Immediate Subordinates Should Be Your Equals"

Bosses should hire subordinates who are "100 percent of them," instead
of picking people who are not quite as good as they are. Too often, executives
prefer underlings who will agree with rather than challenge them.

Geoffrey R. Simmonds, chairman, Simmonds Precision Products, who
stresses this point, is a manufacturer of aerospace and industrial process controls, but there can be no doubt his statement cuts across all business lines.

Simmonds relates how he once told his immediate subordinates he was
satisfied they met his 100 percent specifications but wondered whether they
could say the same of *their* subordinates. When they shook their heads to the
contrary, he chided them:

"If I were to hire you to be 70 percent of me, and you hired your
subordinates to be 70 percent of you, then before we get three layers down in
the corporation we would have pure mediocrity. If I am going out of my way
to hire people who I think are 100 percent of me, what right have you to hire
subordinates who are only 70 percent of you?"

The publicly owned company was started almost forty years ago by Sir
Oliver Simmonds, Geoffrey's father, now retired and living in Nassau. Geoff-
rey, forty-six (in 1975), was born in Southampton, England, came to the
United States in 1949 and subsequently became an American citizen. In 1951,
Simmonds became sales manager of Pinnacle Products Co., a struggling sub-
sidiary of Simmonds Aerocessories founded, but no longer owned, by Sir
Oliver. In 1941, control of the company was acquired by William Enyart, an
American. When Enyart died in a plane crash in 1958, the younger Simmonds
was elected president and chief executive officer of the parent company. A year
later, he obtained the controlling interest.

Simmonds amplifies his views:

Q. If you say that people you hire directly below you should be 100
percent of you, then how do these people reconcile the fact you are their boss
and not the other way around?

A. I think the very existence of the hierarchical system in a corporation
never leaves any question of who is the boss and who is the subordinate. It is
a question of whether you can avoid the practice of people not being candid

because they are the subordinates, of their not challenging the things the boss says because he is the boss. Nevertheless, at no time does this suggest they should be disrespectful of me or of my office, nor that I should be disrespectful of them. It is possible to be candid without getting into a situation where you challenge relationships.

Q. It would seem that a person who feels he is an equal of you may just find himself in a dissonant state. He may feel that some of his ideas, or—since he is your equal—all of his ideas are better than yours. In fact, he may feel that he should be your superior. I don't see how just the fact that you say, "Be candid with me," is going to remove this dissonance.

A. I can tell you an amusing experience we had recently. When we were working on this top team analysis, we started writing down on the blackboard all of the decisions that had to be made by each of the people in the top group. We wrote down the decisions that the president had to make. We were trying to analyze which were "one-alone," which were "one-to-one," and which of them were "one-to-all." I hate to tell you that, by the time we completed an analysis of my job, about the only decisions I make "one-alone" are what time I eat my lunch and when I go to the men's room.

It is very important, Simmonds adds, to set high standards of achievement for the company. He cites the example of the four-minute mile, a record nobody succeeded in breaking for thousands of years. But, within the past twenty years, Roger Bannister of Oxford University did succeed in running the mile in less than four minutes. Soon, other runners also breached the old barrier. Since then, the time has been reduced substantially further.

So it is with corporations, the electronics producer advises.

With both technology and concepts of business management advancing rapidly, Simmonds notes, some people are not keeping up with the company's rate of progress. These people tell you of all the good things they did for the company ten, fifteen, and twenty years ago. The chairman's position:

"Look, we are very grateful for what you did for the corporation in the past. We assume you were well paid for the services you rendered at that time, and we assume the management appropriately expressed its appreciation at that time for the good things you did. You must have been happy with the corporation because you are still here. Now, today, we must address ourselves to your performance today and to the performance you plan to contribute to the corporation in the future. . . . Obviously, where one has an investment of fifteen or twenty years in a man, the motivation is strong to work with him to overcome his deficiencies."

5

THE GOAL IS PRODUCTIVITY

Productivity, People—Two Sides of Same Management Coin

Declining profits, the reflection of a losing battle between higher costs and lower individual and group performance, have tormented many companies for years. Obviously, the problem has worsened during the recessionary period.

High among teaching, consultation, and research efforts designed to help business, industry, and service institutions turn the tide is Scientific Methods, Inc., based in Austin, Tex. The company's founder-heads are Robert R. Blake and Jane Srygley Mouton, industrial psychologists. Blake is a one-time University of Texas professor and researcher; Ms. Mouton, a former student of his.

They have applied behavioral science to exercise of a theory called Managerial Grid. The grid they invented seeks to demonstrate that concern for productivity and concern for people are two sides of the same management coin that must be integrated to achieve optimum results. Their program is carried out on an in-company basis and in public seminars worldwide. The scope of clients includes governments, medical services, and religious institutions as well as industry and business.

Blake explains the five-day managerial and executive grid seminars which require twenty-five to thirty hours of advance work: "We create conditions where people can compare the status quo with standards of excellence. This is routinely a disturbing, difficult but highly rewarding experience. People see what a flabby mentality they've slipped into."

Both the standard of excellence and the status quo are pinpointed on the grid which measures a manager's concern for people on a vertical scale; concern for the task, on a horizontal scale. Five executive types—1,1; 1,9; 5,5; 9,1 and 9,9—stand out on the managerial grid out of a possible eighty-one mixtures (nine times nine).

The grid's inventors define the five types:

1,1 *The cynic.* He believes workers are naturally lazy and sets production standards low so they can beat them. Exertion of minimum effort to get required work done is deemed appropriate to sustain organization membership.

1,9 *The morale builder.* He figures that a comfortable work tempo will let production take care of itself. Thoughtful attention to needs of people for satisfying relationships leads to a friendly atmosphere and work tempo.

5,5 *The compromiser.* He wants to keep employees happy, production adequate—and doesn't want to rock the boat. Adequate organization performance is possible through balancing the necessity to get out work, while maintaining morale of people at a satisfactory level.

9,1 *The production man.* He doesn't let human factors interfere with efficiency. Output outweighs everything else.

9,9 *The rarest of all.* He expects results will be best when managers and workers have a common stake in company goals. Work accomplishment is from committed people in an organization purpose leading to relationships of trust and respect.

Blake reports that, "although the desirable 9,9 manager is actually a rare bird, that's where four out of five managers say they fit before going through a grid seminar. If there really were that many around, U.S. business would be running a lot more smoothly. One out of five still believes he's a 9,9 manager after a week's session, and that's still too high."

Noting that the vast majority fall in the 5,5 style, Blake adds: "Most managers have the compromise mentality. They take their pace from the broader environment, stick their necks out by a standard amount, take home standard amounts of paper, dress in a standard way, and go up the ladder at a standard rate.

"In the executive suite, we find an unanticipatedly large number of 1,1s. They are zombies who have no one else to fight and nowhere else to go, and their interests have turned to the outside."

Avenues to Productivity Improvement

As a concept, employee productivity is universally respected; in practice, it's something else again.

Management and labor each blame the other for lack of successfully sustained productivity programs. This is a failure reflected in the fact that, during the past decade, the United States ranked eleventh in the rate of increase in output per man-hour among major free-world industrial powers.

Saul W. Gellerman, president, Saul Gellerman/Consulting, Ho-ho-kus, N.J. firm specializing in management education and organization development, submits a nontraditional view of the productivity problem.

- Traditional approaches to productivity gains are based on control—that is, on prescribing and proscribing worker behavior. Despite temporary successes, these have not been adequate in the long run.
- The behavioral approach to productivity attempts to establish conditions in which human effort can be effective. However, it encounters resistance because sustained behavior changes require basic changes in the internal culture of organizations.
- The implementation of behavioral approaches to productivity is more of an internal political problem for the organization than it is a technical, psychological, or industrial relations problem.

Yet, this industrial psychologist continues, management and unions tend to fault each other.

Management cites such alleged drags on productivity as limitations on what individual workers are permitted to do, unnecessary workers (featherbedding), rigid seniority rules that prevent rational assignments and stifle motivation, artificial shortages due to restricted apprenticeship programs, work interruptions that disrupt complex schedules, inadequate discipline (notably for absenteeism), and exorbitant wage demands.

Unions retort that productivity is largely a question of how financial and material resources are deployed. Just as "law and order" is interpreted by some disadvantaged groups as a code word for repression, so productivity is seen by some unionists as a code word for speed-ups, lay-offs, and a reduction in both union and worker security.

However, as Gellerman views it, "fault is a useless concept in highly complex interactions such as these." He looks for an answer in cultural differences in the organization—"a more or less consistent pattern of habits and expectations concerning the ways people treat each other. This culture defines the limits of acceptable and unacceptable behavior. It becomes an unwritten but highly effective code that governs conduct within the organization."

Why do labor costs differ between organizations that use essentially the same equipment and methods, and hire from essentially the same labor markets? The answer, of course, is that people work differently in the two organizations. But why? Gellerman's opinion:

"Most people work the way they do—at some level or other of diligence, cooperation, alertness, ingenuity, and effort—out of simple conformity and habit. They do what they think is expected of them—by their peers as much as by their superiors. Thus, whatever standard they conform to is often the effective limit of their productivity because it tends to be reached before the limit of their abilities or tools.

"The most familiar example of conformity to a limiting standard is so-called restriction of output—the tendency of individual production records to cluster around an average commonly acknowledged to be well below capacity. A less familiar but perhaps more important example of conformity can be found in managerial behavior with respect to a proposed innovation. The proposal tends to be considered less for its merits than for its newness and risk. Too often, management's real standard of success is to not fail conspicuously."

Gellerman defines two types of productivity problems:

1. The "classical" problem exists when people are not doing what is expected of them as well as they should. This, in turn, could be due to inadequate training, ineffective leadership, demotivating conditions, or some other failure to apply their potentialities fully.
2. The "cultural" problem has been recognized only recently. It exists when people are doing what is expected of them as well as could be expected, but the expectations themselves are out of touch with reality. In this type of problem, productivity cannot be increased without changing the standards to which everyone in the organization conforms.

The trouble with productivity programs, according to Gellerman, "has nothing to do—at least directly—with productivity itself. The trouble is that productivity improvement often requires more of a change in habits and attitudes than most organizations are willing to accomplish. Willing—not able. Organizations, that want to change, can. But, by itself, productivity is not a sufficiently moving cause to create that desire. Important, yes—even vital perhaps; but moving, no. There is no sex appeal, no pizzazz, no charisma in productivity. It needs help. Not slogans or posters, but internal political help. What makes or breaks a productivity program is the power of its advocates."

The consultant concludes that the strategy having the best chance of succeeding has four elements:

• The program must have strong sponsors in the persons of the managers whose departments are immediately affected.
• Initially, change programs should be introduced only to those units that are most susceptible to change because traditions are lacking or being questioned.

- To sustain the change, the superiors of the affected managers should be tolerant of, and sympathetic to, what they are attempting.
- Once a demonstrable record of improvement is available, the cycle should be restarted, beginning again with new strong advocates and new susceptible units.

Gellerman contends that the real problem of employee turnover is not that there is too much of it but that there isn't enough. And too much of what there is takes place furtively and desperately. Ideally, voluntary turnover, even of key employees, can and should be "managed—frankly, openly, and mutually."

Gellerman begins by summarizing the cost side of turnover:

It creates a need for replacement, which costs money. In large companies, full-time staffs must be retained to recruit, select, hire, and train replacements, even when the company is not actually growing. Productivity may suffer during the interval between the departure of an experienced employee and the attainment of full competence by the replacement.

If turnover is concentrated among younger employees, as it usually is, the effect is to deny the company a seasoned, thoroughly mature workforce. If turnover includes employees who are highly regarded for their potential, as it often does, the effect is to prevent the company, in the future, from adhering to a policy of promotion from within.

If the turnover is among university graduates who are replaced, in effect, by more recent graduates, this often induces salary compression by offering higher starting salaries to the most recent recruits. If the turnover is among employees who have contact with customers, relations with the customers may suffer.

Small wonder that defectors are the personnel manager's perennial headache. After all, he is charged with keeping the company adequately manned, and defectors simply undo what he has been doing. "During periods of high turnover," Gellerman notes, "personnel managers are likely to feel as if they were trying to shovel back the tide. Not a few of them regard economic recessions, when job opportunities dry up and turnover naturally declines, as a well-earned respite."

This psychologist proceeds to the advantages of turnover:

"The most obvious benefit is simply the opportunity to bring new talent, ideas, and techniques into the company. Sometimes, people who make exceptional contributions to a company join it to fill a vacancy created by turnover. But turnover also has subtler advantages which are more likely to occur than the fortuitous hiring of a genius.

"For example, turnover is probably the most common (and most practical) solution to the ubiquitous problems of dead-end jobs and dull work. These are typically high turnover situations, and the sad truth is that, very often, nothing can be done to make them attractive. Job enrichment obviously can work only when it is feasible to use it; and it frequently isn't. Once a certain natural tolerance level for tedium is passed (and if no suitable new opportunity is available) it is best to accept their departure gracefully. In fact, it should be encouraged. Why not offer bonuses to the thoroughly bored employee or the one who has no visible future in a company, if they are willing to seek employment elsewhere?"

Gellerman also cites indirect but not inconsiderable financial advantages of turnover to the company. Turnover, he explains, minimizes the number of employees whose wages or salaries rise beyond the midpoint of their range. The effect is a significant downward leverage on actual payroll costs, in most cases without any significant loss of productivity. The productivity gain that comes with increased experience occurs in most jobs while the individual's pay is still below the midpoint.

This consultant calls pay increases, beyond the experience point where individual productivity does not increase significantly, "merely rewards for not having quit."

Some companies, Gellerman continues, "acquire reputations for excellent training so that a few years of employment become the resume-equivalent of an MBA. Such companies get high turnover rates. They also train, at their own expense, managers and technicians for other companies. On the surface, this appears unfortunate for the companies losing good people. But, beneath the surface, it is apparent that these companies can choose more selectively among jobseekers than less sought-after firms could, and can identify the few star performers and make especially generous arrangements to keep them. For the rest, should any decide to leave, they will usually have more than paid their own way and their departure makes possible a continuing flow of young, eager, highly motivated replacements. . . . The *number* of employees who defect is not nearly as important as *which* employees defect. Most of us, to be blunt about it, are replaceable."

Getting Employees to Be More Than 50 Percent Effective

The typical company head almost invariably wants to change others, but not himself. These others may be the world, the government, the union, colleagues, wife, or children—you name it. Rarely does a president or chairman concede he should first seek to discover if he himself needs to change his ways.

This is a provocative thought voiced by Dr. Alfred J. Marrow.

Marrow is a rare combination of professional social psychologist (Ph.D.) and practical businessman. For many years, he headed Harwood Companies, manufacturer of men's and women's sleep and leisure wear, founded by his grandfather and father in 1897. He is now a director of this publicly owned company. Seymour A. Marrow, Alfred's brother, is chairman and chief executive officer.

Throughout his business career, he was an active participant with professional colleagues in research on laboratory or sensitivity training for leadership by supervisory staffs. Marrow has been a frequent lecturer on the application of scientific knowledge to social behavior and has written nine books. He was the 1964 winner of the Kurt Lewin Memorial Award, highest honor in the field of social psychology. He is now a consultant to industrial, governmental, and academic organizations in the fields of group dynamics and organizational behavior.

Marrow is a founding member and chairman of the National Academy of Professional Psychologists whose one hundred-member faculty conducts postdoctoral seminars at the New School in New York and at a dozen other locations nationally.

Some of the problems with which he has concerned himself are the permissiveness that passes for participation, absenteeism up to 20 percent on Fridays, shoddy workmanship, excessive use of alcohol and drugs, and heart failure linked to job pressures. Their solution is pegged to such examples of humanized management in action as job enrichment, team building, strategies for self-motivation, sensitivity training, assessment centers, mutual respect, and trust and group incentives.

Too little of this knowledge is being generally applied because the present generation of executives "has been unwilling to replace dying managerial traditions and start learning a new system. They still prefer to play it safe by asking for more data and, not uncommonly, to continue to view the professional behavioral scientists with some suspicion."

Marrow argues that "the same man who could program a computer to pay everybody on time and simultaneously keep track of the entire inventory has had a terrible time managing his subordinates. He has not received any training in how to develop and carry through a program to lift morale, resolve conflict, introduce change, build trust, or improve organization performance. A huge number of people with no talent or training in how to manage have succeeded in getting themselves ensconced in the position of 'boss.' "

More than ever before, Marrow points out, we need to develop new and better ideas about how to influence groups, how to plan and expedite change, how to release human organizations from the rigidities of the past, and yet keep the effect of change from becoming too disruptive.

Tradition, he goes on, is no longer the sole guide to our values. Tradition is no longer able to give the answers, whether in industry, science, education, or morality. Certainly not in our product development, technological research, and patterns of management.

All kinds of social change are not necessarily seen as progress by all people, nor do these always lead to greater well-being, enlightenment, or improvement. For example, those people who are dismayed by miniskirts, topless waitresses, quickie divorces, and instant research are not necessarily hostile to new ideas or to improved social practices. They are simply unconvinced that these changes offer an improvement over the traditional way of doing things.

Many heads of companies, as Marrow sees it, are upset because their efforts to improve and innovate have turned out unhappily. Behavorial scientists respond that this was inevitable because the methods used were inadequate for the situation. The program failed because the changers did not possess either an adequate understanding of the process of change or the skills to put change in effect.

Marrow continues:

It is difficult to see how hardship can be avoided during this era of revolutionary change. The process of change itself is threatening to both the organization and individuals. The program costs a lot of money, involves a good deal of risk-taking, forces people to change their habitual ways of doing things, and steps on the toes of powerful groups.

Interlocking causes and effects require prodigious inventiveness on the part of managers to avoid highly emotional reactions—frustration, tension, anxiety. To the people in the organization, there is the matter of pride and fear of failure, exposure to hurt or ridicule, loss of status, threats to security.

Planned change to them, then, becomes something to resist, to block, to prevent, particularly when there are habits of noncooperation and disinterest, suspicions about the motives of management fears about being squeezed out.

Marrow then asks these questions: How can a company create an atmosphere for change that will improve employees' productivity, job satisfaction, and the economic health of the organization? How can the staff be motivated to assume greater risks, make more decisions, be more innovative, and accept greater responsibilities? How can existing negative attitudes be converted to supportive ones? How can a program be designed so that it will increase managerial competence and improve interpersonal relations? In sum, how can a climate be built for changing the total system which includes leadership, supervision, motivation, communication, decision-making, and goal setting, and to carry this out with a minimum of defensive reaction by the employees seeking to protect their own vested interests?

The real solution, he submits, is up to the leaders of each company. If they recognize that only the fittest organizations will survive, then they must risk both turbulence and capital. With the capacity to learn, to innovate, to expand, and to alter those managerial practices that have remained unaltered for generations, and with the knowledge and skills of "managing change" learned from the behavioral scientists, enlightened managers will be able to overcome the complexities with a minimum of disruption. Reflecting continuing antagonism against men from the behavioral science world in industry, Marrow has heard the term "healer-dealer" used a number of times.

Always assuming top management cooperation, Marrow continues, an organization, can be changed in from two to seven years. Instant change is nothing but a fraud. Change can be facilitated if:

1. The persons affected know about it early enough.
2. Those affected participate in planning and bringing it about.
3. The company adopts and publicizes "no injury policies"—for example, selection retraining or relocation with no loss of job or pay.
4. The people who are directly involved should be informed about, and involved in, decisions wherever possible, to protect their interests.
5. Changes can be made more effectively by creating an informational feedback system so that necessary corrections may be made in time.

Is Job Enrichment More Catchword Than Holy Grail?

Like Motherhood and the American Flag, Job Enrichment is a concept with which nobody could—or should—find fault.

Job enrichment is the redesign of a job—effective selection, placement, and technical training; providing a worker with greater responsibility, more autonomy in carrying out that responsibility through a complete job, and more timely feedback about his performance. Who could take issue with that goal?

Yet, a number of social scientists have varying viewpoints about job enrichment's impact on employee morale and productivity.

Frederick Herzberg, Distinguished Professor of Management at the University of Utah and the leader of the pro-job enrichment school of thought, recommends this approach over three other major management philosophies.

Scientific Management, or Taylorism. Under this concept, people are seen as functions, not human beings. Originally, this system worked with a great deal of success. By reducing everyone down to the lowest common denominator, it lowered training and material costs. Taylorism was very efficient—so efficient that two years ago we produced ten million cars in the United States and called back thirteen million. When people say they will not tolerate buying waste and junk, then Taylorism is no longer efficient and is out as a viable managerial philosophy.

The Ideologically Based System. People believe that, if we have common goals, beliefs and values, then a natural process emerges to run an efficient, harmonious nation. The most magnificent of all such systems is Israel, which provided all its organizations with political and military leadership without violation of any humanistic principles, at the same time respecting human dignity and freedom. Israelis came from all over the world, from all walks of life. All were completely equal—the doctor, the lawyer, and the common laborer. The work assignments were the same, and the workers were all equal —equally ignorant. The equality of ignorance is the reason why most ideologically based systems fail.

The American System. We reversed the ideological plan—when we faced a central problem, we developed know-how. We considered the handling of the management of people a technological problem too. And, when we developed a human relations problem, we started with Dale Carnegie courses and escalated them up to sensitivity training, encounter therapy, transactional analysis, and all the rest. Human relations technology is failing because it's become textbook stuff. People are no longer moved by an ideology or a slogan, and they have learned very quickly that what we considered human relations has been merely manipulation. Historical traditions about security are no longer meaningful. Young people have no psychic income from work. The women's lib movement is the end of the obligation "to diminish my life because of male traditions."

Herzberg's fame is based on his identification of two types of work factors—hygiene and positive motivators.

Under hygiene are poor working conditions, poor policies and administration, reshuffling of tasks, incentive systems, and compensation. This psychologist has sought to prove that such factors do not motivate people; they merely satisfy them. If these factors are of high enough quality, employees are not completely frustrated, but little change in productivity results therefrom.

On the other hand, positive motivators consist of:

- Removing controls from the employee but holding him accountable for results.
- Giving a person a complete, natural module (a standard for measuring results) of work, not just adding and subtracting tasks.
- Granting additional responsibility and job freedom.
- Making periodic reports available to him so that the employee may initiate corrective actions, instead of being ordered to do so.
- Introducing new and more difficult assignments so that the individual may learn, grow, and gain recognition for his achievement.

"There is nothing in the climate of retailing, profit-oriented as it is, that makes the interrelated problems of job enrichment, employee motivation and performance, and company survival any more severe than for industry in general."—Scott Myers, organizational psychologist.

"Organization development programs are equally applicable to department stores as to food chains, to electronics as to chemicals. The same concepts, techniques, and strategies apply. The clerk in a supermarket responds just as enthusiastically to the opportunity of becoming involved in problem-solving and decision-making as the clerk in a department or apparel store." —John A. Pare, vice-president, personnel, Northern Electric Co., Montreal, a principal of OD Strategies, consultant firm.

"Job enrichment is required whether we're talking about telephone sales representatives or retail salespeople. We're talking about the human condition, not about any particular industry."—Robert N. Ford, director, work organization and environmental research, American Telephone & Telegraph Co.

This consensus was drawn from the three men following their direction of a participative management seminar sponsored by Frederick Atkins, Inc., store-owned buying and research organization.

Scott Myers, who organized the Atkins agenda, suggested that "company goals can be best served by providing opportunities for employees to achieve their personal goals. It has been traditional for top management to treat people like automatons and call all the shots, putting employees in the position of supporting goals that might not be their own. We believe most people are potentially responsible, creative, and productive. The opportunity must be provided for them to help plan and measure their work, not just do it."

Pare enumerated four management styles or "power structures"—boss, system, peer, and goal.

The *boss-powered style,* most often encountered in smaller companies, assumes employees are passive and outer-directed, have batteries that need to be charged from time to time, and require and want the edicts of a few executives with built-in generators. *System power,* most prevalent in larger companies, depends on rules, regulations, standards, and precedents—"The Book"—and also assumes employees need and want to be controlled. *Peer power*—the "peer group" comprises employees at a level with and immediately subordinate to the manager—replaces the "unfeeling" boss and the "impersonal" system with the "considerate" manager who thinks adequate wages, fringe benefits, and good working conditions are sufficient motivation for his people. *Goal power* accepts employees as inner-directed people who will exercise the necessary self-discipline to achieve goals they have had an opportunity to influence. The goal structure, Pare stressed, is the most effective of the four management styles.

Ford assured the audience that decreased turnover and absenteeism result from job enrichment of monotonous, boring jobs.

"Employees," this social psychologist reported, "are saying more than 'treat me well' with wages, fringe benefits, a pleasant atmosphere, and clean restrooms. They are also saying 'use me well'—the work motivation side of the coin."

MY JOB

It's not my job to run the
train
The whistle I cannot blow
It's not for me to say how
far
The train is allowed to go
I'm not allowed to blow off
steam
Not even clang the bell
But let the damn thing
jump the track
And see who catches hell.

James C. Ozello, manager, personnel development, central personnel, Broadway Department Stores, subsidiary of Carter Hawley Hale, recited this poem as an illustration of management's motivation problems, of getting people to work with greater efficiency and effectiveness. These are problems of on-the-job conditions reflected in absenteeism, attitudes, errors, shrinkage, productivity, turnover, and employee complaints about communication, wages, and fringe benefits.

Ozello was a speaker on "Will Job Enrichment Motivate Your Employees?" at an annual training conference of National Retail Merchants Association's personnel division. He answered the question with a resounding "yes."

Incidentally, the poem is graffiti, author anon., found in an employees' restroom of a large manufacturing company.

Before Ozello came to Broadway as employee relations manager, he was successively college relations manager at AT&T and personnel manager of Mattel, the toy manufacturer.

Job enrichment is essentially an attempt to put back into the work the opportunity for real achievement—and satisfaction. This is accomplished by systematically giving an employee greater responsibility, greater autonomy in carrying out his responsibility, more immediate feedback as to how well he has done and more recognition for doing a job well.

Stressing that job enrichment is a useful management technique for retailing, whether in a one-store operation or a chain, Ozello said that Broadway instituted a pilot program in the customer service department at its headquarters service building in the fall of 1973. It expects to expand job enrichment to all stores at the group manager (sales manager) level. For one thing, these managers will be given total responsibility for merchandise presentation in their respective departments. The program will be extended later to the nonselling areas.

Although this chain does not seek to enrich the salespeople's job directly, Ozello pointed out that "one of the benefits of job enrichment is that it works both ways and, therefore, the process filters down to salespersons."

Job enrichment, Ozello further explained, is designed for managers who wish to create an environment in which people motivate themselves—you can't motivate others.

Ozello credited psychologist Frederick Herzberg with the motivation-hygiene theory of job satisfaction.

Two sets of needs are involved: avoidance of pain (hygiene), and psychological growth (motivation). Factors of hygiene—how do you treat people?—include company policies and administration, supervision, interpersonal relations, salary, and fringes and security. These factors do not lead to motivation but, without them, you have dissatisfaction. Herzberg's use of "hygiene" in the job environment derives from a comparison of the term to public sanitation. Herzberg has observed that water purification and garbage collection don't make people healthy, but they keep people from being unhealthy. Similarly, good wages, hours, and other working conditions don't make employees happy, but they keep them from being unhappy. Based on primary drives of the body, Herzberg's theory proceeds along these lines: "I was hungry this morning. I'll be hungry again tonight. I got a salary increase last year. Now, I need another. And, if last year, I got a $2,000 increase, and this year a $1,000 increase, psychologically, I've taken a $1,000 cut."

Ozello emphasized the distinction between movement and motivation. When managers want people to move, they offer "an incredible number and variety of carrots or jelly beans. But jumping for the jelly beans is not motivation but movement. Motivation occurs only when the employee moves because *he* wants to move. Both approaches—motivation and hygiene—must be done simultaneously. *Treat* people as well as you can so they have a minimum of dissatisfaction. *Use* people so they get achievement, recognition for achievement, interest and responsibility, and they can grow and advance in their work.

"Job enrichment, then, is simply the process of putting back into the job opportunities for achievement, not what the company thinks is achievement, but what the employee thinks is achievement. A basic premise of job improvement is that deep personal satisfaction can come only from the work itself."

Some of Ozello's concluding ideas:

Employees have varying tolerances for the hygiene and varying needs for motivation. Not all people can be motivated for all jobs. First, you cannot motivate anyone to do a job who can't do that job. Most people are more willing to say the company doesn't motivate them than that they can't do their jobs. Motivation becomes the smoke screen.

Second, you cannot motivate anyone to do a job unless the job fits psychologically into his needs, his self-image, and his goals.

If talented, trained people are treated well, but not motivated then the job is sick. And, if the job is sick, you have to clean up the job—which is job enrichment. The argument for job enrichment can be summed up quite simply: If you have someone on a job, use him. If you can't use him on the job, get rid of him, either via automation or by selecting someone with lesser ability. If you can't use him and you can't get rid of him, you will have a motivation problem.

Throw out the Golden Rule which says, "Do unto others what you would have them do unto you." Substitute, "Do unto others as they would have it done unto themselves." Or, in up-to-date terms, use people as they would want to be used, not the way you would want to be used.

Job enrichment, Ozello advised as a final thought, "is a strategy, not a slogan."

Sidney Harman is an industrialist who is seeking to bridge the gap between the machinery of business and concern for the human condition.

Harman is president and treasurer of Harman International Industries, manufacturer and distributor of high-fidelity equipment and automotive and aircraft engine products with a 1974 volume of about $92 million. His background includes separate and intertwined careers as business executive, educator, and politician. From this vantage point, he insists business has it all over any other field as the place for personal growth and constructive social influence.

While in pursuit of his Ph.D. degree, Harman met Michael Maccoby, a practicing psychologist who also heads a Harvard study of work and management character. Harman enlisted Maccoby in helping him to set up a work-redesigned project at the firm's automotive plant in Bolivar, a small town in Tennessee. The plant makes sideview mirrors and is the largest of its kind in the world. The United Automobile Workers and management play equal roles.

Harman cites "a much freer, much looser arrangement in which every man is encouraged to grow to the maximum of his capabilities, to learn a great deal of the work of the other man. Under the guidance of a professional social scientist, small groups of workers and their supervisors talk about their work problems. There is a considerable amount of job rotation in which the opportunity for obtaining broad experience at different levels of management is an active part of company procedure and practice. Job redesign has been effected at all levels through top management.

"The Bolivar project is no longer an experiment. The fundamental principles are being brought to the other divisions."

"We're engaged in a socio-technical reexamination and, in consequence, a transformation. But it cannot be done in a patronizing, paternalistic manner."

Harman reports, "My principal duty is to see that responsibilities of others at all levels are enlarged, that they be allowed to make mistakes so they can grow and really develop, and that I stay out of their way and let them do their jobs. I don't write the Scriptures and send them down the line. Each of us understands the total process in which we operate, our involvement in decisions in which we have to live, and our need for mutual reinforcement. Granted that kind of climate, we all work our rear ends off."

"Basically, it reduces to a genuine conviction—I hope I don't sound sanctimonious—there is that of God in every man, certainly there is that of individual value worth nourishing that deserves the opportunity to grow in every man. No man or woman should be exploited by any other man or woman."

If for no other reasons, the field of job enrichment will continue to grow because of its cost-cutting and profit-raising implications. So says David A. Whitsett, vice-president, Drake-Bean & Associates, psychological consultants.

Job enrichment for management and the college-educated is the most important phase of the future of this process of individual and group motivation. This is the opinion of Robert Janson, vice-president, Roy W. Walters Associates, behavioral science consultants.

Whitsett is a former assistant professor of industrial psychology at Case Western Reserve University where he was a graduate student under Frederick Herzberg. In advancing the cause of vertical loading (job enrichment) over horizontal loading (job enlargement) Herzberg counsels: "Two or three meaningless activities do not add up to a meaningful one."

There are two ways, according to Whitsett, to respond to a question as to the future of job enrichment. The first way:

There must be a very rapid increase in the number and kind of business organizations trying to make work more interesting. Else, industry will have to sustain the steadily increasing costs of not doing anything or simply going through the motions. These costs are of two kinds: a) loss of people actually leaving the organization or b) loss of people in the sense of tremendous disinterest, low productivity, high error rates, absenteeism, tardiness, and boredom.

"More than half of the top fifty to seventy-five industrial firms on Fortune's 500 list and perhaps two-thirds of the entire roster," charged Whitsett, "are not doing anything in job enrichment beyond discussion and seminars. Of themselves, these efforts cannot result in enriched jobs which must comprise three parts: a) a complete piece of work, b) over which the person has as much decision-making and control as possible, and c) through which the person receives frequent, direct, individual feedback."

The second facet of the future of job enrichment:

"Preventive job design instead of patchwork repairs. The most successful job enrichment is being done in new plant start-ups, new office buildings, and massive reorganizations because the best opportunity rests with engaging a large group of people at one time. Major resistance to job enrichment comes from managers as well as rank-and-file workers who are comfortable and secure doing what they're now doing and refuse to change. In consequence, many firms plan or hope to start programs with new people who will be more responsive and productive from the outset."

Whitsett cites an aspect of his prediction that preventive job design will replace patchwork repairs. Up to now, he explained, most companies with job enrichment programs have employed a group of personnel specialists who constitute the patchwork force. These persons, he contends, frequently work at cross-purposes with associates who are assigned to other functions such as systems or work measurement. As job enrichment reaches out from dealing with one job or a small number of related jobs to a large piece of the organization, as Whitsett expects, all the personnel people will have to work together more closely.

In the case of a department store chain, he goes on, the experimental work will probably involve new suburban stores in entirety or whole divisions rather than one or two departments in the downtown main stores. If the innovation works out well in the branches, Whitsett feels, the headquarters command is bound to suggest it be utilized downtown as well.

Janson, who before joining the Walters organization was with AT&T as district manager, says:

"Even though the management level may not be more than 10 percent of the entire organization, its influence is far greater. It will be the most important phase of the future of job enrichment. This future will embrace management-level jobs up to and including divisional presidents.

"At present, very little is being done with the college-educated on job enrichment. Ninety percent of this work is confined to below the first-line supervisory jobs. This is particularly true in retailing which for the most part is still putting young college-educated trainees through two months' training in one department, two months in another, and so on for a year or two. This is called 'exposure to the organization.' In fact, though, the young person is bored out of his mind because he doesn't have any responsibility. This approach is definitely wrong."

"What is the alternative?" Janson is asked.

"The trainee ought to be given responsibility almost immediately upon walking in the door. He should find out what his training needs are and what additional exposure he needs to handle that responsibility. Someone who is a better manager than he is should be trained to act as his sponsor or ombudsman to help in the individual's growth and to make sure he has as much responsibility as he is capable of assuming and that he is performing up to standard."

Department and apparel store retailing, Janson advises, "stand to gain the most from lower-level decisionmaking and other job enrichment efforts. They must be more than McDonald's hamburger stands handing out prepackaged goods as fast as possible. Even Korvettes has found out it must be more service-oriented."

If a higher degree of motivation through added, meaningful responsibility at all levels is not soon forthcoming, Janson warned, the turnover rate will accelerate with the promise of a brightened economic outlook.

His belief in this regard is confirmed by a Gallup Poll among 1,520 workers which finds that those under thirty are substantially more dissatisfied with their jobs than older persons, a degree of discontent greater than four years ago. "A boring job" is a chief reason for the dissatisfaction.

After attending a job-enrichment seminar, a supervisor was convinced it was the answer to his productivity problem. He invited an employee into his office and told the man that, starting the next Monday, the worker would be allowed to plan, carry out, and control his own job. To the supervisor, this meant he would be introducing wanted "satisfiers" into the man's job.

The worker asked if he would get more money. The supervisor replied: "No, money is not a motivator, and you will not be satisfied if I give you more pay. But I do want you to plan and control your own job." Once again, the employee asked: "Well, if I do what you want, will I get more pay?" The supervisor answered: "No, you need to understand the motivation-hygiene theory. Take this book home with you and read it. Tomorrow, we'll get together again, and I will explain to you one more time what will really motivate you." As the man was leaving, he looked back at the supervisor and asked: "Well, if I read this book, will I get more money?"

This actual experience points up the fact that job enrichment is not the complete answer to job enjoyment, as traditional management may believe it to be. Traditional management practices what psychologist Vincent S. Flowers describes as "mirror management"—a supposition among managers that takes two forms: 1) All people have values close to those of their supervisors. 2) The manager looks into a distorted mirror and believes all people can be divided into different classes, each with its own values. As this reasoning goes, blacks are less intelligent, women are not really interested in careers, and young men with long hair are on drugs.

Instead of traditional management, the answer may be existential management—the manager accepts people whose values differ from his own. This is not necessarily to be confused with participative management which conveys an implicit order from the boss to the worker: "You WILL participate and you

WILL enjoy it!" Maybe the employee doesn't want to participate and doesn't enjoy it.

Current studies indicate there is no significant difference in job enjoyment among hourly and salaried workers. This, despite the theory that hourly workers are likely to have routine, repetitive tasks, hence are presumably much more susceptible to dissatisfaction than salaried employees who tend to have more creative, more flexible jobs.

A researcher, who spent a lot of time at his desk scoring hundreds of questionnaire responses, asked a machine operator whether he had a boring, monotonous job. The worker's reply: "I was just about to ask you the same question."

Further evidence of the ambiguous nature of job enrichment and enjoyment is provided by other surveys.

According to studies conducted over a fifteen-year period by the University of Michigan's Survey Research Center and other groups, satisfaction for the working population rose during the early 1960s and remained high into 1973. Ninety-one percent of men aged twenty-one through sixty-five reported themselves "satisfied" with their jobs last year. This percentage compares with 85 percent for blacks, 89 percent for women (who however are increasingly aware of inequities), and 77 percent for workers under twenty-one.

Divergent findings are cited from surveys among a cross-section of workers across the nation. The data have been included in a paperback, *Where Have All the Robots Gone?* by Harold L. Sheppard and Neal Q. Herrick. Sheppard is on the Washington staff of the W.E. Upjohn Institute for Employment Research. Herrick, who was with Upjohn four years, is now director of the Office of Program Development, Employment Standards Administration, Department of Labor.

The authors show a clearly defined generation gap shaping up among white male blue-collar workers. One out of four such workers under thirty is dissatisfied with his job by comparison with one out of ten older employees. In addition, the younger workers are more antiauthoritarian, unhappier with their unions, less trusting of the political process and the two major parties, and less racially prejudiced than their elders.

In a survey of 1,533 workers by the University of Michigan Survey Research Center, good pay emerges fifth among twenty-five elements in job satisfaction. Preceding it are interesting work, enough help and equipment to do the job, enough information, and enough authority to do the job.

Herrick lumps service occupations and the wholesale-retail industry among "pockets of discontent" where he contends chances for job dissatisfaction are nearly one in four.

The ratio is about one in ten in technical, professional, and managerial positions.

Women are more likely to express negative attitudes toward both their work and their lives than any other segments of the American work force. Among men and women in the same income ranges, however, differences in work dissatisfaction tend to dissapear.

Herrick suggests two possible conclusions: 1) The structure of work should change to accommodate young people, or 2) young people should change to accommodate the structure of work. The latter is a popular notion among older folk. They recall their own accommodations (and those of their fathers) and feel it is only proper that the young people of today should change. But this gives rise to two questions: First, is a possibly pathological adaptation to sterile work actually desirable? Second, if it is desirable, are the young people of today willing to go that route?

Herrick's "answer to the first question is an emphatic 'No.' The existence of deadening, numbing, and individually constraining work in the past is no argument for its continuation in the future. The real potential for change depends far more on the answer to the second question. If young people are willing to adapt and to accept the values of the hierarchical work situation (seeking their place in it and striving to improve their situation step by step), we can be assured that little attention will be given to restructuring work. If, on the other hand, young people demand that their employers give them a voice in shaping their work lives constructively, we may see at long last an extension of our democratic principles to the workplace."

Two men at a productivity workshop of The Conference Board took a dim view of job enrichment, a term that has taken on the status of a shibboleth or catchword.

These dissidents are Leonard R. Sayles, professor, Graduate School of Business, Columbia University, and Mitchell Fein, consulting industrial engineer.

According to Sayles, managers, since the early days of scientific management, "have sought the holy grail which would enable them to transform passive, or even hostile, employees into cooperative, hardworking, and diligent workers. Almost every decade has brought a new cure-all; now they are coming even faster. It was once work simplification, then incentive plans, participative management, counseling programs, and, more recently, job enrichment."

Conceding they all incorporate some truths, some useful guidance, Sayles argues they also "represent the search for nostrums, aided and abetted by speech writers looking for sure-fire phrases. Unfortunately, productivity, like profitability, results from a large number of decisions and organizational elements. Further worker 'productivity' is as much or more the result of managerial productivity. Many more employees are 'turned off' by obvious managerial wastage, the ignoring of equipment or procedure malfunctioning, and the tolerance of inefficient methods than by boring jobs."

Sayles denies the existence of any reliable data that managers and professionals are more hardworking, more productive or motivated than workers on the assembly line. As many, if not more, white-collar employees are goofing off, if only because work standards are harder to come by when one leaves the factory floor, he contends.

The Columbia professor thus feels "there are no grounds for shifting the productivity problem to employees. Most of the problems I've seen have their source in managerial decisions concerning job definition, controls, and work flow."

As Sayles sees it, job enrichment itself is simply a code word for most of the human relations techniques recommended to managers since the Western Electric studies of the 1930s: more employee participation, clear work group boundaries and small-sized organizational units, reduced supervisory initiatives, more feedback, use of informal leaders as straw bosses, and managerial attention and recognition. One newer element is the growing realization that extreme job specialization is both less fulfilling and more costly in terms of the effort required to coordinate specialized jobs.

Fein thinks it curious that "a vocal school of social scientists," concerned with work humanization or job enrichment and pressing government officials, legislators, and management on these points, is not supported by workers or unions. "One would think," Fein submits, "that, if workers faced the dire consequences projected by the behaviorists, they should be conscious of the need to redesign and enrich their jobs. Yet, there is a sharp difference of opinion between what workers say they want and what behaviorists say workers should want."

This professional engineer is convinced the behaviorists' stand is largely based on a number of job enrichment histories and studies over the past ten years that indicate workers want job enrichment. However, he continues, when these studies are examined closely, it is found:

1. What actually occurred was quite different from what was reported by the behaviorists.
2. Most of the cases were conducted with hand-picked employees, usually working in areas or plants isolated from the main operations and who do not reflect a cross-section of the working population. Practically all are in nonunion plants.
3. Only a handful of job enrichment attempts have been reported in the past ten years despite the attractive claims made by behaviorists of gains for employees and management.
4. In all instances, the experiments were initiated by management, never by workers or unions.

In that regard, Fein mentions such well-publicized endeavors as a study for the Department of Labor by the Survey Research Center at University of Michigan, an experiment at General Foods' Topeka plant, and programs at Texas Instruments, Polaroid, Motorola, AT&T, and General Motors.

Fein gives two main reasons for his belief "there are no job enrichment successes in ways that bear out the predictions of the behaviorists":

1. The vast majority of the work force, which presumably should benefit, rejects it.
2. A small portion of the work force which would desire job changes is prevented from participating by the social climate in the plant. This group finds involvement in their work by moving into the skilled jobs.

From more than thirty-five years' experience, Fein ascribes much of "the penned-in feeling and the blues" of workers to "their inability to take care of their daily personal problems and needs, such as to make an hour visit out of the plant, make and receive phone calls, come late because someone in the family was sick in the morning, or because of traffic jams, or car trouble, or because they simply just woke up late. . . . Management and the white collar workers have this personal freedom.

"The behaviorists just cannot comprehend why workers do not call for job enrichment as they do for money and working conditions issues. But workers see job enrichment as more beneficial to management than to themselves. Most workers do not come to work for fulfillment from the work itself. They come to work to eat, to exchange their time, efforts, and skills for what they can buy back outside the work place. The jobs behaviorists call sterile and inhuman are looked upon quite differently by workers on these jobs as their source of bread.

"A minority of workers—about 15 percent of the work force—is attracted to job enrichment. But these are mostly in the skilled jobs or on their way up. They are frustrated in the low-level jobs and they want greater autonomy in their jobs. But the social pressure in the plant from the 85 percent noninvolved workers sets the plant climate, and they oppose job changes."

"Much of what you've heard and read about job enrichment is a lot of bunk. Forget projective questionnaires; they're a lot of bullshit. There are two kinds of employee unhappiness and discontent: The first is inequity—workers feel they've been screwed. The second kind is boredom. You have to know the difference between different types of discontent before you seek to enrich the job."

With this blunt language, David Sirota, head of a management consultant firm bearing his name, excoriated many of his fellow behavioral scientists who, in the jargon of the craft, present job enrichment as a panacea for management-labor problems. Sirota is also associate professor of management at the Wharton School. He was formerly director of manufacturing manpower development at IBM.

Sirota addressed a meeting of the personnel division at the National Retail Merchants Association.

"When a worker complains he's unhappy with his pay," Sirota argued, "you don't solve the problem by enriching the job. There are psychologists who claim that, when a worker says he's unhappy with his pay, he's actually saying he has unresolved personal conflicts. But he really is unhappy with his pay. And you should be working on paycheck enrichment.

"Job enrichment is not designed to make marriages better, to make people stop using drugs. The thing to do is to bring the job up to the individual's abilities. The point of job enrichment should be to treat someone as if he has brains. Ask employees in very simple ways how they feel about their pay and their jobs. The issue is not either money or interesting work. People want both things. The best predictor as to whether employees will leave their jobs this year is to ask them just that: 'Are you going to leave your job this year?' Find out what the problem is before you do anything."

The trouble, as Sirota sees it, is that the wrong medication is being prescribed for the disease. Each of the techniques of human relations, participative management, T-groups, and job enrichment can be used to solve a specific employee problem; each has something to offer if, instead of being treated as a panacea, it is carefully applied to the malady it was designed to cure. However, adherence to the statement that cure should be matched with malady has been the exception rather than the rule. Sirota lists the most common causes of malady-cure mismatches:

- Management becomes infatuated with a particular behavioral-science technique, usually after an executive's highly satisfying personal experience, and decides "Let's try it here."
- Management has an erroneous preconception of employees' needs that blocks its ability to recognize the true problem, even when the evidence is overwhelming.
- Management perceives the surface manifestations of the problem correctly —for example, low productivity—but fails to explore thoroughly the causes before deciding on a course of action.

Sirota advises that, "Corporations, like human organisms, are subject to stress, change, attrition, and ailments of mind and body. They also have another failing: a tendency to inertia. To be of most use, a thorough diagnosis should be made in a climate free of prior assumptions by management. The company that waits until it is sick may have waited too long. The company that assumes it is well may not realize rebellion is simmering underneath."

Nine Reasons Why Management Falls Short of Profit Target

Many success-stories have been written about how to achieve employee cooperation in improving productivity. But reasons for failure are rarely publicized. From thirty years of observation of, and talking with, thousands of blue- and white-collar workers, A.A. Imberman, president, Imberman & deForest, Chicago-based management consultants, suggests "chief executives with high ideals and the will to improve employee performance" could learn much from common corporate pitfalls. He submits nine "shotgun" remedies that have missed the target. His compendium and criticism of "corn-cures, shin-plasters, and other popular devices":

1. Follow the Leading Companies. There is no infallible physic for all malaises. Any employee morale improvement theory borrowed from one company requires sophisticated modification before it will function efficiently in the environment of another company.

2. Shift Management Responsibility. There is a tendency toward shifting management responsibility down to profit centers within profit centers. This kind of decentralization will separate top management so effectively from the work force it is supposed to be managing that a major rescue squad may subsequently be required to keep the boat from rocking.

3. Leave It to the Personnel Man. All too often, top managers of both non-union and unionized companies or plants think they don't have to spend any time on employee morale and leave policing personnel relations to the personnel vice-president. There comes a time, however, when this "behemoth syndrome" must come face to face with reality: what the hourly worker thinks and feels about the company. The greater the distance—geographic, sociological, and industrial—between first-line foremen and the men on top, the greater the likelihood of labor trouble, high absenteeism and turnover, poor quality production, delayed shipments, poor productivity—and poor profits.

4. The Work Force as "Fixed Asset." By this line of reasoning in the annual report, "the asset requires attention only when the pay plumbing goes awry, or the wage boiler blows up in a strike. This causes some snorting and frothing in the front office. The failure is patched up with money, the alleged sovereign balm for every itch and twinge." More major executives should make labor relations one of their responsibilities and spend more time in the shop.

5. Speak Through the House Organ. To communicate with the work force mainly through costly house organs containing sonorous exhortations is less demanding on the higher cerebral centers than to tackle tough communications problems that require listening and responding to what employees think about the company. A related device to which managers often turn is the employee attitude survey that can be purchased replete with paper forms and attached pencil. This reduces the inordinately complex to the absurdly simple.

6. Rely on Computer Printouts. To rely on information relayed to the president by a vice-president who gets the story via computer printout is considered by many firms far more dependable than reliance on the opinions of hourly workers expressed orally. This theory derives from "one of the gross superstitions of our times": that any data quantified and processed by a computer is therefore scientific, hence more important than data that cannot be measured.

7. Speed Up the Wheelbarrow. The only elements involved in improving productivity and cutting costs, according to this theory, are labor inputs and "pushing the wheelbarrow faster." The truly successful business is interested in reducing total costs, not particular ones. It should be obvious that, when labor costs rise, any measure that reduces total cost is welcome. Whether this is accomplished by saving labor or capital expenditure is irrelevant. Management can easily get bogged down by concentrating on labor-saving techniques.

8. Job Enrichment as a Panacea. This theory goes hand-in-glove with the belief the typical employee in assembly fabrication feels doomed by his limited, banal and repetitive drudgery, hence suffers from "blue collar blues." The remedy is not a combination of several limited, banal and repetitive tasks.

9. Retain a Consultant. It isn't enough to hire a consultant "who, with novel expedients and extraordinary efficiency, will bring about improvement without involving company management, company policies or executive time. This notion is akin to that of being able to fly through the air without wings or gasoline. The ironic fact is there are excellent consultants already within the ranks."

All avenues of proper personnel administration, all roads toward increased productivity and profit, it is clear, lead from and to top management.

Executive Productivity—A Self-Indictment

It used to be assumed that productivity improvement is almost entirely a matter of focusing on assembly-line workers, clerical staffs, and lower supervisory personnel.

However, a substantial number of top executives cite lack of well-defined organizational or departmental goals and objectives as most responsible for poor productivity in all areas and concede this to be an indictment of themselves. Improved productivity of corporate presidents and other middle-to-top managers, it is admitted, would help in the quest for greater profit and return on investment and ability to attract capital.

This is a major finding of a survey report, "Executive Productivity," by Amacom division, American Management Associations. Authors are Herman S. Jacobs, a principal of Software Sciences Corp., management consulting firm, and Katherine Jillson, a writer.

Material for the report was gathered principally from a questionnaire answered by 530 presidents and 745 managers. Sixty-two percent of the answers are from people in manufacturing industries, 25 percent from service industries, and 13 percent from retailers, government, education and diversified fields.

Although the two most critical causes of productivity problems are lack of clear company-wide and departmental goals and objectives—cited by 46 percent of the respondents—and inadequate managerial leadership—cited by 44 percent—only 36 percent work in organizations that have made some "special effort" to evaluate executive productivity in the last three years.

Middle management is the fourth most frequent choice, after production personnel, supervisory and clerical staff, as the personnel area that experiences the most severe productivity problems.

Executives say their productivity is being hampered by inadequate, ineffective in-house management development programs; different work attitudes and values of younger managers; time required to deal with consumer groups, and government regulations.

Managers and presidents differ sharply on the degree to which "office politics" and "red tape" adversely affect executive productivity. Twenty-four percent of presidents and 44 percent of managers believe office politics are detrimental to executive productivity; 18 percent of presidents and 40 percent of all managers call excessive organizational red tape a factor significantly affecting executive productivity.

Over half of the managers and one-third of the presidents claim "middle management malaise" is adversely affecting managerial performance. Presidents and managers feel security items, such as higher salaries, better benefits, and better working conditions are not likely to improve the quality of managerial performance. They give almost five times as much weight to the following low-security, high-responsibility factors:

1. More meaningful and challenging managerial work.
2. More effective management control methods in the areas of budgeting, scheduling, personnel relations and information flow.
3. Better management-education programs.
4. Financial incentive programs for managers at all levels.
5. Greater dissemination down the line of information pertaining to executive-level decisions and the reasons for these.
6. Increased organizational decentralization wherever possible so as to delegate more responsibility and authority down the line.
7. Better approaches to managerial performance appraisal.

Company presidents and managers differ in their views on managerial deficiencies.

Presidents' reasons: Working at cross-purposes with other managers. Most spend their time in technical areas involving too much detail when they should concentrate on managing work—planning, organizing, leading, and controlling. Failure to keep their operation in proper perspective with relation to its impact on total company performance. Failure to develop people; too many managers fear others' strength. Lack of job experience prior to advancement. Failure to keep up-to-date in management education. Lack of drive. Want to be president at twenty-five. No knowledge of human relations as applied to cost effectiveness. Poor utilization of time. Inability to get good results from subordinates. Avoidance of risk.

Managers enumerate their own most common deficiencies: Necessary fire-fighting (short range) crowds out the required planning (long range). Lack of vertical and lateral communication. Procrastination. Poor definition of goals. No standards for evaluating performance. Isolationism. Problems in setting priorities. Wrong people in the job; technically competent people aren't automatically good managers. Obsession with detail at the expense of overall results desired. Lack of authority to manage. Failure to face up to difficult situations. Unwillingness of one manager to accept a difference of managerial style in another manager and work with that manager productively. Personal "contentedness"—no personal goals, no new dreams.

The respondents make it clear their own understanding of corporate goals and objectives must involve workers in setting such goals and objectives as a basis for sound superior-subordinate relationships. Also needed is logical distribution of work emanating from proper acceptance of responsibility and delegation of authority.

While such valuable concepts as Management by Objectives and equitable payment practices abound in management literature, the authors contend these concepts "are not originating action in the real world of management. The success of management techniques depends on the people who use them; the techniques don't magically do the work."

At least, "the grandiose notion that managers naturally manage properly" has been dissipated, giving way to an all-important admission that all executives—from middle-managers to presidents—need all the help they can get.

6

A QUESTION
OF INCENTIVE

Employee Fringe Benefits Should Produce
Higher Profits

With few exceptions, retailers do not offer fringe benefits that are competitive in the labor market. The average expenditure for retail fringe benefits is substantially less than the 10 percent of payroll for such programs in industry in general.

Such benefits include pension and profit-sharing plans, group-insured medical and group practice plans, group life insurance, disability income protection, and dental and prescription drug programs. In addition, stock options and deferred compensation agreements are often sought to provide additional tax shelters and to act as an incentive for executive and management employees.

Raymond B. Krieger, consulting actuary, Touche Ross Stennes & Co., offers advice on the problem in an article, "Employe Benefits: Beyond the Fringe?", in *Tempo,* quarterly magazine published by Touche Ross & Co.

Krieger submits his views against the backdrop of the unique characteristics of the average store's personnel: relatively high average age, a proportion that is 70 percent female, an average of 40 percent of the employees with less than five years of service, relatively large portion of part-time as well as temporary employees, and salaries representing a high proportion of operational costs.

Among the points made by Krieger:

There are many companies that have major medical programs providing an individual with lifetime maximum benefits of only $15,000. Apparently, these companies do not realize the disadvantage they would be at should another firm offer one of their key men, who has a large family and has had many large medical bills, a position at a similar salary but with major medical coverage providing for $1 million per person lifetime maximum coverage. The cost is actually little more than that for the $15,000 maximum. For one Chicago retailer, such a superior medical plan provided the edge in attracting two key executives from other stores.

Krieger points out that a well-designed fringe benefit program keeps employee morale high. This, in turn, reduces turnover and helps attract top-grade people. It also motivates employees to achieve a higher level of performance which, of course, would produce higher company profits.

The opposite effects were realized in the case of a medium-sized midwestern department store where a fifty-five-year-old-employee who had worked there thirty years had to move away for family reasons. He had risen to executive status, but because the store's pension plan did not provide benefits when an employee leaves before he is sixty-five, the man's years of service brought him no pension benefits.

This would not have happened if the benefit plan had provided for vested retirement benefits after, say, fifteen years of service. The cost would have been reasonable, and the "return" in motivational value would have been well worth that cost. Such vesting, according to Krieger, will not be optional in the future. He expects it to be part of pension reform legislation that may be enacted by Congress.

Like all plans, Krieger continues, pension plans must be kept up to date. He reports the case of a southern retailer who had been on an active acquisition program for five years and had acquired a number of companies. But, when he began to transfer employees between companies, he ran into trouble. First, a large number of people had to spend too much time simply administering the variety of programs. Second, and more important, it became difficult to get a talented manager, for example, to move to a merged company that had an inferior benefit program.

The simple solution was to coordinate the pension plans so that all subsidiaries had the same pension formula for future benefit accruals as well as vesting provisions that gave credit for service with allied companies.

Once the plans are in effect, the benefits must be regularly communicated to the employees. Krieger recounts the experience of a West Coast department store chain. Its pension plan, for a variety of reasons, became overfunded. As a result, the IRS would not permit further company contributions until the funded surplus was eliminated. Meanwhile, employee contributions continued. The problem arose when the store did not have a program of communicating the benefit program to employees. From the "rumor mill," word got around that the company was no longer contributing to the pension plan (which was true) but also that the plan's benefits were being funded only by the employees' own contributions and that an employee could receive a better benefit by putting his money in a bank (which was far from true). Not only were both participation in the plan and company morale low, but a top officer of the store withdrew his own contributions.

Krieger has encountered "cynical retailers who, faced with a serious shrinkage (averaging 1-to-6 percent of sales), sometimes argue that shrinkage should be considered a fringe benefit. It is true that this figure, added to the average size of retailing benefits, would bring the industry's average benefit costs more into line with that of other industries. Indeed, it is argued by some that a good benefit program can be a significant step in solving this industry-wide problem.

"More significant, however, is the fact that, while many benefit programs in retailing were adequate when they were set up, changes in the work force, social attitudes, tax laws, Social Security legislation, and corporate goals have resulted in these plans developing either gaps in coverage or overlapping protection."

For the short run, Krieger predicts, we can expect current coverage will be better coordinated and new coverages, such as dental insurance, will be added. For the long run, one probable approach will be the so-called "cafeteria" or "buffet" system—to meet the differing needs of the individual employees, of older and younger people, of married and single men and women, of married employees with and without children, and of persons at various stages of their careers and salary levels.

Executives Favor Cash in Pocket over "Golden Handcuffs"

What will it be—the golden handcuffs of deferred compensation and bonuses or the freedom of cash income on the barrelhead?

A significant trend appears to be developing in retailing as well as in industry in general toward the latter method of pay for senior and middle-level executives.

Major reasons why upper-bracket executives, with the possible exception of those nearing retirement, see no real incentive for deferring a sizable percentage of their compensation until a later year:

- Reduction of the maximum federal tax rate on earned income from 70 percent to 50 percent (state and local taxes must be added).
- Most deferred pay is considered by IRS unearned income and, therefore, still subject to an up to 70 percent tax.
- The continuing inflationary spiral.
- Executives want greater mobility to move from one company to another— the very mobility that corporate arrangements for individual deferred compensation plans seek to minimize.

The truth is that the golden handcuffs of deferred pay that supposedly make a company hard to raid have been unlocked by rivals many times. Handcuffs don't hold a man but merely raise the bidding. Deferred pay manacles second-raters much more than it does top-caliber persons.

Gerald R. Guralnik, president, ISI-Woodward, Ryan, Sharp & Davis, consulting actuaries, finds that deferred compensation "is considerably less attractive under current circumstances and has fallen in favor among executives."

Guralnik reports that "most retail companies, as well as others, have returned to incentive-oriented cash income rather than deferred compensation plans and qualified or nonqualified stock options."

"Qualified" plans are defined as pensions and profit-sharing plus some stock option programs—always funded (money placed in escrow)—that have been approved by IRS. "Nonqualified" means deferred compensation arrangements with selected managers and other executives that do not have IRS approval and don't enjoy the same tax opportunities.

Deferred compensation experienced substantial growth in industry during the 1950s and 1960s—the era of strong expansion of mergers and acquisitions involving a need for professional management that had to be lured with big money—maximizing dollars and minimizing taxes until a later date of lower earnings and taxes. Retailing was slower to adopt made-to-order pay packages but, eventually, every chain of any consequence jumped on the bandwagon.

Now, the reverse process is underway. As contracts expire and as important job openings occur, executives with clout (profit-making potential) are in position to have much of their pay set up on a current schedule without the moral restrictions of deferred compensation agreements. Their superiors may or may not like the idea but have to accept it with as good grace as they can muster. For other executives not as well endowed with present accomplishment or future promise, the employer remains in the driver's seat.

Guralnik notes that, traditionally, retailing "did not use deferred compensation as extensively as, say, the automobile industry because pay structures are different."

Guralnik also observes that a number of chains, formerly oriented toward nepotism and paternalism, have only in relatively recent times felt impelled to go outside the personal and store family for professional management. Boasts that "all our major executives have been trained by us" aren't heard as often today as in the less competitive, more placid, past. Persons with strong general management experience occupy the chairmanship or presidency of a number of chains instead of men who typically rose to the top through merchandising and, to a lesser extent, the operating route.

Noteworthy in this regard is the presence in chief executives' posts of men such as Sears, Roebuck's Arthur M. Wood, R. H. Macy's Donald B. Smiley and Allied Stores' Thomas M. Macioce who came to retailing by way of law degrees.

James T. Powers, partner, Peat, Marwick, Mitchell & Co., accountants, says that "in the past five years, more good positions have been available than people to fill them. My partners and I are getting twice as many calls from companies looking for top talent."

Underlying Principles in Executive Pay Incentive

The management compensation incentive system at IBM confines participation to fewer than 60 of a total of 150,000 employees, to the approximately three score who make the key profit decisions.

The extremely limited participation includes, for example, the president or general manager of a manufacturing division whose decisions have an impact on profit. However, it excludes the personnel director of the division who may have a major influence on labor costs representing the biggest single expense of the division but who does not ultimately make the decisions. Similarly, staff attorneys have a major influence on the business but always in advisory and counseling capacities and, again, do not make final profit decisions.

Wesley R. Liebtag, director of personnel programs, gave this corporate approach as one of two underlying principles in IBM's incentive plan.

IBM's objective is to provide a management incentive plan that will "optimize annual and long-term profit growth, giving equal weight to each. We are obviously attempting to avoid a cyclical profit pattern that could work to the ultimate detriment of the business."

The second underlying principle is "conscious use" of a "contention" system which Liebtag defines:

"There should be adversaries, each fighting for his point of view, each making certain that the other looks at all the facts. In the case of our incentive plans, we consider an individual business unit to be one side of the contention system and the top corporate management to be the other. The individual business unit is obviously striving to maximize profit in the current budget year whereas the corporate management team is striving to optimize that profit within a long-term, steady growth trend."

Under the contention system, IBM awards units with a par value of $1,000 to a limited number of key decision-makers each January. The ultimate value of those units, which is determined at the end of each calendar year, is based on two different methods, depending on which side of the contention system they find themselves.

In the case of the corporate group, the ultimate value of the unit is based on the achievement of earnings per share compared with those of the prior three years. That is, if in the previous three years the earnings per share growth had averaged 10 percent and if in the year in question the achievement had been only a growth of 8 percent, the value of the share would be 80 percent or $800.

In the case of the business units evaluation system, the value of the awarded unit is based on corporate management judgment of the performance of that business unit. The top management team would take into account the business plan, the outside environment, the responsiveness to new challenges, leadership in terms of both people and technology and other pertinent factors. Once having reviewed all these aspects of the performance of the various business units, the top team would rank these from high to low or, more typically, into top, middle, and bottom performing groups. Values would then be assigned, and the units would be finally paid.

While in both the corporate and business unit plans, some attention is paid the performance of the individual, Liebtag emphasized that, on the whole, the ultimate value of the unit depends upon the performance of the team.

Notwithstanding changes in tax laws and rulings, stock options are "still very much alive and flourishing," according to Jack D. Salwen, partner in the law firm of Rothschild & Salwen. However, he noted, the changes have brought about "substantial modification" of stock option plans. He explained:

The new plans of companies with stock listed on the New York Stock Exchange generally authorize nonstatutory as well as statutory options. The statutory option, when used, will be large and be confined to executives below the highest paid level.

As a result of a recent ruling of the Treasury Department, it is no longer possible for companies to grant tandem or twin options—the "cafeteria or smorgasbord" approach—which enabled the executive to choose between a statutory and nonstatutory option at the time he exercised the option. The company, and the executive if consulted, must now make the choice in advance of the option grant. The nonstatutory option departs from the fixed pattern required of the statutory option. Its provisions vary from company to company and the ingenuity of the plan's architect.

Formulation and implementation of option plans must take into consideration a variety of factors. Included are the effect on company earnings of the grant and exercise of options under the plan, compliance with wage stabilization guidelines, meeting requirements for exemption from the short-swing profit provisions of federal securities legislation and compliance with proposed tax regulations to assure earned income treatment upon exercise of nonstatutory options.

Alternative programs are being developed to supplement or substitute for the stock option plan. One of the most significant plans confers stock incentive or appreciation rights, entitling the holder to receive cash or shares of the company's stock for any increase in value at a designated time. Also important are performance share programs, wherein units equivalent to shares of company stock are allocated to participants with payment made in stock of cash after a relatively short period of years if earned by individual performance and achievement of company earnings goals. Such payment is made irrespective of whether there has been an increase in market value of the company's stock.

Bruce R. Ellig, director, compensations and benefits, Pfizer, Inc., charged that the relationship between corporate objectives and the executive compensation program is "by far the foremost reason most plans are in trouble today."

These, he advised, must be related to industry considerations, corporate objectives and individual performance in a manner that is not only cost-effective but also attractive to the recipient. Since these relationships are fluid, not static, compensation programs must be under continual review to insure their effectiveness.

Middle Management Discontented with Pay, Job Security, Authority

Which segment of the U.S. working force comprises only 4 percent to 5 percent of the total, yet has a significant impact on the other 95 percent including the 1 percent that is top management?

The answer: middle management.

Despite their importance to organizational results, many of the 4 million to 4,500,000 middle-managers are convinced their true worth is not properly recognized. Their discontent is reflected in impaired personal and corporate effectiveness. By the same token, any meaningful efforts by top management to improve the lot of these subordinates must enhance the bottom-line showing.

Emanuel Kay, president of a behavioral science consulting firm bearing his name and based in Marblehead, Mass., has taken up the cudgels in their behalf.

Kay, a Ph.D. formerly with General Electric and Gellerman Kay Corp., defines the scope of middle management: the lower limit excludes first-line supervisors who primarily supervise non-exempt employees. The upper limit excludes the chairman, president, executive vice-president, group vice-president, heads of major functional areas or staff functions, and division general managers with profit-and-loss responsibility. Kay thinks from two-thirds to three-quarters of the supervisory, managerial, and executive population may be identified as middle managers. The largest group of middle managers—the first post-World War II generation to achieve this status—is in the forty to forty-nine age range.

On the basis of many discussions he has held with middle-managers in his consulting work and of seminars he has conducted, Kay finds:

"Perhaps the bitterest complaint of middle managers has to do with inequitable salary treatment. This complaint generally revolves about what is called the 'compression effect.' The compression effect refers to the fact that the differential in salaries between longer-service and shorter-service employees is narrowing and has been narrowing over a period of many years."

The annual rate of salary increase is inversely related to years of service. The net result is that the actual salaries of newer people move closer to those of longer-service people, and the differential continues to decrease over the years.

From a motivation point of view, salary must be regarded as a "hygiene" factor. Hygiene factors are those issues that, if not satisfactory, have a marked propensity for producing discontent. Traditional salary relationships have been upset by unusually large increases in the blue-collar groups and the accelerating starting rates for new college graduates. Wage controls also had the effect of locking these inequities into place.

Concern about job security is the second greatest complaint of middle-managers. During the 1970–71 recession, the unemployment rate among middle-managers went from slightly under 1 percent (1966–69) to about 1.5 to 1.6 percent. Statistics generally support the notion that older people spend more time unemployed than do younger middle-managers.

Another grievance of middle management is their lack of authority and influence relative to top management. They are able to recommend and implement, but the power to decide remains in the hands of top management. In some cases, the authority is withheld explicitly; in others, it takes the form of uncertainty about using whatever authority they may have, thus freezing them into very limited spheres of action.

As still another major concern of middle-managers, Kay cites "their perceived loss of career flexibility. As an individual moves to a middle management position, the narrowness and specialization become more apparent, and he sees fewer lateral experiences available to him. Ill-conceived or poorly executed development programs reinforce the resulting inflexibility. During favorable economic circumstances, the middle-manager is concerned about the obsolescence of his skills, rather than losing his job. The obsolescent manager may be assigned responsibilities in keeping with his perceived abilities, or he may be bypassed when new programs develop in the organization. In more extreme circumstances, early retirement may be encouraged."

Top management, according to Kay, tends to see middle-managers as unrealistic in their requests for facilities, personnel, and new or expanded programs. The top executives attach considerable importance to their own roles as decision-makers and tend to resist incursion by others on this prerogative. Negativism of top executives may be reflected in an attitude of "if you don't like the way this company is run, then go elsewhere"—an attitude that can either persuade the underlings to resign or take fewer risks, and propose and push fewer ideas.

Interest of union leaders in organizing middle-managers is described by Kay as "lukewarm." He explains that the union leaders are not banking on top management voluntarily to recognize middle-manager unions, nor do they feel the middle-managers have enough organized power to bring about a change in the law that would require mandatory recognition of middle-manager unions.

Kay has these impressions about the views held by middle-managers' subordinates: The middle-managers have little or no influence with top executives, they are indecisive and inflexible, and they have undesirable jobs.

7

THE NOW GENERATION

Management's Challenge from/to New Breed of Employees

Do you, as a manager, regard the "new breed" of employees as a problem or an opportunity?

Your answer will reflect whether you are frustrated because you have devoted much misspent effort trying "to change them to be like us" or have changed your own approach and attitude and are meeting the "mavericks" half way.

Stanley Peterfreund, president of an Englewood Cliffs, N.J., management consulting firm bearing his name, discusses the two schools of thought. Before he formed his own concern, he was on the staffs of the Survey Research Center and the Bureau of Business Research at the University of Michigan.

As perceived by many management and supervisory people, Peterfreund finds, the new breed in the American work force—white- and blue-collar employees alike—a) challenge authority, don't follow orders; b) have no loyalty to their employer, no commitment to their company; c) are overly ambitious, impatient to get ahead; d) care only about money, are less dedicated (or "professional"); e) don't care how they look; f) are arrogant and rebellious.

The new breed, on the other hand, see themselves as a) impatient of meaningless work, in revolt against the dum-dum jobs of the world; b) committed to "doing their thing", if they can't find satisfaction doing it in one place, they'll go somewhere else; c) better educated than past generations, more sophisticated, asking the right questions—to the distress of many supervisors; d) wanting to continue self-development and get ahead and not have their talent underutilized; e) having a broader span of interest in the world around them as well as in what's going on in the environment in which they work; f) no less motivated in their work than their predecessors, but more likely to become demotivated by what they see and experience than any work group before them.

Peterfreund submits seven emerging trends that he believes could transform the new breed into "the most potent, most productive human resource ever available to business and industry—if management is prepared for them":

1. The rise of individualism, the drive for personal identity and recognition. Basically, industry is seeing a manifestation of what's going on in the broader society. There is a surge of individualism denoting greater confidence in one's self rather than in the institution, less dependency on an employer for a job, on a union to speak for the worker, on the church for divine guidance, on someone else to tell a person what to do. In consumerism, it's a reaction to dealing with computers or impersonalized service. In industry, it's resentment against being treated as "a number" rather than as an individual.

2. The importance of the work itself. Rebellion against meaningless work will grow. As greater responsibility is assumed by rank and file employees, the job of the first-line supervisor must also change.

3. The mobile employee and changing loyalties. Employees with twenty to forty years of service in a single company will become increasingly rare. New methods of orientation and training will be needed to make employees productive as early as possible so that there can be a maximum return during their tenure. It also means developing people to be flexible and adaptable; there will be far more need for backups and shifting people around.

4. The second career. Growing numbers of managers and professionals are leaving secure positions in their forties and switching occupations completely. New concepts of employment and benefits will be required to respond to this trend. For instance, a national pension pool, rather than individual company plans, is being advocated with growing vigor. New programs will be needed to handle the increasing demand for continuing adult education and self-development opportunities. Greater utilization will be made of tuition refund programs, even for courses not directly related to a present occupation.

5. Options in benefits, jobs, careers. Employees must be given more leeway to try new jobs, new pursuits, within a single company. A set, uniform benefit program may not work effectively. Industry has successfully impressed employees with the concept that benefits are part of their income. Variable benefit programs, with individual options, will come fast—and in the near future.

6. New concepts of work days, work hours. Four-day weeks are appearing with greater frequency. Some firms give employees the option of picking their own hours. Still others assign "a day's work," and the employee is free to go when finished.

7. Equal employment and promotion opportunities. Upward progression of minority group members has been made mandatory by the government. Compliance reviews are being built in to assure that minorities are more widely distributed, vertically, along the organization chart. There is an even greater focus on such opportunity and action for women. Equal employment opportunity, for the next five to ten years, may become unequal employment opportunity for white males unless the program is managed effectively. Nowhere will the problem be more pronounced than among those white male supervisors who must objectively recommend, promote, and transfer people if affirmative action is to work and who at the same time find their own prospects threatened by women and minorities on the move.

Peterfreund sums up with such policies of sound management as:

1. examine the quality and attractiveness of jobs

2. bury sexist job stereotypes

3. more effective communication and participation at all levels in an era of organizational democracy

4. sharper management of individual development and advancement

5. better systems to reward individuals in more direct relationship to achievement

6. better standards of increasing white-collar productivity

7. more demanding management, raised expectations of subordinates

In conclusion: "Laxity, boredom, poor motivational stimulus is what turns the new breed off. The most effective response—and the greatest potential—lies in challenging the new breed more."

Sears Studies Seek to Bridge Generation Gap

Sears Roebuck & Co. is engaged in separate studies among retail management trainees, MBA graduates and candidates, and managerial personnel. If these three surveys have common denominators, they are attempts to establish closer communication of top and middle management with the under-thirty group who will help run the company fifteen years from now, and to identify the generation gap and formulate plans to bridge that gap.

All of the 106 retail management trainees were approached by letter and asked in essence: "What is wrong with big business today? Are Sears and other companies responding to the needs of the times?"

The replies—all signed—"Tell it like it is." The consensus is that business must be more responsive than at present to sociological issues and must divert more money and effort toward solving the nation's nonbusiness problems.

To dramatize the findings, a twenty-minute color film, entitled *Sears Is People,* was produced in the training room of the White Plains store. A dozen of the trainees, who came from a number of Sears' eastern stores, were interviewed in a group session and individually.

One of the respondents—a young woman—says 85 to 90 percent of her fellow trainees agree big business has been derelict in carrying out its responsibility along ecological and other environmental lines. For example, it is suggested that, when Sears takes over a certain amount of acreage for a new store or other facility in an area that may have been used in part for recreational purposes, the company should replace the park space on or near the grounds.

Psychologist Margaret Mead, who also appears in the film, expresses the opinion that the trainees reflect how young people, generally, feel today. The generation that has grown up since World War II, she explains, sees the world differently from its elders. She describes the new generation as "the youngest members of the Establishment." Ms. Mead warns that "business must play a different role in society than before, and something must be done about this now, not twenty years from now when the present younger generation will be top management."

Coincidentally and independently, the psychological services division at Chicago headquarters conducted a pilot study of attitudes among a limited number of MBA students at Harvard and Loyola Universities and twenty-eight Sears managers with ten to fifteen years of service who are holders of the advanced degree.

This survey is still in initial stages of analysis, but the replies indicate a substantial number of similarities to those from the eastern territorial study.

Another attitude study by Sears' parent personnel department has been made among fifteen thousand executives, an overwhelming majority of the management people throughout the country. Results have been tabulated and are now being evaluated. A marked divergence of opinions on sociological questions has been found between younger and older executives. More mature executives take a more conservative position than their youthful associates. Even here, though, there are exceptions in each group. Graphs of the results appear in a film strip called *Business-Oriented Socialization Scale* with the not inadvertent acronym, "BOSS."

This is the first time Sears has conducted a large-scale attitude survey among executives. The company has sponsored such morale studies for years among hourly employees.

Winfield Firman, personnel director for Sears in the New York fashion buying office, and William C. Ashley, director of psychological and attitude surveys at Chicago headquarters, presented some preliminary findings of the three studies.

To point up the perplexing nature of the generation gap, Firman related the incident of a retail sales manager of a large Sears fashion department who suddenly told him: "I'm packing it in. I can't reconcile myself to the business world, so I'm going off with my wife in a camper-trailer for a year and think it all out." The man, who is in his early thirties, had risen to an important position in ten years.

Young men who voluntarily step out of big jobs to meditate on life-goals aren't too frequently encountered. Nevertheless, the story illustrates the ambivalence of the younger generation.

There can be no doubt Sears has confirmed its expectations about the polarization in philosophies of younger and older executives, about a new generation of executives much more concerned with humanistic than profit motives, about trainees' insistence on involvement in decision-making eight to ten weeks after starting their entry jobs. It may be anticipated that, as the company learns more about what makes employees tick, the generation gap will be narrowed, if not bridged.

The War between the Generations: How to Cool It

"Tell it like it really is" is the urgent advice of Edgar H. Schein and Frederick Herzberg, behavioral scientists and consultants, to businessmen, parents and educators concerned about the youth revolution.

Schein is chairman of the organizational studies group, Sloan School of Management, MIT; Herzberg, Distinguished Professor of Management, University of Utah.

Pulling no punches, Schein and Herzberg characterize the older generation as poor developers, motivators, and users of people, hypocrites, and psychologically jealous of the younger generation. Hewing to objectivity, they call the youngsters unsophisticated and naive.

The two professors agree that youth is "anti-authority and anti-establishment, disillusioned and disappointed about our society, truly angered at the phony excuses and untruths" of the older generation. The younger generation, they suggest, wants "open, collaborative relations" with its elders, looks to them to develop a working environment and management skills on a positive basis rather than encourage mutual misunderstanding and recrimination.

Schein and Herzberg also concur in the thought that both older and young people have, and must continue to have, their "facades and self-delusions—no one can face life cold turkey." At the same time, they add, the two generations must be honest with each other about this universal facet of human weakness as about everything else in the complexities of "people problems."

More of Schein's provocative views:

Students are carrying over, to the university and the job, hostilities begun in the home. Nothing irritates students more than the older generation's attitude that the problem in hand is being studied. The young people feel that the older generation must be resisted and, if possible, displaced. It's a dangerous fallacy to believe that the young people will grow up and settle down—riots, sitdowns and other efforts to have adults pay attention show ignoring the problem won't work. Reforms are needed in schools as well as in large business organizations. We have gotten fat and lazy. The answer to the young people is not "You do it" but meaningful, challenging assignments at the outset of the job. Ignore or repress the young at your peril.

And from Herzberg:

The human being has to delude himself and sometimes does it through drugs or booze. (Herzberg prefers booze.) Technology forces us to live life with less self-delusion. What used to be five hundred years of change takes place in twenty-five years today. We now need management by prevention, rather than correction. Fifty percent of the guys who have retired in your company are still with you. We produce the most competent incompetents in the world. There's so much know-how required that we're getting a polarization of sloganeering. There's the hygiene problem: How do you treat people well? But you can't tell people you're treating them well and that they should appreciate it; you're expected to be decent. Two weeks after a person gets a raise, he's dissatisfied. "What have you done for me lately?" always prevails.

You can't motivate people to do something unless they can do it. They can be motivated only if they have talent and competence. Such talent and competence can be developed and should be utilized much more than we're doing today.

These young kids, Herzberg counsels, are not going to go home and beat their wives or eat their heart out. They'll tell the boss to go to hell. Your frustration tolerance must be increased. Adults' concern about the sexual freedom of the younger generation is often psychological jealousy.

In case you think humans are getting better, forget it. Herzberg sees no improvement in human relations since the first apes started hitting one another over the head. Nor does he think there will ever be improvement. We may not hurt people physically, but we will psychologically.

Demand for Young Talent Exceeds Supply

"Our great stores are but as museums of merchandise without good people who like their jobs and who are successful in doing their work— whether they meet the customer at the point of sale or 'service the fleet' from behind the scenes. People are the life blood of our industry."

This is how Henry T. Emmons, vice-president in corporate personnel and previously manager of executive development, R. H. Macy & Co., describes the all-important role played by those in the "people business . . . an area most every business executive likes to get into, and of course he should —it is that important."

This is the climate in which retailing is seeking good people. How to find them?

First of all, Emmons makes clear, "there is absolutely no substitute for a sound company-wide promotion-from-within program. When we go outside the company, we discourage the initiative and ambition of existing staff members. What is more, we reveal our weakness in back-up strength."

On the other hand, the best man should be found in order to satisfy stockholders. As ability is where you find it, a good goal is 90 percent promotion from within and 10 percent outside recruiting of starting executive trainees and executives on a five-year basis. "This will signal to the executive group that they do not just ride up the escalator automatically."

Emmons finds a list of "abilities of successful merchants" invaluable in the selection process. The list was developed in the course of meetings with ten of Macy's top buyers:

1. integrity and intelligence as opposed to "smartness"
2. mathematical ability—facility with numbers
3. drive—competitive spirit
4. optimism—tomorrow is another day
5. maturity—emotional stability
6. ability to press through to the goal
7. ability to "go for broke"—gambler instinct
8. patience and determination
9. sense of rightness or wrongness when looking at merchandise
10. ability to "sell a program" to a store manager

11. good taste—variable because taste means different things to different people
12. ability to work through people for the accomplishment of your goals
13. display instinct, conviction about the "department look"—appreciation of neatness
14. good health and good home life
15. conviction that this is the best job there is
16. interest in the theatre and museums
17. know what to do first and where to be at the right time

Why Do So Many College Graduates Leave First Jobs?

Many large companies lose nearly 50 percent of their college graduates within the first four or five years of employment.

Do these terminations occur among less or more effective employees? How do the early job experiences of terminees differ, if at all, from those encountered by other college graduates who have chosen to stick with their first employers? And how can this high, costly incidence of early attrition be reduced among employees who presumably possess the best potential for advancing into key jobs?

To gain at least preliminary answers, Ford Motor Co. sponsored a study of over one thousand college graduates currently or previously employed by the company.

A random sample was selected of all college graduates who had left the firm during a two-year period with a tenure of four years or less. Letters were sent to them requesting they complete a rather lengthy questionnaire about work motivations, job expectations, and job experiences during their service with the company. Of 564 who agreed to participate, 495 (88 percent) completed usable questionnaires.

At the same time, Ford's personnel research department compiled a list of about the same number of college graduates still with the company who had the same tenure (matched according to date of employment) as the terminees. In addition to asking for brief biographical information, the questionnaire inquired about what they wanted in a job at the time they graduated from college, their employment expectations at the time they accepted jobs with the company, and descriptions of their first and present job assignments in the company. Completed usable questionnaires for this group were returned by 525.

Marvin D. Dunnette, one of three men who conducted the survey, is professor of psychology and industrial relations at the University of Minnesota and director of the industrial psychology program and program manager of the university's Center for the Study of Organizational Performance and Human Effectiveness. His co-authors in this survey were Richard D. Arvey, assistant professor of industrial and personnel management, University of Tennessee, and Paul A. Banas, manager of personnel research at Ford's world headquarters.

Terminees and employees were fairly in agreement on the job features they said were important for satisfaction and overall fulfillment in both "before and after" respects. Most significant job features: feeling of accomplishment, interesting work, opportunity to use abilities, opportunity to get ahead, a good salary.

"A good salary" was the only one of these five areas to come close to meeting expectations for both current employees and those who later left the company.

Least important job features: fair company policies, security in the job, good working conditions, to be in charge of other people, to have high status.

Those who had left the company did not differ from those still with the company in how well they did in college or high school, where they came from, parents' educational levels and other potentially relevant personal factors. The authors conclude that terminees were much the same as non-terminees in basic motivational dispositions and in their patterns of academic and other accomplishments prior to joining the company.

Both groups were nearly identical in what they expected from their jobs at the time they decided to go with the company. The nature of expectations about employment with the company is observed as testimony to the effectiveness of the company's college recruiting efforts. Before joining the company, the respondents believed with a fair degree of certainty they would find security, good pay, and good working conditions, coupled with interesting jobs in which they would have opportunities to utilize their own abilities to attain feelings of accomplishment. Moreover, they agreed, the company would administer programs fairly and provide opportunities for advancement. Most important, those who stayed and those who later left shared these highly optimistic views about their forthcoming jobs with the company.

The first job assignment in the company brought rather sharp disenchantment to both present employees and terminees. In particular, the first job was seen as one that severely frustrated their high hopes and expectations of opportunities to use their abilities. This finding is believed to reflect a supervisory practice apparently prevalent in many large firms—the practice of "breaking the new man in" by assigning tasks either so trivial as to carry the clear message the new man is not yet capable of doing anything important or requiring such specialized knowledge as to make failure inevitable.

Since both groups were almost equally soured on their first job assignments, why did some leave, others stay? Those who stayed apparently moved into later job assignments that much more closely matched preemployment expectations, whereas those who left evidently saw later assignments in the company as more of the same.

Much remains to be done, say the authors, to resolve the conflict between the campus recruiters' "seduction" and the "hazing" followed by many first bosses of these new employees. "College graduates placed in job situations under managers who successfully utilize and challenge, rather than delimit and stifle, abilities, tend to be more effective performers over the long run than men who are either merely put up with or actually put down in those early jobs." Their final word of advice: Supervisors must be given specialized training to equip them properly for helping these high-potential people through the period of adaptation they must undergo.

Successful Young Businessmen
Tell Off Cynics

What do young executives up to a dozen years or so out of graduate school think about the satisfactions and problems of a business career?

Price Waterhouse & Co., the accounting firm, commissioned interviews with thirty young businessmen about twenty-five to thirty-five years of age, selected principally on the basis of recommendations of graduate business school placement officers. The respondents work in Boston, Chicago, Los Angeles, New York, and San Francisco and represent a wide range of industries and occupations. All who were approached for interviews accepted.

The purpose of the interviews was to examine the validity of many undergraduates' statements that business is "for the birds."

Many of the young men have found stimulation, excitement, and intellectual and creative satisfaction in their plunge into business. More than that, they feel they are contributing to the general welfare. While they grant that business has its shortcomings, they add that so does every career.

Of course, this study is not sufficiently widespread to warrant drawing valid statistical conclusions. Nor is it free from bias; the college placement officers who suggested the interviewees probably singled out their most successful younger graduates. Yet, the study succeeded in its attempt to present a sampling of enthusiastic views as an answer to those who ask: "What has business got for me?"

The young men do not envy classmates who have gone into teaching, which they tend to regard as regimented and difficult to change, or into government, which they are inclined to think is a somewhat inefficient and slow-moving instrument. At the same time, they are not scornful of these alternative careers. Some expect to teach or serve the country in government when they have completed successful business careers. But today they are caught up, as one young man put it, in "the rapid pace, the change and the challenge" of business.

Some mention the satisfaction they derive from encouraging the development of the people who work for them.

Several cite financial reward. An assistant buyer of a New York department store says: "You need money if you want to participate in the good life, and business is where the money is."

To a question as to his concept of business's contribution to society, this same young man replied: "I hope that what I am doing now will prepare me to perform some future service for the country. Specifically, I hope to operate in government some day. At my level in business, there isn't much opportunity to make a contribution. You have more social impact at the top."

These young men, it is apparent, are not blind to the faults of business. Many of them, for example, would agree with critics who say that business has not met its public responsibilities sufficiently. But where things are wrong, they want to help improve them.

One individual comments:

"You don't have to conform in industry any more than you do in other fields. Let's face it: If you're a beatnik, you have to conform to the standards of that group.

"A lot of people complain that government is taking over. This isn't an accident. Government has gotten into areas because business has not assumed the responsibility for them.

"A manager is often in the position of salvaging some guy whose growth has been stunted, perhaps by a poor manager. This is really doing something."

Perhaps the central message here is why the career these young men have chosen in business has significance and relevance.

Unless a greater effort is made in this direction, it may be that more and more young men will come to feel that "business is for the birds" despite impressive but uncommunicated evidence to the contrary.

Young Men in a Hurry: "Spoiled Brats of Corporate Nursery"

Eugene E. Jennings describes executives in their twenties who quit as many as three jobs in six years as "the supermobiles."

Jennings, professor of administrative science, Michigan State University and a pioneer in the field of executive career counseling, contends the expectations of these "spoiled brats of the corporate nursery" are out of balance with any corporate opportunity and blames their unwarranted demands on our mobile society, the universities, and the corporations themselves.

He maintains that many of the men in middle-to-top posts in the largest companies are ill equipped to deal with the multifaceted challenges before them.

This authority on executive behavior observes that "the supermobile, whose expectations are so gross he cannot endure the hardship of staying long enough on the job to become competent, represents a defect inherent in a mobile society. Whether he stays or leaves, such a man creates problems for himself and for others. The farther and faster these supermobile young men move, the more they want to move faster. They experience a rising expectations syndrome. A growing chorus of protests and admonitions has been made by top executives who first sounded the alarm in the middle of the 1960s when the general outline of the problem was discovered in several large corporations."

Jennings examines the factors that drive the supermobile manager and the problems he causes.

The problem, he points out, is that "men on fast tracks to the top have their expectations increased faster than their corporations can fulfill these. Moreover, they are bred to be supermobiles." The corporations upset the balance by overhiring and overpaying—procedures that inflate young men's expectations without producing the equivalent in achievement opportunities. This experience, Jennings claims, is not an isolated or novel occurrence in a rapidly growing society and is not confined to young people or to businessmen.

"It may be argued," he notes, "that if a large number of people do not have rising expectations, the economy will lose its bloom. For that matter, a sizable portion of people in a non-growth society can have rising expectations whether they are mobile or not. Even managers and executives in slow tracks to the top may have rising expectations. The problem is not rising expectations per se but, rather, expectations that grossly exceed the standard or base of rising expectations that appear normal and justifiable."

In the premobility era, Jennings reports, it was not common for an aspirant to get to the top by his early forties unless he was specially aided by advantages of family or other forms of nepotism. Today, it is not uncommon for men to arrive at the top by their early forties or even late thirties.

"The grosser the experienced expectations and the greater the perceived blocks to achieving them," the professor continues, "the more likely the young executives will commit aggression by quitting and leveraging. Of all figures dotting the corporate landscape, supermobiles are the least prepared to stay when loss of career time appears imminent. The breeding of fast-track executives seems to draw out the latent career-centeredness in men. Once they become career-centered, the breeder must compete with other corporations for their loyalty."

Jennings asserts that the college graduate, particularly the MBA from one of the twenty or so universities favored by big business who has a "short ladder" complex, comes to the corporation with strong doses of career-centeredness that executive development programs only enhance and intensify. "The attempt to breed out the insider's strain of conservatism and conformity encourages the unintended consequence of mobile men better prepared to leave the known for the unknown. The capacity and willingness to leave the company at the first sign of immobility is greatly increased by extra care and attention paid to youth on the lower rungs of the ladder."

8

RESPONSIBILITY ENTAILS SOCIAL AWARENESS

"What's Good for the Country Is Good for General Motors"

"For years, I thought what was good for our country was good for General Motors, and vice versa."

This statement, which has been widely quoted, misquoted, and derided, was made by Charles E. Wilson, a former president of General Motors, at Senate hearings prior to his confirmation as secretary of defense in the Eisenhower cabinet in 1953.

There are indications that GM is now leaning toward the opinion—and appropriate positive action—that what's good for our country is good for GM, and forget vice versa.

GM's long-time preeminence must have played a part in this super-corporation's adherence, under successive generations of chief executives, to a headquarters policy of rarely admitting to errors of judgment. One exception to this rule was the apology by James M. Roche, then president, before a Senate subcommittee in 1966 for the company's harassment of Ralph Nader, the consumer advocate.

GM hasn't exactly covered itself with glory since. Peter F. Drucker, the management professor and consultant, charges: "GM can be seen as the triumph and failure of the technocrat manager. . . . In terms of sales and profits, it has succeeded admirably, at least in the North American market. (GM is dominant overseas only in Australia. In Europe, it's in fifth place. In Latin America, it's second to Ford.) But it has also failed abysmally—in terms of public reputation, of public esteem."

For years, GM gave only token recognition to consumer demand for small cars. Nor did it take adequate action on energy-related issues of safety, pollution, and public transportation. It has been battered by its worst sales slump since the 1958 recession—a slump from which it is only now rebounding. With the energy squeeze transforming oil into a more valuable commodity than automobiles, Exxon has, not surprisingly, replaced GM as the number-one profit-maker.

Roche, now retired as chairman, acknowledged,

"Business as usual is out . . . we must conform our attitudes to the new expectations with respect to our social problems. . . . The clear challenge to U.S. business is whether or not it is willing to make a firm commitment to do its share in the struggle for a better society and a better world. We must make certain that corporate and societal goals do not collide. If they do, the private sector in the U.S. may be viewed as increasingly irrelevant in our society. Then, business will be the loser because no business or industry can live and prosper without social acceptance.

"When business is challenged or criticized, it must respond. The source of the criticism or challenge is not important. Business must respond by change if necessary, or by providing a proper explanation of its position. I think we have been remiss in both areas on too many occasions. We have not done as much as we could and should have done to meet these attacks head-on by constructive action or a positive answer to the criticism. We should not shrink from admitting our defects, and then work to correct them where necessary. If we do, perhaps the critics will also admit some of our great achievements."

Roche admitted that corporate assumption of responsibility has been deficient on such issues as the minorities, consumerism, the environment, and the plight of our urban centers.

On inflation, he contended corporate profits cannot be blamed for the "very rapid" upward rate of the past few years. Indeed, if all corporate profits were eliminated, it would represent only a small share of the gross national product. Inflation is not partial—it has afflicted corporate profits the same as everything else—and price increases in most cases have failed to cover the additional costs with the result that profits have been badly squeezed."

Roche suggested "five things American business must do—responsibilities we must accept—if we are to maintain a viable, healthy and productive economic system":

1. Develop policies to deal positively and effectively with minorities, the environment, consumerism, and urban affairs. High-level executive responsibility should be assigned for the execution and monitoring of these programs.
2. Strive for improved public understanding of vital issues and their potential effects—favorable or adverse—upon the common welfare of our country. The order of the day is honesty, frankness, and timeliness in our public relations activities.
3. Give top priority to the job of creating a better understanding of the role of profit in our society. Above all, change the all-too prevalent view that profits are excessive and against the public interest.
4. Find new methods to motivate workers and union leaders to cooperate with, and not resist, management efforts to improve productivity.
5. Find ways to accommodate to the growing interrelationship of government and business . . . an atmosphere of encouragement of trade and growth, not one of restriction and regulation that impedes flexibility and the ability to compete.

Roche asserted GM is "doing all these things." He pointed out that in 1970 the company established a top-level committee of members of the board as the public policy committee. Its charter is to examine every aspect of the corporation's activities to determine the adequacy of policies and procedures as these impact upon the public. Roche said the committee is "making an important contribution toward improved public understanding." (More on page 145.)

He conceded, "The management of change, especially in the area of what might be termed social engineering, is a critical but little understood discipline. To a great extent, we are sailing in uncharted waters. In many instances, we must formulate new concepts of decision-making as it pertains to private responsibilities and public obligations. We must accept change, but at the same time, we must manage it for the benefit of everyone."

"What's Good for the People Is Good for Business"

Urgent need for better local integration of social and economic goals was the message of chief executive officers of two leading department store chains.

Ralph Lazarus, chairman, Federated Department Stores, and Stanley J. Goodman, then chairman, May Department Stores, took similar tacks in advising retailers to make greater personal contributions toward community social-issue programs. As Lazarus put it: "New and vital initiatives" are required for "a planned, purposeful effort to improve the life where we and our employees and our customers live." In Goodman's words: "What's good for the people is good for business."

Under Lazarus' definition of leadership, "company chiefs should become community-service Indians." He would have top as well as middle-managers assigned to "day-to-day involvement" in selected local service programs, rather than have top businessmen assume merely "figurehead roles" in community projects.

To point up the critical nature of the challenge and the opportunity, Federated has underwritten an annual award "for initiative in innovative community service by a retailer."

Goodman lamented the "collapse" of public confidence in, and regard and respect for, retailing as well as for the rest of business. "The customer who is 'always right' in the retailers' creed," he contended, "is also the public who thinks business is nearly always wrong."

He commented on opinions that a corporate social audit is equally as important as assessment of financial performance: "Whether or not we will come to live with a social audit is not of pressing importance. Let's get the performance, and the measurement will take care of itself."

To give retailing as an industry "more positive visibility," Goodman counseled more concrete endeavors and results in consumerism, saving the environment, attention to minorities, job opportunities for women, and image with own employees, as well as community social service.

Describing himself as "not a visionary but a pretty tough, results-oriented guy," the St. Louis-based chief executive pointed out: "As a nation we must integrate social and economic goals, and as business managers we must be judged not just for the quantity but for the quality of profits."

Proud to hold high the banner of the American free enterprise system, Goodman asserted: "High profits for the most efficient should never be thought of as going counter to the social needs of our society because it is precisely the companies good enough to achieve high profits in a competitive environment that will be good enough to get results on social problems. Don't expect much of a contribution to society from the business that is struggling for survival. American business management has the energy and resourcefulness to do well for society without doing less well in their business."

Arthur B. Toan, Jr., partner, Price Waterhouse & Co., accounting firm for many retail as well as industrial companies, maintains that business has measured "a fair amount" of its social performance for many years, particularly in areas involving employees and customers. But he finds that degree of interest small compared to increasingly popular ideas of "corporate social responsibility" or "corporate citizenship." He has no doubt "this heightened interest has much to do with the basic social and political unrest of the day as well as such specific business problems as pollution, waste creation, dwindling natural resources, product quality, customer service, minority and female employment practices, and safety."

Toan reports "an enormous increase in the quantity and quality of information being made public" in annual reports or special supplements. He finds "an increase in awareness, in sensitization to issues and alternatives and (in some companies) a more conscious utilization of such information in long-and short-term decision-making and managerial evaluation." He adds:

There clearly is a developed interest in the data, a recognition of the value of providing it, and a considerable effort within these companies to identify issues, clarify positions and gather data. There are problems with the material reported by many companies—it is often cosmetic or too much of the 'good works' variety to be altogether credible. But improving the balance is essentially a problem of psychology rather than the need for a new technology.

"We do not now have—nor are we likely soon to have—a neat set of socioeconomic reports, using a common financial or social unit of value which produces some kind of overall index or measure of a corporation's social performance. Instead, we will continue to have an increasingly valuable set of unconnected, descriptive statements about—as General Motors puts it in a ninety-six-page report—'areas of public concern' and the company's relationship to them."

Toan believes that "the interest in corporate social performance is too deep and too broad, both within and without companies, to expect that attempts to measure and report on it will be dropped. I also believe that, in spite of great technical problems, substantial efforts will be made to improve upon the initial results we are now seeing and that substantial progress will, in fact, ultimately be made."

"Retailing must respond to the new aspirations of the society it serves."

So said Julia M. Lee, retired vice-president for consumer affairs, Woodward & Lothrop, as a panelist at an annual convention of the American Retail Federation. Ms. Lee agreed with other panel members that the bogey of consumerism could be put to competitive use as a tool to enhance the store image.

In similar vein, David Rockefeller, chairman and chief executive officer, Chase Manhattan Bank, told the Advertising Council: "Because of the growing pressure for greater corporate accountability, I can foresee the day when, in addition to the annual financial statement, certified by independent accountants, corporations may be required to publish a 'social audit' similarly certified."

A social audit is an evaluation of the social, as distinct from the economic, performance of a business. The phraseology, "evaluation of business responsibilities," is preferred by Dr. George A. Steiner, president of the Academy of Management and professor of management and public policy and director of the Center for Research and Dialogue on Business in Society, Graduate School of Management, University of California, Los Angeles. He notes that persons and groups outside business have different objectives in making their social audits of individual companies. Generally, however, he finds the end result sought is to make business more socially responsible as individuals and groups measuring the performance see that responsibility.

Steiner enumerates and explains five major purposes of business's social accountability:

1. To identify those social responsibilities a company thinks it ought to be discharging. These can be classified in three different ways: a) actions a company takes partially with a view to helping society achieve objectives it sets for itself; b) internal activities such as equity in promoting or firing employees, and external activities such as improving consumer products and training hardcore unemployed; c) effect on short-and long-range profits.

2. Once the areas of concern are chosen, the company then needs to examine what it is doing and how satisfactory is the performance. As there are few generally accepted standards to measure performance, it is important that business get involved in development of such standards for, if it does not, government and private groups will set these. For some types of activities, such as minority employment, employment of women, meeting pollution standards, or improving worker productivity, it is possible to set up quantitative measurements. But such other activities as quality of advertising or meeting employee demands for job enrichment cannot be measured quantitatively.

3. Once performance is measured against a standard, the next question is: If there is a gap, how far should the company go in filling it? Here, it is necessary to make cost-benefit calculations that are often more matters of judgment than quantitative conclusions. Costs and benefits must be defined in terms well beyond traditional financial or broad economic measures to include, for example, impacts of not doing something (costs) versus advantages to the community in taking some action (benefits).

4. An audit may be designed to determine whether a company is vulnerable to potential criticism and attack. This purpose is defensive. In a large company, activities may be taking place unknown to top management. These might be the cause of severe criticism if the public were informed about them. For instance, a remote plant may be polluting the atmosphere contrary to the policy of the company and the laws of the local community.

5. A company may make an audit in order to inject a social point of view into the thinking of managers at all levels. The idea is to institutionalize social concerns into the job of each manager.

One list of major fields suggested for pursuing social responsibilities: economic growth and efficiency, education, employment and training, civil rights and equal opportunity, urban renewal and development, pollution abatement, conservation and recreation, culture and the arts, medical care, and government. The company providing this list detailed fifty-eight subgroupings in these areas. A firm desiring to focus on problems might include, in addition to those noted, poverty, prices, people congestion, privacy, space and beauty, transportation congestion, minority entrepreneurship, and research and development.

Who should "social audit" and for whom? An outside team might be selected to assure high objectivity. Or a company might set up a team of its own members. Other approaches might be to give the job to a committee of the board of directors or to hire an outside consultant to work with the company's management. Still another possibility is for a group of concerns operating in a common area to employ a team to study all the companies. Each firm must decide, in its own wisdom, whether to make the report, or parts of it, public. If the report were made public, whose standards of performance would be used? Those of the auditors? The chief executive officer? Majority stockholders? Ralph Nader? The SEC? A local housewife? A student?

Steiner sees mandatory social accounting "some distance ahead, but it seems to be the direction in which we may be headed." He grants the possibility of risks that the corporations may be unjustly criticized either for sins of omission or commission and that "society may be less well served if excessive expectations lead companies to do too much. On the other hand, there are opportunities for individual companies and society if acceptable criteria for guiding and limiting businesses' social performance can be hammered out."

If social audits could be made to work for business, Steiner ventures, why not, then, for government, nonprofit corporations, and universities?

If America is fully to realize the promise of the world of tomorrow, businessmen must set social as well as economic goals.

Coming from the mouth of Elmer L. Winter, this is no pompous, pious statement. He's doing something about it.

Winter is president of Manpower, Inc., supplying temporary help and other business services through more than 630 offices in thirty-four countries on six continents. The organization was founded in Milwaukee in 1948 by Winter and Aaron Scheinfeld, his brother-in-law and law partner. Winter is also a prize-winning amateur painter and mosaic artist, and the author of twelve books, principally concerned with various phases of temporary and part-time help. Elmer Winter is a brother of Jack A. Winter, president of the Milwaukee-based women's wear manufacturing firm of that name. The brothers are directors of each other's publicly owned companies.

In 1963, Winter helped form the Milwaukee Voluntary Equal Employment Opportunity Council to make certain his native city's employers open their doors wide to all persons, regardless of race, color, or creed. Many programs have been developed to help members hire, integrate, and advance minority workers in their companies. The council works closely with schools and the Urban League to motivate young black boys and girls to get additional training in preparation for the jobs of tomorrow. Winter has also advised groups in Washington, D.C., and Omaha in their efforts to develop similar councils.

In the spring of 1964, the Social Development Commission of Greater Milwaukee urged the city's businessmen to consider what they might do to help employ some of the fourteen thousand young people, sixteen to twenty-one years old, who would not otherwise be able to find summer jobs. Such a program was felt essential to combat juvenile delinquency, reduce high-school dropouts, and develop the potential of teenagers. It was Winter's idea that, rather than simply providing an adult staff to carry out this function, young people would be better off if they were given the opportunity to help themselves.

He called on "The Other 98," a local youth service group representing the 98 percent of Milwaukee's nondelinquent teenagers, to furnish the high-school and college-age volunteer staff of a June-through-August job clearing house he fathered—public service, nonprofit Youthpower. Manpower rented ground floor space in a building near its headquarters, gave office equipment and supplies and telephone service, paid the salary of a director, and then stepped out of the picture except for being available for advice when asked.

Among standard fields covered by Youthpower referrals are sales and stock clerks, door-to-door salespeople, handymen, car hops, babysitters, and household helpers. Training clinics are held in how to dress and act when job hunting, and in a number of specific fields.

In the years that followed, the program expanded to twenty-five cities. Since its inception in 1964, young people have been placed in more than 100,000 summer jobs by Youthpower. Nearly thirty thousand hours of volunteer time have been contributed by youths to make it all possible.

Elmer Winter, who is also president of the American Jewish Committee, made a $100,000 grant to fund AJC's Center for Human Relations Concerns of Business. AJC is this country's pioneer human relations organization. Throughout almost seventy years, it has sought to protect civil liberties for all people, regardless of race, color, creed, or sex.

In an attempt to forge a closer tie of the business community to every facet of social consciousness, CHRCB is offering its experienced consultative and technical resources as a nonprofit project "to help corporations improve the quality of their response to social issues. It assists business executives in how to use their corporate resources to best advantage in employee and community relations."

Jerome M. Rosow, head of the center's board of directors, is manager for public affairs planning, Exxon Corp. Before he joined Exxon in 1971, he was assistant secretary of labor for two years.

Arnold Harris is director of the center's professional staff. Prior to joining AJC a year ago, he was a consultant for the Coca Cola Co. and before that was a member of the staff of the Department of Justice in Washington.

Among AJC's service areas of expertise that will be tapped by business are urban issues, quotas and affirmative action, women and the feminist movement, housing, corporate giving, educational programs, executive-suite discrimination, health and welfare, transportation, drugs and alcoholism, criminal justice, and public safety.

A dozen full-time professionals in one or more of these fields will be teamed with sixty corporate executives who have been successful in leading company programs on human relations and social issues. In this way, Rosow observes, "companies, with the support of the center's trained staff, will be able to work with one another in formulating approaches and executing programs. Our pool of intergroup relations specialists is available as consultants for corporations seeking to develop, improve, or evaluate community relations programs. They will train management personnel in human relations techniques and in developing new communication systems with ethnic and racial groups."

Rosow reminds that "with the emergence of activists among environmentalists, consumerists, youth groups, women's libbers, and blacks and other minorities, suspicion of the power structure of big business and financial institutions has grown apace. In self-defense, many firms have involved themselves in considerable efforts to demonstrate their social responsibility."

Harris says "some companies have excellent programs in some areas but recognize the center can help them in expanding their consciousness of other areas with which they are not as familiar."

Rosow and Harris know of no other nonprofit organization comprising a network for the exchange of external and internal practices. Conceding many national conferences have been held on these problems, they argue that there has been no continuity until the center was organized.

CHRCB has developed a "problem census of social priorities." This will enable a company to determine the relative importance of specific social issues to each of the constituencies it wishes to poll—customers, employees, shareholders, directors, management, and the community where it operates. Companies may thus make better-informed decisions about needed programs.

The Conference Board sponsors a Council for Corporate Contributions for the exchange of pertinent information. Among the leaders in corporate philanthropy are General Motors, Ford, Sears, Roebuck, IBM, Exxon, and Xerox.

Rosow reports at Exxon to Stephen Stamas, vice-president of the public affairs department. In this department are community development programs which make grants for various public activities. Exxon Education Fund, a trail-blazer in grants to universities, was started in 1955.

By law, a business can deduct up to 5 percent of its net profit before taxes for social programs. yet the national average of such financial aid is about 1 percent. Describing the $100,000 grant to CHRCB as "only seed money," Rosow hopes the center, along with other nonprofit organizations dedicated to the betterment of society, will be accorded substantially higher financial cooperation from corporations.

Rosow concludes that "willingness to contribute money, manpower, and corporate commitments, as evidence of sensitivity to the public for the solution of community problems, is in no sense to be construed as altruism. It is, rather, a means to perpetuate the corporation in society."

Three broad beliefs on the issue of corporate social responsibility are apparent:

1. Milton Friedman, University of Chicago professor and conservative economist, thinks "a corporate executive's responsibility is to make as much money for the stockholders as possible, so long as he operates within the rules of the game. When an executive decides to take action for reasons of social responsibility, he is taking money from someone else—from the stockholders in the form of lower dividends, from the employees in the form of lower wages, from the consumer in the form of higher prices."

2. A.J. Cervantes, former mayor of St. Louis, represents the liberal thought that "it is primarily up to private enterprise and not to government to upgrade the disadvantaged, to provide training for the unemployed, to break down the complexities of job components, to employ the willing to make them able, to push for social betterment, to dissolve the ghettos, to break through the vicious cycle of welfarism, to integrate the poor into an affluent economy and to rebuild the cities."

3. Robert A. Newman, vice-president for community affairs, TRW, Inc., Cleveland-based manufacturer of electronics and other products, expresses for his company and himself an opinion "in between these extreme viewpoints."

"At TRW," he says, "we view corporate social responsibility—perhaps the most complex business issue of the day—as responding to the needs and aspirations of all corporate constituents (employee, customer, shareholder, community, and government) as fully and fairly as possible without penalizing any one constituent in favor of another."

Putting the problem into modern historical perspective, Newman traces the first wave of business' social concern to 1965 with the Watts riots in Los Angeles, followed in the next few years by riots in such other cities as Cleveland and Detroit.

The second wave of social concern, Newman continues, followed hard on the heels of civil rights issues. Topping the wave were environmental problems, first expressed by Rachel Carson's *Silent Spring* and then consumer problems as articulated in Ralph Nader's *Unsafe at Any Speed.* All this was further complicated by the Vietnam War. In this second wave, according to the TRW executive, business appeared to react highly defensively, even indignantly. It retreated behind time-worn clichés to defend itself, using shield words such as "profit" and "free enterprise."

The third wave of social concern, with us during the 1970s, is marked by such broadened issues as women's rights, occupational health and safety and truth in advertising. In the current wave, Newman discerns a more businesslike, less emotional, more mature, more analytical and systematic approach to these problems.

Until Watts, TRW's contributions to society's needs, other than being a good employer, were primarily dollar allocations from the TRW Foundation to higher education and community institutions, as well as employee and management participation in local activities. After Watts, the company "became more involved but mainly project-oriented, without really probing the true depth and the real meaning of the rising tide of public demands." In some of its first efforts, support was given to minority enterprise, health and day care facilities, and disadvantaged youth.

In the third wave, TRW is in a new phase of development in social responsibility. It has ongoing projects but is not as project-oriented as it was in the late 1960s. Newman describes the present effort as "the education-study-research-learning-analysis-planning-philosophical" phase.

At this point, the company has deemed it proper to find out what its various constituents thought about corporate responsibility. It started with a questionnaire to its shareholders. About 10 percent replied.

In answer to the question, "How can a corporation most effectively discharge its responsibility to society?" many agreed the relative profitability of a corporation is the key to its ability to contribute to the betterment of society, whether within or outside the organization. As to how TRW should discharge that responsibility, 35 percent said the company should work in some sort of partnership with government to conduct socially useful projects, 31 percent suggested the company should get involved independently in such projects and 24 percent felt it should commit itself only to making a profit and paying taxes. The remaining 10 percent had no opinion.

To another question, "How do you react to a company that makes a strong commitment to programs in the area of social responsibility?" 42 percent would be more inclined to invest in it, 31 percent said it made no difference and 27 percent would be less inclined to invest in it.

TRW's research "comes to simply this: The vast majority of the public expect from corporations a social performance that relates largely to internal affairs or business practices—not to external affairs or community activities. True, this runs counter to the feelings of many people who believe corporate responsibility means being more active in community problems and issues, giving larger contributions to the over-expanding variety of social causes. However, I'm suggesting that corporate responsibility actually involves every facet of business activity, particularly 'mainstream' issues—such as producing quality goods and services, engaging in fair hiring and promotion practices and controlling pollution."

Newman sums up by submitting these priorities:

1. Consider periodic research to find out what your constituents expect of your company, set targets for improvement where indicated and measure progress against benchmarks.
2. Get top management involvement and commitment, and communicate that fact throughout the company.
3. Concentrate your efforts on the internal, "mainstream" issues of corporate responsibility.
4. On external or community activities, consider the following;
   a) Concentrate in those locations where your company has a presence as an employer.
   b) Get involved in activities where your special expertise can be utilized.
   c) Remember that giving time and talent is often more important than giving money and, when you give money, check out "the return on investment."
   d) Look for involvement in those community issues that tie in with serving your employees, thereby lowering absenteeism and job turnover, and raising productivity and morale.
5. Once you have a successful track record, communicate this fully to your constituents "with accuracy but restraint."

One thing you can practically always count on if you attend the annual meeting of any publicly owned company:

A number of "professional" or other minority shareholders in the audience—never on the dais—will raise questions about the firm's social responsibility. How much time during working hours do officers and other employees devote to outside public activities? How much money does the company donate to philanthropic, cultural, and political organizations?

Complaints of this nature are invariably accompanied by more personalized pleas. When are you going to raise (or declare) a dividend? When are you going to split the stock? These prods have been joined by rebukes that management may not have joined the parade in electing women and blacks to the board.

There can be no escaping the connection in the minds of shareholders between the time executives spend on efforts apart from the job for which they are paid, the effect on bottom-line results, and failure of management to reward self-dubbed faceless, benighted, downtrodden small investors more fully for their faith in the company. The ritual is almost always the same: The chairman assures the petitioners the board is continuing to study the dividend and stock-split situations. And the gathering emits a collective sigh of resignation or resentment to the greater wisdom (and voting strength) of the directors, to be followed by a decision whether or not to keep the faith.

As an indication of the breadth of outside activities undertaken by businessmen, a group of thirty executives spent four hours visiting facilities of New York City's criminal justice system including detention pens and courtrooms. The tour was arranged jointly by Lawrence S. Phillips, president, Phillips-Van Heusen Corp., manufacturer-retailer, and the committee on administration of criminal justice of the New York State Bar Association which hopes to convince the business community to support legislation for court and prison reforms.

Among those who spoke with prisoners and city and court officials were Charles Veysey, president, Frederick Atkins; Julius Kraft, president, Excelsior Import Corp.; and David Linowes, partner, Laventhol, Krakstein, Horwath & Horwath, accounting firm. One of them summed up the consensus: "You can't have riots down the street and expect to have a profitable business."

Henry Ford II, Ford Motor Co.'s chairman, urges that business serve a wider range of human values beyond its basic job of providing goods and services, that it "accept an obligation to members of the public with whom it has no commercial transaction."

Of course, this unselfish interest never loses sight of the fact that immediate and long-range corporate profitability must remain as significant a concern as the issues of the broader society. For one thing, the public image of the corporation affects the extent to which it can attract and hold the cream of the crop of future executives.

As Richard C. Gerstenberg, retired General Motors chairman, puts it: "Only if we do concern ourselves with seeking to solve society's problems, will we be able to remain both profitable and responsible."

With that goal in mind, GM established in 1970 a public policy committee as a permanent standing committee of the board. Its five members are directors but none is an officer of the corporation. Chairman is John A. Mayer, chairman, Mellon National Bank & Trust. Other members are Gerald A. Sivage, director and retired president, Marshall Field & Co.; John T. Connor, chairman, Allied Chemical Corp.; James R. Killian, Jr., honorary chairman, Massachusetts Institute of Technology; and George Russell, a retired GM vice-president.

Purpose of the committee, Gerstenberg explains, is "to give matters of broad national concern a permanent and prominent place at the highest level of management right there on the board of directors which ought to be the first to perceive change and the first to grasp the opportunity of responding to it. The committee's mandate is to inquire into every phase of the corporation's business activities that relates to matters of public policy and to recommend any changes it feels appropriate to management or to the full board."

Meeting regularly every month, the committee requests and receives reports or presentations from management. It also pursues inquiries independent of the corporation, including consultation with outside experts. Gerstenberg has been present for a portion of most of the committee meetings.

GM's former chairman views as "perhaps the most important contribution of the public policy committee its continuing discussion with management. This has assisted immeasurably in strengthening and implementing corporation policies in many areas, including minority efforts, product quality, service, and mass transportation."

Phillips-Van Heusen may be the first profit-making corporation, at least in apparel retailing and manufacturing, to have embraced social accountability through employees' committees for corporate responsibility and environmental policies.

In 1972, Lawrence S. Phillips, P-VH's president, asked each of the presidents of the retail and manufacturing operating divisions in the East, South, and Midwest to nominate a middle-manager under thirty-five years old to serve voluntarily on one of the two committees.

Phillips gives the background: "We believe that, in addition to our profit responsibilities, we have to be concerned about the quality of life in our country, and we want to do everything within our power to become a factor and a force for good. Our sole instructions to the members of the two committees are to set up criteria and make recommendations to our trustees, who generally accept the committees' thinking."

The committee on corporate responsibility is charged with the social audit of some 90 common stocks, bond issues, and government securities in which P-VH's pension and retirement funds have an investment of about $11 million. It recommends to the trustees how the proxies should be voted.

The committee on environmental policies checks on how each division deals with, among other matters, recyclability and biodegradability of materials used. This committee expects to expand its policing to suppliers.

Even before the creation of the two committees, the pension fund invested $250,000 in the Dreyfus Third Century Fund, established to acquire stocks in socially responsible companies. In addition, the proxies for two thousand shares of ITT stock had been given to Clergy and Laymen Concerned, a peace group that asked the conglomerate for disclosure of Vietnam War-related interests. The P-VH committees are also following paths previously taken by investment advisory subcommittees of students, faculty, and administrative representatives at Yale, Stanford, and Princeton Universities, the Corporate Information Center of the National Council of Churches, the Council on Economic Priorities, and the Project on Corporate Responsibility. The P-VH committees are unique in comprising employees who have been granted "portfolio power," close to carte blanche as possible.

The seventy common stock issues held have been divided into sixteen industrial categories. Companies in comparable groups are rated by various members.

The committee has received corporate permission to avail itself of the services of Investor Responsibility Center, nonprofit organization based in Washington, at an annual fee of about $500. The center was formed in December, 1972, by a group of fifty institutional investors, among them universities, foundations, banks, mutual funds, and insurance companies.

After one annual shareholders' meeting, the committee members left for their own regular gathering. By invitation, Lewis Gilbert, the corporate gadfly, went along to give them some of his views.

Upon recommendation of the committee on corporate responsibility to the trustees of the corporation's pension and retirement fund, the fund managers sold holdings in ITT. The committee explained that its action on June 7, 1974, was "based on ITT's irresponsible behavior concerning political contributions and intervention in the political process, both domestically and internationally."

How much of a businessman's social responsibility is based on true concern about minorities and other phases of the public good, and how much is based primarily on the profit motive?

More to the point, shouldn't publicly owned corporations openly admit that both attitudes are equally important considerations instead of playing a game that philanthropy is their sole purpose? Even more to the point, how many of the brave, beautiful words about stress on public interest over private gain expressed by corporate leadership in the period of prosperity have evaporated into bluster and sputter in a time of recession?

Obviously, a decided element of double-talk envelops the entire subject. Double-talk, as in the case of a Georgia law having to do with preventing head-on railroad collisions. The statute reads:

"When any two locomotives of any line operating within the state of Georgia shall find themselves approaching each other from opposite directions, both must immediately stop. And neither may start again until the other does."

Hypocrisy plays a prominent role in how business handles such social issues as employment, job training, entrepreneurial opportunities for minority groups, housing, health, pollution, education, consumerism, mass transit, crime fighting, day-care center facilities, and drug addiction.

The line between hypocrisy and honesty is described by Shelley Winters, the over-fifty year old actress-playwright, in a discussion of on-stage nudity: "I think it is disgusting, shameful and damaging to all things American. But if I were twenty-two with a great body, it would be artistic, tasteful, patriotic and a progressive religious experience."

The muddled question of social conscience in the corporate world is an old one. Julius Rosenwald, Sears, Roebuck's president from 1910 to 1925, served on a special commission studying vice in Chicago. The report concluded that single girls had to make $6 to $12 a week in Chicago, or they were driven into prostitution. However, Sears' salesgirls started at $5 a week, and Rosenwald felt impelled to file a dissent.

This was the same Julius Rosenwald who, as a pioneer in philanthropy, gave away $61 million in his lifetime (1862–1932), much of it to build black schools in the South, and also provided many additional millions of dollars to be disposed of within twenty-five years after his death.

The dilemma of the proper place of business in social involvement has been raised anew by the position taken by economist Milton Friedman.

Friedman pursues the thesis: "There is one and only one social responsibility of business—to use its resources and engage in activities designed to increase its profits." He accuses those executives who plump for social responsibilities of misappropriating shareholders' investments. He also charges such executives with usurping government's functions when they get involved in pollution and urban problems. Nevertheless, the professor grants that modest contributions to causes outside the company are justified in certain circumstances requiring the goodwill of the community.

Editor-columnist William F. Buckley, Jr., concurs in Friedman's philosophy. Buckley says:

"It is the theory of free enterprise that anonymous mechanisms—competition primarily—should work to keep a company's surplus to just the level it needs to be in order to prevent its stockholders from taking their investments elsewhere. The most civic-minded thing a corporation can do is reduce the price of its product."

MIT professor Paul A. Samuelson, a 1970 Nobel Prize-winner for his economic theories and writings, takes issue with Friedman and Buckley: "A large corporation these days not only may engage in social responsibility; it had damn well better try to do so.

Samuel S. Beard, chairman, Capital Formation, a foundation established to assist minority group economic development, also believes Friedman and Buckley "miss the point." His opinion:

"Their view seems to stress that the business of business is manufacturing cosmetics and panty hose (profits are their only god); they overlook the business of constructing low-income housing, the business of training the unemployed or underemployed for jobs, the business of teaching the hard-core to read.

"With incentives from the government, business can meet its social responsibility and make a profit, and it should. These measures worked during World War II and got us to the moon. Why can't they work in Bedford-Stuyvesant, Watts, or Appalachia?"

Businessmen must understand, Beard reiterates, that "their ability to continue to do business depends on the health of the society, and that the health of the society is threatened by serious internal inequities." Observing that efforts to eliminate poverty in the United States are not producing results, he advises: "We talk of the private sector becoming involved, but until there is a profit motive, we should not expect the corporate community to provide more than token resources."

As Beard sees it, business should look at the elimination of poverty as a major new $200-to-$500-billion market. He urges that the private sector be encouraged to meet the challenge by assuring it of a reasonable rate of return on investment.

Minorities Scaling Executive Suite Walls

Martin Niemoller, German Lutheran clergyman, once said of Nazi Germany: "They came after the Communists and I did not speak up for I was not a Communist, they came for the Jews and I did not speak up for I was not a Jew, they came for the trade unionists and I did not speak up for I was not a trade unionist, they came for the Catholics and I did not speak up for I was not a Catholic, and then they came for me and by that time, there was no one to speak up for anyone."

Paraphrasing this message in terms of the American social and economic scene, substantial prejudice still exists against blacks, Puerto Ricans, Chicanos, Jews, women, and other minorities. All are victims of the hypocrisy that insists opportunity solely on grounds of ability is really equal for all. Pastor Niemoller's warning, that unless everyone speaks up boldly and acts forcefully against discrimination there will be no one to speak up for anyone, surely applies to management, whether in business and industry, schools at all levels, churches of all kinds, government agencies, housing, vacation resorts, and luncheon and social clubs.

Too often, blacks, recruited in record numbers on college campuses, find themselves after a half dozen years stuck as assistants to the personnel director, as assistant advertising account executives, and as "urban community" public relations men—"tokens" in the otherwise white-walled, blackballing executive suite. Most companies only go through the motions of cooperating in minority preemployment education, training, and upgrading.

Fewer than one of every one hundred top executives in banking, insurance, public utilities, transportation, steel, and other heavy industries are blacks, Latin-Americans, or Jews. About 15 percent of the alumni of Harvard's Graduate School of Business are Jews, but only an infinitesimal percentage of those enrolled in Harvard's Advanced Management Program, where industry sends top-position candidates, are Jewish.

Executive suite discrimination is being overcome—very slowly—through vigorous steps in some companies to change promotion policies and to recruit more members of minority groups for potential top management positions. Such actions stem from intergroup relations agencies as well as from federal equal employment programs calling on firms with government contracts to end job discrimination on the basis of race, color, creed, or national origin.

The American Jewish Committee, which has played a pioneering role in these efforts for some seventy years, does not believe the problem will be solved by a quota system of hiring, promoting, or upgrading minority group members. However, it does believe a change in attitudes is warranted in much of United States business, simply in the interests of democracy.

AJC's concept of truly democratic job policies and procedures:

1. The corporation should examine itself thoroughly to find out whether a problem of executive suite discrimination exists.
2. Over and above what government regulations require, the corporation should announce a policy to the effect that hiring and promotion will be based on ability, and that this criterion—not race, color, creed, "social station" or even "what others might think"—is the only acceptable yardstick. This policy must be clear and lucid. When executives are confused about company policy, they tend to fall back on their personal attitudes, some of which may be biased. When the rules are unambiguous, prejudice has no elbow room.
3. Personnel departments should be instructed to carry out the equal opportunity policy with the same emphasis as all other company policies. Personnel officers who do so should be commended by management, just as those skillfully executing other company policies are commended.
4. As a rule, the farther down the organizational ladder a man is located, the less familiar he is with company policy. Therefore, executives all the way up and down the line should be frequently notified and reminded, through informal as well as formal channels, of what the rules are and what is being done to implement them.
5. Executives below the top level might well be involved with the actual framing of equal opportunity rules and procedures, since a man will usually follow through on a rule he has helped set up.
6. To demonstrate that it means more than lip service, top management can

promote or transfer minority group members into positions where they will be visible to present and potential employees. This applies particularly to jobs in top management's own ranks.

7. Fears of antiminority pressures by third parties should be examined and, if the pressures prove real, they should be resisted.
8. Personnel decisions made by persons who show signs of being prejudiced should be watched with special care.
9. Misconceptions about the supposed characteristics of minority groups should be corrected.
10. Appropriate procedures for measuring hiring qualifications and promotional factors should be devised and circulated so as to eliminate, or at least narrow down, the use of irrelevant or marginal criteria.
11. The status of minority group members already employed should be periodically reviewed. Periodic progress reports should be required at all levels.
12. Educational and career guidance programs should be started to interest minority group members in all types of careers.
13. A recruitment program addressed to members of all minority groups should be begun with strong emphasis on equal opportunity all the way up and down the line.
14. A special effort should be made to inform minority group members on college campuses that the doors to the executive suite are not locked.
15. Corporate executives should use their influence to help break down discriminatory barriers in the clubs to which they belong.

Recession Hurts Cause of Affirmative Action Programs

The recession has hurt the cause of equal employment opportunity and affirmative action in hiring, promotion and retention of women, blacks and other minorities.

Ronald Michael Green, a lawyer specializing in representing management in labor and EEO problems, cites two recent developments in law that are "of great moment." 1) The U.S. Court of Appeals in New Jersey reversed a lower court which, in the case of a utility company, held the principle of last-in, first-out or last-hired, first-fired had to give way to the concept of affirmative action for minorities and women. 2) American Brands was ordered by the U.S. District Court in Richmond to allow black and female employees to advance within the cigaret and pipe tobacco plants to positions they might have held but for discrimination and, in a "bumping" system, to displace incumbent employees from those jobs as necessary.

"The presumption," according to Green, "is always that women and minorities are available for employment in any position to the same extent that they are represented in the area labor force. If, for example, 42 percent of the New York City labor force between 16 and 64 are women, the burden is on the employer to show why he may have less than that percentage of women in any job. The same burden of proof rests on the employer in the case of the 30 percent of the New York City labor force that are minority groups—blacks, Spanish-surnamed Americans, American Indians or Orientals."

Organized labor is adamant in adhering to the last-hired, first-fired principle, the heart of the seniority system since being incorporated into union contracts in the depression 1930s. The Labor Department argues there must be a substantial reason, other than an economic downturn, for an employer's unilateral decision to get rid of people between 45 and 60. EEOC, on the other hand, concedes that seniority must yield in some instances. Retirement before the mandatory age of 65 as one means to keep women and blacks—the primary victims, on the job—was termed discriminatory by former Labor Secretary Peter J. Brennan.

Green notes "intense competition among the traditional victims of discrimination. There is rivalry among blacks as a class, Hispanics as a class and women as a class. This often places employers in the difficult position of having to select from among these protected groups to the dismay of those who are not chosen. In recession, the businessman's task is all the more difficult because the protected groups contend that the requirements of the law and their redress for prior discrimination should not depend on a healthy economy, that they have the right to insist employment and unemployment be equally shared."

Green also counsels that retaliation against employees who attempt to enforce their rights under federal or state EEO laws constitutes a separate wrong quite apart from the discrimination charge. Thus, even if an employer is successful in defending a charge of discrimination, he is still prohibited from disciplining in any way the employee who brought that charge.

The Equal Rights Amendment, passed by Congress in 1972, requires passage by the legislatures of 38 states prior to an expiration date in 1979 before it can become the 27th amendment to the U.S. Constitution. By mid-1975, 34 states had approved the proposed amendment. The legal principle of equal rights is now in force only in 15 states. The amendment reads: "Equality of rights under the law shall not be denied or abridged by the United States or any state on account of sex." This would appear to protect the rights of men as well as women, but it is obvious the female sex stands to derive the most benefits from a nationwide, uniform curb on continuing discrimination patterns in hiring, promotion, firing, fringe benefits and forced early retirement. Once it becomes the law of the land, the amendment would close a substantial gap in enforcement wrought by varying interpretations by courts or legislatures.

The amendment is supported by a national campaign of the ERA Coalition, an umbrella organization of more than 60 women's groups. Among these are the National Federation of Business and Professional Women and the National Organization for Women (NOW).

Opposing the movement are many women who insist that, regardless of its merits, ERA loses sight of biological, physical, psychological and emotional differences between men and women.

One Fort Worth-based organization, called W.W.W.W. (Women Who Want to Be Women), is distributing leaflets saying in part: "God created you and gave you a beautiful and exalted place to fill. No women in history have ever enjoyed such privileges, luxuries and freedom as American women. Yet, some dissatisfied, highly vocal, militant women insist you are being exploited as a 'domestic drudge' and 'pretty toy.' And they are determined to liberate you—whether you want it or not!"

Among other things, W.W.W.W. warns: Husbands in the armed forces would be forced to share "sleeping quarters, rest rooms, showers and/or foxholes with women" and all public schools, college dormitories and hospital rooms, as well as public rest rooms, would be forced to "desexigrate."

Want the Truth About Prejudice?
Ask a Black!

Only a black really knows what it is to be a member of his race in a white-dominated society. This is the blacks' usual reaction to whites' recommendations on how best to improve economic and social relations between the two groups.

Howard L. Fromkin and John J. Sherwood, professors of social psychology and administrative sciences, Purdue University, bore this chasm in mind in conceiving and editing a book, *Integrating the Organizations: A Social Psychological Analysis.* They asked Dalmas A. Taylor, black professor of psychology, University of Maryland, to join seventeen other college teachers, psychologists, and consultants in writing original essays seeking to bridge the gap between integration research and the practical problems of management. Among these problems: career preference; selection and motivation of minority group members; interracial communication; black culture and personality; and leadership, power, and influence. They deliberately assigned the final chapter—"the last word"—to Taylor, pointing out that he "offers a perspective on integrating organizations that neither the white social scientist nor the white administrator can ever experience."

In presenting his case, Taylor gives a survey of executive positions in the sixty-seven largest California corporations. The results indicate that, of the 1,008 directors, not one is black, none is Mexican-American, one is Spanish-surnamed and he holds the Nobel Prize in physics. Six of these directors are women, of whom three are married to the company president or chairman, and one is the daughter of the company's founder. "There is no reason to believe," says Taylor, "that these data would not generalize to most organizations throughout the country."

Some of Taylor's thoughts:

- The study of prejudice by psychologists has led to concern with symptoms instead of causes, to an inspection of victims instead of perpetrators, and to a focus on intentions instead of consequences.
- When a black family moves into a home in a white neighborhood and is stoned, burned, or routed out, they are victims of an overt act of individual racism that many people will condemn—at least in words. But it is institutional racism that keeps black people subject to the daily prey of slumlords, merchants, loan sharks, and discriminatory real-estate agents. The society pretends it does not know of this situation or is incapable of doing anything about it.
- Blacks or other minorities should be represented among the ranks of those with authority, prestige, power, and control. For this to happen, we obviously cannot believe these qualities are genetically determined.
- Integration, like slavery, is an institution devised and defined by whites for blacks—without black input.
- Blacks who serve on boards in white organizations do not have a black constituency supporting them: their positions are usually a result of appointments by whites. Consequently, to advocate points of view favorable to black interests could result in losing the position as board member. If black membership and participation in boards of directors is going to be meaningful and helpful to the black community, then mechanisms must be developed that permit black people themselves to be involved in the selection of those who represent them. When there is an understanding among blacks within organizations that blacks will accept appointments to boards only when the black community is involved in the process, there will be fewer and fewer opportunities for blacks to be used in the further exploitation of their own people. Since there is no power base behind the black board member, it is quite easy for the white majority to ignore him or her.
- Blacks have pursued integration strategies by seeking coalitions with the white power structure, rich and upper-class whites, philanthropists, entrepreneurs, middle-class white liberals, poor whites and, finally, radical

whites. In all cases, these efforts have met with failure, primarily because 1) internal power relations between blacks and whites were never resolved, 2) hidden conflicts between the interests of poor blacks and middle-class whites were never resolved, and 3) the latent racism of whites has never been adequately confronted.

Taylor's summary of his views:

"The most urgent and pressing task facing the managers of today's organizations is to explore ways of creating avenues for the empowerment of neglected minorities. Unfortunately, power is rarely shared or transferred without confrontation and struggle. In that light, one of the most useful functions this volume could serve would be to facilitate managers' awareness of the wisdom in sharing or relinquishing power gracefully."

In an introductory chapter, Fromkin charges that "the foremost barrier to the integration of minority members into organizations is a morass of inaccurate beliefs commonly held by white leaders. These ill-founded beliefs about black performance limitations not only inhibit the hiring of blacks but are also responsible for pernicious self-fulfilling prophecies inside the organization. At the same time, research shows the major impediment to adequate black performance in organizations is the absence of any real opportunities for achievement, recognition or advancement to managerial levels."

There is more racial animosity in America today than ever before.

A startling indictment, indeed, coming as it does from William H. Brown III, former chairman, Equal Employment Opportunity Commission.

Since the Civil Rights Act of 1964 was passed to end discriminatory practices in jobs for minorities, Brown charges, equal employment opportunity has become "neither universal nor close at hand. . . . Amid the greatest social progress in our history, there is the greatest hatred, and the reason is that the white establishment has failed to honor its promises. . . . Enough of a minority of the white establishment has disobeyed the law as to prevent an undermanned and outgunned federal government from enforcing the law effectively."

The 1964 law has achieved mutual hatred following a frustrating exercise in naivete, disillusionment, and resentment among the minorities, Brown asserts. He contends that "too much of both private industry and the public has been concerned not with carrying out the spirit of the law but rather with achieving minimum compliance. They created standards that treated everyone equally on the surface but had the effect of disadvantaging and screening out certain groups.

"Employment testing must be kept in its proper place—as a tool for personnel management. When testing becomes the major expression of the personnel management, it is no more than a crutch. In most instances, I believe that employment tests could be eliminated entirely in favor of more comprehensive and realistic methods of personnel assessment. Many companies have done just that and have reported no adverse effects."

Brown cites median income disparity to prove that no significant change has occurred. A black with four or more years of college education still earns less than a white with a high school diploma. The income of the average black family with three earners is not substantially different from the family income of the average white family with one earner. In nine industries with relatively high hourly earnings, blacks had 8 percent of total employment but only 1 percent of the higher paid occupations (professional, technical, and managerial).

Brown warns: "EEOC looks very closely at the relationship between hiring criteria and actual job requirements to determine whether an illegal exclusionary effect on minority groups exists. There are too many instances in which criteria are arbitrary, and relationship to job needs tenuous at best."

Kenneth B. Clark, president, Metropolitan Applied Research Center, consultant firm, and professor of psychology, City College of the City University of New York, looks at and behind discrimination patterns. He starts with some broad classifications:

1. There is a deepseated, conscious determination on the part of whites to oppress non-white people for material gains.
2. There is an instinctive repugnance among one race of people for people of different races.
3. There is a genuine and natural feeling among whites that all non-whites are inferior and cannot be entrusted with the rights and responsibilities of genuine participation in a civilization.

Clark argues that these explanations, which pivot around a concept of the innateness of group aversions in each individual, are not adequate in themselves. As he sees it, prejudice is planted in the individual by institutionalized patterns of segregation and discrimination, not inborn.

To illustrate how and why individuals conform to group standards, the black psychologist observes: "It can become fashionable to dislike some group of people for various reasons. [For instance] 'Everyone else dislikes Jews and blacks. I can't be different. I must dislike them, too. If I don't, my friends will reduce me somewhat to the status of these disliked people.' In time, these ideas and attitudes become ingrained in the individual and accepted as a normal, natural way of life."

Clark generalizes that existence of the American pattern of racial prejudice and its attendant injustices has had the following effects upon the white population.

- Guilt feeling and moral conflict occupy a central role in this reaction pattern. This guilt feeling results in heightened emotionality, irrationality, and suspicion in dealing with blacks. Such stabilizing devices as rationalization, repression, and stereotyping are used as an escape from disturbing interracial realities.
- Many whites are reluctant to have racial issues faced and discussed realistically, since this tends to focus attention upon the split between democratic ideals and the facts of existing injustices.
- This pattern is complicated and irritated by the existence of many whites —albeit a minority—who for political, personal, sentimental, or humane reasons, attempt to view the problem rationally from the standard of simple human justice.

"Rarely," Clark continues, "can one view this problem in terms unencumbered by the dominant and subtle tendencies and racial attitudes of American background and culture. When an individual does appear to have succeeded in freeing himself from these attitudinal and behavioral determinations, it is quite likely he will lose his status or have his prestige or power modified in the white group. In order to regain it, he must make concessions, however subtle, in the direction of the crystallized pattern of racial attitudes. Few personalities are able to withstand these permeating pressures."

In blacks, he reports, existence of this racial cleavage often gives rise to bitterness and extreme racial sensitivity, to aggression against "white" values, institutions and, sporadically, "white" property, or to apathy and acceptance of an inferior status. In each type of reaction, there is a desire for protection against a society that continuously bombards the black with threats to his survival. Clark urges the following point of view upon executives:

A single standard of performance should prevail for blacks and whites in business, industry, and education. Any compromise in favor of blacks, any special treatment accorded them through double or triple standards, can only prove to them they are still not being taken seriously. This tends to intensify, not alleviate, all the problems of racism.

Clark resigned as a trustee of Antioch College in protest against what he characterized as abject capitulation of school authorities to black students' demands for courses of study completely separated from the regular college curriculum.

This educator is a leader of the moderate school of thought among blacks that they should operate within the framework of liberal-minded society in seeking to change from a disadvantaged to an advantaged minority.

If blacks are held to lower standards, specially set for blacks and other racial minorities, Clark warns, they will not respect the motives therefor but "will exploit this kind of fuzzy-minded sentimentalism and try to outdemean the demeanors." Any program "that visibly isolates and separates any group, whether in industry or colleges, brings with it built-in problems."

Clark is quick to emphasize that he doesn't expect blacks to achieve meaningful integration and equality in business overnight. Programs of pre-work education and job preparation and training, he asserted, are essential preliminary steps.

No. 1 target, explains this psychologist, whose mother once worked in an apparel plant and as a union organizer, is the problem of "flawed" education in our public schools. Business and industry, he continues, should take the lead in this regard "because the schools have sloughed this off and businessmen are paying a substantial part of the tax dollar for inefficient education."

Job preparation and training, Clark advises, must be differentiated from the job placement that follows. Once the youngster is placed in the job, he stressed, that person must be held to the same level of job performance as anyone else.

The business sector of American society, he adds, "is really the heart of the system. There is very little room for romanticism in our electronic age. My advice to black students is that 'soul' studies won't help them when they enter business. They should be ruthlessly competitive in a ruthlessly competitive society."

Clark makes clear his antipathy for the euphemisms of "culturally disadvantaged" for "lower status, minority people, for the most part black," and "law and order" and "safety in the streets" for "we must find some way to control the ghetto blacks who are acting up." He charges that racism, in terms of supposed genetic differences, "dominates the thinking of the masses of Americans. The average American does not really accept the recommendations of the more sophisticated social scientists that primary attention be paid to external environmental controls."

The blacks' only effective weapon, according to Clark, is "the toughest kind of realism that Martin Luther King, Jr., knew so well—to move tortuously toward egalitarian relations. There is no possible way that the blacks with one-tenth or one-ninth of the population can effectively change the situation on the basis of racial polarization."

Once business has dissipated its hang-up about special job conditions for blacks, Clark counsels, it should then go all the way in helping surmount problems of the northern urban black: residential degradation, deteriorated housing, filthy streets, menial jobs, low incomes, and high infant mortality.

The Black Man and Woman in White America's Business

Frank Reynolds, narrator for the American Broadcasting Co.'s one-hour documentary *Black Business in White America,* said in his closing remarks:

"It is a fact that our system of free enterprise is more free for the enterprising white man than for the enterprising black man. The white businessman can get a bank loan and secure financial credit more readily than the black businessman. The white man can select the location for his business more freely than the black man. The white man can buy adequate insurance coverage when the black man cannot. It is of course true that black Americans are participating in the economic life of the nation to a greater degree than ever before. But we still have a long, long way to go before opportunity is really equal. Perhaps we can be optimistic because money, unlike some other things, is color blind."

Two events served as sounding boards for the ABC program and Reynolds' comments. One was a talk, "A Realistic Approach to Minority Training," by Eugene A. Toomer, vice-president urban affairs and employee relations, Alexander's. He was a speaker at a National Retail Merchants Association Personnel Division conference on training and management development. Seven hours later, Reverend Jesse L. Jackson, national president, Operation PUSH (People United to Save Humanity), was the keynote speaker at the annual awards dinner of BRAG (Black Retail Action Group).

BRAG is composed of more than two hundred associates mainly with New York area-based stores and chain headquarters but also with other retailers in cities across the country. Its goals:

"To promote the total acceptance and participation of black men and women at all levels of the industry. To attract black high school and college students as managerial and executive candidates. To insure that the industry is responsive to the problems facing the cities, especially those of the disadvantaged. To bring to the buying public's attention those enterprises not responsive to the needs of black Americans to participate in the mainstream of the economy."

The association's self-help projects take such forms as scholarships, workshop-seminars, career counseling, job referrals, research, and a planned mathematics skills institute.

BRAG was founded in 1969 by Brenda B. Schofield, its first and only president, who was then at Abraham & Straus where in six years she was successively an assistant buyer, training executive, and manager of community training. She then went to Johnson & Johnson as manager of organization planning. She is now corporate manager of affirmative action at Clairol.

Ms. Schofield will not be "really satisfied until and unless blacks advance not only in merchandising posts but also into the executive suites and board-rooms in numbers proportionate to their presence in the working population as a whole."

From inside knowledge as a black himself, Toomer gently but firmly stressed the need of special education and training for white supervisors and other associates of minority people. He asked for sympathetic communication and patience with employees from deprived backgrounds who are often "a first generation in the business environment."

Toomer, who has a bachelor's degree from Kentucky State College and a master's from Wayne State University, joined Alexander's as director of human relations in 1968 after having been a history teacher in the Detroit schools.

Importance of the commitment of top management cannot be overem-phasized if a viable program is to be assured, continued Toomer. "Unless top management reiterates the stand that changes are long overdue, the program will be increasingly diluted the farther down the line you get."

Many blacks come to New York, enter banking or other industries as well as retailing, stay a month or a year, and then quit because their color has prevented them from being promoted, Toomer added. As he sees it, this is not a deliberate oversight by management, but it's what black writer Ralph Ellison has called the "Invisible Man"—you just don't see the black who's right under your nose. "Every man must be given his opportunity to fall flat on his face. Because the black may have had bad experiences in school, he may have to be taught to learn. If he is not promotable at a certain time, he should be told the truth. Everybody knows men who sell their blackness, not their perform-ance, and this must be handled as a personnel, not a racial problem."

As if things weren't difficult enough for blacks and Puerto Ricans trying to climb the executive ladder, Toomer charged, the retail industry is very abrasive. People speak to each other as if they were about to kill each other half the time. We don't say "thank you" or "please!"

Jackson lashed out in typically fiery, caustic manner that scored self-centered blacks as well as callous whites. He attacked black middle-class persons who think they have it made economically and have virtually forgotten they have a stake in correcting ghetto problems.

Crusading Jackson conceded that before blacks can participate much more fully in the economy as owners and top executives they must have the knowledge required to make a profit. He submitted that BRAG must have more members with businesses of their own before it can carry on "the real fight between the haves and have-nots, between the elite and the oppressed. The time must come when everyone will admit business comes natural to blacks, just as it is admitted [here his voice took on a sarcastic tone] they are natural singers and dancers."

When Gloria Hartley started visiting the market a dozen years ago, she rarely if ever saw another black face she could recognize as that of a fellow buyer. Over the last five years or so, she's seen an increasing number of black buyers. However, she notes, blacks in retailing "still have a hard row to hoe." Even now, she finds, there aren't more than two hundred black men and women in buying, merchandising, and management jobs throughout the country.

Ms. Hartley, buyer of women's sportswear, Alexander's, gave this appraisal of the slow growth of black retail executives as a panelist at a marketing workshop, part of a conference for minority-group business students on career opportunities in management. The all-day meeting was sponsored by the Association for the Integration of Management (AIM) and the Alfred P. Sloan Foundation. Attending were 350 students, including not only blacks but also Spanish-surnamed Americans, Oriental-Americans, and American Indians.

AIM is seeking to accelerate the advancement of present and potential black managers into middle and higher levels of major corporations. Its program runs the gamut from educational projects and services for black college students to self-development on the job.

Ms. Hartley, a board member of BRAG, is a graduate of Bronx Community College, has taken courses at NYU's School of Continuing Education, and is now studying political science and American foreign affairs at the New School.

She was with Allied Stores Marketing Corp. for eight years but left it for thirteen-unit Alexander's "because I wasn't in the mainstream. I wanted to see the customers and learn directly what they want. So I gave up my nine-to-five job four years ago for Alexander's where buyers sometimes put in twelve-hour days six or seven days a week and up to sixteen hours a day in the period from Thanksgiving until after New Year's. However, the years at Alexander's have been more exhilarating and productive for me than working in a buying office."

For the relative handful of blacks who've made it in retailing, Ms. Hartley observed, handsome compensation and bonuses are the rewards for hard work, long hours, and sacrifice of leisure time.

Jacqueline Krygar, buyer of women's sportswear and intimate apparel, Family Fashions by Avon, direct-mail apparel division of Avon Products, agreed with fellow panelist Ms. Hartley on retailing's attractive job prospects.

Ms. Krygar, a graduate of Moore College of Art and Science, in Philadelphia, started at Alexander's, went on to Sears, Roebuck as assistant buyer, rising to buyer of better junior dresses, and then joined Avon's new venture in apparel.

Halvan J. Lieteau, black general manager of the Brooklyn plant of IBM, the keynote speaker, offered his views on the effect of a slowed-up economy on minorities.

"Nobody's busting the doors down to hire people. Even the EEOC people are somewhat realistic. When survival of companies is at stake, they've got to see what they can do to protect the bottom line. IBM is manifesting social responsibility, but it's still in business to make money.

"If there's a national 7 percent unemployment rate, I've got a pretty good idea who will lead in the jobless."

Still, Lieteau insisted, "the job prospects for you aren't all gloom and doom. Career planning and objectives should be approached with realistic immediate and later goals in mind. Enjoy your work; you'll be in it a long time. So, if you don't like a job, move on."

With a background in financial management, Lieteau joined IBM in 1967, was promoted to senior technical assistant in Brooklyn a year later and assumed his present post in 1971. He heads a plant manufacturing such products as cables and power supplies. Most of the four hundred employees live in the Bedford-Stuyvesant district in which the factory is located. The number is small, he conceded, compared with the 450,000 blacks who live in the area. Lieteau submitted, "There should be hundreds of such plants scattered through the inner cities of America, but they're not."

James S. Spain, a founder and executive director of AIM, stirred the young people with the remark that "the past twenty years have been the beginning of the process of the principle of self-respect for black men and women. Our goal is survival on meaningful terms of blacks and other minorities in the private sector, not as extra or superfluous people in the society. You must be trained, equipped, qualified to fill vital roles in the system. You can have a successful career in the mainstream of economic activity through building a reputation, solidly based on performance, with superiors, peers and subordinates. You must do all you can to change the terms and conditions under which we live and work. You can then get a fair share of the good things of life for yourself and for successive generations."

A black, who aspires to stand out and rise to middle-to-upper management, has to play the white man's strategy game for all it's worth.

Beyond adequate educational preparation and diversified on-the-job background; beyond intelligence and industriousness, the black—or any other ethnic minority—must bring into constant play such executive skills as guts, risk-taking, visibility, manipulation, infighting, mobility and politics. Of course, a white also has to use all these guns to gain access to the management fortress but, for him, it's easier—much easier.

Frank advice along these lines was given by black managers to minority-group business students at a career-opportunities conference and workshops sponsored by AIM.

AIM drew 175 students and 25 deans and coordinators from twenty-six primarily white or black colleges and universities in the East to as far south as Atlanta and Nashville. A scattering of the attendance was Spanish-surnamed or of Oriental descent. Sixty-five percent of the collegians were undergraduates; the balance, MBA candidates.

Robert Gudger, employee relations manager and ombudsman, Xerox Corp., struck the key note of the meeting in advising "brothers" how to make it in a white man's world.

From broad experience in labor, personnel and public relations positions in business, social service and government, Gudger told the students he would pick business as a career. He explained that, although business poses greater risks, it also offers greater rewards for the relatively few who rise toward the top of the management pyramid and "become decision-makers, not decision-takers."

How can more blacks scale the management walls? The Xerox executive's recommendations:

"Have both two-year and five-year plans in short and long-range goals of self-development. Try to get your first experience in the field before going to a staff job. Select a fast-moving department such as marketing or finance. Don't just be satisfied to do the work. Learn everything you can about the people with whom you work so you can talk to them better and get things done better. Try to develop rapport with your boss. But marriage to a department, division or a corporation isn't necessary. If you're incompatible with your boss or associates, don't stay there.

"First, however, take a good look at what you're giving up. Young people are less concerned about pension plans than about stock options. You may have to make a trade-off. See if your organization has a lateral position in which you can develop skills in another kind of job. If you leave one company, don't close the door behind you." (Gudger had separate three- and four-year tours of duty at American Airlines.) "Do something to be visible. Visibility isn't hard for you." (This, with a wry smile.)

"If you want to succeed, you must take risks but, on balance, you'd better be more right than wrong. There are politics in industry as in everything. Remember, white senior staffs of corporations are by no means brothers under the skin. The competition is so severe some don't talk to others.

"You can be either a specialist who manages things or a manager who manages people, who has a staff and a budget and is a decision-maker. No matter how high you climb, your education is never really over."

Gudger, forty-six (in 1975), has a degree from New York Law School. He joined Xerox in the Rochester office in 1971 and also has filled the post of ombudsman since 1972. The use of ombudsmen was started in Scandinavian countries and has spread to Harvard University and one of the General Electric plants, but this is a first for a major American business corporation as a whole.

As ombudsman, Gudger talks to employees on a confidential basis about their grievances and seeks better ways of doing things. To show his is not a black-oriented function, he pointed out he has handled from two hundred to three hundred cases, of which only from twenty to thirty have been with blacks —"a proper proportion to the population."

Gudger's decision is "final and binding," subject only to possible overruling by Donald D. Lennox, president of the Information Technology Group and a corporate director, to whom he reports, and by C. Peter McColough, chairman.

In Gudger's own short-term plan, he has "one and one-half financial moves to make to go to vice-president which pays a minimum of $55,000 to $60,000 a year. He thinks (the conference took place in April, 1974) he'll be in his present post eighteen months or so more, then move on, in a mutually planned program, to the corporate office in Stamford, Conn., probably in personnel or public relations. "It's not important," he asserted, "if I make vice-president then, as long as I'm in decision-making. I'm already in the stock option plan which puts me in the ballpark." His five-year plan calls for "further growth."

To underscore the advantages of mobility, Gudger observed that Xerox, a multinational organization, has brought into top jobs men with special skills from Ford, IBM, and General Electric. His own boss has made fifteen moves in nineteen years. McColough, he continues, makes over $400,000 a year and has staff members earning several hundred thousand dollars. Women as well as men are starting to enter the "fast-track, pivotal job area."

In a final word, Gudger cautioned: "The company exacts blood. A nine-to-fiver can't survive at Xerox. But, then, no one works for philanthropy. It's always for money."

Women, Blacks on Boards: Are They Still "Tokens"?

More and more corporations have capitulated to social and ethnic pressures and consciousness-raising by electing a woman or a black, sometimes one of each, as directors. If they haven't done so already, they seek to take the heat off with the explanation "we're looking."

Edward W. Littlefield, chairman, Utah International, mining, land development, and shipping company, is the exceptional chief executive officer who has the temerity to take a contrary stand. At a Conference Board meeting on "New Realities for Corporate Directors", he said:

"I have no tolerance for constituency representation on the board. Each director should be there to represent all the shareholders. I favor selecting those individuals who appear to be the best qualified to act on behalf of the shareholders, to protect their interests, and to enhance the affairs of the corporation, regardless of sex or color."

Margaret Hennig, associate professor of management and organizational behavior, Simmons College, is opposed to choosing a woman as a director primarily because she is a female. She goes so far as to express the conviction that a retail corporation does not automatically require one or more female directors as a reflection of its strong orientation to women customers.

Ms. Hennig's sole criterion for a woman director: "She must be as qualified as a man is. Only as a person, only if there's a role to be filled professionally, not because of her sex, does a woman belong at the seat of power—and then she certainly belongs there."

This management authority, who has both master's and Ph.D. degrees from the Harvard Business School, finds it regrettable that some companies, which she declines to name, have appointed women to their boards regardless of their lack of particular competence for the jobs. She calls it "rape" to hire a woman, who's not qualified, for any position, merely because it's a woman. To Ms. Hennig, "this is the worst kind of racism or sexism and is programmed for failure."

The forward march of blacks and females to boards goes on although they account for hardly more than a ripple in the estimated total of some fourteen thousand directors of the nation's one thousand largest corporations.

Jerome H. Holland, former president of Hampton Institute and former U.S. ambassador to Sweden, leads all other blacks with nine directorships, among these AT&T, Chrysler, Manufacturers Hanover Trust Co., and the New York Stock Exchange. Also on Chrysler's board is Martha W. Griffiths, lawyer and former Democratic representative from Michigan, who is also a director of Burroughs Corp., National Bank of Detroit, and Consumers Power Co. Also on Burroughs' board is Clifton R. Wharton, Jr., black president, Michigan State University, and a director of Ford Motor Co. and Equitable Life Assurance Society. On Equitable's board is a second black—Andrew F. Brimmer, a visiting professor at the Harvard Business School, a former member of the board of governors of the Federal Reserve System, a director of E.I. duPont deNemours & Co., and a trustee of the Ford Foundation.

On the AT&T board is Catherine B. Cleary, president, Milwaukee's First National Bank, who is also a director of General Motors, Kraftco, and Northwestern Mutual Life Insurance. A fellow director at General Motors is black minister Leon Sullivan, also a director of Girard Trust Co. and Philadelphia Saving Fund Society.

Luther H. Foster, president, Tuskegee Institute, is a director of Sears, Roebuck & Co. Sears has had a succession of women, one at a time, on its board for many years. The current female director is Norma Pace, vice-president, American Paper Institute. Vernon E. Jordan, Jr., executive director, National Urban League, is a director of Xerox, J.C. Penney Co., Celanese Corp., and Bankers Trust Co. Penney also has a woman director: Juanita M. Kreps, vice-president, Duke University. Dr. Kreps is also a director of R.J.

Reynolds Industries, Western Electric, and Eastman Kodak. Eleanor Thomas Elliott, chairman of the board of trustees, Barnard College, is a Celanese director.

Marcor Inc., parent company of Montgomery Ward & Co., also has a black man and a woman on its board. The black is W. Leonard Evans, Jr., publisher, Tuesday Publications and founder of the National NNN radio network of black radio stations. The woman is Marina von Neumann Whitman, economist and former member of the President's Council of Economic Advisers.

Ernesta G. Procope, founder-president, E.G. Bowman Co., largest black-owned insurance brokerage concern, is on the board of Avon Products where she joined Cecily Cannan Selby, a scientist. Patricia Roberts Harris, partner in the law firm of Fried, Frank, Harris, Shriver & Kampelman, New York and Washington, answers the quest for a woman and black in one person. She is on the boards of IBM, Chase Manhattan Bank, Scott Paper Co., and the National Bank of Washington.

Other black directors are Samuel R. Pierce, Jr., partner in the New York law firm of Battle, Fowler, Lidstone, Jaffin, Pierce & Kheel, at General Electric Co.; Henry Parks, sausage manufacturer, at First Pennsylvania Bank, Magnavox, and Macrodyne-Chatillon, aerospace instruments company; and Clifford L. Alexander, Jr., lawyer and former government official, at Pennsylvania Power & Light and the Third Century Fund.

Additional women directors are Martha E. Peterson, president, Barnard College and a Columbia University dean, on the boards of Metropolitan Life Insurance Co. and Exxon; Mary Wells Lawrence, head of Wells, Rich, Greene, ad agency, on the board of Sun Oil Co.; Ruth Patrick, board chairman, Academy of Natural Sciences, Philadelphia, on the board of Du Pont; Barbara Scott Preiskel, vice-president and legislative counsel, Motion Picture Association of America, on the board of Textron, Jewel Companies and Amstar; Kathryn D. Wriston, Federated Department Stores; and Gertrude G. Michelson, senior vice-president for consumer and employee relations, Macy's New York, a director of Quaker Oats Co., Harper & Row Publishers, Chubb Corp., insurance firm, and the New York division of R.H. Macy & Co.

Others are Jane P. Cahill, vice-president-communications, IBM, director of Chesebrough-Pond's; Anne Armstrong, former counsellor to the president and cabinet member, director of American Express Co. and Union Carbide Corp.; Mary Gardiner Jones, University of Illinois professor of law and of business administration and former member of the Federal Trade Commission, on the board of American Airlines; and Sister Jane Scully, Roman Catholic nun and president of Carlow College, Pittsburgh college for women, on the board of the Gulf Oil Corp.

Ms. Cleary, the banker, insists "I do not represent women. . . . I can't say if I'm a token director but, if I thought I was, I wouldn't be on boards."

Black directors divide themselves into two distinct groups: those who consider themselves black directors and those who claim they are directors who just happen to be black. The majority view themselves as spokesmen for the black community as well as being qualified by business or professional background.

Evans, the publisher and Marcor director, finds it:

"unbelievable that corporations are capitulating to social and ethnic pressures to elect board members and, if so, who is applying the pressure—or is it all imaginary?

"The day of tokenism, in my opinion, is over. Most certainly, as far as one Leonard Evans is concerned. We at Tuesday Publications do not take token advertising from advertisers, nor do any of our officers take token appointments.

"I know more about marketing in a special segment of the major forty markets than a hundred other directors of other companies because of my experience and background. I see no reason to be apologetic for that expertise. The market I am most familiar with spends more than $46 billion in consumer expenditures. As president of a company that is interested in the bottom line, I think this experience reflects my decisions at Marcor, which is interested in profits.

"I did not accept the nomination to the board of directors of Marcor Inc. to represent any particular group or faction, and most certainly it was not a result of either ethnic or social pressure."

Robert K. Mueller, vice-president, Arthur D. Little, management consultants, comments on minority group directors:

"With recent social pressures forcing recognition of all sorts of minority groups and 'affirmative action' interests, there has been a scramble to respond with a sprinkling of race, color, creed, and sex representatives as directors. The problem here is at least twofold: finding qualified, interested candidates and getting the traditional establishment board to change its thinking sufficiently to go beyond tokenism and welcome responsible seating of a minority group director in the inner board circle. The frequency of such elections is increasing in the more progressive directorates, but the long-term problem will be to find qualified candidates."

Myths about Women

Myths and stereotypes persist about women's personality traits as compared with men's.

At a meeting of the Association for the Advancement of Psychoanalysis, the consensus of a panel of two men and one woman was that, despite widely accepted generalizations: Men are not necessarily strong, tough, assertive, objective, courageous, logical, constructive, independent, unsentimental, une-motional, aggressive, competitive, diligent, disciplined, level-headed, con-trolled, practical, and persuasive. By the same token, women are not neces-sarily weak, passive, irrational, emotional, empty-headed, unassertive, subjective, illogical, dependent, fitful, devoted, self-effacing, impractical, artis-tic, and receptive.

Dr. Harry Gershman, dean of the American Institute of Psychoanalysis, reported that "all these qualities can be observed among men as well as women."

But this isn't the opinion of most businessmen. The male philosophy to the contrary was expressed in the classic line of Louis XV of France, "After me, the flood," which ignored the existence of Mme. Pompadour, his mistress. The king's reasoning was that women are welcome in the bed chamber but not in the council chamber. Almost two centuries have passed, but the same reasoning is adhered to by most "kings" of commerce today.

Dr. David Robbins, attending psychiatrist, New York Hospital-Cor-nell Medical Center, Westchester Division, sought to take apart some of the rationalizations for sexual discrimination as a commonplace in Ameri-can business:

"First, the issue of time off for family problems. Only a small proportion of working women have very young children likely to need extra attention at unpredictable moments. Women with older children are as reliable as men; with advancing age, women may actually need less time off for health problems than men.

"We are often told that women are too emotional and unstable to manage complex responsibilities. There is no proof that this accusation is universally true. Nor is there any evidence that such instability is genetically linked to gender. Our acculturation-socialization process teaches little girls to be emo-tional and also insists that logical scientific thought is male.

"American industry managed to employ women freely when an ex-traordinary need existed—for example, during World War II. Other nations, at congruent levels of technological and industrial complexity, freely utilize women in a wide spectrum of jobs. So the real issue is a willingness to tran-scend unnecessarily rigid stereotypes and allow the growth and fruition of talent, regardless of irrelevant physical and cultural variables including sex, race, ethnic origin, theology, etc. When discrimination and bias are removed from the world of work, each individual will be free to choose the quality, the quantity, and the locale of their occupation commensurate with their skills."

According to columnist Sylvia Porter, the antidiscrimination law should finally set at rest these "myths":

1. It isn't worthwhile to hire a woman instead of a man for a high-placed job entailing substantial investment in training in view of the prospect of more absenteeism among women.
2. There is a faster job turnover rate among women.
3. Men prefer to work for men.

   Proof to the contrary:

1. A study by the U. S. Public Health Service indicates that women average 5.4 days of sick leave per year against 5.6 days for men.
2. In one year analyzed by the Bureau of Labor Statistics, 11 percent of the men changed jobs one or more times, while only 8.6 percent of the women workers changed.
3. Admittedly, most men who have never worked for women insist they wouldn't want to do so. Yet, an examination of attitudes, published in the *Harvard Business Review,* finds only one man in seventeen "strongly unfavorable" to the idea of female managers. Actually, one in ten is "strongly favorable." The other attitudes range from "mildly favorable" to "mildly unfavorable."

In many cases, women are satisfied with being subordinates. Generally, they don't have the same driving ambition as men for advancement and authority. They don't want the hypertension, backaches, spastic stomachs, and other psychosomatic ailments that plague so many aggressive men who are fighting to reach the top or stay there.

Working wives have divided loyalties and responsibilities. The husbands are the major breadwinners and their success is all-important. If the husband gets a job in a different city, the wife almost invariably goes with him. For this reason alone, there is less certainty that she will stick to the job as long as a man would. By the same token, she won't be tempted by out-of-town offers for herself unless, by some chance, her husband is included. Fact is, even single women resist being uprooted more than men do.

Granted, departure from business for marriage and home-making is the chief reason why women don't rise higher. But what about women—perhaps small in percentage but looming large in absolute numbers—who remain unmarried or are divorced or separated? What about the steadily increasing ranks of wives who return to work after they have cared for their children through childhood?

Mere superiority of numbers gives men the competitive edge, the vote, for most jobs. And the men comprising the vast majority of middle-to-top executives make the decisions as to who will be hired and who will be promoted. Any doubt as to the better choice is usually resolved in favor of the man. The male boss knows the man better than he does the woman candidate, feels more comfortable with him. Even the woman executive is often inclined to give the nod to the man.

Many in top management hold it to be almost axiomatic that men won't take orders from a woman, that women resent supervision from another female. Women just don't have as many doors open to them.

Frank J. Devlin, of the School of Business, John Carroll University, Cleveland, submits this view as to whether women have the qualifications to hold managerial positions:

"Much depends on what may be considered managerial qualities. Men are generally larger and physically stronger than women. But women are constitutionally stronger than men, live longer, and hold up better in a crisis. So far, superiority of one sex over the other in intelligence has not been established. And historical usage, custom, tradition, preference, and all other superficial measures are in violation of Title VII."

Germaine Greer, in her book *The Female Eunuch,* says:

"Considered as a whole, female employment in Britain and the United States displays the same basic character—that of an inert, unvalued, though essential force, considered as temporary labor, docile, ignorant, and unreliable.

"Because more than half the working women are married, the assumption arises that the family is their principal concern, that work outside the home brings in a little extra spending money, that they have no ambition. Not only are women paid less than men in most of the instances where they do work identical with men, but most women work at a lower level than men in the same industry, so that the question of parity can never arise.

"In England, the long struggle to elevate women's work to equal dignity with men's has slowly but surely gotten under way after years of fitful skirmishing: the stimulus to action has been passed on from the professional women to the workers. In America, the concern of the liberal new feminist to see that her sisters are allowed keys to executive washrooms must seem bitterly irrelevant to those three-quarters of the female population who have an income of less than $4,000 a year."

Felice N. Schwartz, president, Catalyst, a nonprofit organization to expand career opportunities for college-educated women, says:

"Women are motivated to enter the work force in this order: 1) a desire to earn money, 2) to feel useful, 3) to be recognized in their own right, and 4) to utilize their minds and education more fully.

"In short, they want to feel productive and self-respecting and contribute to the support of their families. Increasingly, women enter or re-enter the labor force as their home and family responsibilities require less time or are shared with their husbands."

Women, according to Dr. Ruth B. Kundsin, Harvard bacteriologist, are too often placed in one of two categories by male colleagues: If the woman is attractive, the men are flirtatious. If she is unattractive, their merciless appraisal of her appearance takes precedence over what she has to say.

The placement director of a midwestern university confides: "Now, instead of saying 'no women,' there is a tolerance for having them on interviewing schedules. But I do not think the situation for women has improved."

A sociologist cites findings that "the actual personality of women executives seldom corresponds to the stereotype, but the stereotype persists."

It is a mixed blessing that during the recession there has been a significantly smaller jump in unemployment among women than among men. The reason: concentration of females in white-collar jobs that have been less strongly hit by the economic slowdown than have blue-collar jobs most frequently held by males.

Signs that women are finally beginning to make it in a man's world:

1. The Supreme Court has ruled that women may not be excluded from jobs because they have children unless men are too.
2. In South Dakota, the Attorney General has ruled that women may work the same number of hours as men.
3. In both North and South Dakota, women are now permitted by law to be jockeys at horse races.
4. A number of states have eliminated laws that women may not take jobs requiring them to lift only thirty to forty pounds.
5. The police departments of Peoria, Indianapolis, and Miami are sending women out on regular patrol.

When Gertrude D. T. Schimmel became the first woman captain in the New York Police Department (she is now an inspector) she was asked at a press conference whether she thought a woman would ever be appointed police commissioner. "Yes," was her reply in the presence of then Mayor Lindsay, "by a woman mayor."

It now works both ways. Men have won equal job rights as airline stewards and nurses. And a male food handler successfully sued for the right to keep his shoulder-length hair if he wears a hairnet required of female employees.

If this trend continues, you'll hear men calling women female chauvinist sows.

Margaret Hennig, associate professor of management and organizational behavior, Simmons College, and director of the Prince Program in Retail Management at that college, conducted a five-year study of "Development for Women Executives." The original research was among 125 females who are presidents or senior vice-presidents in line capacities at medium-to-large corporations. In her final report, she concentrated on thirty-five women with whom she spent from fifty to sixty hours each in in-depth interviews.

Abilities she found outstanding in these women:

To take risks, to deal with and live with conflicts, to handle confrontation, to endure loneliness, to initiate rather than react, to make independent decisions, to be disliked and live with it, to live with being different.

All these qualities, Ms. Hennig pointed out, are technical, human, political, and conceptual skills previously identified with men, but "very few of these skills have any sexual meaning."

All the women in the study were either their parents' only children or the first-born of all-girl families. Their relationships with both parents were equally strong. All attended college, but none went to graduate school. All are now in their fifties and with the same companies twenty-five years or more. Until they reached middle management, they had made it as technical specialists. Slightly more than half are married, but all would have wanted marriage. Most wanted children, but none had any.

One of the women gave as a self-conception: "I would say my total success as a person would be if people spoke of me as 'one helluva executive and one helluva person' rather than as 'she's a bitch and I wouldn't marry her.' "

Ms. Hennig observed that "stereotypes are still with us, and this is true of both men and women. The fact that "few women are executives is due to the women themselves as well as to men." One of these obstacles: many women don't want to move to other geographical locations or their husbands object.

Too many firms, Ms. Hennig went on, won't put a woman on the management training program and make it clear nobody will rise in the organization unless they've gone through the program. "Women have not been helped to internalize, to create yardsticks of performance."

Ms. Hennig disparaged what she described as "the Queen Bee syndrome among women in top posts. She explained this attitude as:

"After all is said and done and I make it to the presidency of the company, I'm still affected by my acculturation and socialization. I very much enjoy being the only woman executive in the company."

Dr. S. G. Huneryager, associate dean and coordinator of the management department at the College of Business Administration, University of Illinois, Chicago, contended that women are "not a minority in work discrimination in the same way that blacks and Jews are, but they do face job discrimination." He asserted that very little research has been carried out on the man-woman working relationship. In this limited research, he went on, most commonly accepted impressions about women are psychological beliefs that are not supportable. He derided such opinions as that a woman is too emotional for a top position, that she can't make rational judgments, that she is only a temporary employee waiting to get married to leave the work force.

"We must develop selection techniques and programs," Huneryager suggested, "that will demonstrate there's no discrimination between men and women. Because most men don't have any awareness of the problems of women in the world of work, we must expose male managers, as IBM is doing, to sensitivity programs bearing on women. It's nice to put legislation in the books, but I'm not so sure this changes attitudes. Companies should sponsor training and development programs for women who are home raising children —programs that will capsulize the growing body of knowledge and ship it to them so that, when they return to the job, their skills will not be obsolete."

How does a woman at the lower rungs of the executive ladder survive and rise in a male-oriented company in which even other women may give her the evil eye?

This was one of many questions discussed by fifteen females at a two-day seminar on "Principles of Supervisory Management for the Newly Promoted Woman." The meeting was sponsored by The Distaff Group, Inc., subsidiary of Executive Enterprises, an organization in the field of management education with concentration on seminars. The registrants were sent by eleven companies (one company sponsored four employees, another two).

The fifteen women hold such titles as supervisor of general accounting, supervisor of personnel records, personnel department coordinator, corporate employment manager, benefits adviser, director of supervisory training, and manager of personnel services.

It is quite likely their employers, who represent both large and small companies in a cross-section of industries, have been influenced to develop these women at least as much by Equal Employment Opportunity Commission sanctions regarding training and promoting women for management positions as by a completely voluntary desire to improve the lot of businesswomen.

True, the law may persuade a firm to choose a woman over a man for a certain job, but the registrants concurred that a selection on the basis of sex alone is to be disparaged. Too often, women in supervisory jobs are still "tokens" in much the same way as blacks in similar positions.

Program leaders were Pauline McGee-Egan, assistant professor of psychology, St. John's University, and Henry Hein, a New Rochelle consultant who is also affiliated with Robert Saunders Associates, New Fairfield, Conn.

Dr. McGee-Egan contended that, "aside from a problem of over-involvement with subordinates, there are no innate problems peculiar to females. All other problems are man-made or woman-made. There are no problems inherent in women that prevent them from rising to any job."

Hein posed the question of many women who are reluctant to take a bigger job "if there's no precedent in the company. But it has to start with someone and, then, the dam breaks wide open." At the same time, he recognized that legal pressures on an organization tend to cause the firm "to promote a woman into a job and take out some of the responsibility because the woman isn't prepared for the responsibility. We see, here, a pincer movement between tokenism and ability to perform the job."

Prof. McGee-Egan attributed continuing stereotypes and myths about women to "traditional cultural bias—perceptions held by many females as well as men." Women, she reported, are often found acceptable only as "barefoot and pregnant" dependents. They have been taught it's proper for a woman to cry but not for a man. "Emotionality of women is a little more overt. It's better to talk it out. Your emotions can debilitate you."

Arguing for equal opportunity, the youthful professor nevertheless told her audience: "This is not to say we're not different. Women are more sensitive to other people. They are more willing to listen to personal problems than the man who rebuffs such discussion with: 'You've got problems? You're here to do a job.'"

Ms. McGee-Egan agreed with a registrant that "women managers may have a problem of drawing the line on how friendly they should be with employees; they may show favoritism to some over others." The professor's rejoinder: "This is one of our biggest problems. You may be too gregarious. There's always a tendency to take advantage of a friendship. You must maintain a certain air of authority without being a snob. You must separate yourself from subordinates at times. You must not get too involved with your people's private lives. You shouldn't become one of the boys—that's one of the worst things you can do. You can't loosen up too much because you can't then tighten up when you have to."

Among problems enumerated by the registrants as being high on their lists of things to accomplish:

1. establishing a closer relationship with subordinates
2. coping with supervisory changes from above
3. establishing a good relationship with more experienced women managers
4. the male-female relationship—getting men to accept women as peers
5. motivating subordinates to take on more responsibility
6. delegating work loads
7. constant improvement of oneself
8. maintaining your cool under extreme provocation

The university teacher observed that "the feminists have harmed women's position in that they have overemphasized our demands and underemphasized our abilities." To demonstrate her own objectivity, she proceeded to talk about the problems of being a woman supervisor and about the advantages and disadvantages of women compared with men.

Ms. McGee-Egan referred to "the challenge of the male ego—men who refuse to accept a woman's authority or peer status." She also mentioned men who question a woman's motivation—"Is she a potential threat to me?" and the extra burden of the "token" woman who, if she doesn't make good, makes it harder for another woman to step up the ladder.

This Ph.D.'s concept of female advantages over males: "A woman can often help another woman better than a man can. But the sad thing is, there are so few women mentors around to ask and we have to go to a man whose predictable solution for any problem is 'Don't worry about it.' Women have a greater eye for detail than men have. Ask a man what someone wore, and he'll answer in generalities. A woman sees and remembers. This is part of her sex. Women have physiological advantages over men. Stress factors do not affect women as greatly as they do men." The difference, she ventured, may be female hormones that may help women escape heart attacks "to which men are more susceptible because they keep things bottled up."

What are women's shortcomings? "Change upsets women more readily than it does men. In a change of location, women are more worried about the cafeteria and restroom than men are. Women may be more afraid than men to improvise in the job environment. Women, more than men, need constant reassurance. Women tend to be more timid about asking people to carry out assigned projects."

To a query from a registrant as to the emotional effect of menstrual periods on the average woman, Ms. McGee-Egan responded: "Cyclical changes in a woman make her more sensitive, more tense, at that time. There are no corresponding physiological phenomena in a man. Some women would be well-advised to defer important decisions at that period."

To a woman who admitted timidity in dealing with subordinates who complain about their work load, telling them she'll do the job herself, the professor retorted: "You were chosen to be a supervisor, so lead. Clarify the policies under which everyone on your staff has to work and enforce them. Discipline them when necessary but do it privately. Of course, there are women who want decisions made for them, but that's the way the culture wants it."

Is there a problem of home versus the job? One woman's view: "My child comes first, but any real emergency requiring me to rush home occurs very seldom." Another woman: "Men, too, go home in a crisis. They take a day off to take a child to the doctor more than women do."

At another point, the psychologist advised: "Malingering is not confined to women."

Miriam Meyers Ritvo, dean of students, Lesley College, set the stage for her talk at an American Management Associations meeting by telling a riddle:

"A man and his young son were seriously injured in an auto accident and had to undergo surgery. After the son had been prepared for the operation, the surgeon started to wield the scalpel but stopped upon seeing the lad's face and cried out: 'My God, I can't operate on him. He's my son.' How could this be when the boy's father was also about to go under the knife?"

Ms. Ritvo invited answers from the gathering. Only one man came up with the right answer: the surgeon was a woman. The speaker pointed out, "Women can't answer the riddle any more than men can. They just don't think along lines that a surgeon could possibly be a woman. The fault lies in the fact that a woman manager, such as I am, represents a token person."

Ms. Ritvo, a Ph.D. who is also dean of students at the Cambridge, Mass., college, reported that, earning a high salary and substantial fees, she has "made it in management in a man's world, and that makes for problems with men." In an updated version of a cliché, she quoted one man asking another: "Would you want your brother to marry a woman manager?"

Some of her shafts directed at the status quo:

- The man's view is that the traditional superior-subordinate role, sexually, makes it hard to switch roles in the executive suite.
- A lone woman or even five in the executive suite are under extreme pressure because they're token people. The woman has to try to be one of the boys. She's supposed to be flattered when she's told she thinks like a man, but she must still be feminine. She can't be a castrating person.

Ms. Ritvo volunteered: "Running a home is a little different from running an office. I feel I must have an impeccable house to prove to the world at large I can fill a dual role and not neglect my husband (a radiologist), children, and home."

In open discussion, men in the audience disputed Ms. Ritvo's need for a career outside the home. One charged that "matriarchy and momism are rampant at home. Why do women want to make it in the office as well? Why is there a need to unseat the male?" Ms. Ritvo's rejoinder: "Why must it be either you or me? Why should it be thought the woman wants to displace the man?"

The Problems of Integrating Women into Executive Ranks

Integrating women into responsible jobs in business and industry falls into three major areas, according to Sharon N. Kirkman, vice-president, Boyle/Kirkman, management consultant specializing in equal-opportunity and affirmative action programs for females. Barbara Boyle, president, and Ms. Kirkman founded the firm in 1972 after having been associated in similar work at IBM.

The three areas:

1. Inherent discrimination in the corporate organizational system. This includes universities as well as industrial or retail organizations. This bias takes such forms as having all women enter as secretaries.
2. Management attitudes. The top managers, the great majority of whom are males, may be free of bias and want to correct any inequities, but there is the problem of transforming corporate policy into organizational practice. The basic attitudes that prevail in discrimination are those of the majority of men in lower-to-middle management. Most men in a company do not plot to keep a woman from rising to a responsible job, but perhaps only unconsciously, they believe all the stereotypes about women even after these have been disproved. The men have been conditioned that men's place is in business; women's, in the home. There is no factual evidence to corroborate the myths that women do not want challenging promotions, that women with husbands and grown-up children do not want to relocate geographically, that women with husbands and young children do not want jobs that require them to make frequent out-of-town trips. They are not given the choice of saying: "I'll take it" or "I don't want it." Instead, the boss acts as if he knows what's on her mind, as if he knows what's best for her. At the very least she should be asked.
3. Even if the system is cleared up, there is the problem of women themselves. The great American dream decrees that they'll fall in love, get married, have babies, and live happily ever after. This thinking is changing, but the changes are minor, not dramatic. Many little girls are still being raised to believe in that future. Daytime TV and kids' books serve to perpetuate the myth. Of course, there's nothing wrong with the American dream except that it doesn't happen to everyone. Young men may not make enough money to support a family. Children may need special schooling. There are divorces. Husbands die. Many women don't get married or, being married, don't want children.

   For many women, the real-life story may create a tremendous lack of confidence which will interfere with any desire to carry out a successful business career.

Boyle/Kirkman's seven consultants work with some twenty-five corporations in setting up and implementing awareness, development, and action plans. Managers are helped to gain essential insight that will cause them to review their thinking and take the talents and abilities of specific women into full consideration the next time a responsible job opens up.

So far as the women are concerned, the consulting firm provides training programs to reverse a too-prevalent low esteem on their part. Most people limit themselves to what they think is attainable. If women do not aspire to jobs beyond lower-to-middle management, it's because they think there is no probability they can reach the top positions. Where a woman does hold a top job, more women under them will seek bigger things themselves. With women's rights and sights being raised by both government and private-group activities, a growing number of women are likely to push for more of the upper management posts. Boyle/Kirkman is committed to a positive answer to the perennial question of businesswomen: "I've trained my tenth male boss. Why can't I have the job myself?"

Ms. Boyle enumerates ten basic steps in a viable affirmative action plan:

1. establishing ultimate responsibility for the program
2. pinpointing the problem areas through statistical study
3. top management participation
4. identification and tracking of women with potential
5. job restructuring
6. setting realistic, measurable goals
7. recruiting for a broader range of positions
8. management development and training programs and specialized seminars
9. lower-level management awareness
10. study of personnel policies

Ms. Kirkman finds the recession affecting women in three ways:

1. Women outside the work force are not being hired.
2. Women now in the company have an opportunity they wouldn't otherwise have. With hiring freezes at many companies, when someone is let go, everybody left in the department has to do more. Women are getting opportunities for the experience needed for promotion, and this will pay off at the end of the slump.
3. Where women have been advanced into skilled technical jobs through equal employment opportunity, they may now have been displaced through the union seniority system.

The number of women in management will triple in the next five years, Ms. Kirkman predicts. The explanation is women's increased educational level and awareness of legal and social factors as a result of "assertive" training.

Ms. Boyle was with IBM for fourteen years. In 1970, she established the company's first affirmative action program for women. While with IBM, Ms. Boyle brought out *Fifty-One Per Cent,* a film that may be rented by other companies. The film is accompanied by a video-tape discussion guide Ms. Boyle produced with Frederick Herzberg, the psychologist who is the father of the job-enrichment theory. Ms. Kirkman, who was with IBM for ten years, developed its program of equal employment opportunity for women, and then went to American Express Co. for one year as personnel relations manager to set up an affirmative action program for women and minorities. Ms. Boyle and

Ms. Kirkman were encouraged to go into their own business by David J. Mahoney, chairman, Norton Simon, who gave them a substantial advance payment as their first client.

In private life, Barbara Boyle has been the wife of John L. Sullivan, Jr., marketing vice-president, Computer Sciences Corp., since August, 1974. His firm is based in Los Angeles; hers, in New York. Like a growing number of other couples who work in cities far removed from each other, the Sullivans try to arrange their travel schedules to meet weekly.

Vicious Circle Keeps Women from Top Retail Jobs

In eighteenth-century England, a fad developed among women to become preachers. When writer-critic Samuel Johnson was asked what he thought of females in the pulpit, he replied, "Sir, a woman preaching is like a dog walking on its hind legs. You are surprised to see it done well but even more surprised to see it done at all."

So with women as top executives in retailing in general and department stores in particular.

In an industry in which they play dominant roles as customers, women only infrequently rise to general merchandise managers and vice-presidents, and presidents are so rare their appointments are page one news.

In theory, at least, certain women have the drive, intelligence and ambition to rise to any position. A few have demonstrated this in practice. However, most females, even those possessed of aggressiveness, haven't reached upper-echelon positions because they haven't been afforded the necessary opportunities. Tradition and prejudice have conspired to keep them as specialists, instead of encouraging them to raise their horizons and become the generalists essential for high-officer rank.

Richard P. Hauser, president, The Broadway division, Carter Hawley Hale Stores, expects women to achieve top posts in retailing in the near future. "I think women are more aware than they've ever been that they have opportunity. Because women are more aware, so are managements of various retail businesses more aware that women are every bit as capable as men for any of the top jobs. As women get the kind of experience that leads to the presidency, more qualified candidates for any top jobs will be found among them as well as among men. Before 1980, there will be more than one woman [Geraldine Stutz, Henri Bendel] to whom you can point as a store president."

Asked about the place of women in the J.C. Penney Co. hierarchy,

Chairman Donald V. Seibert commented: "We are putting a lot of emphasis on improved mobility of women. Quite a number of women were at our 1975 management conferences. The company has one woman vice-president, Satenig St. Marie, director of consumer affairs. Other women hold important divisional merchandising, buying, and technical positions. We don't pretend to say we're satisfied. We were late in taking advantage of this management resource, but we now have more women in training than ever. We expect to have a significantly larger representation of women at our next management conferences."

Women are often first assistants to males who head up merchandising and operating functions. As more than one female views this: "The women do most of the dirty work while the men play the political game and grab all the credit."

Within the past four decades, fewer than ten women have become presidents of major department or specialty stores. In chronological order: Hortense M. Odlum, Bonwit Teller; Beatrice Fox Auerbach, G. Fox & Co.; D. D. Brown, Brown, Dunkin Co.; Dorothy Shaver, Lord & Taylor; Marion Armstrong, Weinstock, Lubin; Margaret Gollan Jelleff, Frank R. Jelleff; Geraldine Stutz and Mildred Custin, Bonwit Teller. Of this group, four were members of controlling families, and four made it primarily on their own.

The only one of the eight now at the helm is Ms. Stutz who became president of Henri Bendel in 1957. She was previously vice-president and general manager of I. Miller's retail division for two years, and before that fashion and promotion director of Miller's wholesale division after having been associate editor of *Glamour* magazine. I. Miller and Bendel are owned by Genesco.

An example of keeping it in the family is Margaret Scarbrough Wilson, chairman of Scarbroughs, an Austin, Tex., department store. She is also a former chairman of the American Retail Federation, first female to hold that post. Mary Helen Byck is chairman of Byck's, Louisville, Ky., specialty store. Barbara H. Freed is president and chief executive officer of Flah's, Syracuse, N.Y.-based specialty store chain. She was previously executive vice-president. In her current post, Ms. Freed succeeded her husband, Bertram H. Freed, now chairman and chief financial officer.

Two women left retailing in 1974 to become presidents of pattern-making companies. They are: Mary Joan Glynn, who at forty-five went to Simplicity Pattern Co. but resigned within a year to become a consultant, and then joined the Marcella Borghese division of Revlon as general manager; and Jane Evans, who at thirty joined Butterick Fashion Marketing Co., a division of American Can Co. Ms. Glynn came from Bloomingdale's where she was vice-president and director of communications. Ms. Evans was previously with Genesco where she was successively president of I. Miller & Co. and international marketing vice-president.

Proof of how seldom female presidents appear on the retail scene is underlined in the regularity with which a question as to the number of women reaching retailing's summit mainly through their own efforts is answered with: "What about Dorothy Shaver?" Ms. Shaver was president of Lord & Taylor from 1945 until her death in 1959. She was a protégée of Samuel W. Reyburn, a distant relative, fellow Arkansan, and president at the time she joined the company in 1924 as a comparison shopper. She made her reputation as America's No. 1 career woman and attained a then relatively astronomical salary for either sex of $130,000 by developing an individual personality for the store.

Mildred Custin was born in Manchester, N.H., in 1906 and was graduated from Simmons College. She began her career in Macy's controller's office in 1928 but soon thereafter went to Shepard's, Boston, as secretary to the general merchandise manager. Her new boss asked her to find someone to run a new art-needlework department. "I've always been an eager beaver," she later recalled, "and I told him I could do both jobs. I would do everything, and it was known that I would. That's the keystone of my life."

Her next step was to R. H. White's in the same city as buyer of gifts, china, glassware, and lamps. In 1935, she relocated in Philadelphia as John Wanamaker's gift buyer and rose during the next twenty-three years to ready-to-wear and fashion accessory merchandise manager and vice-president. In 1958 she became president of Bonwit Teller, Philadelphia; in 1965, president of the entire Bonwit chain, and from 1969 to 1970 chairman and chief executive.

Ms. Custin credits Albert M. Greenfield with making her president of Bonwit Teller, Philadelphia, when Bankers Securities Corp., the complex he headed, bought that firm. She bows to the Jarmans—W. Maxey and Franklin M.—for elevating Ms. Stutz to Bendel's presidency, herself to the presidency of the New York-based Bonwit chain, and now-retired Catherine Case to the top post at Gidding-Jenny, Cincinnati.

So far as can be ascertained, no woman executive in American retailing now equals the $130,000 salary paid Ms. Shaver in the 1950s.

During her Bonwit regime, Ms. Custin, now a consultant, rose to a salary exceeding $100,000, probably the highest pay for a self-made woman in retailing in that period. Ms. Stutz makes an undisclosed salary under the $100,000 figure.

A dozen years ago, Ms. Custin said she could not have risen to the top from the 1930s through the 1960s "if I had not kept my eye on the ball. I was old-fashioned enough to think a woman's place was in the home, that I couldn't manage running a home and forging an important career for myself. I wouldn't have been a good wife or mother. There's nothing about my life, in retrospect, I would change."

Ms. Custin has mellowed so that today things are different. If she had been born several decades later, she now admits, she could have made it to upper-echelon stature without closing the door on also being a housewife. Very important, she notes, top management has gone along with that philosophy.

From her special position in the retail firmament, Ms. Custin advises how women can rise as far as she did, even to a department store chain's presidency, "on their own, without family influence":

They must have "an overview of the entire store—merchandising, operations, and control. It would be better for all concerned if top management picked and trained them for their all-round potential long in advance of possible successive promotions. Superiors should invite more women buyers, divisional merchandise managers, and sales promotion people to higher-level meetings on a scheduled basis. In addition to their technical skills, high-caliber women possess female characteristics of grace, charm, intuition, imagination, and creativity. A person with talent in retailing stands out like a shining light. In our business, you can't miss if you're head and shoulders above the rest. If women have the requisite track record, neither men nor other women are likely to quarrel with working for them."

However, Ms. Custin finds, "even today, many women are their own worst enemies. It's a two-way street. Not only must store principals be inspired to give women buyers an opportunity to advance to the top, but the buyers themselves must be inspired to consciously set their sights higher for the opportunity that is there. For a woman to get the same job as a man, she has to work harder than a man—and perhaps be twice as effective—or the man will get the preference. You can't expect a man completely to change his point of view overnight. It has to evolve from a requirement that the woman be twice as good to a woman being equally as good as a man. In any event, I thoroughly believe women should receive equal pay for equal jobs.

"Retail men in high places," she is convinced, "will be looking increasingly for women for divisional merchandising jobs, then general merchandise managers, then presidents, if for no other reason than the sheer numbers of women in the working population. It must also be true that the success of women as college presidents, corporate directors and in other key jobs in Wall Street, advertising, and government will have its effect on retailing."

Summing up with the statement, "there should be no sex in retailing," Ms. Custin, nevertheless makes it clear, "I'm not a women's libber. I'm opposed to the methods of protestation and demonstration of reformist and radical groups and would substitute dedication for declaration. I honestly believe I was liberated when I started out in retailing more than forty years ago. True, I was a phenomenon of my time, but I have never stopped believing women have only to prove themselves to make it."

Prejudice against women in retailing, Ms. Custin finds, "has broken down, but that still leaves tradition in most department store organizations to fall by the wayside." However, she still believes "too few women are willing to assume the responsibilities of the top jobs. They just don't want to face the headaches, the heartaches, the hazards, and maybe even the hard work that come with bearing the ultimate burden of running a business. It is up to them to take that final giant step."

As stated, women, other than members of a controlling family, who have become store presidents may be counted on the fingers of one hand. Most women who rise beyond rank-and-file employees do so as fashion buyers in stores and resident offices. However, beyond the buying, store management, personnel, and sales promotion divisions, the number of women falls off sharply. Most women aren't prepared for certain positions or divisions—for instance, general merchandise manager, controller, or display head.

Women holding other upper-level positions include Rita Perna, assistant vice-president and national fashion coordinator, Montgomery Ward & Co.; G. G. Michelson, senior vice-president for consumer and employee relations, Macy's New York; and Helen Galland, president of the Trucraft division of Wamsutta Mills, a division of M. Lowenstein & Sons, and previously senior vice-president and general merchandise manager of Bonwit Teller.

Top retail posts under presidential rank for women command compensation in an estimated range from $40,000 to under $100,000, with stress on the up-to-$65,000 level. There are numerous female buyers of middle-to-large-size department stores whose pay runs anywhere from $15,000 to $50,000. Bonuses and fringe benefits may raise the base pay substantially.

On the whole, retailing has given women a better financial break— certainly, so far as buying positions are concerned—than many other branches of industry where equality is still largely an empty phrase.

From more than twenty years of interviewing, hiring, and training women, Ray A. Killian, vice-president and director of personnel and public relations, Belk Stores, southern department store chain, raises these provocative points:

- Women are often their own worst enemies in regard to their opportunities and job performance. The most serious impediment to the equal treatment of women is the way women act once they are employed. If a woman expects special treatment, a bending of the rules in her favor, or lowered performance standards, and if she won't accept responsibility and resists supervision, she is essentially undermining the basic equality for which she struggles.
- The most stable employee is the woman over thirty-five, either married or single, who is career-oriented. In comparison to younger women, she is more poised, requires less supervision, is less likely to change jobs, is more dependable, is absent less often, has learned to dress and converse intelligently, has fewer family problems, is more easily trainable. However, most companies continue to prefer young blood.
- If the supervisor clings to basically untrue notions about women, such as that they have physical limitations, are frail and easily fatigued, cannot stand noise, dirt, or drafts, and have to go to the washroom too frequently, his attitude will show through and will be easily recognized. Clichés of this kind are usually one part truth and nine parts nonsense.
- All companies should prefer a competent female supervisor to an incompe-

tent male any day of the week. But the sad fact is this is not always the case —incompetent men have been promoted over competent women for years.

Killian has called 'em as he sees 'em. Neither biased for nor against females, he expresses the hope that more women will be accepted as individuals, not as stereotypes and, like men, will be promoted strictly in accordance with their own abilities and skills, not penalized for others' shortcomings. Who could ask for anything more?

Nevertheless, a female middle-level executive finds fault with the fact that a listing of thirty-six top retail executives receiving from $150,000 to over $400,000 in compensation in 1973 did not contain the name of one woman. She herself is in her thirties with a salary and bonus in the $30,000 range.

Some of her beefs:

"Many retailers pay women less money than they pay men despite the law that stipulates equal pay for equal work.

"Why aren't company planes available to me for market and store trips on the same basis as they are to men? I usually have to take commercial planes. I admit I miss the camaraderie.

"Many men don't know how to treat women as good friends—and nothing more. Of course, there's a sex problem.

"Why is it a highly qualified, single woman I know who was being interviewed by a top executive for a middle-management position was advised at the outset that the company makes a substantial investment in training new people and getting them used to the system? He followed this up with questions as to whether she planned to get married and what method of birth control she used. With that, she stood up and walked out of the room.

"Why aren't more women sent to management courses at the Harvard Business School and other schools or association-sponsored programs?

"Why do the same men who see *Business Week* on my desk ask me why I read that magazine when the question would never occur to them about *Vogue* and *Harper's Bazaar?*"

Her concluding comment: "My company is one of the best, so far as women are concerned, but it's still not good enough."

Heads of executive recruiting firms serving retail companies agree that, in many cases, tradition and prejudice in varying combinations prevent or curtail women from holding the same jobs at the same salaries as men. On the one hand, most jobs at the very top—president, vice-president, and general merchandise manager—are virtually closed to women. On the other hand, most women shy from these responsibilities, aspire no higher than buyer and, less frequently, to divisional merchandise manager. The recruiters insist that a major obstacle to the upward move of females in significant numbers often lies in their relative lack of ambition, aggressiveness, competitiveness, and dedication as compared with men. If more women were so motivated, the recruiters are convinced, there would be a substantial increase in their representation among upper-echelon executives.

One definition of a dedicated career woman-wife: "She has her baby Friday night and returns to the store Monday morning."

When the average retail company is looking for a president, according to Edward A. Raisbeck, Jr., senior partner, Thorndike Deland Associates, pioneer firm in retail executive recruitment, it isn't enough that a man has been a merchandise manager. Candidates must know finance, building, store openings, and many other operational phases as well as management. It's often hard to find a man, let alone a woman, with the requisite background. Most women who reach top positions have done so through creative, artistic, and fashion qualifications, more than through administrative skills.

If more women were in top jobs and performed outstandingly, Raisbeck concedes, there would be greater interest in promoting more of them. The problem remains: how does a woman gain the all-round experience that leads to the top if she's only seldom given the chance to prove herself beyond a buyership or similar operating level? It's a vicious circle!

Women are other women's severest critics. So let's see what three females with long experience as retail executive recruiters have to say about the negative as well as positive characteristics of their sex.

Alice Groves was until her retirement in 1973 head of her own business for eighteen years and for seventeen years previously was with Associated Merchandising Corp. as personnel director of the New York office and executive placement director for member stores. She states:

"Generally speaking, traditional thinking, rather than prejudice, explains why women, with scattered exceptions, haven't climbed to top jobs in larger stores or to such other positions as controller, or furniture, fur, or piece goods buyer. Those who reach positions from merchandise manager to president have learned how to handle other women. One female wants to work for another only if the superior is exceptionally talented. Nor does a man want to work for a woman unless he has great respect for her. The top woman executive must be as highly creative, as strong in figures, as a man—with something plus. And always retaining her femininity, she should temper determination with graciousness, whether she is dealing with a man or a woman. It is also true that many women, particularly working wives, don't want to work as hard or as long as men do and are satisfied to be assistants."

Ms. Groves, who sold the firm bearing her name to Raymond J. Leavee, retired merchandise vice-president, Macy's New York, notes that "in the last decade, women have made great strides in retailing. In 90 percent of instances, stores don't care whether the buyer applicant is a man or a woman. It used to be 50-50. Stores will take a qualified woman applying for a merchandise manager of ready-to-wear, accessories, intimate apparel, or children's wear 50 percent of the time. It used to be much less.

"Today, more than ever before, many women are readily combining careers, marriage, and family responsibilities. Among shattered myths are that women do not want to work for another woman, that men do not want to work for women, and that women are not as indefatigable workers as men." Ability, not sex, is the criterion, she is convinced, lauding certain stores for courses and seminars that have helped produce these results.

(Just to prove that women don't agree among themselves, Muriel James, a Ph.D. in adult education, consultant in communication and human relations, and director of the Transactional Analysis Institute, Lafayette, Calif., has this to say: "A woman would rather work for a man than for a woman for the same reason that a man would rather work for another man than for a woman. In each case, they want to get away from their mothers. Besides, men are easier for women to manipulate than other women are.")

Lillian Horinbein, retired president, Business Careers: "Many women have difficulty delegating authority and responsibility. Many others are not willing to dedicate themselves to the intermediate jobs that lead to the top. But women don't have any innate weaknesses for any position.

"Too often, retail management still picks a woman as buyer on the reasoning: "We can get a better woman at $10,000 than a man at $12,000 to $18,000."

Patricia B. Astor, executive searcher:

"Women can be the sharpest, most miserable people in the world. To a larger or smaller degree, they think more emotionally than men do. A good executive should be logical. As a rule, women don't like to work for other women. Top women executives have to soft-pedal when it comes to running other women. The concept that men don't like reporting to women is overplayed. A female who is respected can and does win men's admiration for her talents. A woman can handle any retail function, although it is true she may be more comfortable in some than in others."

Ms. Astor casts a jaundiced eye at men who think "we'll upset the applecart if we bring in a woman," that there are more fishwives and prima donnas among women, that women have less endurance, that women can't be as dedicated and astute in business, that women can't be both feminine and tough.

Prejudice against women executives has eased through the years, in Ms. Astor's opinion. However, she still discerns it in many old-time department stores where few women rise beyond buyers and floor and section managers.

The consensus of the searchers:

- It is only peripherally true that one reason leading chains and independents may choose a woman over a man is that the former may be hired for less money.

- Women's Lib has been a psychological aid in the past five years or so in upgrading jobs and salaries for females.
- Many women don't want the pressures and hours that go with prime responsibility. They would rather rise to assistant to a top executive and shoulder tasks short of risking the psychosomatic ailments that so often assail driven men. There are numerous outstanding women who fit the description of capable first or second assistants.
- Conventional department stores have many more women than discounters at the middle-management level. Women as a rule shy away from the long hours and "knock-down and drag-out" environment of discounting.
- Many married women are tied to the cities in which their husbands work and don't have the mobility that men can exercise. This sometimes inhibits their earning capacity when it is considered that many stores pay more when they go outside for people than when they promote from within.

Rosalind Gersten, former ready-to-wear and accessories vice-president and fashion administrator, Macy's New York, exemplifies women placed in a quandary when their husbands are called to higher posts in distant cities. Melvin Jacobs, Ms. Gersten's husband, was promoted by Federated Department Stores from Bloomingdale's executive vice-president of women's and children's apparel to president and, later, chairman of Miami-based Burdine's. At the time of his appointment, Jacobs said: "We won't be moving down immediately. I'll be commuting for the next six or eight months." Ms. Gersten remarked then: "At the moment, there are no plans to change the status quo. One thing I can say, I intend to remain in the fashion field." The Jacobs' plans revolved, in part, about their under-teenage daughter, a student in a private school within easy access of their Manhattan apartment.

Subsequently, Ms. Gersten joined Federated as merchandising consultant for fashion accessories, cosmetics, and shoes. She resigned within two years to become a retail consultant and production and research assistant at WPBT-TV, Miami.

Retail stores are always rife with rumors about illicit love affairs and other instances of hanky-panky between middle-to-top-level male executives and female underlings.

Unfortunately for the behavioral scientists, there is no authoritative body of literature on the subject of eroticism in any branch of business or the professions. There is no infallible index whether retailing is more susceptible on this score than, say, manufacturing, banking, government service, or education. This much is beyond dispute: The problem—or, at least, recurrent gossip —centers in all fields where men and women are thrown into close daily association. That's why you hear about it constantly in the apparel and accessories industry, resident buying, motion pictures, advertising, and radio-TV. One thing you may be sure of, however, sex has no occupational boundaries.

Let a girl get into the car of her boss or another married executive who is merely driving her to the bus station. Let a girl lunch in a quiet restaurant with a married male superior—with the only thing on their minds the upcoming college-shop promotion. Or let her go dancing with him at a night club—for whatever reason, he thinks he needs a platonic friendship with a female associate. Heaven help the poor working girl if somebody from the same company happens on the scene.

The next day, bursting with the burden of newfound knowledge, the person who had chanced on the hapless pair postpones any thought of work until the choice morsel has been passed on to one and all within earshot. The grapevine does the rest. Within a few hours, the place is buzzing with the news that Mr. Jones and Ms. Smith are engaged in a liaison.

There are all kinds of reasons sex scuttlebutt gains rapid, widespread circulation. First of all, such titillating topics are welcome relief from everyday tedium for both Puritans and prurients. Then, assuming gossip is equated with gospel, people may be afflicted with a case of sour grapes—jealousy, if you're an available, complaisant female, that the other woman got to him first; envy, if you're a man with a roving eye, that the other man got to her first. We must also expect all the skepticism, cynicism, malice, and plain orneriness that warp the fairmindedness of many persons in a highly competitive environment.

Objective observers (whatever that means) are inclined to deny credence to such hearsay. On the contrary, they say, the wonder is that clandestine romances don't flourish as often as rumor hath it. Face it, they explain, the retailing way of life lends itself to more than ordinary temptations for married men to stray from the straight and narrow. The nature of the business places high-powered men and attractive women in close proximity day after day—late evenings, Saturdays, and, sometimes, Sundays and holidays—not only in the store but wherever in the world the job takes them. The chemistry of propinquity may well perform its magic and turn dilly-dallying into dalliance. Very human emotions have to be stifled—and most often are.

Even if most men think of women, the great majority of them are too scared to do anything about it beyond talk. Certainly, when they reach the latter middle-age stage of Tired Businessman, home and/or the cocktail lounge and golf course are the only places they use for relaxation. Or, if they see themselves in the mirror as having a few good years left in them, they may occasionally resort to extracurricular female companionship—but for admiration and sympathy, that's all.

Of course, affairs of the heart between a married man and another's wife or with an unmarried girl become a matter for top-management's attention when the woman in the case is helped up the career ladder out of order and outside of merit. This is the really sticky part for the man.

He doesn't want to jeopardize his future by on-the-job sponsorship of the woman who is lavishing her favors on him unless he is quite certain she has the necessary ability for a higher post. When the word gets around how she got the promotion, staff morale tends to become demoralized, the store becomes a hotbed of discontent, employee performance is impaired. The man's tripping up the primrose path can't be winked at. The woman who has shaped up as a sweetheart has to ship out as a bad influence, for it's usually the woman who pays with her job. Other women vying for her position and thirsting for her blood will make such a loud noise the company may have no alternative. The man "resigns" less frequently, sometimes only after he has been put on notice but hasn't stayed a good boy. Rather than risk the possibility of fouling his own nestegg, the man who insists on such shenanigans will indulge himself only with women outside his company.

Any attempt to estimate the incidence and intensity of such entanglements, it must be clear, would be meaningless. Most couples are discreet and sophisticated enough to keep this side of their lives private and secret.

Of this much, there can be no doubt. Subrosa affairs have been, are, will continue to be, part of the social history of retailing, as of the business community in general. Only the two concerned know for sure—and they're not telling.

Sears, Roebuck is doing its part to combat the "sexist attitudes" of its officials and managers, Charles F. Bacon, vice-president of personnel, testified before the U.S. Civil Rights Commission. He mentioned sensitivity courses being conducted by the chain in an attempt to overcome "any existing sexist or stereotype" views. However, he conceded, in a company of Sears' size, "it would be ridiculous to assume someone hasn't goofed."

Bacon cited a week-long human relations awareness course being continuously sponsored for Sears' senior management across the country. "Specific elements of this training program," he explained, "are addressed to the subject of sexist attitudes and the need to alter ingrained stereotyped notions about the kinds of jobs women should hold."

Sears has retained a firm to conduct training programs for senior corporate managers, Bacon reported, "to uncover and correct negative attitudes regarding women in the work place."

A movie, *51 Percent,* is being used in various Sears units "to further sensitize the attending executives on the need to overcome existing sexist and stereotyped views." The chain's *Parent News* employee publication ran a feature article, "Fracturing a Fairy Tale," with the same aim.

At one point during the commission hearing, a clerical employee at Sears Tower testified she was required to make the morning coffee, get the boss's lunch, and order merchandise for his family. Bacon rejoined that male assistants to female bosses perform the same duties.

Bacon agreed that "like the rest of American society, we have our male and female chauvinists, and it necessitates a constant policing program, which we have. The problems that this commission is investigating are deeply rooted in the whole fabric of American society. The place of women in society is not only the product of the American business system but of schools, churches, social clubs, governments, and labor unions as well. All of these groups share responsibility. Sears accepts its fair share of that responsibility."

Why are there virtually no women in such high-income retail jobs as selling appliances?

Many managers sincerely respond: "It's a mechanical item—women don't understand cars, so they won't understand a washing machine."

Sounds logical. But when the same question is asked about such other "big-ticket" lines as furniture and rugs, usually sold on commission, the explanation is: "Furniture and rugs are heavy to lift, and women aren't strong enough."

Take the TV repair expert, the engine tune-up worker—blue-collar jobs frequently paying considerably better than beginning white-collar jobs. Management's reasoning for not developing women for these technical positions: "They don't like this kind of work," "It wouldn't be safe for them to be making home calls," and so on.

Ray J. Graham, director of equal opportunity, Sears, Roebuck & Co., calls the reasons for low female representation in these kinds of work "the ability to rationalize irrational factors and reach logical-sounding illogical conclusions." Sears, he says, has "exposed the fallacy of these stereotyped notions about what women can and cannot do, jobs they should and should not hold, ambition they may or may not have."

Both of these examples, Graham submits, are "proof of the belief held by many that much of workplace discrimination is based on economics. As long as we could save money by hiring minorities and women, we did so. Now that that's no longer legal, any argument to exclude them from all our jobs becomes spurious."

Against the background of affirmative action programs, Graham dwells on the general problems of moving greater numbers of the minorities and women "into the better-paid, more responsible and, unfortunately, traditionally 'white male only' jobs."

The Sears executive's reply to management's complaint that many minorities and women do not have the requisite skills to be considered for promotion: "An honest answer in many, many cases is simply that our previous policies of exclusion have not made it possible for them to gain the experience and, thereby, the skills.

"Another problem is the attitude built in by culture, custom, and tradition, making it difficult for many managers to sincerely encourage minorities and women to actively seek to change their role and their status in the organization, and making it equally difficult for members of the affected groups to picture themselves comfortably ensconced in a new and unfamiliar role."

Graham recommends five specific guidelines in upgrading, transferring and promoting present employees:

1. Don't exclude any source, any activity within your company. Past practices have not only forced talented and ambitious people (who happened to be

minority or female) into relatively unrewarding jobs, but also have virtually blinded many managers to the fact that talent and ambition exist in groups other than white males.

2. Put out of your mind non-job related qualifications resulting from the "chairman of the board" syndrome that everyone in the organization must eventually be promotable to the top job. There just aren't that many "super" people around, even "super" white males.

3. Don't make any assumptions, before talking to your people in the in-house talent search, about their desires, ambitions, ability, mobility, willingness to transfer and so on.

4. Conscious, deliberate steps must be taken to insure the success of minority and women employees in the new job. Artificial barriers may be erected by associates. If the job should not prove to the liking of the promoted person, a transfer back to the previous activity should be arranged without penalty.

5. The final guideline could well be the first: top management support for both the spirit and letter of the law is vital.

Once Sears started actively seeking women for commission sales jobs, Graham says: "we found the barriers tumbled rapidly. Both managers and co-workers discovered that customers are really more interested in buying merchandise than they are in the sex of the salesperson."

Graham adds that, "when we had made it perfectly clear women would be developed for technical jobs, our people found a way to get the job done. They began by calling together all of the clerical people (women) in the various service activities on the reasonable assumption that their familiarity with the general nature of the work (typing and routing service calls, for example) might relieve some of the apprehensions. When these women were told of the company's desire to train them for these slots, half of them indicated a desire to be considered. From that small beginning we now have a significant number of women driving service trucks, working on repair benches, and, generally, reminding us that manual dexterity has no sexual boundaries."

What's Required of Women Reaching for Top Posts?

Why is it that so few women are running major corporations?

The question becomes particularly pointed when directed at the so-called "women's industries"—fashion, fabrics, fragrances, home furnishings, retailing, advertising, and communications. Even where women own companies, it is men who have the power, who set policy and make decisions.

Amelia Bassin, president, Bassinnova, cosmetics marketing firm, raised the question as chairman of a committee of the Fashion Group that conducted a symposium on "Women in Management: Your Time Has Come!" Before she went out on her own, Ms. Bassin was with Faberge for twenty-one years, where she rose from art director to senior vice-president and creative director.

Ms. Bassin ascribed the appearance of only a few women "up there in Management Heaven" to the failure of females in general to prepare themselves for the upper-echelon jobs. The Fashion Group, she explained, "views with alarm the rampant disinterest of so many of us, so many bright, smart, ambitious women caught in a kind of ego trap. We have been so totally involved in what we call the 'creative' end of the business—the spirit, heart, soul, look, feel, smell, excitement of it—we're leaving the business end of the business, the vital backbone of business, to those dullard bookkeepers."

Obviously convinced a speaker can, and should, inject humor into a basically serious subject, Ms. Bassin said:

"Those dullard bookkeepers know that the backbone is connected to the bankbone, and the bankbone is connected to the bossbone—and that's how the dullard bookkeeper gets to be chairman of the board, while here we sit cozily cocooned in our snug, smug, little gilt-edged security blankets.

"Believe me, you can't lick 'em, so join 'em. If you really want to make that big jump to the top rung of the ladder where the decisions and policies are made, where the power is, your time has come. Power is the magic word, the big masculine trade secret—the passkey they hand you along with their B.S. degree (that ain't necessarily Business School).

"Please don't think, as I once did, that power is an unclean word. Power is the difference between truly top management and where most women executives are today. When Henry Kissinger observed that power is the ultimate aphrodisiac, he said it all. It explains not only what makes even a fairly repulsive person instantly irresistible to the opposite sex; it condenses into five words volumes about motivation and management and the masculine mystique.

"In today's turbulent economic mess, in this new Age of Precarious, the time has come for us women to join our male colleagues in making corporate decisions that will fashion the future of our company and our economy. But it can never happen unless we gear up for power drive, unless we get clout. Combine our executive experience and expertise, our position as genuine consumers, our so-called feminine talent and intuition, with a sound basic business-administration backup—figures can be fun—and we are invincible."

Ms. Bassin asked her audience to "think positive—not to play sexorcist and blame such evil spirits as the corporate chauvinist or the boys in the stereotypist pool. . . . We have met the enemy—and he is US."

Herbert Mines, president, Business Careers, executive placement firm, suggested that women, "who are now happily and productively employed, do not have to reach for a higher rung on the ladder, and many perhaps should not. Many men reach this conclusion in their careers as well." But for those who want to compete with men for the top jobs, he recommended that line, rather than staff, positions are the best roads to follow. He gave such examples as being a buyer, not a personnel manager, in retailing, and being in the marketing department, not in public relations, in a cosmetics company.

If the woman is married, Mines continued, she must weigh the effect of travel requirements and night work on family life. If single, what effect would this have on the woman's social life, and how important may this be to her?

If the woman is determined to attain the promotional steps above her, the executive recruiter advised she "seek out the best courses in the best school directly related to the area in which she wants to improve, whether or not it leads to a degree."

Louis D. Volpp, professor and former dean, Columbia University Graduate School of Business, quoted figures indicating that 70 percent of women with business degrees abandon business careers "in favor of something else." He also stated, "the quality of the trip is more important than the destination." He was referring to the fact that, "the world is moving so fast that nobody today can plan a specific career pattern and destination. The particular positions will not be the same for a person in the years to come as they are now. Therefore, the length of the woman's career should not be as important to her company as what she puts into it while she's there."

Volpp differed from Ms. Bassin's viewpoint that, "If you can't lick 'em, join 'em," with the advice: "If you can't join 'em, lick 'em."

Outwomaneuvering Men Up the Executive Ladder

"Women in business are victims of the 'Sleeping Beauty' syndrome. They mistakenly believe that, if they do a good job, their bosses will promote them.

"To gain promotion, however, a woman must compete and not just cooperate. If she wants to move up in management, she must understand her appropriateness for supervisory responsibility is judged by a male role model. To achieve the status that goes with power, she must establish a game plan to be a prime mover. She must play the political game just as men do. With all this emphasis on adopting the male pattern of job behavior, she must still find a way to retain her femininity while proving that biology is not destiny."

DeAnne Rosenberg, consultant-lecturer-college instructor, stressed this viewpoint in conducting a three-day seminar at American Management Associations on "Management Skills for New First-Line Women Supervisors and Administrative Assistants."

AMA has been sponsoring conferences for women managers since 1967. It has held about two dozen seminars under this title throughout the country. "Once women have been promoted," notes James L. Hayes, AMA president, "there must be management backing to continue educating them in supervisory skills if they're going to succeed. The people we have really had to sell our training programs to have not been the women participants but their bosses, who in most cases are men. These men are showing signs of responding. Attendance at our women manager conferences has risen sharply in the past few years.

"Because of social pressures," Hayes adds, "business may think it has been quite noble in providing jobs for women. But that's not enough. Many companies are appointing women to jobs which give these firms the legal headcount but they're not directing them into careers. Top management should make it clear it doesn't want men under them who, perhaps subconsciously, hope the new woman supervisor will fail so they can appoint a man or that the new black supervisor will fail so they can appoint a white.

"The trick is to furnish careers through continuous training within the organization and development of management skills in outside courses and seminars. Companies must at all times exert positive efforts to treat and evaluate women equally and promote them on that basis."

The participants in her seminar, said Ms. Rosenberg, represent thousands of female management novices—some have made it as "a reward for endurance," others because of Equal Employment Opportunity Commission pressures, and still others strictly on expertise—who in many cases face more complex problems than are encountered by their male peers.

Ms. Rosenberg enumerated among a woman supervisor's "special hassles": "prejudices of both sexes—women who prefer working for men and men who dislike women bosses; the woman's own cultural conditioning that may make her wonder if she's up to the demands of the job, the degree of aggressiveness she should exercise on the job and in the effort to get ahead, and the feeling, right or wrong, that the job may be a 'token woman' situation and a dead-end street for her."

In common with all new supervisors, the woman has to increase the speed and success-ratio of personal input into problem-solving and decision-making. In so doing, she must develop interpersonal skills as a coach, counselor, delegate duties and appraise performance properly, be effective in communication and negotiation with subordinates, peers, and superiors, enhance her motivation and her people's productivity—in short, minimize the management-by-crisis that reflects lack of planning.

The male-role pattern requires the woman supervisor to stand on her own feet in competing with peers and taking responsibility for results. Still, the better part of valor in a man's world might be for the new female manager to express her thoughts in the form of a question rather than a statement. "A year down the turnpike when she's established credibility," the consultant explained, "she won't have to resort to a subterfuge. Establishing credibility with male peers is probably the biggest barrier to her success."

Alluding to the part played by politics in achieving and retaining power, Ms. Rosenberg asserted that the question a woman should ask herself is not "Shall I play politics?" but rather " 'What kind of politics should I play?' There's dirty politics—hurting others—and clean politics. An unethical politician eventually loses out."

Among tools recommended by Ms. Rosenberg for improved political image and increased power in the struggle for the diminishing supply of top positions—always with the knowledge "it's not necessarily the best man or woman who wins out":

1. Do stand-out work.
2. Look loyal.
3. Remember that your immediate superior is the most important person in your job life. Help him get ahead, and he'll help you. W.I.I.F.M. (what's in it for me?)—you do me a favor and I'll owe you one—is an essential way of life.
4. Learn everything you can about your job and those of your peers and superiors.
5. Become visible by getting into the "in" group and on a task force with the president and by writing for the company newspaper.
6. Show respect for everyone—friends and foes alike—even if it kills you.
7. Avoid the boss who is dead-end and get yourself transferred.
8. Be fluid, not rigid. Take your job seriously but look at it with humor.

As corporations try to comply with government and feminist pressure to move women into more responsible jobs, the consultant went on, "more and more women are finding themselves in new positions with fancy titles. But a title doesn't insure responsibility. Many managers are told by their supervisors to hire or promote more women, and the manager does what he is told but still makes the plans and decisions himself. He uses a female supervisor as a mascot. His attitude is: 'You're the first woman in your spot—don't make waves.' Such 'overkill' managers actually hurt the woman's chances for growth.

"Then there is the sink-or-swim manager who takes the attitude: 'Okay,

you're hired, so do it.' Under such circumstances, women have a 50 percent
chance of failing."

On the subject of a possible romance with the boss, Ms. Rosenberg
warned: "There are all kinds of books on how to be a friend or a lover, but
none on how to be just a business associate. It's the woman who pays the price
of mixing business and romance, who leaves or loses a job when the situation
gets out of hand."

On the bright side: "Women have made great strides in the past five years
or so away from being regarded as sex objects and to being recognized on
merit."

9

PHYSICAL HEALTH

Should an Executive Conceal Physical, Emotional Ills?

Not so long ago, an upper-level executive of a department store chain suffered a stroke or heart attack—the grapevine was never clear on this—soon after he moved over from another company. He was out of commission several months and returned to his new duties on a much reduced basis.

In July, 1975, Secretary of the Interior Stanley K. Hathaway resigned after six weeks in office "for reasons of my personal health." He entered Bethesda Naval Medical Center with "moderate depression due to overwork and physical exertion." The former Wyoming governor, then 51, who never quite got around to coping with his heavy responsibilities in the energy and environmental fields, underwent psychiatric treatment. He was also found to have "mild diabetes."

Everybody knows of someone who passed a physical examination with flying colors but was incapacitated the next day with a serious heart attack. Everybody knows of someone who supposedly had no emotional problem but, one day, past the breaking point, disappeared from his home or failed to show up at the office. Unfortunately, people with emotional difficulties still tend to keep these to themselves instead of admitting stressful pressures out of their control with as little embarrassment as if they had broken an arm.

Aside from such incidents that occur without advance notice to victims, families, friends or business associates, it would be a much better world if people with a secret emotional disability would seek medical attention. The stresses accompanying unrecognized or unacknowledged depression may find an outlet in alcoholism, absenteeism, poor leadership and impaired productivity.

President Ford was asked how he was able to maintain a generally relaxed manner. He replied: "I have learned that, if every problem is an ulcer-generating one, you don't have good health, and if you don't have good health, you can't work at the job."

Too bad the President didn't apply this criterion to Hathaway. So far as is known, the secretary was subjected only to the routine FBI field check made of all presidential appointees. Ron Nessen, the President's press secretary, evaded the issue when asked whether Hathaway had undergone a "personal profile" that might have revealed incipient mental depression. Nessen's testy rejoinder: "I feel compelled to say that Mr. Hathaway has never had a previous history of similar illness."

Ford is one of the healthiest presidents the nation has had in this century. But such predecessors as Woodrow Wilson, Franklin D. Roosevelt and John F. Kennedy concealed grave ailments. Theodore White, in his "Breach of Faith—the Fall of Richard Nixon," concludes that the President was "an unstable personality" whose behavior before his resignation had become increasingly erratic. White traces evidence of Nixon's faults of emotional health over many years of public office candidacy and occupancy. The late Georges Pompidou, president of France, died of cancer after months of visibly failing health and incapacity to carry on his duties. In the last year of his life, he told his cabinet: "My succession is not open. My health is my own affair."

Where has it been written that politicians can decide for themselves they can play fast and loose with their constituents whose servants they are—at least in theory—in such vital matters as the state of their health? By the same token, should an individual in a high business post feel he should retain his office in poor health against the organization's interests?

Almost without exception, the duties of executive recruiters are confined to drawing profiles of the abilities, character and motivation of best-qualified individuals for particular openings. They are not expected to check up on the possibility of a candidate's emotional disturbance except if this should show up in their interviews.

At a New York-based department store chain, pre-employment physicals are required for all middle-to-higher-level executives beginning with buyers and department managers. Once a year, physicals are given at outside medical examining facilities.

At another national chain, corporate headquarters has no overall policy on the matter. Each division works out its own system. At one division, for example, every job applicant has to pass a medical examination. Major executives get an annual physical at a hospital clinic.

At still another department store chain, the New York headquarters employs a corporate physician who comes in once a week to examine applicants for $15,000-and-up positions. Executives who earn over $20,000 are given annual exams at their own option at the doctor's office. The corporation becomes involved at divisional operating levels only in cases of managing directors.

At a general merchandising chain, pre-employment physicals are given to applicants for both "ledger" level jobs—those not on time-cards, and to candidates for the "private" payroll—position in the $30,000-and-up category. Once hired, they are eligible for annual physicals.

Because of the confidential nature of the annual exams, there is no exact knowledge of how many ailments have been uncovered and referred to personal physicians, of how many lives may have been saved. The head of one clinic claims that, of those getting their first checkups at his office, more than half have been found to have defects that, if undetected and untreated, would have eventually resulted in serious illness or death.

Emotional checkups, conducted by a psychiatrist, are much less often part of the diagnosis than purely physical exams by general practitioners or internists.

In the best of all possible worlds, executives and their employers would know that mental depression is the most treatable of psychiatric ills, that perhaps 85 percent of such setbacks run their course in from two to four weeks under treatment. In the world of tomorrow, a troubled executive would feel free to go to his employer without shame, without fear of the superior's contempt and, if need be, obtain a suitable leave of absence for treatment and convalescence.

Your Ten-Year Chances of Survival
Often Up to You

Will you be alive in ten years?

Your offhand answer with a forced grin would probably be "Only God knows." But, according to Life Extension Institute, a person's life span lies to some extent in his own hands.

With that ray of hope in mind, LEI is now studying prospective or predictive diseases as well as preventive medicine to bolster the periodic health examinations it gives business executives and others.

Obituary columns repeatedly carry stories of businessmen well under to just past sixty who die of heart ailments, cancer, or other diseases or, presumably healthy, pass away "unexpectedly" in their sleep or at work. The question is whether any of these deaths could have been delayed by years if complete physical charts of the individuals had been regularly updated and monitored.

The concept of health care called prospective or predictive diseases seeks to forecast what diseases a person will be likely to suffer from and what disease he will be likely to die from. Preventive medicine, as a logical follow-up to that health-care development, tries to defer, if not prevent, these diseases.

The attack on prospective diseases features "health hazard appraisal—an assessment of what can be done to reduce or eliminate the risk plus required actions if desired end results are to be realized." At the same time, "the greatest single resource of underutilized, yet highly qualified, talent available in the health-care field is tapped: active participation of each of us in our own health care."

Without fear of contradiction, LEI points out that "life is a risky business. Each day of our lives, we face risks—of illness, accident, injury, disability, or death. As we grow older, many of our risks increase. This is not merely an opinion. It represents a conclusion resulting from a twenty-year study into the deaths of hundreds of thousands of persons—men and women, white and nonwhite. It includes findings of many medical research teams about the causes of death. The end result is a conviction that no one is immune to the perils of living."

Putting its case right on the line, LEI warns: "People have been killing themselves by not availing themselves of appropriate early treatment and, even worse, by failing to curb some of their 'habits.' Studies that led to the establishment of prospective medicine—coupled with discoveries about cancer, heart disease, and many other deadly diseases—allow no room for even the most skeptical of disbelievers. Some people will always laugh at the facts as readily as they disregard laws of jaywalking, speeding, overtime parking, and the like. When they carry over this gambling instinct into their medical care and health habits, they are flirting with premature death or disability.

"The evidence is in—whether you live or die is often squarely in your own hands. Granted, we face risks all of the time but this does not mean we cannot do something about them—we can. We cannot guarantee you will not have a disability, but we can reduce the risks. The concept is based on the fact that, while you may suffer an affliction or even be killed by any one of a long list of health hazards, at each point in your life there are only a few conditions that comprise the major part of the risk. If these major hazards are identified and quantified and if they are then combined with a computerized bank of health, illness and death data, a list of specific threats to your continued good health can be identified. Once these are out in the open, a plan can be developed to reduce or eliminate them."

The LEI doctors tell how it's done:

"In analyzing the natural history of any disease, six stages are found. Stage 1 is the time when you are at no risk from the disease. Stage 2 is the time when you are at risk due to your age or the environment in which you live. Stage 3 is the time when the agent that causes the disease strikes and you are in danger of acquiring that disease. Stage 4 is the time when signs of the disease become present, signs the physician or laboratory may identify but you do not. Stage 5 is the time when you can recognize symptoms. Stage 6 is the time of disability or death."

Most traditional medicine is practiced in stages 5 and 6. Periodic examinations and multi-phasic (with many phases) health testing deal with stages 3 and 4. Prospective medicine, using health hazard appraisal, attempts to intervene at stages 2 and 3. The method used to intervene in the natural course of a disease in stages 2 or 3 is as follows:

"First, your ten-year chances of survival are determined by developing a personal health forecast, compiling your present risks and estimating your future risks for every major cause of death. Any known prognostic characteristics which affect this disease are then identified. Using actuarial help, characteristic risk factors are assigned. The results tell you how you differ from the 'average' individual with regard to your risk of death in the next ten-year period.

"Next, the prognostic factors that can be changed are isolated and the corrective actions necessary are outlined. Conceding the fact that you will heed the advice and take the necessary intervention action, a new risk profile can then be accomplished for you. This whole procedure allows you to compare your chronological age with your calculated 'real or risk age' and shows you what you can do to alter your risk age by intervention and compliance.

"Finally, it makes possible an ability to calculate for you a new age estimate—your 'compliance age.' "

A sophisticated computer program has been developed to assist LEI in implementing this portion of prospective medicine.

Coincidentally, the increasing role of computers in health care and clinical medicine is being discussed at seminars and workshops in cities throughout the country. Co-sponsors are World Health Organization, an affiliate of United Nations; American Hospital Association; State Hill-Burton Agencies; and U.S. Department of Health, Education, and Welfare.

Who says the American business executive is an unhealthy specimen sacrificing himself on the altar of success and dying prematurely for the glory of his company?

To Dr. Harry J. Johnson, retired chairman of the medical board, Life Extension Foundation and Life Extension Institute, this popular opinion is an old wives' tale.

True, he concedes, the average executive eats, drinks, and smokes too much to be in top-notch condition; nevertheless, his health is good.

The sixty-year-old, New York-based organization examines about fifty thousand executives each year for more than twelve hundred corporate clients throughout the country. This medical executive's experience is that only about 14 percent of executives have annual examinations on their own, but company-sponsored health checks raise participation to about 85 percent.

"Overall health of our executives is good," Johnson insists. "They have the potential for physical fitness. All we need is a change in a few established habits and the determination to make the change permanent."

This executive-health specialist seeks to dispel the widespread belief that executives die earlier than those lower down on the business ladder.

"This is so much nonsense. We can assure everyone that Mr. Executive is an average healthy person with a better-than-average life expectancy."

Still, Johnson admits, business executives lack overall fitness and stamina as a result of economic affluence and sedentary work. He explains:

"When income is adequate to ride instead of walk, to smoke, eat, and drink without regard to expense, physical fitness suffers. Add to this insufficient sleep because of multiple extracurricular activities, and we have a way of life that lends itself to unfitness."

Other "myths" enumerated by Johnson and "why they are wrong":

Myth No. 1. Most executives work under too much tension, and this is jeopardizing their health.

"Tension and pressure are essential to a full and productive life and are healthful unless continued too long. In a study completed a little while ago, we found only 13 percent of six thousand executives worked under tension that could be considered harmful to their health. Excessive tension carries the warning signs of fatigue, sleeplessness, indigestion, and headache."

Myth No. 2. Executives are particularly prone to ulcers and coronary heart disease.

"Let me emphasize that there is no disease to which an executive is prone by virtue of his job. Incidence of ulcers and heart trouble is no higher among executives than among blue-collar groups. There is no special hazard to being the boss." Dr. Johnson cites a study of eighty-six thousand Du Pont employees showing that the lowest rate of coronary occlusion (heart attack) was found in the top management group. Most executives, he insists, have a higher-than-average life expectancy."

Myth No. 3. "Relax, take it easy" is a good prescription for off-hours.

"Fifty years ago, men needed weekends and evenings to relax and rest physically. The usual work week was forty-eight hours, and everybody's job involved considerable physical activity. The present thirty-five-hour work week involves practically no physical activity. A larger proportion of leisure time should therefore be spent, not relaxing, but in some physically active pursuit—a brisk fifteen-minute walk two or three times a day, weekend golf, tennis, or swimming."

Myth No. 4. The best way to lose weight is to go on a crash diet and take pills.

"The only way to bring about a cure for obesity is to lessen the intake of higher caloric foods and possibly eliminate some for life."

Johnson's estimate that only 14 percent of all executives have regular health exams at their own expense is disputed by a survey of 165 top-level executives by *Business Management* magazine.

About 80 percent of the execs had undergone thorough physicals this year or last, and more than 60 percent of them had paid for the exams out of their own pockets.

Their principal health complaint is fatigue. Forty-three percent said they frequently feel tired, ascribing their weariness to various factors: job pressure (61 percent), increasing age (49 percent), and excessive work load (25 percent). A few blame personal problems, excessive travel, or recent illness.

Almost half of these executives smoke—usually cigarettes—and at least 20 percent of those who don't smoke stopped recently. About half of the respondents say they drink moderately, some 30 percent drink only at parties and other social occasions, and 15 percent don't drink at all. Only 2 percent confess to more than five drinks a day.

Exercise has many adherents among these men. Forty-six percent get regular exercise of one kind or another. Golf, tennis, bowling, and similar recreational exercise are most popular, but walking, bicycling, and calisthenics also have many followers.

What about overweight? More than 40 percent of these executives believe they are fit and trim. Another 40 percent are either on a diet or planning to go on one in the near future. A small percentage had tried to take off poundage but failed.

Reporters, writing about a well-known person, often say: "He looks ten years younger than his age." Certainly, this is flattering to the older man concerned.

But it is doubtful that reporters, any more than other laymen in general, really know how a man of forty, fifty, or sixty should look. The superficial standards applied in this regard—ten years are automatically added if a man is prematurely gray or bald—mean little to the physician.

There are certain physical aging characteristics, Johnson explains, that are known to any doctor: the condition of the skin and the area underneath the eyes, suppleness, briskness of movement—how the man and his body perform. And individual performance varies widely.

"One of the big disservices done to all of us," Johnson continues, "is the constant emphasis on our chronological ages. Almost daily, we are reminded how old we are, through the filling out of forms, through stories about people 'over forty,' through retirement programs with the conventional sixty-five-year cut-off."

In certain occupations, this longtime industrial physician observes, people try to disguise their ages because they are immediately downgraded in the estimate of their colleagues or employers. Some men, he adds, live in terror of being out of work after fifty—in some industries, much earlier—when actually they are at the peak of their powers and should be so judged. Other than as a statistical guide, Johnson insists, old age is a meaningless term. There should be only two stages in life—youth (growing up) and adulthood, a fairly level plateau through life without any severe drop-off until the end.

Too many people, he finds, talk themselves into premature old age. Once settled on a regular job, they begin to behave according to a preconceived standard as the years go by. After forty, they believe, they must slow down. They think they must ride, not walk. When they walk, they shuffle. Soon they *look* old *and* are old.

The truth is, Johnson counsels, that, once adulthood sets in, we all begin an inevitable deterioration affecting the teeth, eyes, hearing, and bone structure. However, this is very gradual, almost imperceptible, and dentures, eyeglasses, hearing aids, and other health appliances enable the average person, following normal rules of health, to move with relative comfort through the years. It must be emphasized, though, that, to maintain that normal, slow rate of letdown, you must use your physical machine regularly.

Aside from the possibility of such diseases as heart failure, cancer, or stroke that may come at any age, preventive maintenance can keep a body in good working order. Average life expectancy may still remain at seventy years —longer for women—but the later years can be as productive and enjoyable as the middle years. The pattern for a successful "old age" is set in early adulthood.

Despite the fact that a growing number of the fifty states have laws banning employment bias against forty-to-sixty-five-year-olds, it is still true that one out of every two jobs opening up is not available to persons over fifty-five; one out of four, to those over forty-five.

A typical letter from a man who cites his excellent background in education, business, and health, yet finds himself an unsuccessful jobseeker in his fifties:

"On the business of men over 50 (maybe 45 would be equally applicable), my experience has been that 'the establishment' is totally uninterested and, in fact, has tacit but clearly understood rules for those in position to hire such men. I am not talking about those fairly rare cases of men who hold top level executive positions and are sought out by other firms by reason of their unusual abilities (or reputation for such) having no bearing on age. I do refer to those who have left top level executive jobs for any reason and are obliged to enter the active competitive market for similar jobs in their own fields. Unless these men have had the foresight or the good fortune to maneuver themselves into another job before separating from their present employment, they immediately hit the downgrading process. It is similar to the 'instant depreciation' of a new car as soon as it has been driven out of the dealer's showroom.

"The saddest aspect of this phenomenon of really capable executives who have, so to speak, passed the midfield stripe, is the potential waste through disuse of talent that has taken twenty-five or thirty years to acquire.

"No matter how many articles you write or quote from speeches of the giants of our industry, referring to the desperate need of retailers for top and middle management executives, I take the position that this kind of commentary is about 90 per cent lip service.

"There is a sort of wolf-pack attitude toward men who are out of jobs, almost with total disregard for the reason. Granted, of course, these reasons often indicate weakness that militate against the individual's chances of success at new jobs at the same or equivalent level. But how many really good men are forced to quit jobs due to intolerable pressures from unfair bosses, intricate political situations within companies, elimination of a job due to merger or acquisition, and other perfectly valid reasons having nothing whatever to do with the man's basic abilities to perform?

"It would almost appear that employers and corporate employment managers, recognizing the vulnerability of an unemployed executive past fifty, deliberately see how far they can go in discovering the degree of 'desperateness' that can be ferreted out by offering the man a position obviously far below his capabilities, or a salary much below the point where his pride (if not his purse) demands it be refused."

Heavy dependence of business on employees who are from thirty-five to forty-four years old—prime working ages during which executives are being developed—may well undergo a change toward greater use of older people. However, this would be for practical rather than humanitarian reasons. Because of the particularly low birthrate in the depression years, the number of male workers who reached thirty-five to forty-four years old in 1975 were 700,000 fewer than the comparable number in 1966, and women in this age group are also likely to be somewhat fewer. But the over forty-fives can't wait patiently for this turn of events.

To conclude with a pertinent comment from Dr. Johnson: if only some way could be found to purge this country of its fixation on chronological age, more older people would demonstrate there's a lot to the old saw, "You're as young as you feel."

Executive Health Plan Is
Hard-Nosed Investment

Preventive health programs for executives should be of greater concern to company ownership than such more easily replaceable assets as buildings, machinery, and equipment.

Who would deny that more efficient management comes from executives in good physical and mental health than those with significant diseases or disorders? The motivation is even more urgent when it is recognized that most persons who supervise others and make decisions are in the age group where many ailments show up. Why should companies start thinking of health plans only upon the unexpected death of an important man in the organization?

Despite overwhelming evidence of the need for maintaining maximum effectiveness of managerial talent, studies by Commerce and Industry Association of New York demonstrate there is no specific executive health program in from 47 to 59 percent of the companies examined. The higher percentage applies particularly to smaller firms.

There are three basic methods for establishing an executive health plan, according to Dr. Harold Brandaleone, industrial physician:

1. "in-company" in which the examination is performed by a member of the medical department;
2. hospital or diagnostic clinic;
3. private physician.

From the background of four decades in practice and experience as medical consultant to such groups as Commerce and Industry Association, Kimberly-Clark, and Grey Advertising, Brandaleone elaborated upon these three methods:

The in-company method is suitable for organizations that maintain professional staffs and equipment adequate to carry out these checkups. Facilities for x rays, electrocardiograms, diagnostic, and laboratory determinations must be available. A qualified internist should perform a careful, detailed examination and evaluate the physical and emotional findings. The physician should have the privilege to refer the patient to other specialists when necessary. The company physician should have a close relationship with the patient's private physician. Some organizations with a medical department prefer to send their executives to an outside private physician or diagnostic clinic in order to assure secrecy of findings. However, a well-run company medical department should be able to keep records confidential. Each company must evaluate its own program according to its facilities.

Reasons for choosing the in-company plan: a) economy, b) convenience,

c) better relationship between medical department and executive, d) company doctor's ability to observe the patient's stresses and strains closely over a long period.

A hospital or diagnostic clinic should have the staff and equipment required for a comprehensive checkup. Luxury programs are sponsored by clinics in resort areas. These combine relaxation and golf with the examination.

A private physician emphasizes the basic idea of the patient-doctor relationship. It is usually best for the company to select a well-qualified internist who has the necessary equipment as well as a good knowledge of the executive and his business environment. The physician should be able to communicate with the executive's private physician. Complete confidence should be the rule unless the patient gives the doctor permission to discuss his problems with members of his company.

Use of an outside physician is of value when: a) there is a lack of adequate facilities in the company medical department, b) there is geographic dispersion, c) there is a lack of specialists in the medical department, d) the executive desires complete privacy, e) executives feel they can relax more with a physician outside the company.

Dr. Norman Plummer who retired in 1969 as general medical director, New York Telephone Co., prescribed similarly for people in general. "An executive's health," he observed, "isn't much different from anyone else's."

Americans, he warned, "are eating themselves to death, smoking themselves to death, killing themselves in automobiles."

What should be done to protect ourselves? Plummer's recommendations:

- The American diet should be altered. We're eating too much. More men have been slain by their suppers than by the sword. Men should strive to stay fifteen to twenty-five pounds under average weight for their height.
- Cigarette smoking should be curbed, if not eliminated, as it causes cancer of the lung and arteriosclerotic diseases.
- People should exercise in reasonable amounts. With this, there must be proper sleep, rest, and relaxation.
- Most important, the older man must be philosophical, face the future with optimism, want to live a productive life, and be so motivated by others.

Enough is known about incorrect diet, smoking, and other wrong habits, Plummer continued, to be certain there is a corollary between our ways of life and the "alarming, astounding" incidence of the cardiovascular diseases, particularly hypertensive and arteriosclerotic types. He urged executives to "lead people away from the scourge" of these trends.

Don't fool yourself that serious physical defects begin at middle age, Plummer further counseled. Practically all American males have some degree of heart or blood vessel damage at thirty. This is not so true of women or, for that matter, of men in other parts of the world. The best solution is to start before you're born; pick your parents. The next best thing is to stop harmful patterns of living before they control you. From that standpoint, adolescence is the most important period of your life. That's the time when people take up practices inimical to their physical and emotional well-being.

You can't wait until you're thirty, certainly not until the forties and fifties, when you're likely to be in real trouble. Perhaps 25 percent of men by age fifty have some evidence of heart failure. Nevertheless, even at fifty, all is not lost.

Plummer ranks cardiovascular defects, next to mental and emotional illness, as the most serious health problem today. The diseases of the heart and blood vessels may lead to strokes and sudden coronary attacks. These cause more deaths than any other physical ailments.

Cancer is second to arteriosclerotic and hypertensive conditions as a cause of death in this and many other countries, reports Dr. Emerson Day, former director, Strang Clinic. Here, too, the mortality rate is going up. Most of these fatalities, led by lung and colon-rectal malignancies, could be saved by early knowledge, Day's long-specialized background convinces him.

Up to 40 percent of apparently healthy executives enrolled in periodic health examinations are found to have diseases or defects previously unknown to them.

A compilation of over 100,000 such initial or subsequent examinations shows obesity to be the No. 1 enemy of health. Not far behind are the arthritic-rheumatic ailments. These are closely followed in order of frequency by hypertension, arteriosclerosis, hemorrhoids, and "anxiety" disorders. Other recurrent conditions are rectal or colonic polyps, peptic ulcers, inguinal (groin) hernias, and anemia. Also discovered are an appreciable number of defects of the eyes, prostate, varicose veins, and skin lesions; and occasional cases of congenital or rheumatic heart disease, tuberculosis, and cancer.

In from 50 to 90 percent of these incidents, therapy is available that, if applied at the proper time, can be expected to remove or arrest the condition or retard further development. However, if unchecked, many of these disorders are likely to produce major disability or death.

In the face of this evidence crying for more widespread sponsorship of preventive medicine, at least half of all companies—appreciably more in the smaller-size group—have no specific executive health program. This is an estimate arrived at in surveys by the Commerce and Industry Association of New York.

Dr. David H. Goldstein, of NYU's College of Medicine and a pioneer in environmental medicine, offered many of the foregoing facts and figures, derived from various sources, to an executive-health symposium presented by the Commerce and Industry Association. Goldstein said: "Performance of a periodic health examination may be ever so much more difficult than appraisal of an obviously sick person. My own philosophy in such an approach to a seemingly healthy client is: 'You are guilty until proven innocent.' " The physician in industry, he also pointed out, should supplement, not interfere with, the family doctor. Even with the most thoroughgoing alertness, he warned, the human being is so vulnerable that incidents occur—happily, only occasionally—of the man who gets an "A" on his health report today and a death certificate tomorrow.

Frequency of illness is found to be substantially less among executives than among other employees. Lost time is 25 percent lower. The fact that short-term absences are less among executives is interpreted as a difference of motivation.

It will come as a comforting thought to many executives that incidence of most diseases is no greater in their ranks than in other grades of employment. Cardiovascular disease, Goldstein reported, attacks both executive and white-collar nonexecutive groups with similar violence. However, blue-collar workers have a higher incidence of disease and mortality than white-collar workers.

Dr. Clinton G. Weiman, head of the medical department, First National City Bank, reported that a study of one hundred vice-presidents and one hundred middle-management people revealed there are twice as many smokers and twice the incidence of disease in the latter group. The two groups compare almost identically in age, but the vice-presidents are somewhat heavier.

"Our executive health program, started in 1949, has proved worthwhile as a hard-nosed investment; it pays off." Charles B. Delafield, retired vice-president for finance, Consolidated Edison Co. of New York, so advised other business executives and industrial physicians at a symposium on executive health. Delafield was ably abetted in discussing the company's program by Dr. S. Charles Franco, retired assistant vice-president and executive director of the medical department, Consolidated Edison Co. of New York, now the company's executive medical adviser.

Delafield lays the whole question of executive health checkups on the line as a dollars-and-cents proposition:

"Management should not have to worry about spending public funds in this manner. It should find some measure to prove it has a medical program that means something, so that the ax won't fall on the program some day.

"When the pressure is on profit margin, particularly where investor interest is the lifeblood of growth, it certainly would be helpful if management in general had better statistical information on health and mortality records of executives, both those exposed and those not exposed to a medical program. There is now no ready yardstick to measure the effectiveness of different programs. Con Edison thinks a soundly conceived program does pay off."

Agreeing that, from the health viewpoint, there appears to be no particu-

lar occupational hazard in being an executive, Franco yet warned that degenerative diseases start in the thirties and forties and are full blown in the fifties
and sixties. The best one can do, he advised from over thirty years' experience,
is to seek to control these ailments and live productive lives; "cure is not in
the realm of degenerative diseases." The biggest plus of an industrial medical
program, Franco said, is increased health-consciousness among executives.

Doctors employed by business organizations are making the transition
from industrial, to occupational or preventive, to environmental medicine.

The "environmental" description of this branch of the medical profession points up the broadened horizons of interest and responsibility reached
by the physician and psychiatrist in full- or part-time practice in industry.

The change in the making has been given impetus at New York University Bellevue Medical Center.

Goldstein is confident the term, "environmental medicine," must eventually prevail in view of incontrovertible evidence that a man is the creature of
his own environment. Adjustment as a total person is subject to stresses,
strains, and tensions wherever and whenever these may occur—in the home,
on the golf course, driving a car, playing cards, or in dozens of other places
or pursuits, as well as in the business environment. One important adjustment,
as Goldstein puts it, is "to family and to the boss, marital and/or mercantile."

Tying in with this philosophy is the definition of health contained in the
basic charter of the World Health Organization: "A state of complete physical,
mental and social well-being and not merely the absence of disease or infirm-
ity." Health, so defined, is obviously a goal that most persons can only aspire
to, a condition realistically attainable only by a lucky few.

Three Decades of Health
Maintenance Programs

Periodic health examinations could save or prolong your life. When large
numbers of mature males are thoroughly examined, about one-third are found
to have some potentially significant disease of which they are unaware. Every
doctor who conducts such examinations can cite case histories of a half-dozen
or more patients who are well today, long after usually fatal disorders were
discovered in an early stage and proper treatment begun. Only from 10 to 25
percent of those who seem healthy are really entirely so. In the great majority
of those examined, health-related practices or habits might profitably be altered.

These statistics are cited by Dr. Ralph F. Schneider, retired medical director, Exxon (formerly Standard Oil Co. of New Jersey), world's largest oil company, which has sponsored health maintenance programs for about forty years.

He joined the Esso medical staff in 1946 upon leaving the Navy as a lieutenant-commander. Before entering the service, he was in private practice in internal medicine. His first Esso tour of duty was two years with affiliated companies in Peru. He returned to New York in 1948 as an assistant medical director with responsibility for South American affiliates. He became medical director in 1954.

In other parts of the world, the Exxon medical department uses more than two hundred full-time or part-time doctors, most of them nationals of their respective countries.

American employees overseas whose illnesses may require further investigation are referred back to New York medical headquarters when they come back on furlough—or sooner, if necessary.

All Exxon affiliates are decentralized from corporate and operating standpoints. Decentralization includes the medical department. Each affiliate's medical director reports to a member of his own board of directors.

The function of Exxon's medical director is to assist the various medical directors and, through coordination and consultation, carry out the basic policy of uniform health maintenance. Aiding in this "two-way street" of communication is the *Medical Bulletin* published three times a year and devoted to a wide variety of articles by doctors and other professionals outside as well as within the company. Regional meetings are held periodically. Overseas doctors come to the United States when there is need for special instruction on clinical or administrative matters.

The company instituted examinations on a "more or less regular" basis about thirty years ago. Previously, periodic examinations were on a selective basis. Management and the medical department had their work cut out for them trying to convince employees of the personal benefit of health evaluation.

Dr. Schneider believes the company's medical department is "unusual for industry from the standpoints of degree of standardization and coordination of international medical service and the number of employees involved. . . .

"Our [staff's function] is to apply measures of preventive medicine to carry out a uniform program and policy of optimum health maintenance of employees. We start off by examining all persons who apply for positions. We want to ascertain, so far as can be evaluated at the outset, whether the individual's physical and mental capabilities are in keeping with the job.

"Once the person is on the payroll, he is invited to undergo an all-inclusive periodic examination, supplemented by a health questionnaire and any laboratory procedures the doctor thinks may be needed. The examination should not be obligatory, but should be confidential. One way we have always found to convince employees to take the examination voluntarily is for their bosses to set an example in this respect.

"Doctors know that a person's environment has a lot to do with his health. The air and light around him, machines, equipment, and procedures to which he is subjected, social relationships, habits, are all factors that relate to physical and emotional well-being. All these are discussed with the employee during the examination."

Employees are asked to come to the medical department on a schedule depending on age, previous findings, and interval health history. In general, a person over forty-five is invited every year; a younger man, every two or three years. All employees—executives and underlings alike—get exactly the same care.

When necessary, patients are sent to a psychiatrist who in most instances reports back to the medical director. Fortunately, he says, most of the people he sees don't require this specialized attention. He points out that a man may have emotional problems but, most frequently, can resolve these himself during his examination.

The medical department does not employ clinical psychologists. The employee relations department uses industrial psychologists.

Once the examination is completed and all findings in, the doctor reports back to the individual with his recommendations. Where definitive treatment is required, the personal physician is advised of the situation, but only with the employee's consent. Even where findings don't suggest a follow-up, permission of the patient is obtained to send a copy of the report to his private doctor.

Schneider comments:

"Our knowledge about the strains that stress places on organic and emotional health is surprisingly limited. As a matter of fact, we still lack good tools and techniques for measuring it, and so are not even certain that the executive is subjected to any extraordinary amounts of it. In my opinion, we do not today have valid evidence that the executive is prone to any particular diseases as a result of stress or any other aspect of his work. We know even less about the potential benefits of stress.

"However, we do know that, of the many known environmental (as opposed to hereditary) influences on our physical and mental health, a pleasant proportion is wholly or partially subject to our control. We cannot change our individual inheritances with respect to health, but even so, we are at times able to influence their effect upon us."

Exxon's former medical director offers this prescription for maintenance of executive and nonexecutive health:

1. Our attitude toward health should be realistic.
2. We should have and use a personal physician.
3. We should have periodic health maintenance examinations regularly and

attend promptly to any new or persistent symptoms developing between examinations.

4. We should receive such immunizations as are appropriate.
5. We should be enjoying and performing effectively our roles in our family, our work, and our community.
6. We should be getting exercise regularly.
7. We should have a number of sources of satisfaction to pursue in our leisure time, and we should arrange to have leisure time.
8. We should avoid over-eating, over-smoking, over-drinking, and over-exertion.
9. We should have some privacy.
10. Lastly, except in importance, we should have faith and a faith.

Can Coronaries Be Identified in Advance?

Scarcely a day goes by that obituary pages fail to carry news of the deaths from heart attacks of men of achievement in their forties and fifties.

Did these untimely passings occur without prior warning signals? Is there something in the way these men lived that foretold the way they would die? Couldn't these calamities for families, friends, companies, and associates have been averted?

The unhappy questions come much more easily than the necessarily ambiguous answers. Generalizations can only be confusing. Each disability and fatality must be considered separately. True, diseases of the heart and blood vessels are the No. 1 killer. But application of medical statistics to any single individual is both misleading and erroneous.

As the aftermath of excessive, unpleasant tensions, the man's blood pressure may remain too high too long, his appetite dulled, his muscles tightened. He's all wound up with no place to go.

The all-too-revealing story is told of an executive who underwent a minor operation. True to form, he kept a log at his bedside showing that, at the end of three days, he had spent seventy-two hours in the hospital, his doctor had attended him for six hours and thirty-four minutes, his nurses had looked after him twelve times. Finding fault with the system, he wrote a letter to the hospital superintendent setting forth his grievances and recommendations at great length.

General belief is that the dynamic, quick-tempered, over-aggressive, hard-working person, one who is or aspires to be top dog, develops more coronaries than does the person who is placid and easy-going.

Subject, as his popular profile makes him, to nervous tension, frustrations, and anxieties, fear of criticism or failure, this man thinks he must take his work home in his briefcase. He turns lunches into business conferences. He doesn't know how to delegate authority or to share his fears and doubts with subordinates. His day is a not-so-merry-go-round of dealing with difficult people with worries of their own. He is overwhelmed by the task of making decisions, of being constantly confronted at least in mind's eye with the injunction: "The buck stops here." He can't take or enjoy a vacation. Friction in his domestic life not infrequently complicates his office problems. He has no hobbies, no outside interests, but eating and drinking. To him, healthy relaxation spells danger; somebody may be ready to pounce on his job.

To particularize for a moment about retail executives, the established image is of a man who works too many days and too many nights. He attends too many meetings. He is held personally responsible for short-range results as few executives in industry are. He is always enveloped in a crisis atmosphere. With the self-pity that often characterizes the middle-to-top-echelon man who feels his contribution is not fully recognized, he may say only half in jest: "Don't ask me how I live, but how I stay alive."

A Man's Best Friend Is His Doc

Medical statistics concerning the life span after a heart attack contain many variables.

One in four suffers a second attack any time from one day to twenty years after the first incident. Yet, it is difficult, if not impossible, to predict recurrence of coronaries in a given case with any certainty.

Proof that medicine is sometimes working in the dark in the field of cardiovascular defects is implicit in the fact that more than 50 percent of all heart attacks take place while the person is asleep or at rest. Only 2 percent are connected with unusual exertion, such as shoveling snow or running for the train.

Some medical authorities assert the supercharged, harried business executive, lawyer, and physician are more often—or sooner—victims of heart failure than are the truck driver or manual laborer. Reasoning: as responsibilities and incomes go up, so does blood pressure. Many others contend that those who do hard physical labor are the first to lose their health.

There are also those who insist you just can't fit people into convenient occupational pigeonholes for such purposes. Some argue that tensions, whether controlled or uncontrolled, are the lethal enemy. Others say fierce competition and attendant stresses and strains can be good for people, depending on how they react to these.

Men who have had a first heart attack must learn to live in moderation. They must strike a balance between their work and home life, diet, exercise, relaxation, and vacations. They must compromise with any previously held conviction that a large part of every man's life is a continuous effort to escape the possibilities of being fired, or of failing and falling down in the eyes of colleagues, family, and friends. If you're a top executive, you must select the most capable men you can find to whom to delegate authority and responsibility. Then, keep hands off; don't take over compulsively to prove how indispensable you are.

However, to complicate matters, abandonment of bad habits after a heart attack may set up a new emotional disturbance even worse than the physical condition.

Happily, thousands of cases in doctors' files illustrate the recuperative powers of the most seriously impaired heart muscles and prove that one or even several heart attacks are not of themselves marks of invalidism. A man with a coronary is not necessarily handicapped when he operates under judicious conditions—conditions custom-made for his own needs.

Most of the progress in medical science of the past one hundred years has been achieved in infant mortality and contagious diseases. For middle-aged and older individuals, though, things haven't changed much from the 1800s. A century ago, men of fifty had a life expectancy of 21.6 additional years. Despite all advances since, the man of the same age today has added only two years to his life expectancy. The man of sixty has made practically no gain— 15.64 versus 15.6 years.

In other words, once our pre-Civil War antecedents passed the hazards of being born and of childhood diseases, they compare well in longevity with the current crop. Then, it was the survival of the fittest. Today, the not-so-fit also survive. Chronic diseases are the major problem of our middle-aged and older groups.

Long-term preventive medicine is the answer. The doctor, in both industrial and private practice, is a man's best friend. A personal health program is required—one that will anticipate and prevent, or at least arrest or control, "stress diseases"—physical and emotional afflictions caused by heavy strains throughout a man's life, in line with the individual's own limitations and potentialities.

Such programs are certainly in order for executives—men in the thirty-five-to-sixty-five age range, at one and the same time most susceptible to coronary and other degenerative diseases and most important company-assets.

Top Executives: Take Heart, You Outlive Your Doctors

Want to live long and strong? Of course, you do. Your chances for healthy longevity are much better if you are a top corporate executive or a leading scientist or politician than if you are a doctor, journalist, or telephone company worker. Here's proof:

A West Coast study contrasted eight hundred oil, bank, and insurance executives employed by large companies with eight hundred physicians, most of them self-employed. Over a twenty-year period, twice as many doctors as executives had heart attacks.

A former president of the American College of Cardiologists, Dr. George C. Griffith of Los Angeles seeks to explain the discrepancy on the ground that the executives "get ahead just by keeping their noses clean and don't have the economic drive for subsistence" of doctors who make it on their own. Doctors' susceptibility to heart attacks is a costly price for their average national income exceeding $40,000.

A sociologist took a sampling of men whose biographies were included in *Who's Who* and followed their mortality figures for the next twelve years. Adhering to the appropriate actuarial adjustments to obtain a single statistic for the death rate of each professional group, he found that scientists listed in the book had a mortality only 79 percent that of all persons in *Who's Who*. Comparison of the famous scientists with the whole roster of their colleagues of the same age shows that the better-known ones have a mortality only one-third as much as that of the entire profession.

Coming out worst of all were journalists, with 210 percent of average mortality.

The beneficial effect of success on a long, vigorous lifetime is observed in a seven-year study of 270,000 male employees of the Bell System. The survey sought to ascertain whether stress generated by tensions of ambition, competitiveness, and overwork is prelude to disabling coronary disease. High executives had a heart attack rate of only 1.85 per thousand per year. The comparative rate for telephone workers and foremen was 4.33 heart attacks per thousand per year.

Executives at every age from thirty-four to sixty-four experienced a little less heart disease and accounted for fewer deaths from that cause than laborers and foremen and, by retirement, had substantially fewer heart attacks than their subordinates.

Dr. Lawrence E. Hinkle, of the Cornell University Medical College in New York, who headed a staff of investigators in this survey and analyzed the data, reported that the onset of heart disease is closely related to a man's inherited body build, social and educational background, and smoking and eating habits. Incidence of heart disease among holders of college degrees was 30 percent less than that for those who had not gone beyond high school.

The results, according to Hinkle, "didn't come out the way we had anticipated."

Yet, similar studies at Du Pont, Exxon, and General Motors confirm his findings. He now believes that the statistics for the telephone company employees, who comprise about 1 percent of the U.S. male work force, are valid for the majority of large American corporations. In the absence of definitive studies of smaller firms, Hinkle declines to extend his thinking to such companies.

Another study of 270 men, sixty to ninety-four years old, indicates that "work satisfaction and good morale" are better predictors of longevity than proper exercise, physical fitness, smoking history, diet, or parents' age at death. Y' pays yer money and y' takes yer cherce.

Program Survival for Wives of
Heart Patients

Heart attack in a relatively young man—in his thirties through fifties— is the single most common health cause of radical change in family life in America.

Happily, thousands of cases in doctors' files illustrate the recuperative forces of the most seriously impaired heart muscles. Proof is abundant that one or even several heart attacks are not of themselves marks of invalidism or precursors of premature death. Men with coronaries are not necessarily handicapped, so long as they operate under ground rules custom-made by their doctors.

Proper attitudes and actions of the patients' wives are all-important to a prognosis of a return to lives on as nearly normal a plane as possible for all concerned.

With this in mind, Jane Schoenberg and JoAnn Stichman have written *How to Survive Your Husband's Heart Attack*.

In addition to a longtime friendship, the co-authors have a common bond of husbands who suffered heart attacks in their forties. In 1967, Arthur Schoenberg, then forty-six, was in charge of manufacturing at Theodor of California, handbag firm in Gardena, a Los Angeles industrial suburb. He was water skiing in the Pacific off Santa Monica when he was stricken with a massive coronary. His young daughter and two sons pulled him out of the water into the family's motor boat. He was taken by ambulance to a hospital for emergency treatment and then to another hospital where he remained seven weeks.

Before his heart attack, Schoenberg had been an ardent tennis player, golfer, and water skiier. He was outgoing, able to take stresses in stride. Five feet 10 1/2, weight 173, he was a nonsmoker, supposedly in excellent physical condition and theoretically not a likely candidate for a heart seizure. In hindsight, though, doctors ascribed his coronary to a combination of factors: heredity—his father, who died at seventy-eight, had previously suffered a number of heart attacks; and cholesterol—it was determined for the first time that Arthur had a high cholesterol level.

Schoenberg was permitted to go home for several months' further recuperation before returning on a gradual basis to his work. He later rose to the presidency of the company, which had been founded by members of the Schoenberg and two other families in 1946. In 1974, he resigned to join Thermwell Products Co., Paterson, N.J.-based manufacturer of weatherstripping and other do-it-yourself products as manager of operations in the Los Angeles warehouse.

Ms. Schoenberg spoke about how she and Arthur, married since 1950, have rewoven their lives.

The book is the outcome of a research project the two women undertook as fellow students in a sociology course at UCLA. They had returned to college after their husbands' heart attacks.

Asked by their professor to write papers bearing on personal involvement in community affairs, they hit upon a joint program of interviews with other women going through the same emotional ordeal. They called their UCLA Medical Center project *Women Who Have Been Through It Helping Women Who Are Going Through It.* The study was expanded to include taped interviews with hundreds of other wives of heart-attack and heart-coronary patients.

Dr. Selwyn Bleifer, Schoenberg's cardiologist, and Dr. Michael Thorner, Stichman's cardiologist, advised the authors during the writing of the book. In 1971, these and other doctors assisted Ms. Schoenberg and Ms. Stichman in forming The Heart Wife Counselors at Cedars-Sinai Medical Center, Los Angeles, the institution where Arthur Schoenberg had been confined in intensive care and coronary care units. The counselors, who include a number of volunteers, meet weekly with Heart Wives whose husbands are still in the hospital. Heart-Wife Counselors speak from actual knowledge of the traumatic experiences and selfish thoughts from which Heart Wives are suffering, and can provide the comfort of wives whose husbands have recovered. Medical and social-work professionals attend the sessions.

A $5,000 grant was made to The Heart Wife Counselors by a man who had a heart attack before the program started and felt his wife would have been spared many hours of torment had she been able to avail herself of such aid. The concept may be extended to other hospitals.

According to the authors, "the real problem of a heart attack is not the possibility of dying; it is the much greater probability of living. The problems are a result of the very human reaction of nearly all patients to certain effects on the body—and more important—on the mind. Your husband does not know if he will be able to work as hard or as well as he did before. Or at all. He may not be able to earn the money he did before. He will have to stop smoking, watch his weight, give up many foods and activities he used to enjoy. We are talking about a personality and behavior change as well as a distinct change in life style. How long must you expect these changes to continue? For the rest of your life.

"You play the key role in your husband's recovery. You set the tone and atmosphere. Your attitude toward the adjustments you must make directly affects the adjustments he must make. Commit yourself to accepting the fact your husband has had a heart attack. Then help him accept it. That is the first step in surviving it—for both of you. The next step is not in what happens to you, not in the thoughts and emotions that sweep over you, unbidden and unwelcome."

Cogent counsel is given on a wide range of subjects, among these the children, his care at home, his diet, setting up a communication system to get help in an emergency, divorce "cardiac style," and, perhaps most significant, "how to be a shrew with delicate grace and charm."

Never flinching from their advisory roles, Ms. Schoenberg and Ms. Stichman devote a chapter to sex: A heart attack, they advise, has absolutely no physiological effect on a man's sexual ability. The psychological effect of a heart attack on a man's sex life is a different matter. Husbands who come home from the hospital may become "uncontrollable" sexually but are likely to return to a normal sex life once they think they have proved themselves. At the opposite end is impotence due to the husband's apathy or fright. Each case must be considered individually—and by the couple's own doctor.

The Schoenbergs used to belong to a once-a-week bridge group and regularly attended the theater with friends. They have considerably modified their social activity. They now play bridge and go to the theater "only when we feel like it, not because we have a precommitment."

A year after Schoenberg's attack, Jane, then thirty-nine, made up her mind to get a college degree, the lack of which she had always keenly regretted. She decided a college education would be helpful should the day ever come when she might have to support herself and her three children. Her last contact with formal education had been in her late teens when she took courses in English and dental assistant training at the University of Southern California in Los Angeles. At seventeen, she had come from Paterson, N.J., and worked as a model and dental assistant. She married Arthur at twenty-three. Besides being a wife and mother, she was engaged in community work.

When she decided to return to school, she registered at UCLA with one or two courses, accelerated her program, went to summer school, and in four years won a bachelor's degree in sociology. Arthur, a graduate of the University of Michigan, enrolled for evening courses in accounting at UCLA's Graduate School of Business Administration.

How is Arthur Schoenberg doing? Just fine!

10

EMOTIONAL HEALTH

The Enigma That Is the Human Being

Human beings persist in acting like human beings. As such, they are enigmas to themselves as well as to others. This poses a major problem for industry.

Management is comfortable with measurable, predictable things. Machines, materials, money, and manufacturing and retail operations are not uncomplicated, but they are susceptible to measurement. Even the most astute executive, with a high degree of intuitive understanding of people, wishes he could measure and manage the "people" part of his business as confidently as he can the "material" part.

Dr. Robert B. O'Connor, now retired vice-president, health services, United States Steel Corp., described this challenge as a speaker at an industrial mental health conference sponsored by the National Association of Manufacturers.

It is important to bear in mind, he advised, that mental health carries no connotation of loss of individuality or conformity to some concept of an "average" or "normal" man. All of us are likely at one time or another to have an emotional problem of a greater or lesser degree of seriousness. A search for an average man in an industry is as absurd as a search for an average book in a library.

M. Ralph Kaufman, now retired psychiatrist-in-chief and director, Department of Psychiatry, Mount Sinai Hospital, New York, concurs.

Since the dawn of civilization and before, Kaufman says, what's inside a human being hasn't changed much. Yes, human tensions take different characters and forms of expression in different periods. It is true there's a certain open acceptance of sexuality today that was repressed in the "underground" Victorian Age. Sex in general depends on which facet of society you belong to or are looking at.

People seem to be expressing themselves more openly, but at the same time, there is more conformity. The current adolescent is no more rebellious than in previous generations. As always, a young person gets along better with his grandfather than with his father, and the grandfather better with his grandson than with his son. An old saying still holds true: "The enemy of your enemy is your friend."

"You can't generalize whether open expression is good or bad," Kaufman warns. "You can't say that, because there's this, this inevitably leads to that. I'll let you know in twenty years when I know where these kids have gone."

For 150 years, Mount Sinai's former psychiatric chief observes, psychiatrists have said: "Life is much more complex now." Trains "rushing through London at eight miles an hour" were once cited as a factor in the increase in insanity. It's the fallacy of the Golden Age—each generation finds the Golden Age is the one two generations back.

Only in absolute numbers is there any more mental illness than at any other time. Frustrations and need for adaptation are part and parcel of the process of living.

By and large, there is a more understanding attitude, a more sophisticated approach, toward mental illness now. Some of the stigma has disappeared but by no times all of it. Psychiatric illness is still less acceptable than physical disability.

Individual Mental Health—Greater Corporate Effectiveness

Dr. (Ph.D) Harry Levinson has been concerned for two decades with the relationship between people and the organizations in which they work, with promoting the mental health of individuals and the effectiveness of companies or institutions in which they are employed.

In 1956, Levinson began conducting seminars for executives and industrial physicians at the Menninger Foundation, Topeka, Kan., where he created and directed the Division of Industrial Mental Health. In 1968, he was appointed Thomas Henry Carroll-Ford Foundation Distinguished Visiting Professor, Harvard Graduate Business School. For the past few years, he has been president of The Levinson Institute, Cambridge, an association of clinical psychologists and psychiatrists for management education and consultation.

The institute sponsors five-day seminars on psychological aspects of management for organizational leadership.

Levinson gives the underlying philosophy that brought the seminars into being:

"Being an executive is as agonizing as it is exhilarating. No executive is free of the pains and struggles of motivating, guiding, and integrating people into an effective organization. The failures and frustrations of executive work stem largely from those efforts. An executive cannot dismiss such difficulties lightly for his competence lies in being a leader of men.

"This task, always difficult, is becoming even more trying. It is hard enough to find good people, let alone make judgments about how well they might perform. It is even harder to understand the changing expectations of younger men and to maintain the vitality of experienced managers. And how does the executive get people to adapt willingly to tomorrow's needs when they are still trying to solve yesterday's problems?

"What about one's colleagues and boss? Relationships with them are critical to an executive's success. Most important, how well does the executive grasp his own needs and aspirations?"

Thousands of long-time executives face the chilling realization they're no longer effective in their jobs. And their seniors are caught up in conflicting emotions about still loyal but now incompetent subordinates.

Even where the men themselves are stimulated by personal or company action to take specialized advance training, the task is endless. The fact is that any new professional knowledge has a half-life of ten years—that is, half of what a man knows is obsolete within that time.

What should the individual and the organization do to cope with the steadily increasing complexity of higher supervisory positions, of executive obsolescence?

Levinson makes some suggestions:

• Every man should prepare himself for maximum flexibility. He should specialize only after gaining as broad a college education as possible. The broader a man's education, the more flexibly he can adapt to changing circumstances.
• Every person who pursues a career, as distinct from a jobholder, should expect to continue his education for the rest of his professional life.

Some companies urge executives to attend one or another learning program annually. Many send men to university refresher courses. Larger firms have their own in-service or management development programs.

Even relatively small organizations pay tuition for advanced courses relating to the business.

Career men should have specialized knowledge of a second field they might enter should their first choice not work out. Those who establish alternative competence not only have the equanimity that goes with not having to bear a chronically difficult or demeaning situation but also have something to turn to as a major activity when they retire.

- A man's own feelings are the most powerful agents of obsolescence. The two most formidable barriers to flexibility are the factors that usually are the most significant in creating obsolescence: passivity and fear. Every man must fight these attitudes to survive; in middle-age, they can be paralyzing.

Levinson gives as an illustration of passivity his experience at a university offering two advanced graduate programs for executives. One group of men was between thirty and thirty-eight; the other, between forty-five and fifty-five. The older group seemed less willing to learn and less able to look at alternative courses of action. They seemed to have more at stake in already fixed positions that they did not want to examine but, rather, felt impelled to protect. Compared to the younger men, they had already given up in self-defeat. The psychologist was not surprised when several of the older men later sought his advice in finding new positions.

For a manifestation of fear, Levinson cites a company undergoing drastic management changes and rapid expansion under competitive pressure. The president asked the management group for a critical review of the organization and its needs. To stimulate their thinking, he invited several outside experts to present contemporary management concepts.

The almost one hundred management men then met in small groups to discuss three questions: 1) What did the consultant say that is relevant to the organization? 2) Of whatever is relevant, what is most important to the firm? 3) Who, specifically, in the organization should do something about it?

The management group had no difficulty with the first question, some with the second. But none of the executives named a specific person or department in response to the third. They were afraid to respond to the president's invitation, even though he was not a punitive man.

When the discussion centered on innovation, the management group, in effect, abdicated. They said that the survival of the organization depended on the imagination and drive of younger men who were yet to come. They expressed no confidence in their own ability, nor did they seem troubled by abandoning the field to unknown rivals.

Some executives, Levinson observes, say they cannot afford to develop alternative expertise or methods to retain their flexibility. Sometimes, they are right. Companies do not always allow time for such efforts. But Parkinson's law holds all too often: Activity expands to fill the time allocated to it. Some men have had their fill of going to school; they would rather watch TV.

They should clearly know the consequences, the ex-Menninger psychologist warns. Some have the illusion that, if they just work hard now, the future will take care of itself. It won't. Whatever the excuse for inaction, the problem remains: How to build in and maintain adaptive flexibility that will serve a lifetime.

Executive obsolescence is to a company as rust is to metal. Continuous attention is required to avoid layers of corrosion that tend to change companies into rusting hulls.

Another phase of this problem—managers who balk at assuming greater responsibility—is discussed by Levinson. Levinson divides such people into those who have been suppressed by bosses inhibiting initiative and independence and those who have become overly dependent on others who make the decisions and take the risks.

What should the executive do who takes over a previously highly controlled or autocratically managed organization and who now must make it more flexible?

1. He will have to examine his own attitudes to avoid tripping over his own doubts about subordinates.
2. He will have to deal with the generalized problem of limited perceptions his subordinates have of their roles.
3. He will have to review specific cases to ascertain whether given men are lethargic because they are satisfied, afraid, dependent, or inhibit themselves.

In sum, Dr. Levinson says, many people who seem reluctant to assume initiative can be helped to do so. Many others cannot change significantly. There is room in every organization for the man who holds things together. Sometimes, those who have no power aspirations for themselves are the only ones who can be trusted by their more competitive colleagues.

Levinson offers some thoughts on loyalty within the organization:

It is often said that loyalty—even the need for loyalty—of subordinates to superiors, of managers to presidents, has disappeared. Job hopping in middle management has shot up 500 percent in the past five years. Loyalty, of itself, this line of reasoning goes, is no longer rewarded. It is the most effective, not the most loyal, who reach the top. Loyalty of a growing professional class is to goals, the particular institution simply a means to the goal.

Truth is, a different kind of loyalty than in the past is—or should be— very much a part of the environment, whether the scene be business, industry, unions, universities, the church, or the military. The difference is that paternalism, however disguised, is going, and ways of achieving the loyalty that was characteristic of paternalism no longer work.

What were the old ways? Preaching loyalty, inducing guilt, reinforcing it by tight controls and severe penalties, keeping people dependent and grateful. The tradition in management circles is that, if the employee is paid reasonably, the work place is adequately comfortable, and the boss is "nice," the employee should do as he is told, and do it cheerfully. The employee should stand behind, and for, the man who provides his bread and butter, else he is not loyal.

And the new ways? Freedom for ideas to be examined, freedom to define the problems to be solved, and freedom for all in the enterprise to direct their energies to solving these. When those conditions are met, a manager, a company will never have to ask where loyalty went.

Changing conditions, Levinson explains, have made paternalistic concepts of loyalty obsolete for many individuals and many organizations. Three sets of circumstances stand out:

- Drastic change in the ability required to rise in the ranks and in the rewards that loyalty alone can confer. Becoming a top executive is no longer a matter of rising on a fixed ladder in a stable organization to a command position. It is rather leadership of highly diverse specialists toward ever-changing goals. Such leadership ability is relatively rare and, when the choice must be made between unquestioned loyalty and unquestioned competence, today's organizations usually opt for competence.
- The second drastic change is in people's expectations. The very success of American enterprise has changed the relative pressure of psychological needs. With almost continuous economic growth for twenty-five years, many Americans, particularly those in the managerial and professional groups, found it comparatively easy to meet their basic needs. To a lesser degree, this was also true of the working class.

  As a result, employees turned to their organizations for fulfillment of higher level needs—needs of safety, protection, and care. The organizations responded with seniority provisions, health insurance, pensions, and the like. Need, in turn, moved to a higher level. Respect, status, self-fulfillment, psychological rather than material needs have become paramount. If people can't fulfill higher level needs in one organization, they may turn to another. Only in and to such organizations will they give more of themselves in the form of innovation, creativity, and investment of energy.
- The third drastic change is in the way American families live. Just as erosion has taken place in family ties—grown children are often separated from their parents by many miles—just so has erosion, although an ambiguous one, taken place in the individual's relationship with the company. The very mobility that thinned family ties made the organization more important to the employee. However, demands placed by such employees on their employers were often greater than the company could fulfill. In disillusionment, individuals who had previously severed close ties with parents and home towns found it possible, though painful, to move from one organization to another.

To create the conditions for loyalty, Levinson recommends:

- Be open with subordinates. The omnipotent boss is going fast. Pseudo-omnipotence is a form of manipulation, and those who are subject to it are

rightfully contemptuous when the same boss talks about loyalty.
- Make it possible for people to meet together as responsible adults to solve common problems. If the problems are worthy of their effort, and if the leader provides guidance and support, he won't have to worry about loyalty.
- Offer people both the opportunity and the challenge to be responsible both for their work and the fate of the organization. Don't try to con them by equating opportunity with money, and responsibility with doing what you want them to do.
- Recognize that loyalty is no longer to be equated with blind obedience. The most loyal person may well be the most fervid member of the loyal opposition. The person who raises questions about how things are done, what assumptions are made, what changes have to take place, what is coming in the future, what things anger and discourage people, is the man who helps the organization survive.

Add "jackass fallacy" to the lexicon of personnel relations and the literature of "people" problems.

Levinson has coined the phrase which he defines as "the assumption in managerial practices and most behavioral science research that people are motivated by reward and punishment—"the carrot and the stick." He charges that this "fallacy" corrupts the techniques of management appraisal, underlies the conflicts of family business, contributes to failures of mergers and is at the root of the crisis of middle-aged managers and of misunderstanding of the proper meaning of Management by Objectives.

Two factors—the great jackass fallacy and the bureaucratic organization structure, warns Levinson, are formidable obstacles to organizational survival. They are essentially self-defeating if what an executive wants from his followers are spontaneity, investment, dedication, commitment, affiliation, and adaptive innovation.

He contends, "Effective management must get rid of this invalid motivational assumption and revise the anachronistic organizational structure in order to recapture the momentum toward unlimited possibilities and stimulate the inherent potential of people and their willingness to solve problems, to achieve goals and to reach for the stars."

This psychologist relates the inception of the "jackass fallacy" to executive seminars he conducts. He frequently asks the participants what the dominant philosophy of motivation in American management is. Almost invariably, they quickly agree it is the carrot-and-stick philosophy: reward and punishment. Then he asks them to close their eyes for a moment and form a picture in their mind's eye with a carrot at one end and a stick at the other. When they have done so, he asks them to describe the central image in that picture. Most often, they respond that the central figure is a jackass.

"Obviously, the unconscious assumption behind the reward-punishment model," observes Levinson, "is that one is dealing with jackasses, that people are jackasses to be manipulated and controlled. Thus, unconsciously, the boss is the manipulator and controller, and the subordinate is the jackass.

"The characteristics of a jackass are stubbornness, stupidity, willfulness and unwillingness to go where someone is driving him. These, by interesting coincidence, are also the characteristics of the unmotivated employee. Thus, it becomes vividly clear that the underlying assumption management unconsciously makes about motivation leads to a self-fulfilling prophecy. People will inevitably respond to the carrot-and-stick by trying to get more of the carrot and by protecting themselves against the stick. This predictable phenomenon led to the formation of unions and to the frequent sabotage of management's incentive efforts as well as to the characteristic employees' suspicion of management's motivational (manipulative) techniques. Employees obviously sense the carrot-and-stick conception behind management's attitudes and just as obviously respond to the communications built around those attitudes with appropriate self-defending measures."

While the bureaucratic structure with its heavy emphasis on internal competition for power and position is often touted as a device for achievement, Levinson continues, it is actually a system built for defeat. As he sees it, fewer people move up the pyramidal hierarchy at each step. That leaves a residual of failures, often euphemistically called "career people," who thereafter are passed over because they have not succeeded in the competition for managerial positions. They constitute a heavy burden in most organizations for they are no longer motivated by competitive spirit.

There is little need in their eyes to learn more; they simply do as they are told. They usually stay until retirement and are frequently described as the "deadwood" that needs to be cleaned out when a new management takes over.

In one large company where just that task was undertaken with the hope the forty-year-olds would respond with unbridled enthusiasm when the fifty-year-olds were cleaned out, the younger men failed to respond. They saw in what was happening to the older men their likely fate in ten years.

"Legacy of Neglect": Industrial Mental Health

Emotional illness, psychiatrists believe, is the result of many illnesses; one single cause is quite impossible to determine. Nevertheless, they estimate, from 80 to 90 percent of psychiatric disorders in industry stem from difficulties traceable to the home situation or early life pattern. Because work takes up most of a man's waking hours, industry must play a role in helping the man cope with mental problems that may be evidenced in such disruptive factors as absenteeism, accidents, alcoholism, anxiety and tension symptoms, poor morale, inordinate employee turnover, and lowered productivity.

The authors of *The Legacy of Neglect* think attribution of the great majority of emotional disturbances to the home is misleading. Management misinterprets such statements to mean there may be only a single cause of emotional insecurity, that this occurs primarily off the job; therefore, the company should shoulder little or no responsibility.

However, the truth is there are job-related contributory forces that tend to trigger or precipitate emotional instability sooner or later. So long as work is important in aiding a man to identify himself, the authors add, his inability to adjust satisfactorily to job-created stresses will continue to induce emotional illness.

Leonard Himler, an industrial psychiatrist, corroborates this view:

"It is well known that, sometimes, even minor and ordinary and insignificant conflict situations at work can act as releasing factors for tensions engendered in the individual's earlier experience."

Psychiatrist Robert S. Garber believes, "it is impossible and illogical to suggest that one can separate job life and home life into categories, each with assigned probabilities of emotional disturbance. Who can deny that, daily, constantly irritating factors as a result of interpersonal relations, promotional changes, decision-making responsibility, automation and variables in wages can create emotional stress on the job?"

Programs already functioning successfully, Dr. Garber notes, embody such services as employee counseling, referral for treatment in the community, supervisory training in education, preemployment and psychological testing, employee performance appraisal, accident prevention, provision for rehabilitation, psychiatric research and personnel policy reviews. One of the primary functions of such programs is prompt identification and treatment of emotional disturbances on the job. For example, he observes, Du Pont has introduced a process known as "front line therapy" for the less extreme forms of emotional illness.

Garber reports "tremendous progress" in insurance coverage for psychiatric illness.

If company management wishes to deal with such problems, Garber continues, there are a number of alternative methods of implementing a mental health program. Assuming that the most important company assets are money and personnel, the decision for management then becomes allocation of financial and human resources to a mental health program so as to provide the greatest long-run benefits to the firm.

"Disturbances in mental health of workers usually appear in the form of physical illness, behavioral disorders, and impaired production. High rates of industrial absenteeism and accidents appear to be related to disturbed mental health. Special problems are posed for industry by high incidence of alcoholism among workers, unsatisfactory utilization of older workers, need for reassignment and rehabilitation of those displaced by automation, and planning for those approaching retirement, in addition to rehabilitation of sick or injured employees.

"Responsibility for mental health in industry is shared by everyone in the plant, including both management and labor. Leadership and direct responsibility usually rest with the medical department, the personnel department, and top management. It is a collaborative effort and an investment on the part of all three.

"Research in the fields of human relations and occupational medicine is continually adding new knowledge that is being put to practical use, but there is a vast need for increased research in this field. . . . Expansion of activities in the field of mental health and human relations in industry will undoubtedly be shown by improved health, improved morale and, particularly, in increased productivity which, spelled out to industry, means more profit in dollars and cents and a vast savings of expenditures in the long run."

Prophylactic psychiatry, the equivalent of preventive medicine, is long overdue in business and industry.

Nine essential elements for a comprehensive mental health program:

1. Complete and thorough top management support. Not only does the psychiatrist need channels for upward influence, but top management's interest and acceptance is a necessary example for all employees throughout the corporate organization.

2. There must be an explicit statement of the strategy and objectives of the mental health program and the role of the psychiatrist in the program. This statement must be jointly agreed to by top management, the personnel department, the medical department, and the psychiatrist. There should be a good climate for communication. Often a forum for reevaluation and discussion is required for continual communication—problem employee seminars made up of management, labor, and medical personnel is one possibility.

3. There should be a procedure for the in-plant identification and referral of the emotionally ill employee to either the industrial physician or the in-plant psychiatrist. This normally involves the training of first-line supervision. Secondly, there should be a procedure for referral to psychiatric expertise for diagnosis—the psychiatrist may be full-time, part-time, or a consultant.

4. There should be provision for treatment—in the community clinics and hospitals for severe cases, and in-plant for minor emotional disturbance.

5. There should be a procedure, set by management in cooperation with the personnel and medical departments (and organized labor where it is pre-

sent) which provides for returning the ex-mental patient to the job for trial periods. Generally, no distinction should be made between physical and mental illness, and the employee's past mental illness must not be a barrier to future employment as long as his intelligence and skills have not been impaired. There must be a liaison between the community treatment facilities and the corporation; this is normally the joint responsibility of the psychiatrist and the industrial physician.

6. There must be a procedure by which, if the employee does not perform up to standards after rehabilitation, it will be possible to remove him from the job without reflection on management. There is a limit beyond which management cannot go in good faith without losing control over their own functions and being burdened by employees unable to perform. The medical personnel must never suggest that all emotionally ill employees can be salvaged.

7. There is the need for education and training programs for all employees designed to overcome the stigma associated with psychiatric care and to increase overall sophistication in the entire area of mental health.

8. Research on the results of the programs, the causation of emotional illness, the improvement of treatment techniques, and many other factors are a valuable part of a comprehensive program.

9. There must be provision for financing and administering the programs. Where will the programs be centered in the organization—the medical department, personnel department, or a separate staff function? How should labor participate?

On-Job Conflicts: Effects on Individual Performance

Effects of on-the-job interpersonal relations on emotional and physical stresses and strains and on individual effectiveness are coming into clearer focus.

Robert L. Kahn, Ph.D., director, Survey Research Center, Institute for Social Research, University of Michigan, and Sidney Cobb, M.D., and John R.F. French Jr., Ph. D., program directors at the institute, have written integrated papers on the subject.

Kahn cites a number of job-stress studies conducted among people representing the full range of employment from first-line supervisor to corporate officer in several organizations. Purpose was to explore the degree of conflict or harmony, ambiguity or clarity, in role requirements.

Kahn defines ambiguity as "the amount of information a person has and the amount he requires to perform his role completely." He associates this discrepancy with "dissatisfaction with the job, job-related threat, and low self-esteem."

Almost half of all the respondents report being "caught in the middle" between two conflicting persons or factions more or less frequently. Nine out of ten of those involved in conflicts note that at least one of the parties to the conflict is above them in the organization.

People complain that, while they are willing to meet the demands and expectations of others, even to acknowledge them as separately reasonable, they are unable to meet them simultaneously or within the prescribed time limits. "Qualitative and quantitative overload," observes Kahn, "must be differentiated—these forms of overload are clearly associated with symptoms of psychological and physiological strain."

Kahn suggests that persons experiencing a great deal of role conflict should be given the right to convene those who make excessive demands on them, confront them with the conflicting demands, and work out an acceptable solution.

Cobb divides responsibility into that primarily involving persons—their work schedules, their rewards, and their futures—and that involving things—money, equipment, and projects. The "people" responsibility is the one most likely to produce strain.

"We have modest evidence," the physician contends, "that responsibility for persons, particularly for people's futures, rather than for things, contributes to coronary disease risk among those who are overconscientious. Therefore, we might say that the conscientious person is encouraged to take on responsibility for people and their futures, is rewarded for it with increased status and income, and pays the price of increased risk of myocardial infarction."

Cobb discerns scattered evidence that diabetes, hypertension, and myocardial infarction as well as peptic ulcer are "unduly common among persons subject to heavy, close personal responsibility for the lives of other people. . . . Further investigation will be required before we can be sure that responsibility is the central problem because it is commonly associated with work overload which may well contribute in its own right to the health problems noted."

French studied managerial stress in six large companies. Managers who suffer from a lack of clarity about job scope and responsibilities experience lower satisfaction and higher tension than do those not subjected to such ambiguity. The same failings are attributable to role conflict—people torn by conflicting demands or who hold opinions different from those of their superiors, and by those who have either work overloads or underloads.

Discussing the relation between job stress and individual strain, French enumerates such factors as "the extent to which your superior is willing to listen to your problems, . . . the extent to which your superior has confidence in you and trusts you," and "the extent to which you can trust your superior and have confidence in him." Items measuring relations to the work group include "the extent to which persons are friendly and easy to approach, . . . the extent to which persons are willing to listen to your problems," and "the degree of cooperation in the group." The measure of relations with subordinates includes similar items and also mutual expectations with regard to the quantity and quality of work.

For men who have poor relations with their subordinates, there is a significant positive correlation between role ambiguity and serum cortisol. Diastolic blood pressure is related to work load but only among those who have poor relations with their immediate superiors. Relations with subordinates have even stronger conditioning effects on systolic and diastolic blood pressure and on serum glucose. There is a positive correlation between work load and smoking among men having poor relations with their superiors.

In many cases, French summarizes, "the effect of job stresses on individual strain is eliminated by the buffering effect of good supportive relations with one's superior, one's work group, and one's subordinates."

This psychologist submits six general conclusions that may be drawn from research by Kahn, Cobb, and himself:

1. Progress has been made in distinguishing between conflict and overload, between quantitative and qualitative overload, between responsibility for persons and for things as more specialized aspects of the work load.
2. Different measures have been developed for different stresses.
3. More differentiated and improved measures have paid off in new findings previously masked. In general, the hypothesis is supported that specific kinds of job stress interacting with specific personality characteristics result in specific psychological and physiological strains and psychosomatic diseases.
4. The goodness of fit between the characteristics of the person and those of his job will influence the effects of job stresses.
5. New measures of psychological and physiological strains and of disease entities have been added.
6. As more refined knowledge of the nature of role stresses and their effects is developed, researchers will be better able to design intervention programs to prevent their undesired effects on mental and physical health. Well underway is a study of the feasibility of reducing the risk of coronary heart disease by altering role stresses.

Taking out Guesswork of Costs of
Problem Employees

Much has been observed, spoken, and written about the high incidence of emotionally disturbed employees in business and industry. It is believed that:

- about one in four United States workers has a personality disturbance ranging from minor to major;
- at least half of the two million people in this country who are absent from work on any one day on account of sickness are suffering from some form of mental disability;
- from 80 to 90 percent of all accidents stem from psychological causes;
- more than two million American workers are problem drinkers;
- from 60 to 80 percent of all dismissals are due to emotional inadequacy and social maladjustment;
- annual economic costs of direct or indirect mental illness in the United States total at least $12 billion.

All such statistics, alarming as they are, are only estimates; actual costs have been difficult, if not impossible, to trace and pin down.

Now, for the first time, we have accurate measurements for taking out some of the guesswork in estimating costs of problem employees—employees whose emotional disturbances are reflected in loss of work, accidents, imperfect products, and other penalties inflicted on employers, themselves, and the community. Thanks for this socioeconomic contribution are due to a five-year, industrial mental health study, "Some Economic Estimates of Job Disruption."

The seven-page report was completed by a six-man team representing the Department of Psychiatry and the Department of Environmental Health, College of Medicine, University of Cincinnati, and Xavier University's Department of Economics.

The study, supported in part by a grant from the U. S. Public Health Service, was conducted by medical and social scientists in two companies—one employing three thousand; the other, six hundred—both white- and blue-collar workers.

Methods of calculating economic estimates are used for three matched samples of nineteen employees each. First sample shares evidence of excessive or frequent drinking. The two other samples are matched according to sociocultural background, age, marital status and number of children. The three samples are respectively designated: "Suspected problem drinking," "miscellaneous problem," and "problem-free."

The miscellaneous problem sample is chosen from a pool of employees with such problems as short- or long-term absenteeism, repeated accidents, manifestations of interpersonal friction or inefficiency on the job, or frequent visits to the medical department without evidence of problem drinking. The problem-free sample is obtained from a pool of employees considered by the personnel department to be free from work problems.

Two of the authors spent considerable time gaining a first-hand knowledge of the administration and accounting methods employed in each of the companies. They ferreted out hidden costs that could be related to various kinds of job-disruptive behavior.

For example, an employee involved in an accidental injury resulting in two days of lost time accrues a measurable cost to the company and himself. Not only does the company have to replace the employee for two days, but personnel time is involved in the medical department, administering medical aid and keeping records. Personnel time is also needed to record the incident and fill out the appropriate compensation claim forms, not to mention the salary loss to the employee, even if he is partly compensated by the Workmen's Compensation Bureau.

Problem drinking, it is indicated, is responsible for the greatest costs to industry. This is closely followed by miscellaneous problems.

Problem drinkers at the two firms cost a loss of $32,000 a year; miscellaneous problems, $31,000; problem-free employees, $16,000.

Some may be tempted to conclude immediately, the authors say, that the problem-drinking employee and other problem employees are too costly to be kept in the working group, that the wise solution would be to discover and dismiss them as soon as possible.

"Experience," they contend, "does not support this. It is very difficult to discover any but the most grossly impaired alcoholic, particularly if fellow employees and even supervisors know it is the policy of the company to dismiss problem-drinking employees upon discovery. A policy of this kind often results in the alcoholic being even more carefully hidden. If a company were to start a 'witch hunt' with these groups to decrease costs, it would eventually eliminate many valuable employees who might be in a temporary, reversible state of impairment and, as recent experience demonstrates, have a reasonably good chance of making a recovery."

Boredom Hits Both Executives
and Workers

Pity the poor, bored top executive who has to take work home with him every night!

So says James M. Roche, former chairman and chief executive officer, General Motors Corp. He claims "the blue-collar blues" is a long-time problem that afflicts almost every job in America—not only workers on the assembly line but also the top-echelon spots. "What's more boring," he asks, "than lugging home a big briefcase of papers to be read every night?"

Roche, sixty-eight (1975), started with GM at twenty-one as a statistician. He served as chairman from 1967 through 1971 and is still a director and member of the bonus and salary and finance committees. For his final year before retirement, GM paid him a salary and bonus of $550,000. The year before, the company had a bad profit performance due to a union strike. Roche, a victim of circumstances he was unable to control, lost his bonus and had to make do with $200,000 compared with the previous year's $600,000. In 1970, he was much more frustrated than bored.

A study by the Department of Health, Education, and Welfare estimates that only about three thousand workers in the United States are involved in company experiments seeking to counteract boredom and alienation. Among the employers are General Foods, AT&T, Polaroid, Texas Instruments, Corning Glass, and General Electric.

At a pet food plant of General Foods in Topeka, Kan., for instance, the sixty production workers get a chance to do every major job from unloading with a fork lift truck to making complex tests in the quality control laboratory. And they have been granted the latitude to decide, free of supervisors, how to apportion their time. In the two years the plan has been in operation, plant productivity has been 30 percent higher than that of a comparable facility without such a setup. Absenteeism averages 1 percent and turnover about 5 percent a year, considerably lower than elsewhere.

The same aim of making the work environment and the job itself more pleasant in the endeavor "to get better milk from more contented cows" is behind three and four-day work weeks generally running from thirty-five to forty hours. It is believed that more than fourteen hundred concerns in the fifty states have adopted programs of this nature. Riva Poor, who has studied the trend, finds that the four-day week has proved most attractive where two hundred or fewer employees are affected.

Group Health, Inc., nonprofit organization, was the first union shop in New York City to sponsor a shorter work week. A three-month trial period was extended to a full year in the light of a 20 percent drop in absenteeism and a 50 percent reduction in work errors among 750 employees. Most employees work four-day shifts, beginning Monday or Tuesday—nine hours a day the first three days, and eight hours the fourth, plus 45 minutes daily for lunch. For the thirty people in the electronic data processing section, there are two twelve-hour shifts, one eleven-hour shift, and then four days off.

U.S. Senator Jacob K. Javits addressed himself to the subject of industrial boredom in a talk before the Tax Section of the New York State Bar Association. He cited a HEW report on "Work in America" that "significant numbers of workers are dissatisfied with the quality of their working lives" and that "dull, repetitive, seemingly meaningless tasks, offering little challenge or autonomy, are causing discontent among workers at all occupational levels."

The report suggests that the redesign of jobs, resulting in greater humanization of work and greater potential for individual job-related growth, is vital for dealing effectively with this expanding alienation. Also enumerated as major goals are job security, economic rewards, and more leisure opportunities.

The New York Republican advised that "one of the proven ways of getting workers more involved with their jobs is by dovetailing employee profit-sharing and stock ownership plans with greater responsibility-sharing." He submitted alternatives for stimulating expansion of programs for broader worker incentives:

1. compulsory profit-sharing or employee stock arrangements;
2. tax incentives;
3. collective bargaining;
4. the "Kelso" proposal for transfering stock to an employees' trust, paid for by a loan to the trust from an outside lender.

"We must all recognize," Javits warned, "that improving worker morale is not just a matter of turning up the Muzak and fattening the paycheck."

Senator Edward M. Kennedy heads a group of lawmakers renewing a legislative effort to alleviate job boredom and dissatisfaction. A $20 million research program is proposed to investigate the problem and possible technical assistance to unions, companies, workers, and state and local governments.

Boredom has reached epidemic proportions if we are to believe a survey by *Today's Health* showing that from 60 to 80 percent of workers suffer from this ailment. A list of the "ten most boring jobs in the world" compiled by *Employee Relations Bulletin* singles out: assembly line workers, operators of self-service elevators, pool typists, bank guards, copying machine operators, keypunch operators, highway toll collectors, car watchers in tunnels, file clerks, and housewives.

Executive Tension Marks the Man, Not the Job

Executives in distribution fields feel they operate under excessive tension, that their job demands are continuously too heavy. But, perhaps, these yokes aren't really that burdensome: distribution executives sleep more soundly at night than any other group—or so they say.

These are findings of a survey on "Executive Tension in Business" conducted from February to September, 1971, by the Life Extension Institute among two thousand executives in distribution, production, personnel, administration-finance, sales, and other occupations.

Of the approximately 260 executives who report themselves under constant tension, 17.4 percent are in distribution. Following are 17.2 percent in production, 15.3 percent in personnel, and 13.6 percent in sales. Slightly under 9 percent of the distribution executives complain about their job demands. The next highest figure is a little over 8 percent for personnel executives.

Comparing the current study with a similar one it completed in 1958, the institute finds those describing themselves under excessive tension to be about the same number in the two periods—12.9 percent in 1971, 13.3 percent in 1958. Interestingly, LEI now takes a different stance about results. The 1958 report ended on a positive note—gratification that 87 percent of the executives were not under excessive tension. In the 1971 report, the reverse side of the coin is stressed—"Management should ask itself: is 13 percent of the executive population under severe tension a tolerable figure?"

Some differences between the two groups:

In 1958, the survey asked: "Is there someone with whom you work whom you would like to 'drop off a bridge'?" The replies: 18.2 percent, yes: 81.8 percent, no. In 1971, a similar question, "Do you work with some people whom you dislike intensely?" elicited responses of 20.7 percent, yes; 58.9 percent, no; 20.3 percent, neutral.

In 1958, the survey asked: "Do you feel your superior is stealing all the glory while you do all the work?" The replies: 5.6 percent, yes; 94.4 percent, no. In 1971, the question, "Does your superior often take credit away from you?" drew these answers: 11.1 percent, yes; 70.3 percent, no; 18.5 percent, neutral.

In 1958, 6.2 percent felt they were not getting enough recognition. In 1971, this percentage advanced to 9.4 percent, and was 13.3 percent for personnel executives.

In 1958, 85 percent said their jobs were secure. In 1971, only 68 percent were that positive.

In 1958, only 6.5 percent were dissatisfied with the progress they were making in their jobs. In 1971, this figure jumped to 39.5 percent.

In 1958, 82.1 percent said their wife's attitude toward their career was encouraging and helpful. This percentage declined to 72.8 in 1971.

In 1958, 89 percent claimed they had no difficulty getting to sleep, and 86.6 percent slept an average of seven hours or more each night. In 1971, only 60.7 percent have no difficulty in getting to sleep, and only 70 percent average seven hours or more sleep. Practically the same percentage (3.3 percent now versus 3.2 percent) admit taking sedatives.

In 1958, 10 percent regularly had cocktails at lunch. This has risen by about 50 percent.

Slightly over 36 percent of the 1958 respondents had a regular predinner cocktail. This has risen to 48.7 percent.

In 1958, 47.3 percent smoked cigarettes, two-third of them over a pack a day. This figure has dropped to 30.3, but again two-thirds smoke more than a pack a day.

Underlying causes of excessive tension are attributed to the man, not the job. LEI's comment:

"The incidence of tension varies so widely among occupations that no significant pattern can be established on the basis of these characteristics—creative, analytical, personal contact, multiple responsibilities."

Among those who report constant tension, boredom with the job is 355 percent greater than among those reporting little or no tension; job insecurity, 174 percent greater; dissatisfaction with business progress, 155 percent greater; dislike of business entertainment, 59.2 percent greater; aversion to business travel, 44.7 percent greater; distaste of business homework, 31.5 percent greater. And 60 percent of the high-tension group would like to retire at age fifty-five.

Fear of self-expression is 633 percent greater among the group under constant tension than the others.

One out of five of the men in the high-tension group get no recreation whatsoever. Eighteen percent have no hobbies.

The survey shows that seven out of every ten men under constant tension report some significant personal problem. About 175 percent more of the high-tension group than the others have office problems, and 75 percent of these have business personality conflicts.

The institute concludes tension is not caused by age, occupation or job demands but "is clearly identified with the personality of the individual executive and stems from within the man rather than from the outer forces of his living or working environment."

On balance, LEI believes "the popular concept of the harassed, ulcer-ridden, overworked executive is a myth."

Four Types of Rigid Executives Have Anxiety Problems

People need other people as much as they need food, water, and air. Yet, everyone has problems relating to people. Everyone wants to get close to others but is afraid of being hurt. Everyone needs intimate, confidential relationships but is afraid to let others come too close because they may reject or take advantage of him. These desires, doubts, and fears are completely normal and everyone has them. But some people have stronger doubts and fears than others and, in consequence, usually behave rather rigidly. Which is where a universal problem really assumes hard-to-handle proportions.

There are three "very different" ways of solving the problem, according to psychologist Alan N. Schoonmaker who argues: A man can move toward people (dependency), move away from them (aloofness) or move against them (hostility). Most people lean toward one approach but are flexible enough to use all three at different times. The people who are most anxious and rigid rely almost exclusively on one method. They form four well-known executive types: "The tough guy who moves against people, the nice guy who moves toward them, and the gypsy and loner who moves away from them. Although they use different methods, they all began with the same feeling, and they all end with the same problem—loneliness." Schoonmaker describes the four types:

The Tough Guy. "I'm not paid to be popular. I'm paid to get production, and I've got to push my men to get it." Two standard questions may be asked to find out what causes this executive's toughness: Is he aggressive, domineering, and autocratic when these attitudes are obviously inappropriate? Does this kind of conduct cause problems with other people—problems he ignores? If he bullies everyone, he is probably exhibiting the rigidity of defensive behavior, even if he ruins his career or home life. The rationally tough executive is much more flexible. He may be tough on the job but gentle with his wife and children, or tough when subordinates make mistakes but understanding when they have personal problems.

The Nice Guy. "My group gets good production because we work well together, and we work well together because we like each other." The defensively nice executive will be friendly even when he should be firm or tough. He will avoid criticizing a subordinate who needs criticism, let his desire for popularity reduce his unit's efficiency, give overly generous performance ratings and salary increases, or retain incompetent subordinates. His behavior is therefore as rigid, ineffective, and defensive as the defensively tough executive's. Fortunately, the extreme type of "nice guy" rarely becomes an executive. Many executives, however, have some of these characteristics.

The Loner. "I can think better and get more done when I work on my own. Besides, I don't have time for office politics and gossip." His aloofness protects him; it also makes him feel lonely. Usually, he prefers loneliness to involvement.

The Gypsy. "I know people say I move around too much, but each time I've changed jobs I've moved up. And getting ahead is what this ballgame is all about." Most gypsies, especially the very defensive ones, change many other things in addition to their jobs. Some have been married two or three times or have had several love affairs. Many change houses, cars, or hobbies regularly, always ready to try something new. Whenever such a person finds himself becoming too attached to something, he becomes anxious, breaks away and tries again. He is trapped in a vicious circle and can't get out.

Schoonmaker breaks down these four executive types into seven other categories: the puritan, the rebel, the optimist, the pessimist, the drinker, the conformist and the go-getter. How each class views itself:

The Puritan. "I am paid to work, not to fool around. If other people would take life more seriously, we would all be better off."

The Rebel. "Rules aren't sacred. If I can do my job better and help the company by breaking a few rules, I'll do it."

The Optimist. "I may make some mistakes by being optimistic, but it is the only way to be. It helps me to solve problems other men wouldn't even touch, and it keeps up my group's morale."

The Pessimist. "I think people should be more careful. Most men make mistakes by rushing into things without even knowing what they are getting into. I have saved the company a lot of money by being careful."

The Drinker. "Don't worry about me. I can hold my liquor. And a couple of drinks help me think better."

The Conformist. "I follow the rules because, in a company like this, there would be chaos if everyone did what he wanted to do."

The Go-Getter. "When I entered the business world, I swore I would make it to the top, and I'm not going to let anything stop me."

Well-Rounded Man Is a
Management Myth

Peter F. Drucker, the management professor and consultant, is not convinced there is—or need be—more stress in a large organization than in a little one, in a big metropolitan area than in a small town. Executives, to him, are just like other human beings subject to the stresses of the world we live in.

Some other views of this iconoclastic business advisor:

All the talk about the well-rounded man, the whole man, the mature person, is in tones of disrespect and contempt. These are just euphemisms for "I have no use for human beings." They merely make people products of a machine.

Historically, management knows only one way to recognize people: promote them to executive and administrative positions. But a great majority of people don't want to be managers. Many people are highly schooled, but that doesn't necessarily mean they're highly trained.

It would have been sheer horror for Albert Einstein to have been the principal of a junior high school. And who would think of making a junior high school principal head of the Institute for Advanced Studies at Princeton? A good tax accountant should keep on achieving in the field he knows best. If he's a good tax accountant, he shouldn't have to get along with people and probably wouldn't make a good manager. We're taking too many chemists and making them research directors. We need more research men.

Only thing in universal supply is incompetence. Of that, there is no shortage. The enormous number of tests to select people are useful only in ascertaining the most obvious misfits.

Much as we need managers, we're overstaffed with men who coordinate and understaffed with men who do the work.

A man can be useful in one job and wrong in another. If he is patently misplaced, he should not be retained in it. It's not kindness but cowardice to leave him where he is. This is responsible for hurting, maiming, paralyzing, destroying more people than anything else we do.

The worst thing a man can do is to try to be someone else. There's nothing worse than the controller who tries to be affable at the company picnic, or the executive who's one of the boys at the Christmas party.

A man reaches the top by being task-focused, not people-focused. The village elder, the wise man of the tribe, the father confessor is a role outside the work environment. The relationship of manager and subordinate should not be confused with that of therapist and patient. The manager is not qualified to carry out a job that should be done by a psychologist or psychiatrist. If the professional is not available, better it shouldn't be done at all. Beware of the boss with self-assumed insight. You can't build an essentially clinical relationship into a work-oriented relationship. The attempt on the part of the boss to be an analyst is a drive for power, slightly camouflaged. Managers who try to be lay psychoanalysts can do real harm.

The job of a manager or administrator is to make a man a little stronger, a little straighter, a little more secure than he would be on his own. People learn most, are developed most, by superiors who expect subordinates to perform on their own, who help if needed but don't take over the work. Best results are where relations are cool, not warm. But don't ever be nasty, brutal, or blind.

An organization shouldn't generate any more stress than any other part of a person's environment. It should be a tool to prevent a whole class of stresses. Why not seek to assuage the stress in business and the professions? Why not seek to find out how the organization can best use the strengths of a man for his individual achievement?

11

STRESS AND DISTRESS

Each Man Has His Own Breaking Point

Different persons react to the same pressures in different ways. Each of us can take varying amounts of pressure without cracking.

But each of us has his own breaking point—a certain line deep within our physical and psychological beings that, once breached, triggers the danger signs.

Hundreds of influences are brought into play—heredity (inborn pluses and minuses), environment (personality traits acquired that help counter or make one prey to stresses), as well as such related factors as intelligence, self-evaluation, and diet. Truth is, doctors are less surprised by the number of people who crack under pressure than the fact that many more don't buckle under physical and emotional strains.

Bearing in mind that we begin to age the minute we are born, it should come as no surprise that the middle-aged man is not the specimen he was at twenty, twenty-five, thirty, or thirty-five. This vital fact he must interpret realistically—by how much work and other stresses he can tolerate or endure, what and how much he eats, drinks, and smokes.

At age forty to forty-five, certain normal changes occur—a man grows more obese, his skin tends to dry, he becomes aware of symptoms in his heart and blood-vessel mechanism and other organs, or thinks he does. He can't work from ten to twelve hours a day with relative ease as he used to. He is increasingly subject to fatigue. With added years come added actual or fancied ailments. During the critical period of life—from forty to sixty—worry should be minimized, relaxation emphasized. A good measure of all-round health at this point is whether the individual reacts to these changes with equanimity or alarm.

Outside relaxation should not be confined to weekends and occasional vacations. You should give up singles in tennis and handball and other strenuous, competitive games. Even in golf, fretting over your poor play—or your partner's—may more than overcome fresh air benefits. Ask yourself whether you are on the golf course to raise your income, or lower your score, or—what you should be there for—just to enjoy yourself.

Follow more noncompetitive sports and hobbies—swimming, fishing, horseback riding, gardening, painting, photography, carpentry, bricklaying, playing a musical instrument, stamp or coin collecting. And participate actively in public affairs and social work. When all is said and done, though, the best exercise a man in the "dangerous age" range can take is to push himself away from the table.

Whether in business or in private life, the neurotic competitor is readily identifiable: he's so busy putting on an act that he's as good as ever, he's ashamed to reveal any weakness, he mustn't give in.

Many diseases and disabilities can't be prevented, but their complications can be averted or delayed. With early diagnosis and proper treatment, people in general can be helped to live a happier, healthier, longer life. Severe economic loss to patient, family, and community could be reduced, and valuable executives retained at the peak of efficiency, trained workers at the height of productivity.

Management shares an essential role with medicine, voluntary and public agencies, and research institutions in applying known solutions or palliatives to specific instances of physical and emotional problems.

One Man's Stress Is Another's Stimulus

A widely held concept of hard-driving executives is that of men contributing more than their fair share of candidates for a heart attack in their forties and fifties.

It should be clearly understood, however, that there are numerous exceptions to this popular image. It isn't necessarily true at all that a high-strung individual won't live as long as the placid person. Stress is not automatically incompatible with sound health. One man's stress and strain is another's stimulus, motivation, even pleasure.

Many executives tackle one tough problem after another, manage to take all in stride, whether they conquer these or not. Because they are flexible, well-adjusted to themselves as well as to others, they rebound with undiminished vitality from stresses that might leave others with migraine headaches, upset stomachs, or other neurotic aftereffects. They prove that hard work, of itself, is not harmful for any normal person, but that a man's reaction to it may be. Their tension helps them function at top capacity and achieve results commensurate with talent—theirs and that of their colleagues and subordinates.

Executives who really know and do their jobs are too big to devote themselves to the earnestness of being important. Whether it is money, power, or prestige, or a combination of these, that makes them run, they have learned to live with occupational obstacles. They know enough to slow down before they blow up.

The man on top in more than name only is often able to carry his workload well because he has an understanding family, a wife who has matured with her husband, who senses when to leave him alone and when to help persuade him to taper off.

The fact remains that stress is too nebulous an influence to permit a definite opinion on its cause-and-effect relationship to physical and emotional ailments. Actually, there is no conclusive medical evidence that the pace of modern living inevitably results in coronaries, that no previous generation had it as bad in this respect. After all, the possibility of being scalped by Indians must have caused the original white settlers of this nation considerable stress and strain.

Occupation is no guide. Nor, for that matter, is whether the man be president or porter. There just is no clear pattern of a personality type more susceptible to heart failure or cerebral hemorrhage than any other.

Dr. Marvin Stern, NYU professor of psychiatry; Dr. Marcel Tuchman, NYU professor of clinical medicine; Dr. Norman H. Martin, professor of management, NYU Graduate School of Business Administration; and Dr. Jeremiah Stamler, former director of the Division of Adult Health and Aging, Chicago Board of Health, former director of the board's Heart Disease Control Program, now with Northwestern University in similar work, spoke at a conference on "Executive Stress: The Individual and Job."

STERN: People who get depressed are generally of an unyielding type. They are often middle-aged persons who realize they're not what they used to be and aren't going anywhere. Tensions may be evidenced in headaches, eye trouble, pains at the back of the neck. These may be reflected in lack of sleep and, then, appetite disturbance. Have you noticed how alert your people are when they come to work in the morning? Narcotization—alcohol, barbiturates, and other drugs—may be relied on as a relief of symptoms. Alcohol seems to work for a time. It may take ten years to find clinical effects of heavy drinking. Effects of barbiturates are much more rapid.

TUCHMAN: The state of stress is vital to every phase of our lives. The factor of stress, of itself, is not enough to produce disease. A small minority are immediately susceptible by virtue of genetic heritage, personality traits, and an environmental situation conducive to development of diseases of the gastro-intestinal or other systems subject to stress.

MARTIN: Knowledge of exactly what a man's position and status are is a major reason for stress. The top executive has a many-sided job which he performs in a goldfish bowl. Everybody's dependent on him, and he's dependent on subordinates and on the public at large. But, in the final analysis, his is the position of responsibility. He is the author of the direction taken by, and destiny of, his organization, a society of individuals to whom he is tied. Through his lack of action and decisions, blunders are made, and corners are entered into. He must be sure his successes are greater than his failures. He can turn only to himself for ultimate guidance. The art or science of management is such that he has no clear mandates. This is the executive role, and that's why executives are paid as much as they are.

STAMLER: Organic illnesses—coronary artery and atherosclerotic diseases—are no more frequent in executives than in the population in general. It's a myth that these are diseases of executives. Seventy percent of all deaths are heart-related or due to cancer. Similarly, peptic ulcers are incorrectly called executive diseases.

There is a difference in the incidence of these diseases as they affect men and women; and this applies to male and female executives. For one woman, there are twenty men before ages forty to forty-five who suffer a coronary disease or heart attack. The difference lessens gradually thereafter.

At Du Pont, a ten-year study, constantly updated, shows the top-executive echelon has the lowest coronary incidence rate. The difference between the top executives and others is small—15 to 20 percent. Coronary diseases are still the No. 1 health problem of executives.

Premature coronary disease tends to run in families. If it doesn't in yours, watch out for such factors as diet, smoking, alcoholism, diabetes, high cholesterol, hypertension, marked obesity (25 to 30 percent above your most desirable weight), and sedentary living—habits, traits, and abnormalities that lead to increased likelihood to develop coronary disease before age sixty-five.

Regular, frequent, and progressively intensive exercise is good for an executive, but by itself, it won't buy a lot of coronary prevention. It's good in combination with other positive factors.

It isn't enough to detect the abnormality of disease early. Something must be done about it. Treatment must be started. It's possible to change the risk factor, and the incidence rate of the disease can also be influenced.

Do Executives Take Enough Vacation?

Thirty percent of companies surveyed by Arthur Young & Co., the accounting firm, have special vacation schedules for executives. Fifty-three percent of the executives are required to take their vacation. Most companies require that the vacation time due be taken in the same year; it cannot be accumulated. As a control mechanism, the banking industry makes it mandatory that four weeks be taken—two weeks at a time at different periods.

Executives' vacations are getting longer—more than 75 percent of the surveyed companies give four or five weeks of vacation. Vacations after minimum service: two weeks, 2 percent; three weeks, 10 percent; four weeks, 45 percent; five weeks, 38 percent; six weeks, four percent; over six weeks, 1 percent.

Many businessmen claim they take short vacations because they prefer them to long, uninterrupted holidays. Some are afraid they'd be missing something if they stayed away too long. Others "start climbing the walls" after a few days of idleness.

Rodney D. Strong, chairman and chief executive of Sonoma Vineyards, says: "I like my work and I really hate to be away too long. After the fifth day, I start climbing the walls. A friend of mine just left on a six-week cruise. I'd have to be drugged to do that." Instead, Strong takes some long weekends and extra days throughout the year and usually takes some paper work along with him.

John R. Beckett, chairman and president, Transamerica Corp., cites a practical reason for limiting his vacations to just one week at a time. He asserts that the work piling up in his absence forms "an almost psychological barrier" to staying away any longer. William A. Marquard, chairman, American Standard, leaves on long weekends and sometimes a one-week vacation devoted mostly to tennis and golf. He points out, "I can relax fairly quickly. A four-day weekend is great and, if I can do that three times each summer, it's enough. After the fourth day, I start to get itchy."

Fletcher Byrom, chairman, Koppers Co., says he urges his subordinates "to take all their officially allotted time, but I don't think they ever do. Most of us enjoy our work so much we don't feel the need for it." As for himself, he thinks he's "officially" entitled as chairman to four or five weeks of annual vacation, but he reports he's never come close to taking that much time off.

Dr. Richard Call, medical director, Union Oil Co., believes regular vacations of at least two weeks are "absolutely necessary to break the pace." Executives who fail to do this "run the risk of ruining their health." He advises company executives to travel at least one hundred miles away from their headquarters. "Any closer," he suggests, "there's a great temptation to call in every day, check the mail, and worry about not being there." This medical director admits he has had only limited success in enforcing his opinion on Union Oil executives.

Dr. Jonas Cohler, New York psychoanalyst, submits that company-sponsored trips or even an afternoon tennis match with office colleagues are not good substitutes for real vacations. He argues that "so long as an executive is among his colleagues, he's onstage and can't really let his hair down and relax." His recommended alternative is at least a two-week vacation away from business associates. "Most companies," Cohler observes, "know this but pay only lip service to the idea. In fact, they do nothing to help their people relax. It seems they'd rather burn them out quickly and then replace them with someone else."

Stress, Anxiety May Be Okay but Watch Out for Panic

"Stress" and "anxiety" are two words the layman thinks of in negative terms. Yet, applied in proper amount, each can be healthful. "Panic," which is at the opposite end of the spectrum from "anxiety," is something else again; it's the real trouble-maker.

This is the advice of Dr. John McCann, president and medical director, Life Extension Institute. Before joining LEI in 1971, he was chief of the aerospace medicine group in the life sciences section of the Convair division of General Dynamics and director of the parent firm's health, safety and security. For twenty-four years previously, he was with the U.S. Air Force Medical Corps.

The tall, friendly industrial physician, whose sixty-year-old organization serves fifty thousand executives each year in six New York and California facilities, says, "Stress gives a person a real zest for life. Without stress, the heart deteriorates. Applied in proper amount, it lends strength and vigor to the entire body."

McCann finds that breakdowns are "pretty nearly spread over the general population." This, despite the presumption that the men and women who come to LEI are in management jobs and equipped to handle physical and emotional problems better than the general run of people.

In this day and age, says McCann, "the major threat confronting us all is chronic disease." Apparently, this is the penalty for a life expectancy that has increased since the beginning of the century from about age forty to about the mid-seventies. The doctor points out that life span and life expectancy aren't the same—"Life span hasn't changed since the beginning of recorded history."

Gradual physical decline starting in childhood is not apparent to the casual observer, according to McCann. He reports that average peak capability of vision and hearing occurs before the teens, that resistance to disease reaches its peak in the early teens, muscular development in the mid-twenties, and peak intelligence at twenty-one.

Congenital defects, infectious diseases, and accidents account for most deaths into the teens. From thirty-five to fifty-five, arteriosclerotic heart disease is the number one enemy, and it remains so into the seventies. This is followed by cirrhosis of the liver, motor vehicle accidents, and lesions. Other major killers in middle age are pneumonia, tumors, rheumatic heart disease, and emphysema. Suicide from early teens to age sixty-four, as a result of failure to cope with stresses of day-to-day life, always falls in the ten chief causes of death.

On an individual basis, McCann observes, there can be a marked difference in the physiological and appraisal ages of persons in the identical chronological age.

A number of conditions identify with coronary disease. They are heredity, age, sex, cigarette smoking, high blood pressure, high level of blood fats, stress, overweight, and lack of exercise. Heredity, age, and sex cannot be altered. But it means that, if you are a man between forty-five and sixty-five, your chances of a heart attack are much greater than for a woman in the same age range. It is widely regarded as more than coincidental that heart disease has been increasing during the same period that Americans are riding more and walking less. Yet, doctors concede that 75 percent of the reasons for heart attacks are still unknown.

Ten years after the Surgeon General of the U.S. issued a report citing cigarette smoking as a major hazard to life and health, cigarette sales are at a record, per capita consumption is rising, and three thousand teenagers are becoming new smokers each day. The ranks of smokers have increased from fifty million in 1964 to fifty-two million today. Forty percent of men and 30 percent of women are smokers.

Smoking and alcohol, McCann asserts, "are two bad habits men have passed on to women. Changing living habits of females, formerly believed to be relatively free of heart and other lethal ailments in midlife, have caused women to take on the same kind of health profile as males."

On the favorable side, the LEI head contends, "The cigarette and cigar have almost completely disappeared from corporate boardrooms."

McCann says, "The exercise nut doesn't have any measurable advantage over others who are physically active—who walk two to three miles a day, climb stairs, work in the yard, participate in some sort of sport. But the

individual who denies himself any physical exertion is asking for something."
Other McCann thoughts:

- A continuum of growth and aging is constantly with us. Each phase in life has its particular rewards. Without question, some depressing things occur when a man realizes he can't do some of the things he did ten or fifteen years ago, when his libido begins to fade out.
- The man who hasn't gone through a good emotional maturation period through his life is affected in middle age. He becomes quite frightened when he knows there are fewer years ahead of him than behind him, when his ability to influence and alter his future has become extremely limited, when his way of life is "pretty much poured into concrete."
- Ten to 15 percent of the population will either periodically or even permanently develop habits or mental problems that will prevent them from coping. The man or woman who turns to excessive use of alcohol, who becomes inordinately depressed, who loses his or her drive and enthusiasm to participate in life—these are all phases of panic.
- Panic is not a single isolated occurrence. It is the constant inability to deal with problems, to the extent that depression that is really panic sets in. Depression has been characterized as "the common cold of mental illness."
- It's not proper to categorize a particular group of men and say they have a predilection for certain kinds of diseases or a particular immunity.
- The fact that a man has reached the top may be an indication he can handle stress better than blue-collar workers can. One of the hallmarks of a successful rise is that many executives have learned how to manage stresses that lead to breakdown in the body system. They give ulcers, they don't get them.
- The man on the assembly line or in an office can get stomach ulcers as much as can the executive. The man at the bottom of the economic ladder who is trying to make both ends meet is very likely under as much stress as one who is managing a large company.

Executives are certainly subject to domestic problems as much as are rank-and-file workers.

McCann puts the sexual problem in perspective:

"The male continues to produce viable sperm right up to eighty or ninety. The difference is between the male aging sexually and the female who loses her ability to re-create herself. Both go through psychic changes. The female in her early forties who approaches menopause senses this emotionally and quite often reacts by exhibiting an increased amount of sexual activity. This is the reason for a fair amount of children being born during the woman's early 40s. The woman wants to exercise one last urge to be a mother.

"After menopause, the woman may wind up with a partner who has experienced the male climacteric and can't quite fulfill her demands and needs. There is a great need of mutual understanding of the physical changes they're both going through. When they let panic in, then they begin to decompensate.

"Anxiety can be defined as the first time you can't rise up to the requirements for seconds, sexually speaking. Panic is the second time you can't come up for firsts."

Raising Questions Is 50 Percent of Management's Battle

Like the human animal in general, the manager is neither rational nor irrational but a mixture. How do we mobilize the rational part for greater achievement?

Merely raising questions—about relationships, about resolving dilemmas, what is my effect on the other man's behavior—is 50 percent of management's battle. One question never to be asked: "Why the hell aren't you doing what I want?"

Stress isn't necessarily a bad thing; it can be good. But when the resultant anxiety is overwhelming, and there's no escape, remember the axiom: when the kitchen gets too hot, get out of the kitchen.

These were some of the provocative thoughts Dr. Roy Menninger left with executives, management consultants, and others attending the New York University conference on "Executive Stress: The Individual and the Job." Menninger is director of preventive psychiatry and co-director of the School of Mental Health, Menninger Foundation. He is the third generation of his family in psychiatry.

Scheduled to speak on "Sources of Mental Stress for the Administrator on the Job," Menninger chose not to make a conventional address. Rather, he engaged the audience in a "dialogue"—he threw out questions, opened the floor for comment, and gave his views when he felt these were in order. To his query: "What constitutes the sources of mental stress?," various participants replied:

- Union negotiations—stressful conditions arising from alternating criticisms both from the union and from associates "who feel I'm giving away the possibility of ever being profitable; no matter what I do is unacceptable."
- There is the challenge from below—the manager is always worried about the guy down the line who's trying to undermine his efforts.
- "Is my competency recognized? Or is competency enough to develop in the organization?"
- Dilemma of persuasion versus coercion.
- Problem of the younger executive's relationship to older people under him.
- Strong sense of responsibility for people working for him and for their

families. "We feel we're carrying the whole world, as if we were a father concerned about our children."

• Unrealistic demands from above or outside. "It is part of the mythology of management that achievement is based on unrealistic demands. . . . Plain fear of retaliation, losing an account, being fired keep managers from saying it can't be done."

• There are no more autocrats. The executive has responsibility but not power. He's not independent and he's not self-sufficient. He has shifting problems in trying to keep the ship above water.

Menninger's advice on the "father-son" syndrome in business:

"Subordinates bear a symbolic representation to the way a son thinks of his father. But the symbol is not the reality. There's a hidden danger of paternalism that places people in a position of infantilism. The executive shouldn't wonder why people aren't grateful for placing them in this position. It is the executive who takes the totalitarian view who is the most insecure. He can't tolerate having men grow up to be as good as he is. It's believed but not true that all psychiatrists say you have to love every son of a bitch. But there are limits. The problem is to find the mature way to deal with subordinates that is somewhere in between the extremes."

"The little child in us keeps us quiet in discussing issues. Neither the boss —the King of the Mountain—nor his subordinates wants to risk loss of love. Instead, there's supplicating, conforming, fawning."

On the all-importance of how executives' relations impinge upon others in the environment:

"Ninety-nine percent of an executive's stress comes from his relationships to himself and to others. The executive must first ask himself why something wasn't done and then carry his search for what is wrong to the other persons affected. But the executive's inclination is to look for plausible explanations outside himself."

On whether a myth of invincibility attaches to being an executive:

"Lives and experiences of men cause them to internalize thinking, to develop self-mechanisms, to count on their ability to perceive and their sense of values and, finally, to resort to independent action. Isolation is the price they pay. They've got to match performance with aspirations. Once problems are solved, demands are escalated."

On various kinds of executives:

"There is the autocrat who answers questions as to whether his performance is up to his aspirations with 'By all means, and let there be no doubt about it.' There is the egalitarian executive who worries too much, who feels failure of performance to meet aspirations is his fault."

In conclusion, Menninger said:

Ask yourself the questions: "What am I in the business? What am I after?

You will have made tremendous strides merely by asking the questions. If you can go a step farther and get some answers, you're well on your way to handling stress—the stress of making the demand and the stress of obtaining compliance."

World of Difference between Occupational Stress, Distress

There's a world of difference between healthful occupational stress and harmful distress. Without some degree of stress, there would be little productivity and, almost certainly, there would be boredom. When stress becomes distress, the individual is in real trouble. Yet, so much confusion prevails on this score in psychiatric-psychological circles, as well as among laymen, that it might be wise to strike the word "stress" in its present loose meaning from the lexicon of science.

This is the advice of Alan A. McLean, clinical associate professor of psychiatry at New York Hospital-Cornell Medical Center's Westchester division, head of the division's Center for Occupational Mental Health and, eastern area medical director, IBM.

Until several years ago, this industrial psychiatrist was "relatively comfortable" with the negative concept of stress—a disruption of equilibrium creating fear, anxiety, and mental and physical health hazards; reactions from moving up in management, obsolescence of skills with advancing age, outside problems reflected in a man's work, and other adverse influences. He held a concept, not far apart from that of many of his colleagues, that stress is any work-related factor producing faulty adaptation in an individual. Stress, by that definition, includes effects on job performance and interpersonal relationships as well as psychosomatic disorders.

Now, however, "my faith in this simplistic set of notions has been shaken. Both the term 'stress' and its relationship to adaptation at work are used by different authors in such widely varying ways as to suggest we abandon the word entirely. At the very least, each writer should be forced to clearly define his use of the term. I am reminded of the old computer concept 'garbage in, garbage out.' There is a tremendous amount of garbage in the literature—a great deal of fuzzy thinking."

He now thinks "stress," particularly "occupational stress," should be extended to a very broad class of problems—"any demands that tax the system whatever it is, physiological, social, or psychological, and the response of that system must be included. Each discipline must develop its own terms to refer to the specific concepts of its own analysis. Each researcher and clinician must define his frame of reference and his terms in such manner as to be intelligible to those in his professional audience unfamiliar with what has gone before in his discipline. Clarity, definition, and exposure; cross-pollination and acceptance of these differing concepts as deeply held values are necessary if we are to further our task."

Perhaps, McLean suggests, the concept of stress will remain useful in the same general sense as the concept of infection. But, by the same token that no specialist in infectious diseases would be satisfied to diagnose a patient as simply having an infection, it should no longer be sufficient to say a patient is suffering from social stress or that a particular environment is stressful.

McLean quotes Dr. H. Beric Wright, British specialist in problems of executive health, and others who have noted that "the term 'stress' derives from engineering and implies an inherent capacity to resist or stand up to a defined amount of strain. Increasing the loading on a girder beyond a certain point will inevitably bend it. Individuals, too, have their breaking point and, if this is exceeded, they will also bend or break."

Wright calls this "a complicated situation in which the individual's reaction is the final common pathway between his training, attributes, and personality and the various specific and cultural pressures that the environment—work, home, and community—are putting on him." The British physician is concerned that this approach leads to the total neglect of the beneficial aspects of stress.

McLean also cites Dr. Graham C. Taylor, Canadian industrial psychiatrist: "We think of stress as something that is harmful or deleterious to performance and, in general, we wish to eliminate it. However, we would do well to note that stress is often accompanied by, and indeed may be a necessary part of, the process of change and growth. It is a paradox that many of our actions are designed to reduce stress, but consider what would result if we achieved all our goals and eliminated all of stress. When the stress factor is nonexistent, we are dead."

A demonstration by Lennart Levi, director of stress research, Karolinska Institute, Stockholm, Sweden, shows that stress, as defined by Wright and Taylor, increases during pleasant emotional reactions such as laughter and sexual arousal. Moreover, many individuals deliberately seek stress in the form of adventure, excitement, challenge, and opponents worthy of their steel and seem to enjoy it. Clearly, McLean finds, "stress may very well occur and, consequently, the rate of wear and tear on the organism may increase even when the individual experience is a pleasant emotional reaction. The immediate effects are also desirable from the viewpoint of society such as in the case of great devotion to work."

For the interests of all concerned, McLean concludes, all the disciplines, working together, must distinguish between the physiological reaction pattern that is stress and the psychological syndrome that is distress.

To the question: "Does boredom, frustration come with greater leisure time?", he contented himself with the succinct reply, "Not necessarily."

What effect does our changing lives have on our ability to take it? His answer:

"Change is a common denominator of stress. The pace of change, at least as a generalization, tends to be stressful. More people react to change and, presumably, there is then a greater incidence of psychiatric disorders. Reflecting varying personality makeups, the ways people take it don't change. There will always be people who look at the world through rose-colored glasses, others with a chip on their shoulder, some who get sick, others who stay healthy, some for whom certain things are stressful, others for whom things are not."

Hypertension—excessively high blood pressure—affects at least twenty million Americans and is a factor in the deaths of three-quarters of a million people annually. Yet, most people with hypertension don't know they have it. Various pressure-lowering drugs, diet and exercise may bring the blood pressure back into a normal range.

The trend toward heart attacks in young men has been increasing steadily during the past twenty years. The coronary death rate for men between twenty-five and forty-four has gone up 14 percent in that period. For those between forty-five and sixty-four, the mortality rate has rise by 4 percent during the same period. Some 176,000 of the 675,000 Americans who will succumb to coronaries this year will be under sixty-five.

"Strategy of Living" with Anxiety, Fear, Ambition, Envy

What would you do if a doberman pinscher advanced threateningly on you? Would you start running and probably get bitten in a mad effort to escape the dog's fangs? Or would you relax, show no fear, and tame the dog into submissiveness?

Just as these questions apply to dog vs. man, they also apply to man vs. man. When panicky employee meets panicky boss, the results can be catastrophic.

The parallel is drawn by Dr. Ari Kiev, head of the Cornell Program in Social Psychiatry, Cornell University Medical College, New York, and a clinical associate professor of psychiatry at the college. He is also in private practice.

Major stresses of humans, this specialist in "people problems" observes, are stresses of human relations and communications—the management of people—rather than anxieties specifically attributable to business and economics.

This long-held opinion of his has been confirmed by a mail survey he conducted among 150 top executives of companies on Fortune's "500" list. More than fifty personal, in-depth interviews were held with executives in the New York–New Jersey–Connecticut metropolitan area. Kiev sought to find out the nature of stress in various types of business organizations; how presidents with ostensibly successful careers cope with or break under stress, and whether these experiences are applicable to other people. Underlying all this was an attempt to obtain independent confirmation and guidelines as to whether his clinic's perspective in its educational therapeutic program for patients is subscribed to by businessmen coping in terms of our society.

The top managers who participated in the study seem to bear a common stamp of persons who have always recognized that true strength lies within themselves rather than with the outside trappings of security, with the symbolic significance of the power and authority of the office. The indications are these men were not stressful when they were middle-managers. They did not wait for someone else to cue them on how to respond to a particular question. They always did their own thing.

But the middle-level managers, used as a check, as a group seem to be less relaxed, more stressful, than their superiors. Decentralization through delegation of as much authority as possible is an ideal, but stress is created where middle-level executives think they are still doing "donkey work" instead of having a sense of real authority.

Chief executives who are "comfortable with themselves" recognize their own limitations and don't want to be all things to all men. They focus on what they do best and try to resist the temptation, the "seduction," to intrude when subordinates appeal to their vanity and ask for guidance. The boss must tell them: "It's your job, you do it." It takes self-control to get others to do what they may do better than you.

The man who has built the company doesn't feel obligated to his staff, to the board of directors, or to stockholders in the same way that a professional manager does. The man who brought the company into the "500" list doesn't believe he has to adjust his style of doing things, to behave in a way that must meet others' approval. The hired professional, on the other hand, is often under stress to prove himself, is fearful he won't be able to perform properly, is troubled about the risks he is running and how he's being judged. He is always questioning himself: "Will I be able to cope?" Still, a certain kind of stress and challenge is salutary at all management levels.

Some industries make more demands on individuals, are more stressful, than others. There may be a particular urgency in meeting deadlines relatively absent in less dynamic industries. Executives in the more stressful industries have "to build more cushions," to give up some omnipotence, to allow external stimuli to be handled in a more regulated manner. A lot of stress builds up in conglomerates. There are all kinds of problems with presidents of subsidiaries who don't want to give up their authority and have to be supervised with delicacy but firmness.

In every case, the stress is not so much a question of the industry or the size of the company as it is one of each person's temperament, constitution, the way he feels about himself, and his general way of handling things. As in the case of the doberman pinscher, distress occurs because of distressing feelings, not because of adverse environmental considerations.

Kiev suggests: "A man should not resort to a mechanical formula, emulating others, to solve an anxiety-producing situation but must search for the method most compatible with his own way of life. The more he relies on his own assessments and solutions of each problem—new situations require new solutions—the stronger he will become."

Psychiatrist Kiev classifies successful executives by their varying methods of reaching the top of the ladder.

1. One able leader knows how to pick lieutenants who can be trusted to run their particular shows without breathing down their necks or sending inspectors around to spy on progress every so often. Such lieutenants not only take over the responsibility for performance of their duties but can also be trusted to wield authority so that they can issue commands, make decisions, and deal with unexpected emergencies in their own bailiwicks. These are not yes-men; the resultant success or failure is a team effort. But the chief executive gets as much personal reward as if he had directed every move.

2. This type of executive is too much of a one-man show. He attempts to carry all the details in his own head, not because he distrusts the opinions of others, but often because of his phenomenal success when the company was small. As the details connected with running the business increased, he spent extra hours reviewing matters that someone else, whose time was less valuable, could have easily handled for him. This type of leader is a hard worker who attempts to make both small and large decisions. Unless he has exceptional ability, he will find he has neglected much of his potential. Many of his best talents have been wasted. He has spread himself thinner and thinner over the years attending to matters that are not only tedious but unsuited to his temperament and capabilities. He often has a monumental ego and obtains great satisfaction from the feeling he has done things "all by myself."

Medically, Kiev thinks, this type of executive experiences excessive stress and strain. Surely, he suggests, life would not be interesting without some of each. However, he adds, there may be a type of chronic mental fatigue that acts as a kind of warning signal. Those who are competitive and aggressive may pay a steep price for their solitary success—a kind of cumulative fatigue that could easily trigger a heart attack.

Kiev believes there is probably a third type of executive worth mentioning in this respect—one who always seems to have a new project to start the minute he has finished the last assignment. Frequently, this is a man who does not have any distractions from his work. Because his work may be his real hobby, it also satisfies his ambition. As a rule, his health is excellent and he just seems to skip from one problem to another, obtaining great satisfaction in their solutions. This type of executive is rare.

This psychiatrist argues that "most executives have the greatest difficulty in coping with strong emotions such as fear, anger, greed, envy, hostility, uncertainty, and depression. Unfortunately, these emotions seem to be a natural outgrowth of a competitive environment and are inherent in most human relationships. The less control an executive has over these feelings, the less able he will be to appraise a problem objectively and determine the most appropriate course of action. An honest emotion such as anger is sometimes interpreted as 'strength' but more often than not elicits negative responses from others. These responses demand from the executive both time and energy and usually increase his anger. Because loss of control evokes anxiety in others, these people will habitually respond in inappropriate ways that are designed to allay their own anxiety. Their reactions may then directly expose the executive's most vulnerable points.

Kiev concludes with a half dozen general principles:

1. Corporate and personal goals should not be confused.
2. Motivation by fear of authority and excessive dependence on old school ties should be avoided.
3. Authoritarianism, arbitrariness, and exploitation should not be tolerated.
4. Ideally, individuals' roles and temperaments should blend.
5. Resentments and conflict, usually based on misinformation or inadequate information, are neither useful nor productive.
6. The individual should be encouraged to assume responsibility commensurate with his capacities.

12

THE MIDLIFE CRISIS

Middle Life: Challenge or End of the Line?

Are you a middle-manager between the ages of thirty-five and fifty-five and going through a series of personal, job and societal challenges, tensions or crises?

If so, you're in "middlescence," the actual or potential malaise of the 4,500,000 middle-managers who comprise about 5 percent of total U.S. employment. One of their problems is that the higher up the career ladder they go, the less room there is at the top—only 1 percent of American workers scale the heights of the pyramid. That leaves 94 percent of the labor force—the rank-and-file employees who, theoretically, escape the pressures and psychosomatic ills which plague so many executives.

To bring widely diversified problems and opportunities into focus, American Management Associations held a briefing entitled "Middlescence: The Manager and the Midlife Crisis."

This portion of life, it was the consensus of the speakers from the fields

of organizational behavior, psychology, medicine, family counseling, and employee communications, may have a positive or negative meaning. It may be
better or worse than adolescence and infinitely superior to, or only a hairline
removed from, senescence. Middlescence also bears more than a faint, not
unintentional, resemblance to obsolescence.

It all depends on how the individual copes with the extent of his personal
achievement—how much he cares if he's still in the running for senior vice-
president and beyond or that he may have reached the end of the line, and how
he handles his career anxieties.

It's not what he eats but what's eating him that matters.

On the negative side, do you repeatedly lash out at your peers and
subordinates—and, if you dare, at superiors? Are you inordinately depressed?
Are your nerves at the breaking point? Do you repeatedly make erratic decisions? Are you ignored in the decision-making process? Do you have continuing conflicts with people who work under you? Are you a victim of organizational politics? Is your family life unhappy? Are you involved in
extracurricular sex in an effort to prove you're still young, attractive and virile?
Do you drink, eat and smoke too much? All these and more are symptoms of
negative middlescence.

On the positive side, do you look at middlescence as a season of life with
values and virtues of its own, a period that may be a critical turning point but
need not be a disaster? Have you refused to give up on self-development?

If you're one of the fortunate few, your physiological age is less than your
chronological age, your job-appraisal age compares well with that of current
and would-be younger associates.

Or, accepting the possibility you may not be as good as you were once,
you might ask for, or find elsewhere, a job assignment more compatible with
your abilities. You might take a sabbatical—a foreign trip, an educational
program, a teaching, social-endeavor, or political post—to broaden your horizons. If you're not prepared to live with salary immobility for the future, you
might consider outside investments requiring your personal attention. Or you
may opt for early retirement in favor of new vocational and avocational
interests.

You might, for example, work for improvement of the physical, social,
and cultural environment. With any of these alternatives, you must learn to
come to terms with your normal bodily decline and with your mortality.

Suppose top management of your company offered to guarantee you—
a middle-manager in your late thirties or forties—your present job for the next
twenty years! What would you do? Would you accept the proposition with
varying degrees of reluctance, jump out of the window, or quit?

Emanuel Kay, an industrial psychologist, put the question to more than
five hundred managers. Responses took such forms as:

1. I'd leave.
2. I'd stay and redirect my efforts in the hope of changing the boss' mind about my potential.
3. I don't think this would ever happen.
4. "So what?"
5. No reply at all.

Kay conducted his poll to point up the quandary of middle managers in their thirties and forties, perhaps undertrained and overpromoted, who have "plateaued out" in their jobs and face the prospect of remaining at the same level for twenty to twenty-five years or more. Their problem is that the national total of upper management positions is under 900,000, less than 1 percent of the work force. Obviously, the odds are prohibitive against a man reaching the top of the job pyramid. Middle management accounts for an additional 5 percent of American workers.

Observing that "education equals expectations," Kay ventured: "It may be there is a greater supply of college and higher-degree graduates available than are needed in middle management. Perhaps the 5 percent of the work force comprising that group should be reduced to 2 percent."

Men who have climbed the ladder to middle management on the strength of technical, not managerial, skills, Kay went on, see younger people with greater generalist abilities moving up ahead of them. "Usually after ten to thirteen years of a fast rate of pay increases, there's a break in the upward salary curve and it then goes up at a leveled-off rate and even less so at about age fifty-five. Somewhere along the line, the middle-management man and the fairly recent college graduates come together in pay. The older men become frustrated, insecure, and anxious and may think of a change that might correct what they consider salary inequities. Actually, there are more changes now in middle management than in the last ten years.

"The dilemma of those who are passive, the unhealthy response, is from the men who stay on, stagnant and deadwood, blocking up key positions. Companies cluttered with them sometimes resort to early retirement plans and, in some cases, offer several preretirement years of job and financial counseling. At General Electric, for example, there is a very attractive retirement plan for those about fifty-five which has been called 'the platinum bullet' and a less attractive plan, termed 'the silver bullet,' for men about sixty.

"Then, there are the healthy ones who search for greater fulfillment elsewhere. We have the phenomenon of second careers for dropouts from the middle-manager ranks, most of whom go into service types of occupations that may afford a smaller income but promise a happier life. They open a wine and cheese shop, a camera repair business, a country inn, a marina, or go the educational route."

How can companies help middle-managers to get out of "impacted" jobs and continue as productive employees? Kay's suggestions:

"If a company can provide an environment in which its middle-managers can increase their development and productivity, the effectiveness of the entire organization multiplies. In too many cases, unfortunately, the middle-managers begin to lose their steam at some point in their careers and their value to the company ebbs.

"Opportunities for lateral movement diminish because 1) the individual lacks experience in other functions to which he might be moved, and 2) his salary is too high to move him to an area where he would be regarded as a beginner. It usually appears less costly to train a real beginner who is paid a lower salary.

"A number of companies have voluntary rotation policies at no loss of job level or salary. Top management realizes that, for the time being at least, the middle-manager will probably be overpaid, but this is considered a direct investment in maintaining the continued motivation and expanding the skills of a key person. Should he fail, he is not penalized but is permitted to return to his former area, although not necessarily the identical position.

"Job enrichment also represents an alternative that might result in long-term or permanent solutions to the boxing-in problem."

Roger M. D'Aprix, manager of employee communications, business products group, Xerox Corp., addressed himself to the same problem which he described as: "How does the individual keep himself from being ground up in the organization and being spit out?"

D'Aprix submitted some forces conspiring to defeat the middle-manager in middle age:

"A lot of men got their first experience in the 1950s or earlier in an industrial world that no longer exists. They're confronted by young people engaged in a convulsive change that can only be characterized as a silent revolution against our organizations and institutions. We're becoming an anti-system, anti-authority society. Nobody now seriously expects corporate loyalty. Loyalty to one's career, yes, but not to the organization."

Can the middlescent manager be his own man in the organization? Yes, says D'Aprix.

In an era when the highly structured company with a rigid policy manual is passe, he views "the instructive, creative, flexible middle-manager as an intermediary between the old-line senior manager and the young people who often come into the business with unreal expectations." The older man, serving as "a catalyst to help pull things together in a meaningful way," would certainly earn his keep, D'Aprix is convinced.

He realizes the increasing effect of affirmative action programs which may force white males to go through the anguish of having blacks and women promoted over them, of seeing their own careers interrupted, if not plateaued or ended.

D'Aprix concludes that companies "are at an historical crossroads where they must mirror society. They are moving from people-using to people-building, from the entrepreneurial, bureaucratic organization to professional management and innovation."

If a middle-management man is going to "make it" in business, he has to get into the corporate executive structure and earn at least $50,000 by the time he's forty.

Two significant influences that may help him fulfill his dreams and ambitions are a series of "mentors" during his twenties and thirties and a "special woman" who may be his wife, lover, or friend. The great majority of others, who don't climb far up the ladder of success, too often look back upon what they've lost as traumatic and tragic portents, instead of looking ahead with excitement to future possibilities.

These are among the findings of a continuing intensive study, of forty men in the thirty-five-to-forty-five age range and the changes they underwent in that decade of their lives and since. The men are in four occupational groups: business executives, blue- and white-collar workers in industry, academic biologists, and novelists.

Daniel J. Levinson, professor of psychology, department of psychiatry, Yale University, is also director of the research unit for social psychology and psychiatry at the Connecticut Mental Health Center which is conducting the study.

Some of his opinions:

- Midlife transition is not necessarily to be equated with midlife crisis. It can be a positive period, extending its benefits into late adulthood—sixty and over.
- A "mentor," ordinarily six to twenty years older than a "mentee," should take a younger man under his wing, impart wisdom and criticism and, above all, "bestow his blessing." Workers and men in middle management don't get much mentoring because of the competitive situation and rivalry.
- In many ways, the "special woman" parallels the mentor. Just as the mentor gets a man out of the father-son relationship, the "special woman" gets him out of the mother-son relationship.
- If a man doesn't admit to passing through a period of job and personal turmoil in his thirties and forties, he may be kidding himself.

Gerald Sabath, clinical psychologist and psychoanalyst, said: "Midlife crisis is a universal problem that can be found at any point in recorded history. It revolves about the question: 'Have I achieved or not achieved what I set out to do?' It is a matter of job and personal relationships, confusion about life's meaning, depression, uncontrolled anger, alcoholic intake, headaches, a series of colds or other troublesome ailments."

Larry Greiner, professor of organizational behavior, Graduate School of Business Administration, University of Southern California, took a potshot at the promote-youth-fast syndrome.

He was alluding to the problem of men who may have been promoted to key jobs in middle management before they were ready and may be doomed to stay on the same job for many years until retirement. He suggested that men who become middle-managers at thirty or thirty-five might be better prepared for such responsibilities at forty.

Greiner advised that developmental programs for men in midlife might include placing them on task forces to give them a companywide perspective and "talk-back" sessions of middle and top managers.

The professor argued the case for improving professional standards of technical men "with proper rewards" so as to dissipate the belief that the only way to "make it" is through the managerial route. Even now, he pointed out, "there are lots of foremen who don't want to make it to middle management, and lots of middle-managers who don't want to make it to top management."

Greiner emphasized the double-edged question that applies across the board: How does the organization get work done well and yet make it satisfying?

James O'Toole, assistant professor of management, Graduate School of Business Administration, University of Southern California, cited the problem of "the health, education and welfare of unhappy people in key jobs in midlife, men of forty and over who bear two crosses: their age and their jobs."

He explained: "While the company depends on them to carry out top-management policies and plans and they have a certain amount of financial security and expertise, they don't make rules but simply enforce them. They may be indecisive because they don't have the authority. They have poor relations with others. They realize they have peaked and will never make it to the top. The company is telling them they're not worth anything anymore.

"They have a sense of expendability, of being marginal men, and are bothered by a low level of self-esteem. They are troubled by the thought it might be possible to organize a company that could eliminate middle management and have top management supervise workers directly.

"They may have difficulty making new friends to replace those they've lost. Sexual powers wane in middle age, but masculine ego and boredom may be reflected in extramarital activities. The incidence of divorce rises.

"Psychological stress impairs the thinking process and leads to rigidity of behavior. Depression that comes from all these things makes people vulnerable to illness. Cardiovascular disease, often due to stress, is the leading cause of death in middle age, substantially higher than at the beginning of the century. Men know they must come to grips with the overwhelming problem at this time of life—the inevitability of death."

O'Toole left this reassuring message: "Do the skills of managers become obsolete? No! What we call obsolescence is human beings who are bored and threatened. But a human being is never obsolete."

Within the next five years, the problem of midlife transition "will become one of the hottest concepts in American industry."

This is the prediction of Gerald Sabath, psychologist and psychoanalyst who heads Human Resources Guidance Systems, a team of psychologists, psychiatrists, businessmen and an attorney providing business and other organizations with management and personnel consultation.

As he views the pressures and psychosomatic ills that plague so many middle executives, "midlife can be a tremendous opportunity. It need not mean going downhill, as people are inclined to think. It should be a period of growth.

"The problem is not entirely chronological. It's one that besets a man who is not happy with himself at any time of his adult life. It may start at twenty when a man may begin losing his hair, and this propels him into a concern about what's happening to him. On the other end of the age scale, a person of seventy-five may not have the proper perspective on what it's all about. But, as an arbitrary figure, the age range of midlife transition, also called middlescence, is generally considered from thirty-five to fifty-five."

Literature throughout the ages abounds with tales of crises of midlife. To take only one example, Dante, the Italian poet (1265–1321), wrote this passage in *The Divine Comedy* at the age of thirty-seven:

"In the middle of the journey of our life, I came to myself within a dark wood where the straight way was lost. Ah, how hard it is to tell of that wood, savage and harsh and dense, the thought of which renews my fear. So bitter is it that death is hardly more."

Sabath submits six components of the process of introspection, self-examination, and self-evaluation that may lead to emotional and physical strains, stresses, and ailments:

1. Earlier expectations. A man may be unable to handle either failure to reach his goal or success beyond his hopes. Of course, most people who become upset have fallen far short of their dreams for themselves. But there are others who become panic-stricken at their success. There is a little bit of the *nouveau riche* phenomenon in this. For example, a prosperous retailer may be unhappy because he hasn't opened a certain number of stores by a particular time. There are still others who handle success very well and enjoy it for all it's worth.

2. Formative experiences. There are unresolved needs in growing up. Certain wants have been subordinated because there's no way the young person can take care of these. A parent dies and a youngster has to go to work. He may have to put aside leisure interests until retirement. By this time, the person may feel very depressed about his longtime deprivation and unable to enjoy his leisure. The opportunity in retirement for a husband and wife to become closer may boomerang into tremendous friction.

3. Physical aging. Losing your hair, getting gray, suffering from backache, difficulty in playing tennis singles can really set a man back. He doesn't have to go through a heart attack to feel he's only mortal. He should have sufficient awareness of the passage of time to recognize things as they are and take advantage of all the midlife opportunities and relationships open to him.

4. Growth of personal expertise and wisdom. An older man should be able to teach younger people the ropes from his experience. It would be well if he approached this task from the viewpoint of, "If I knew then what I know now, I would do things in a different way."

5. Changes of inner personality functioning. Loss of contentment and of absorption in work which fails to have a sense of meaning and has become drudgery. The work may be as desirable as ever, but the man's reaction is different. Programs of job enrichment to improve morale may prove effective.

6. Midlife transition. A man may be a well-balanced individual but could get hit with the midlife problem as a result of external changes that have nothing to do with his own condition. These could be changes in the economy, in life styles, in social values. The man has to adjust his inner feelings to the changing demands of the outside world. Questions of women's rights and equal opportunity in general could adversely affect the power of supervisors to function properly. A similar failure to adjust, occasionally to the point of nervous breakdown, was evident in the 1920s and 1930s when some management persons were unable to handle changes in labor relations.

In dealing with these problems, Sabath's organization has set up programs of structured workshops, goal-setting, reorientation and evaluation of results. Psychotherapy programs are also being carried on.

The HRGS head contends these programs "have better results when the chief executive officer and the chief operating officer are not only in on the whole thing but personally participate in sessions. A lot of corporate presidents have a great deal to learn. They are excessively authoritarian and can't delegate and share responsibility or tolerate a variety of opinions other than their own. They may even enjoy humiliating and making life generally miserable for underlings. In some cases, they may go through the motions of encouraging lower-to-middle executives to handle subordinates properly, but they themselves spit on people.

"The enthusiastic cooperation of these top men is essential if consultants like ourselves are to accomplish best possible results."

As Sabath sees it, "It's really an intersection of career and team development and other phases of management development. It is a question of getting to the heart of the matter rather than just touching the surface. Too often, however, Band-Aids are brought in when radical surgery may be needed."

If you're somewhere between thirty-five and fifty-five, the coming of a new year may trigger a process of introspection, self-examination and self-evaluation on whether you are achieving your goals. If you decide you've fallen short of your aspirations, you may penalize yourself with emotional and physical pressures, stresses and ailments.

Sabath contends that midlife transition "is not necessarily a point of crisis but can be a period of mild upheaval or none at all."

He believes these transitional years "can be one of the greatest opportunities of a person's life. Unhappily, though, probably no more than one out of every twenty-five persons makes the best use of that period. They waste their time, the opportunity passes them by and an out-and-out crisis may develop. Perhaps one-fourth of all persons are really hit hard both emotionally and physically."

For whatever small comfort it may afford, Sabath observes that the problem, as a universal syndrome, has always been with us—it is found in the Bible, in Shakespeare and repeatedly in other literature.

Sabath divides midlife transition into two sets of phenomena—intrinsic and extrinsic.

"The intrinsic," he explains, "is the biological clock in all of us, all the things that are physical. You may have a backache or a series of other discomforts and you know time is passing. A parent, a brother or friend dies and you know you have to face your own demise some day. But denial that your own time has finally come is a very common happening.

"The extrinsic are the lifelong experiences and goals that press upon you in midlife. People can't face things psychologically. They become more introspective. They feel sorry for themselves. Denying the pressures of this period, afraid to face reality, they may get too involved in sex or drinking in an effort to keep up their morale. They worry about these excesses, but what they should really be worried about is their denial of reality.

"To pretend it isn't there, to try to push it out of their minds, that's unhealthy. They must evaluate all the resources they have built up and decide whether persisting problems are solvable and livable. The turmoil of self-examination should really be a healthy reaction to arriving at this time of life. It should be acceptable in the same way that sweat is expected in playing tennis."

With a background that includes consulting to retail companies, this psychologist is convinced retailing is an unusually challenging business. He notes, for instance, that the seasonal nature of an apparel chain puts executives on "an emotional roller-coaster" that those in nonseasonal businesses don't have to go through.

"Let's consider a man from forty-five to fifty-five with some substance who's very upset. He may be in retailing, manufacturing, sales or advertising. He could be a writer like you or a psychoanalyst like me. Natural forces at work—forces about which he doesn't dream about at the age of thirty—compel him in midlife to become more introspective. He may confess to having a problem, but the problem to which he admits may be a cover-up for something else. He may blame a brother for problems that he really has—or had —with his father.

"A lot of the time, he's not even aware he's bringing his domestic troubles into the office. If an executive has an argument with his wife in the morning, he may come to the office and yell at his secretary. Or, if he has trouble with his kids, he'll blow off steam at his younger associates."

Sabath points out that there are many younger people who don't want to rise beyond middle management or even junior executive.

"They don't want to be president," he observes. "They want more free time, more leisure, more out of their personal lives. It used to be that, without being asked, a man was moved from one location to another for training that presumably would groom him for bigger things. It rarely occurred to his superiors to give him the chance to decline the honor. Now, there's a tendency to ask him in advance and suggest he talk it over with his wife. He is permitted, without immediate danger to his future in the company, to turn down a particular promotion or move to another city. This trend, in an incipient stage in the 1950s, has become stronger in the past ten years."

Sabath has counseled some people in midlife to work four instead of five days a week and take educational courses, teach or do something else in which they're knowledgeable or to which they'd like to extend their interests.

Such preretirement steps, he assures, often redound to the benefit of the company as well as of the individual and his family.

You're forty or thereabouts. You have been an active, outgoing individual not inclined to waste time in idle introspection. You have worked hard to succeed and have won the respect of your associates as well as material rewards.

Now that you've made it, you may be wondering for the first time, "Why am I doing this?" and, "Is this what I worked so hard to achieve?"

For some inexplicable reason, your attainments look better than the reality—to you. Your inner voice is goading you with the question, "What's next?"

Richard C. Hodgson, organizational behavior professor, School of Business Administration, University of Western Ontario, describes these symptoms as being part of the "midlife crisis" phenomenon.

People at a certain stage in the life cycle, Hodgson reports, have felt that way since time immemorial. For a high proportion of our forefathers, death "solved" the problems of middle age. Now, we have more leisure and proportionately fewer people in the Western world die in their forties and fifties. The midlife crisis has become both a relative luxury representing a potentially profound and beautiful opportunity for personal growth and a period of possible pain and danger. The opportunity "is easily overlooked or misinterpreted by persons entering the 'silly season' of their middle years."

Pointing out that "ours is an age of overstatement," Hodgson thinks the term "crisis" is "somewhat melodramatic" as a characterization of the evolution from young adulthood to mature age. He would substitute "quandary" as more appropriate for the feelings of perplexity and doubt that arise as one's life begins to change in ways that are not well understood and as it becomes increasingly difficult to motivate oneself and retain or obtain a positive mental attitude.

This organizational behavior specialist notes that, around the age of forty, the individual who has expended great conscious effort to carve out a career often begins to pay the price of having lost touch with his deeper self. This is what Carl Jung, the psychiatrist-psychologist, defined as the battle during adolescence and young adulthood between the "ego"—the center of the conscious mind—and the "subconscious"—the real you—which incorporates many of the weaker, darker properties of one's nature. In seeking special achievements and status, the young person makes significant sacrifices at considerable expense to the subconscious. The forces of the unconscious can be excluded from consciousness for considerable periods of time, particularly in the lives of highly successful individuals in whom much personal repression and denial have been highly rewarded by society.

In the second half of life, though, "the pent-up forces of the unconscious begin to break through the defenses built around the ego, resulting sometimes in outbreaks of bizarre behavior among those who are not growing older gracefully. Or more and more energy is required to maintain ego defenses, thus reducing the amount of energy available for work and social relations and leading to the depression and that 'tired feeling' so often reported by the middle-aged."

However, Hodgson continues, the person who continues to develop himself into and past middle age begins to play the game of life differently than he did before he was forty. In a process of personal growth called individuation, he "begins to relax the censorship he has placed upon the properties and forces of his unconscious and to integrate them with the more socially acceptable strengths of his ego.

"Illusions and self-deception start to disintegrate. He develops a more accurate understanding of who he is and who he is not, what he wants and what he does not want. He becomes reconciled to the probabilities of what he will accomplish and what he will not accomplish in life. Then may be formed the integrated personality of the mature adult—conscious and unconscious, strengths and weaknesses, likes and dislikes, successes and failures. The person now sees himself for what he truly is—'warts and all.'

"Of course, he will still be surrounded by people telling him what he should do, how he should feel, what he should think, who he should be. Somehow, "he is much less tractable than he used to be. Increasingly, he goes his own way at his own pace. He begins to experience a peace that passes his understanding. He looks on the gesturing and posturing of adolescents and young adults as, in the words of author James Gould Cozzens, 'a sort of disease.' He would not trade his newly developed sense of self for their youth and vigor for anything in the world."

Hodgson does not minimize two major pressures that probably make the process of individuation more difficult for managers than for professionals or unionized employees. "Managers have bosses and subordinates. Professionals and unionized employees frequently have only one or neither. Managers are caught between the often conflicting expectations from their boss and demands from their subordinates. Managers' careers are not infrequently balanced on the knife edge between both.

"Self-development in managers, itself a difficult process, is rendered more difficult by the 'more-is-required-but-less-provided' situation facing them for prolonged periods of time in mid-career. It is their response over the long term to this situation that makes or breaks many managers."

"More men than women are trapped by life, by a feeling of discontent, hopelessness, despair, and depression. More women have friendships with other women in whom they can confide their troubles than men have with other men. I hope that men and women will come around eventually to being companions and friends."

This is the view of Eda L. LeShan, psychologist.

Discussing marital stress in midlife, she cites the illusions of newly married couples in the past who thought they would live happily ever after. But much disillusionment is now experienced among middle-aged couples who think they've failed in their relationship because they're having problems with their children and each other. The man has lost touch with his children and the wife is answering all their questions. There is avoidance of confrontation and communication between the pair for fear of hurting each other. The shattered dream of lifelong romance is reflected in confusion, loneliness, and isolation. Also, in much use of alcohol and other means of excitement. Outside sexual relations may be sought.

Another provocative point made by Ms. LeShan:

The man of forty-five should not be satisfied to be what he was at thirty-five but must continue to grow. She quotes a man in terminal illness who said: "I'm not crying because I'm dying, but because I've never lived." There is also the middle-aged man who confessed to her: "I'm not the man I used to be and I guess I never was."

Condemning "the obscenity and immorality" of business and public life, Ms. LeShan advised: "Survival in a dehumanized, depersonalized business is not enough. People of all ages are self-destructing. Apathy and unhappiness are not due to technological phases of industry but to the lack of responsibility people are willing to take for the state of this country. How can you interpret the nature of work to make it more human? You must look at things morally. You must take an active part in doing things that will both exhilarate you and help create a better physical, social, and cultural environment."

Youth Worship in American Society—Its Pros and Cons

Senator William Proxmire freely admits he has undergone a hair transplant and facelift to make himself look better. In a TV interview, he proudly reported, "My transplant makes me look younger." He was 60 on November 11, 1975, and is a regular jogger.

A men's hair stylist says 95 percent of his hair-coloring patronage is from middle-aged businessmen trying to look younger, in some cases because they have much younger girlfriends. Plastic surgeons are busier than ever not only with hair transplants but also with nose, eyelid, bags-under-the-eyes, and chin jobs.

It's all a reflection of the youth orientation of American society at large.

Much of this youth worship stems from feelings of inadequacy or inferiority associated with the job market. Many firms have made age a critical factor in hiring and firing. This has been so widely practiced that in 1967, the federal government enacted legislation designed to protect workers from forty to sixty-five in obtaining and retaining jobs except for good cause—serious medical problems, deficient on-the-job performance, and so on. Only within the past few years, the government has stepped up enforcement of the law and has won impressive back-pay settlements from Standard Oil Co. of California, AT&T, Pan American World Airways, and major steel producers—with many more to come.

Labor Department solicitor William J. Kilberg notes that "people in the forty- to sixty-five age group tend to earn higher wages, they tend to be vested in their pension rights or to be close to vesting, which boosts pension costs, and so it is often more profitable to discharge the older, rather than the younger, worker."

Apparently, many firms are still following illegal practices in this respect. If the Labor Department ever catches up with them, they may expect to gain a sympathetic ear only if they can back their retaliatory charges of outrageously poor performance with actual sins of commission or omission. This

could include men and women who have plateaued, who simply go through
the motions from one payday to the next and are going nowhere. It should be
noted this happens with younger as well as older people. In the case of rejecting
the over forties as job applicants, companies may have to prove the older
persons are not as qualified as younger ones.

Of course, there are forty-year-olds who are concerned about growing
old and fifty-year-olds who seemingly aren't worried about the prospect. It all
depends on the individual.

Youth is not necessarily to be equated with good health, or middle age
with deterioration. An inordinate number of impaired hearts were found in
autopsies on American casualties in Vietnam.

Similarly with a popular belief that forgetfulness, living in the past, even
senility, are signs associated only with old age. A social psychologist at the
University of Denver produced several of these "characteristics of aging" in
young people participating in laboratory studies. All he had to do was to take
persons in their twenties and thirties, consistently ignore them and discount
or ridicule their opinions over a number of days. After this ordeal, they began
to exhibit behavior patterns attributed only to older people.

Does the middle-aged person live and work in a healthy environment?
Does he take tension in stride, even thrive on it, and prove the best executive
is the one under the most pressure—but self-generated? Does he keep in
topnotch shape by eating, smoking, and drinking in moderation and doing the
right kind and amount of exercise? Did he pick the right parents and grandpar-
ents to give him the physical fitness—sustained agility, flexibility, endurance,
and strength—that serve as insurance for his own longevity? Is he one of the
fortunate few whose physiological age is less than his chronological age? Does
his job-appraisal age compare well with that of younger current or would-be
associates? Is he a neurotic competitor, busy putting on an act he's as good
as ever and must not give in?

Numerous men and women recognize they can't be, or don't want to be,
president, merchandise manager, or store manager and have come to terms
with that understanding. They may want more leisure time, more out of their
private lives, and don't think they'd have this with what they consider the
twenty-four-hour job preoccupations of middle-to-upper management.
They're satisfied to be small frogs in big ponds. They don't mind relatively
modest positions, but many of them would like to think they're making a
contribution through being drawn into the decision-making process.

If they're lucky to have fairly stable, relatively happy home and social
lives too, they are able to stand apart from the emotionally distraught—the
ill-mated couples, the alcoholics, the drug-abusers, those with psychosomatic
ailments, those with poor interpersonal relations, who provide the frightening
statistics that make headlines.

"Outplacement"—Help for Person, Saving for Firm

An estimated 80 percent of executive opportunities occur in the "hidden job" market—problem areas needing new individuals to solve them. Often, however, top management and personnel departments have not specified these openings. This majority of middle-to-upper-level jobs not in the open market —as distinct from those in "help wanted" ads or listed with executive searchers —is the happy hunting ground of "outplacement" firms. At the expense of the former employer, terminated executives are individually provided with planned job seeking campaigns designed to bolster their morale and strengthen their chances for re-employment.

Frederick G. Atkinson, consultant and chairman of Thinc. Career Planning Corp., a pioneer outplacement service, hazards the 80 percent estimate for the hidden job market versus 20 percent for conventional recruitment.

Before assuming his present post in 1973, Atkinson had retired after a 30-year career at R.H. Macy & Co., as senior vice-president of personnel and industrial relations and a director. He has been a Thinc. director since inception of that company in 1969. More than 1,000 displaced executives from 200 corporate clients have been enlisted in the Thinc. program. Six of these clients are retail organizations.

Atkinson emphasized that the need for outplacement is not applicable solely to a recessionary environment, that "the problem has to be faced from time to time in good economic weather as well as bad. In today's world of increasing complexity, galloping technology, mergers, divestitures and changing product lines, few companies can afford the luxury of holding on to inadequate executives. If the current economic adversity dictates re-examination of policies and practices, that is just a salutary by-product of recession."

Most well-managed companies, Atkinson continued, have some system of executive performance appraisal but most are "less than satisfied" with it. The dissatisfaction relates more often to the lack of candor and objectivity reflected in the interviews and appraisals than to the design or concept of the process. This weakness has an effect on the experience of executive separation —in awkwardness, embarrassment and a sense of injustice. He mentioned the recurrence of incidents of a top line officer charging that Mr. X is not pulling his weight and has to go, only to find, on consulting the personnel folder, that the same person less than six months before had been rated "very good" and given a handsome increase in salary.

If this person has really been inadequate for some time, his brighter subordinates would probably perceive the fact before the front office does and wonder why the top boss puts up with it. Sentimentality may continue to obscure hard-headed realism. Facing up to the issue may be delayed until next year. Eventually, the decision is made and the question of financial and other considerations for the severed executive arises. The variety and combination of provisions can be lavish—a "consulting arrangement in which no service is expected or wanted from him; there may be a commitment to a lump sum or stretched-out payment equivalent to a year's or two years' salary; there may be an agreed-upon delay in his departure, perhaps fictitious duties or a specious title such as assistant to the vice-president for special projects. All this may turn out to be just another form of 'cutting the dog's tail off one inch at a time', a doubtful favor.

Critics of outplacement may be cynical about a company's motives, but objective observers argue that the man who isn't measuring up in one position may not be helped by a lateral or other transfer within the same company. They often advise a clean break, certainly in the case of a person in his 40s or 50s who has that much better chance for reemployment than an older job candidate.

"The quality of management," according to Atkinson, "varies widely among different companies. An executive, who is no longer wanted by Company A, might indeed 'average up' the quality of management in Company B."

What about the predicament of the executive when the ax finally falls? The interview at which he gets the bad news can be evasive, ambiguous, confusing or demoralizing—or all four. But, even if the separation interview is conducted with skill, it is still normal for the displaced executive to experience dismay, resentment, disbelief—traumatic, emotional shock. He may not have had any occasion to seek employment in many years and simply doesn't know what to do, where to look or how to begin.

Should he make the rounds of the executive searchers, mail out resumes, call up old friends? Certainly, he needs someone who can tell him to "forget it" if he indulges in self-pity, resentment or despair, wastes time speculating about who was his enemy at his old office, or proposes that now would be a good time to take his wife on that long-deferred vacation. He must understand that finding a new job is itself a full-time job. He must formulate a "marketing" plan and get on with effectuating that plan.

The ex-employer and Thinc. see the person through four stages: 1) Decompression and emotional adjustment. 2) Analysis and assessment of his marketable skills and likely opportunities in and outside of the industry from which he comes. 3) Planning his approaches and campaign. 4) Conducting the campaign to a successful conclusion.

What is Thinc.'s track record? Atkinson said about 80 percent of the displaced executives they have aided have been placed within 60 to 180 days of their start on the program, a high proportion at salaries equal to or better than their previous compensation.

What are the economics of this plan for the employer-client? Assume that the displaced executive was paid $50,000 a year and that his remuneration allowance was the equivalent of one year's pay. The company offers him, instead, an outplacement service that continues him on salary and group insurance benefits for a tentative four to six months, with the understanding these arrangements cease when he accepts new employment. Even if he takes six months to relocate, the company will have saved $25,000, less the fee paid the counseling service. "It is not often," Atkinson pointed out, "that an employer can provide a new and humanitarian benefit and save money by doing so."

Atkinson devotes one week each month to his outplacement and consultant duties, the rest of his time being spent at his Aspen, Col. home.

Where Does Early Retiring Leave Off and Firing Begin?

With "early retirement"—generally at sixty—being increasingly adopted in the executive suite, the question arises whether the step is entirely voluntary or a euphemism for "graceful firing." The line of demarcation is sometimes quite indistinct.

Pushed-ahead pensioners may reflect the fact that management jobs have grown in complexity, profits are harder to come by, and talented younger lower-to-middle-rank executives are pressing more than ever for accelerated recognition and status. Many middle-to-top managers in their late fifties are sore beset to justify their continuance with the company in any capacity, let alone promotion from their present posts.

Only occasionally does it happen that a man, having risen to a certain position, is willing to step back to his previous assignment. One example that comes to mind is a department store executive who found himself unhappy soon after being elevated to executive vice-president and asked to be returned to his former vice-presidency.

Usually, a man resigns for "personal reasons" or "because of his health" or retires "to pursue a second career." The real reasons may be one or more of these: 1) He is not performing well. 2) He doesn't have the same point of view as his superior as to how his job should be carried out. 3) There is a personality conflict. 4) The company has an embarrassment of executive riches at his level, and the big boss and board prefer someone else for the next promotion.

Self-esteem, dignity, vanity, envy, sense of injustice may well enter into a man's decision to resign in his forties and fifties or to retire if he's a bit older but still short of the mandatory sixty-five. Presumably, this is the age of the beau geste, not of ruthless tactics. But, no matter how delicately the pink slip is handed out, the dismissed man who wanted to stay on knows the knife has been twisted in his back. He can only hope against hope that very few people except the executioners know it too.

Of course, the retiree may not feel aggrieved at all but rather breathe a sigh of relief he has been able gracefully to relinquish a job he has found too hot to handle. Sometimes a top man really believes corporate interests will be best served if he steps out at sixty and gives way to younger management. He's ready and willing to change his life style to a concentration on leisure-time activities. But there are many others who, if they had their say, would choose to continue indefinitely with at least part time work instead of being completely shunted to the sidelines.

Early retirement is encouraged by liberalizing benefits to sums that would ordinarily accrue to a man at regular retirement. Substantial added costs are involved when full benefits are given years in advance of normal retirement date. However, all things considered, the outlay may prove a bargain if the retiree's successor shows materially improved bottom-line results.

Cynics—the industry abounds in them—often refuse to buy company releases that men resign of their own volition when figures dip too deeply into the red or when policy and personal conflicts in the corporate suite reach the breaking point.

What kind of preretirement counseling and other aid should companies give employees to help them make the most of their leisure years?

Meaningful answers become particularly difficult as greater numbers of younger, better educated men and women enter the ranks of retirees. The rate of retirement of those under sixty-five is 70 percent higher than only a dozen years ago.

Seeking to provide guidance for its members, The Conference Board conducted a seminar. Panelists were drawn from organizations which, at the board's suggestion, had previously held "mini-seminars" of their own on the multifaceted subject.

Among the panelists: R.E. Barmeier, personnel planning and research director, Sears, Roebuck & Co.; William S. Christiansen, benefit planning and development director, Eastman Kodak Co.; Stanley L. King Jr., assistant vice-president, AT&T; J. Joseph Kruse, secretary, Textron; and Willard W. Peck, vice-president, Metropolitan Life.

Excerpts from the participants' comments:

BARMEIER: I don't know how much of a "climate" you can create with a geographically dispersed organization such as ours with over three thousand units, many with ten employees or less. But what we do have is a "package" about retirement which covers in essence what we would hope anybody about to retire would give serious thought to. Such information is given automatically to each person who reaches the age of fifty-five. The unit manager is supposed to talk with the employee at this point and offer to answer any questions about the company's retirement program. Beyond that, the degree of individual counseling that can be offered—in-depth information to provide motivation—depends inevitably upon the particular location.

The philosophy that has prevailed at Sears is that it's very important for the organization to continue to bring people in who are younger and will bring more vitality to the organization. We could lose the ablest among them if they felt their opportunity for moving up the ladder was limited by lack of continuous openings in higher level assignments. Of course, every time there is a revision of the Social Security Law, there is a great debate: What's magic about sixty-five? Why should that be the cut-off date? And what's the reason for holding that seventy-two is the age beyond which you can do anything you want without risking a reduction in your Social Security? The relationship between chronological age effectiveness is dependent on so many factors. It's a difficult issue.

Especially in the rapidly growing service sector of the economy, I think there are great opportunities for retirees. Areas such as health and recreation, for example, are going to grow very fast in the next fifteen to twenty years, and I would say that part of the corporate role is to generate new service occupations geared specifically to certain segments of society, older people included.

A corporation could think in terms of sponsoring any number of useful activities. For instance, it could be part of a consortium created to generate programs in service occupations. It could make financial and manpower resources available to get projects going, with the aim of making them ultimately self-sustaining. In selecting them, management could set up a list of priorities, based on the degree of community need and the extent to which it was being met. It would not be very different from what is going on today, on an informal basis, in the unpublicized activities of executives across the land. But it could be put on an organized basis.

You've got to generate something that is structured. You can't just say to someone who's retired, "Go find part-time employment." But, if you say, "Here's an ongoing organization that fills a great need—and needs you," this will be a very productive kind of thing.

CHRISTIANSEN: Kodak, like many companies, has a tuition aid program. We pay 100 percent of the cost of courses taken in recognized educational institutions, and there is no limit to the number of courses one can take—so long as they are related to one's job or to a job one aspires to within the company. I have begun to wonder whether it might be a good idea to liberalize, to some extent, the restrictions on the content of the courses our employees can take under our program, especially in the case of applicants of fifty-five and older. Perhaps an employee approaching retirement should be encouraged to take avocational or specialized courses that would be helpful to adjustment after retirement.

PECK: Responses to questionnaires we mailed to 250 former employees who had retired in 1967–70 indicated very definitely that those who had been active before retirement—in community affairs, in education, in the company hobby program—were most satisfied and happy after retirement. Those who had been inactive before retiring tended to be inactive after they left the company. . . . We have a Self-Development Center where we are trying to find ways of helping our retired people. Some two thousand of our home office employees, at every level of the company, take advantage of offerings that include about one hundred different subjects ranging from sewing to advanced calculus. We also promote all kinds of hobbies—from bookbinding to judo— and many retired employees use the skills they acquired not only for interest but also for profit, thus supplementing retirement income.

KRUSE: We have a personal improvement program in the corporate office. Two officers of the company are selected each year to go for three months, at full pay plus a small stipend, to do whatever they want to do—with no preplanning and no report to be made when they return. The average age of the participants is about forty-eight. This is a true "retirement experience." For one thing, they realize the company can do without them. Secondly, they have an opportunity to be with their families on a continuing basis, and so they begin to examine their personal situation in light of their future retirement. With the success we have experienced to date, we suspect our divisions may also adopt such a program some day.

KING: We have in the Bell System an organization called Telephone Pioneers of America, made up of employees with at least twenty-one years of service. About 95 percent of our employees at all levels who reach twenty-one years of service decide they want to be Pioneers. When one retires, he becomes a life member of the association. The Pioneers provide the retiree with many opportunities to fraternize with his friends and companions from his working years. In Florida, for example, we have over six thousand retired Bell System people organized by the Pioneers into thirty life member clubs all over the state. Each club meets monthly.

Emotional Problems of Men in Retirement

Liberal, early retirement plans of corporations are encouraging more and more executives to leave the working world at sixty or even sooner. Statistically, these persons may look forward to at least seventeen more years at leisure.

H. Beric Wright, honorary medical adviser to the British Institute of Directors, asks the question: "Can an executive's wife survive his retirement?"

John McCann, president and medical director, Life Extension Institute, zeroes in on sex after the male climacteric and the female menopause.

In present-day society, Wright observes, individuals are largely classified by the job they hold, by the position they have attained. Once a person retires, he tends to lose status and identity and to become a "non-person." To a work-oriented businessman, "this may cause a state of purposeless shock."

The "non-person" described by Wright is akin to the retired man who, for want of something better to do, went into a post office and looked at the pictures of the ten most-wanted fugitives from justice. As he turned to leave, he said to himself wistfully: "It's nice to be wanted."

Retirement, according to Wright, starts with the need for married couples to face honestly the necessity of seeing quite a lot of each other. Up to the actual retirement, they may have been able to get along without too much obvious friction. Now, however, the man of the house may be at home most of the time so that fundamental difficulties in the relationship cannot be so easily swept under the rug. These difficulties must be brought out into the open and, hopefully, resolved.

Many wives, Wright reports, are justifiably worried about their husbands' fear of retirement and what it might do to their marriage. They may also "resent being burdened with a new full-time tenant in the house."

Wright advises: "This is a time of life that requires much thought, planning and readjustment. A well-organized retirement can be tranquil, enjoyable and a well-earned reward for a lifetime of effort. A sensible wife can, and should, start prodding her husband into considering what he is going to do in retirement and how he will make his priorities fit in with hers."

The doctor's suggestions:

Retirement planning largely involves activity. The first is the extent to which wives want—and to which it is possible for them—to get involved in their husbands' working lives. The second decision for a wife to make is what she is going to do with herself as the children grow up and her role as domestic drudge and child-minder is no longer full time. If she is sensible, she will develop activities—either paid or unpaid—that take her out of the house and back to the local community. Otherwise, she may become an obsessive housekeeper, needing lots of appreciation and becoming rather dictatorial about her domestic schedule. This is boring to live with and may cause friction.

In order to achieve a realistic balance, Wright continues, the husband should participate in the domestic chores and other responsibilities. He should learn some simple cooking so that he can get his own meals. "Having to look after her husband is no good reason for a woman to cut herself off from her previous activities. In return, the wife must realize that the house is for living in and messing up at all hours of the day. Another useful effort is for the couple to try to see that they develop some interests they can pursue together rather than separately. Ideally, some of the activity should be physical and out of doors."

Where should the couple live after the husband's retirement?

Wright is "strongly in favor of staying in an area where one is known. The bungalow in the wilds of nowhere, with a steep hill up to or back from the shops, is no place for the winter of retirement. Older women generally resettle in a new area and make new contacts with more difficulty than their husbands. The sudden departure from home—leaving the contacts of a lifetime a great distance away—coupled with the husband's loss of work identity can be disastrous.

"A large, older house with too big a garden is a poor place in which to grow old and arthritic. It is well worth considering a more convenient and economic house, since aging is inevitable and does bring restrictions. Choose a house that would be livable for a widow or widower."

Wright seems to be ignoring the attractions of the hundreds of "leisure villages" that have sprung up all over the United States, but particularly in Florida and the Southwest. He is sympathetic to the move of older couples from suburban houses, where they have brought up families, to midcity or near-city apartments now that their children have grown.

13

HARD CORE PROBLEMS

Bernie P.—A Compulsive Gambler Who Kicked the Habit

Bernie P. has just been promoted by a Broadway dress manufacturer from salesman to sales manager over a staff of five.

Bernie is an ex-convict who a dozen years ago joined Gamblers Anonymous and forswore the criminal career he had led since boyhood as a way to get money to gamble and to pay his gambling debts. He has since been a responsible and respected businessman. He suggests the recital of his own rehabilitation might help others.

Bernie was born in Chicago fifty-five years ago, of struggling parents who had emigrated from Russia with a son and two daughters. He recalls, "When I was eight years old, I was shooting craps, playing cards and stealing money. I was convinced legitimate people were suckers and there was no percentage in trying to make an honest living.

In 1934 in the middle of the depression, he quit high school after three-and-one-half years. He started boxing as a lightweight in preliminary bouts at neighborhood clubs. He fought "only to identify myself for bookmakers." Six years later, he suffered a broken jaw and left the ring.

"I was always a wise guy looking for an edge. I had no scruples. I got married to avoid the draft and went into the piece goods black market—anything that would bring me a buck. Meantime, I was gambling in floating crap games, always in trouble with tough guys. I had to steal to give them back what I owed them—with exorbitant interest." His wife bore him a son in 1942 —his only thought being to get a further draft deferment.

In 1947, he was apprehended by the law in a swindle for the first time. Family and friends made restitution and the case was dismissed. Until then, his wife had thought he was a salesman. He continued "stealing and manipulating, still looking for the big hit that would allow me to get rich and retire."

He next defrauded a Pennsylvania steel firm out of a large sum of money, was extradited from New York and served a year in prison. Upon his release, he and two partners stole $230,000 from a firm in another confidence game. They went to Las Vegas "to break the bank" but "we lost everything in four days. We wrote bum checks and forged credit cards to pay for bills and get air tickets back to New York. We were caught and sentenced to two years in state prison. I learned nothing in prison except how to commit more crimes."

Nothing was too low for him to stoop to. When his father was killed in an accident and the story appeared in the papers, he got loan sharks to lend him $7,500 "to give my father a beautiful funeral" but instead lost all the money at the race track.

December 1, 1962, is a day Bernie will never forget. A friend to whom he had gone for financial aid somehow got through to him. "I was a sick compulsive gambler who needed help." Bernie went to his first meeting of G.A. and "I found what I needed. Compulsive gamblers are the same as compulsive drinkers—they're never cured, but they can keep their illness in an arrested state. G.A. achieves its aim through group therapy. Between meetings—I go to one a week—I'm fighting the urge every day. I don't play cards. I don't buy raffle tickets."

Founded fifteen years ago, G.A. is a completely self-supporting group with five thousand members in seventy chapters in this country and Canada. Thirty-one of the chapters are in the New York metropolitan area. There are also members in Britain and Australia. Bernie cites statistics indicating there are anywhere from four million to eight million compulsive gamblers in the United States. Bernie devotes evenings and weekends to helping others in G.A. He has cooperated in founding G.A. chapters in a number of penal institutions, and he wrote *Compulsive Gambler* with William Bruns.

He is on "very friendly terms" with his son, who is married and has a child, after an eight-year period of estrangement.

Bernie, who has been with his present employer about a year, credits the various bosses he has had since his rehabilitation for "giving me the chance to prove my worth." He and his present wife live on Park Avenue.

Problem-Drinking: Industry's
Billion-Dollar Hangover

Alcoholism is one of the three major diseases. Two are killers—coronary heart disease and cancer. Alcoholism incapacitates.

The dimensions of alcoholism may be measured by awesome figures:

- An estimated nine million American alcoholics are responsible for a multi-billion-dollar hangover—half-men or half-women on the job.
- The estimated economic costs of alcohol-related problems for the nation are more than $25 billion a year, more than a two-third increase over figures for the 1960s. Alcohol abuse results in on-the-job damage taking such forms as absenteeism, lateness, accidents and poor performance in general.
- At least half of each year's average of 55,500 automobile deaths and half of the one million major injuries suffered in auto accidents are directly trace-able to a drunken driver or pedestrian.
- Ninety-seven percent of alcoholics are executives, workers, professional people, and housewives. They are found in offices, factories, schools, and in the home. Generally speaking, the more educated, the more urban, the better-salaried Americans are, the more they drink. Only 3 percent of the total number of people in the United States suffering from alcoholism are on "skid row."
- The increased number of people who are drinking more than in the past includes those in their twenties and thirties and the under-twenty-one age group.

In the 1950s, one of every five alcoholics was a woman; the ratio is now at least one woman for every three men. There is also an alarming rise in combined use of alcohol and other drugs by adolescents.

The man or woman who drinks excessively is usually trying to escape something. Tensions of a highly competitive business system are illustrated by the person who is passed over for promotion or who gets the bigger job and is terrified he can't handle it, the middle-aged executive who has to prove himself all over again if his company has merged in another, the man who's vying with associates half his age. Then, there is the man with an unhappy married life or problem children, or who is beset by fear of old age and sickness.

Dr. Morris E. Chafetz, psychiatrist and director, National Institute on Alcohol Abuse and Alcoholism, Rockville, Md., is disturbed by the tendency of too many executives to resort to drinking when particularly troublesome business situations require maximum alertness and sharpness. Citing the $25 billion economic costs of alcoholism, Chafetz concedes that as recently as

1971, the institute estimated the total costs at $15 billion. On the brighter side, he contends that there is no evidence of harmful effects from the steady intake of moderate amounts of alcohol, notably by older people.

Chafetz enumerates five essentials of successful early identification programs for employed problem drinkers:

1. A written policy that specifies the procedures for identifying and confronting employees who may have drinking problems. This should include explicit recognition by the organization that alcoholism—called "problem-drinking" in the employment setting—is a health problem and that employees with such problems will not be penalized for seeking help.
2. Specific channels within the work organization where employees with identified job impairment, resulting from problem-drinking or other difficulties, may be motivated to accept available resources.
3. Training of managerial and supervisory personnel regarding their responsibilities in implementing the program.
4. Education of the entire work force concerning policy, procedures, and the provision of help-without-penalty for problem-drinking.
5. Cooperation and participation of labor through all stages of program development and implementation.

Dr. William B. Terhune, head of a clinic which has made a long, intensive study of alcoholic patients, is convinced that "alcoholism is now epidemic." He bolsters his charge with statistics that 10 percent of the population are alcohol-dependent—the stage preceding alcoholism. Victims, he notes, include many who run a business or hold a job but who, to escape anxiety, boredom, frustration, tension, fatigue, and other evidences of severe neuroticism, must resort to drink before and during lunch, immediately after work, before dinner, and before bedtime. Another 5 percent, Dr. Terhune adds, have become true alcoholics, for whom there is no cure. Even if they remain on the wagon indefinitely, they are still nondrinking alcoholics.

To Dr. Terhune, these are heart-rending facts and figures for which prevention offers the sole solution. "Only the individual who has learned to drink moderately, who never uses alcohol to escape difficulties and tensions, and who knows the safe techniques of drinking, can use alcohol pleasantly and harmlessly," Dr. Terhune concludes.

Dr. Robert S. Garber, medical director, Carrier Clinic, Belle Mead, N. J., private psychiatric institution, is of the opinion that alcoholics run across the board of executives and rank-and-file workers. About women, his estimate is that their ratio of alcoholism is 1 to 3 for men "and may even be close to 1 to 2." Years ago, he recalls, the ratio was 1 to 10. His reason for the revised figures: Women's problems in this respect are coming into the open as more and more of them enter the business world.

Dr. Robert L. Meineker, psychiatrist, discerns alcoholism in every industrial grouping. He suggests there may be more cases among rank-and-file people than executives on the supposition that most persons who show themselves so emotionally unbalanced don't rise beyond mid-management. He notes that the problem seems to increase about middle age. He suspects "there is more to the problem in general than we know." There is a vast conspiracy of concealment about alcoholism.

A bright side of this No. 1 blind spot of society at large is the growing number of persons in the public eye or in executive posts who openly identify themselves as recovered alcoholics so as to encourage a similar fight by others still in the throes of the emotional and physical sickness.

Politicians who have so described themselves include former Senator Harold E. Hughes and New Jersey Senator Harrison Williams, Jr.

Congressman Wilbur D. Mills has publicly acknowledged he is a victim of alcoholism. Mercedes McCambridge, the actress, another recovered alcoholic, has made public appearances in behalf of the National Council on Alcoholism. Robert Young, Dick Van Dyke, and Gary Crosby are other entertainers not ashamed to say they went through the ravages of the dread disease and freed themselves from its bondage.

Examples in the world of business are Thomas J. Swafford, vice-president, program practices, CBS Broadcast Group, member of the council's board and chairman of its public information committee, and Thomas P. Pike, vice-chairman, Fluor Corp., engineering and construction company for the petroleum industry. Pike, who after twenty-seven years of complete sobriety still describes himself as "an arrested alcoholic," is first vice-president and a board member of NCA, a trustee of Stanford University, a regent of Loyola University, and a former assistant secretary of defense. He has testified at hearings of the Senate Subcommittee on Alcoholism and Narcotics under Hughes' chairmanship that "the enormous economic and human waste is primarily due to attitudes founded on prejudices, ignorance, and apathy which grow out of certain popular myths and misconceptions."

"I think one of the members of my staff is an alcoholic," says an executive of a large company. "The man is frequently absent, his eyes are red, his hands tremble, he's often irritable. Should I call him into my office for a man-to-man talk about his drinking?"

Definitely not, advises Ross A. Von Wiegand, director, labor-management services, NCA. "The manager," he explains, "must handle alcoholism just as he would any other disease that affects output. After all, a manager isn't qualified to diagnose or treat any other illness—then, why alcoholism?"

The first important fact to understand is the great difference between social drinking and alcoholism. A person who can take a drink or two or three, but who can stop drinking any time he wants to, is a social drinker. An alcoholic, on the other hand, cannot control his drinking. He must drink for the effect it produces. His body and mind are soothed by drinking, and wracked with pain when the drinking stops.

The second important fact is that the problem-drinking that leads to alcoholism is a disease whose cause is not fully understood by doctors. However, it is known that the "chemical balance" in the alcoholic's body creates a craving for alcohol. There is a physical reason why most persons remain social drinkers all their lives while one out of twenty becomes an alcoholic.

The third fact is that alcoholism cannot be cured in the same sense that measles or a broken arm can be cured. The underlying causes of alcoholism cannot be removed.

Most important of all is the fourth fact: it offers the hope to the alcoholic, his family, and his company that the condition can be arrested, and the patient can live a comfortable, useful life.

But, to do so, the problem-drinker must stop drinking completely. An alcoholic can never hope to become merely a social drinker.

NCA was founded in 1944 as a voluntary, nonprofit health agency. It was started nineteen years after Alcoholics Anonymous. NCA has a management consultant team which works with a company to help eliminate the usual stigma attached to alcoholism so it may be handled like any other illness that hurts individual efficiency and effectiveness.

Confronted with an employee who may be an alcoholic, what should the man's superior do? Von Wiegand's recommendation:

He should carry out his responsibility—observe job and behavior performance, maintain minimum work standards and act only when the employee's work falls below this minimum. Industry's only clues to alcoholism are irregular behavior or work deterioration.

"The manager," the NCA official continues, "should document all cases of absenteeism or behavior disorders that affect the employee's work. Then, when he has built up a concrete case, he should call the man in and show him the record—but without mentioning alcoholism."

Rather, the executive should tell the subordinate something along these lines: "You're not doing well. I think you've developed some kind of problem, so I've referred you to the company doctor (or consultant). Unless you and he can find out what's happening, your job will be endangered."

This puts the diagnosis in qualified hands. If the employee doesn't take steps to correct the trouble, the manager must be ready to recommend his discharge. Alcoholic employees dealt with in this way are said to have high recovery rates—50 to 70 percent recovery that enables the employee to be retained as a valuable, dependable worker.

Yvelin Gardner, special consultant, NCA, says the problem "cuts across all lines from the tunnel sandhogger to the president of the company, from people who work for the government to professionals, in equal proportion to their presence in the population. The stereotypes are generally wrong. Creative people, sales executives, come out about the same as others who lead more placid lives."

Studies indicate to Gardner that those of Scandinavian and Irish ancestry are more susceptible to alcoholism than any other ethnic groups, those from Mediterranean and Latin countries are in between, and Jews are least affected. However, this cultural-religio pattern is changing as the older generation gives way to the new and "everybody is getting into the act."

Alcoholics Anonymous, with from 650,000 to 750,000 members, has done at least as much to treat problem-drinking as any other organization. AA was founded and is run by alcoholics who don't drink anymore but recognize no alcoholic is ever cured. At best, he remains a nondrinker, one who can never return to "social drinking." AA's basic technique is a weekly group meeting designed to strengthen the members' resolve to stop drinking. Somehow, it often works.

Faced with the alternative of firing a valuable, trained employee or attempting to help him, a growing number of concerns are opting for coming to his aid. On the basis that alcoholism may be arrested, although never cured, about 60 percent of those who accept treatment are helped and able to hold their jobs.

Incidence of alcoholism, it is stressed, is greater among executives than rank-and-file workers, and the difficulties of identification and control increase at the higher echelons of management.

Group medical policies of all major insurance companies cover the cost of alcoholism as of any other illness.

Perhaps four hundred major companies comprise the sole examples of successful policy and practices on alcoholism. Among these firms are Consolidated Edison Co. of New York, Du Pont, Union Carbide, Eastman Kodak, American Airlines, General Motors, Kennecott Copper, Allis-Chalmers, Northern Pacific Railroad, Equitable Life Assurance Society, Kemper Insurance Group, and Pacific Telephone & Telegraph.

Their programs run along lines of the three-step program advocated by NCA:

1. Education—getting across the fact that alcoholism is a disease and must be treated as such.
2. Early detection of the alcoholic by supervisors who are told about symptoms of short concentration span, nervousness, irritability, or other evidences of emotional and physical disorders.
3. Referral to treatment centers.

General Motors and the United Automobile Workers, in cooperation with the Detroit Health Department, are sponsoring a pilot drug-abuse program in five plants employing thirty thousand workers. Under this program, which is being operated with a $260,000 federal grant, employees are helped on a confidential basis without fear of disciplinary action against those who seek rehabilitation. GM had previously been working on the problem through some one hundred union-management committees in other plants through the United States and Canada. More than three thousand employees have been treated during the past few years.

Rowland L. Austin, who directs GM's program, thinks "the alcohol abuse problem is probably much more serious than drug addiction in terms of scope and size." He reports that as a result of the GM alcohol program about 60 percent of the workers who have been treated have shown "substantial" job improvement.

Chrysler Corp. started an alcohol referral program in 1968 and a hard drug program in 1970. Employees are referred to community agencies for rehabilitation.

Ford Motor Co. has an alcohol and drug abuse program offering aid in contacting professional agencies. Like the other two major auto companies, Ford arranges medical leaves and company insurance benefits if extensive treatment is needed.

Consolidated Edison Co. of New York is widely acknowledged in industrial-medical circles to have one of the most effective alcoholic-control programs of any company in the country. Certainly, it sponsors one of the oldest such programs.

In late 1947, Con Edison officially recognized chronic alcoholism as a medical condition and adopted a company procedure for its control. The decision was based on a policy that "we would meet the problem openly instead of perpetuating the outworn pretense it did not exist." Aim is threefold:

1. Early recognition of the employee with a drinking problem.
2. Rehabilitation of the employee if possible.
3. Establishment of a consistent basis for termination of employment when rehabilitation efforts prove fruitless.

Since 1952, Con Edison has underwritten the major cost of the Consultation Center for Alcoholism at NYU's University Hospital.

Dr. S. Charles Franco, with the company twenty-nine years, latterly as executive director of the medical department, comments on the necessity for a company procedure on alcoholism:

"We have had it amply demonstrated to us that alcoholism is a hidden disease. The common concepts of the alcoholic often do not apply in industry. Not only does the medical situation tend to confuse the picture, but the ability of the alcoholic to manipulate those about him accounts for the failure to gather factual information. Some alcoholics are covered by certificates provided by their family physicians. Others are hidden by industry itself because of years of faithful service or the idea among supervision that there is no adequate treatment. Medical experience discloses that, unless there is actually a company program in operation, management cannot have any accurate knowledge of the extent of the alcoholism problem."

Detailed analysis of the work behavior of the alcoholic employee at Con Edison, undertaken in 1962 by Professor Harrison Trice, indicates "very definite impairment of work performance in two areas: 1) increased absenteeism; 2) decreased work efficiency."

Two years prior to recognition, the alcoholics showed both significantly higher rates of incidence of absenteeism and actual days lost than did the normal employee group. For example, using ten days or more as a cutting-off point for "abnormal" absence, the normals had 5 percent above this point, and the alcoholics 29 percent. During the year before diagnosis, the alcoholics increased their absences further to nearly 33 percent and the normals stayed at 6 percent. The year of actual diagnosis saw a further increase and, at this point, 37 percent of the alcoholics were above the ten-day-per-year point. Following therapy, the cases still with the company dropped precipitously in both absenteeism indexes.

Analysis of on-the-job accident records provides interesting findings. Despite the differential exposure of the alcoholics because of their manual job assignments, only 9 percent of the alcoholics, as contrasted to 6 percent of the normals, had one or more lost time accidents during the five-year period prior to formal diagnosis. In an effort to find indirect evidence about off-the-job accidents, all medical diagnoses on alcoholics were recorded for an eight-year period prior to formal diagnosis. These revealed alcoholic employees diagnosed significantly more often for contusions and other minor injuries.

While alcoholic employees lack uniqueness where on-the-job accidents are concerned, they show it clearly in credit problems. Whether the credit deficiency is garnishee assignment or levy, they consistently have substantially more of these than the normal employees. For example, 20 percent of the alcoholics had one or more garnishments during the five years before diagnosis, while only 5 percent of the normals were in similar difficulties.

"Companies with a similar program are in the minority," Franco points out. "Imagine," he concludes, "what the problems are in companies without any procedure on alcoholism."

Dr. Thomas J. Doyle, Con Edison's assistant vice-president and medical director, concedes that the company's figures of known alcoholics jibe with NCA's estimate of 3 to 5 percent of the nation's work force. Con Ed's payroll totals twenty-five thousand, more than 85 percent of them men. About three hundred employees are in the alcoholism program at any one time.

Treatment begins with detoxification at a hospital. Usually, this is a ten-day period of special diet and medication and both supervised and unsupervised group therapy. Blue Cross covers the first few days. The rest is shared by the employee and a fund of the Con Edison Employees Mutual Aid

Society. The hospital has special counseling sessions for the alcoholic's family. Should future visits be called for, the employee pays the entire bill. So long as the worker follows the required treatment and rehabilitation, Con Edison pays his wages or salary.

Upon initial release from the hospital, most employees spend up to thirty days at a New York resort facility for the rehabilitation of alcoholics. This center offers no medical cure but operates on principles of AA. All costs are borne by the patient, but Con Edison keeps him on the payroll. When the man returns to work, he must report to the medical department at least once a month and must affiliate with an AA group. Visits to the medical department gradually taper off to one every six months. "If he can stay off liquor for two months," says Doyle, "we feel reasonably sure he has things under control."

Con Ed has a full-time counselor, a former chief line man, who works with the families of employees in the rehabilitation program and with employees who completed the program in the past but still have difficulty.

Du Pont company records indicate a salvage or rehabilitation rate of 67 percent of alcoholic employees who want to be helped.

How does the company uncover alcoholics? Through posters, other publicity, and safety talks. The doctors always describe alcoholism as a disease. You can't be a little bit alcoholic anymore than you can be a little bit pregnant is the way they put it. It often frightens the victims into applying for treatment of their own volition. Or relatives, friends, and neighbors may alert the doctors. In the final analysis, the alcoholic must be persuaded to help himself; no one can help him unless he himself wants to stop drinking to excess.

AA has proved extremely helpful in effecting improvement and keeping the person "dry." Du Pont has assigned an employee—a recovered alcoholic and member of AA—as a full-time member of the medical division's staff. This man interviews active or potential alcoholics and gives lectures to employees and supervisory groups.

"It must be obvious", the du Pont doctors asserted, "there are no easy, short-cut systems of mental or physical exercise gymnastics which will effect a cure-all or short-cut to mental health. There are as many different situations as there are people, and people will differ in their reactions to stressful situations. Each case needs to be individualized, analyzed, and considered in a personal light and from its own standpoint. There can be no 'catalog' therapy of emotional or mental disease."

Treating alcoholism as "a manageable illness is the twentieth-century thing to do. People must be contemporary in looking at such social problems."

Thus does G. G. Michelson, senior vice-president for consumer and employee relations, Macy's New York, describe the alcoholism clause in the new contract with Local 1-S, Department Store Workers Union RWDSU. Unprecedented for a New York-area retail company, the agreement provides workers with sick benefits for absence due to alcoholism under medical treatment. This is the same way the company assumes costs for other disabilities requiring employees to stay away from work. The sick benefit period of two-thirds of wages for hourly rated people is limited to twenty-six weeks, after which employees still under doctor's care and unable to return to the job go on unpaid leave.

Macy's extends the same pay hikes and other benefits to nonunion employees.

Ms. Michelson does not think the added sick benefit for the approximately eight thousand salespeople in the six (of fourteen) Macy's New York units covered by the contract will be a "significant" cost.

Prior to this agreement, she reports, "we have had considerable success in referring employees to Alcoholics Anonymous or to other therapeutic or medical facilities."

Alcoholic Macy executives "under appropriate care" have been informally compensated in the past with the same understanding on management's part that inordinate drinking is an illness amenable to treatment. Without having made any study of the incidence of alcoholism among executives in general, Ms. Michelson doubts that retailing, with all its pressures, presents as much of a problem in this respect as, say, the advertising business.

Alcoholism in retailing may pose far less of a problem than it does in heavy industry. The normal expectation in heavy industry is that a minimum of 6 to 8 percent of the total employee population—assuming an average age of forty-two and less than 5 percent of females—will suffer from some stage of alcoholism. In retailing, on the other hand, 70 percent of the employees may be female and the average age about thirty-five, with the result that the frequency of alcoholism may run far lower.

Drug addiction was also discussed during the recent negotiations, but the diversity and complexity of this problem apparently eluded ready translation into possible contract terms. In this regard, Macy's is following in the footsteps of other companies that handle alcohol, although not drugs, as a sickness, but presumably are watching the situation. Inability to reach a meeting of the minds was coincidentally reflected at the first national Drug Abuse Conference in Chicago. More than two thousand drug treatment specialists left for home with much greater accord on the changing pattern of narcotics abuse than on what to do about it.

A major flaw in all these programs is that they apply primarily to rank-and-file workers. For the most part, middle-to-top executives remain immune because they are not supervised in the usual sense and can indefinitely postpone paying the ultimate penalty of job dismissal.

Only when all members of the work force from chief executive down are included in programs to arrest alcoholism—there can never be complete recovery—will the disease be brought under control.

Causes of Drug Problems More Vexing Than Symptoms

Some 30 representatives of business, industry, government agencies, and the health-related professions met at American Management Association's headquarters to discuss "Drugs as a Management Problem."

Psychiatrist Ari Kiev told the audience: "Distress and depression are worldwide. People cannot admit their unhappiness, they must mask it. So, we have alcohol ingestion in the older age group and drug addiction in younger people."

The drug problem, it was made clear, is symptomatic of a malaise throughout the country and, indeed, in all of Western culture. The cause is many times more important than the symptom. The situation bears comparison with an iceberg, only a small portion of whose mass is on the surface. It is not enough to deplore the drug epidemic. It is necessary to probe to the enormous, concealed portion of the iceberg to analyze what is destroying the quality of life and proceed to do something meaningful about correcting the manifold faults of society.

Young people, who comprise the largest population on the drug scene, want to escape their elders' double talk and their own boredom, to be part of and accepted by the crowd, to feel big and unafraid.

In the world of business and the professions, reliance on drugs to ease the burden of everyday living is traceable to the materialism of the American way of life, to an intensely competitive drive for success not necessarily synonymous with performance. This is evidenced in frequent in-fighting—men stepping on the fingers of actual or potential rivals or enemies as they seek to scale the ladder of achievement rung by rung. Or is it wrong by wrong?

Use of drugs by elementary-school pupils, high school and college students, Vietnam veterans, and jobholders of all ages is increasing sharply. There are some observers who have written off the present generation as a lost cause.

Kiev warned that "a drug is a drug is a drug" isn't so. They all have different effects, he explained. But potential harm always outweighs seeming benefits. He urged that other avenues of relief be sought to avoid lasting serious physiological and psychological results.

His assessment of various drugs:

Heroin, most perilous drug of all, slows down drive and energy, makes a person apathetic, withdrawn, and passive. The addict is not likely to commit a crime then. But he may do so in the withdrawal stage, usually several hours after the last dose.

Barbiturates, useful when prescribed by doctors to induce sleep or quiet anxiety, can be dangerous. Thousands of deaths are due to overdoses taken in a confused state. Among celebrities who died in such a condition were Marilyn Monroe, Judy Garland, Alan Ladd, and Dorothy Kilgallen.

Amphetamines or pep pills are also prescribed by doctors in small amounts to relieve tiredness and depression. Athletes are among those resorting to pep pills in increasing numbers. If taken for kicks, the heart often beats irregularly, muscles jerk, and convulsions may follow.

LSD, one of the most potent hallucinogens, destroys judgment, makes some people think they can fly or that they are God. There is danger of permanent brain damage.

Marijuana, the most popular hallucinogen, distorts sense of time and stifles ambition. While it does not cause addiction—the disruption of the body's chemical balance to the point where the drug is needed to stay well physically —chronic users become dependent upon it psychologically.

Volatile solvents are being sniffed by youths to obtain the effects of euphoria, excitation, and exhilaration also derived temporarily from the more expensive drugs. Among these solvents are airplane glue, spot removers, gasoline, benzene, kerosene, hair sprays, and the gas produced in aerosol cans.

The leading cause of death in the age group from fifteen to thirty-five in New York State is acute narcosis—drug abuse of all kinds.

Among the speakers were Willard W. Peck, personnel vice-president, Metropolitan Life Insurance Co., and Raymond F. Sasso, corporate compensation manager, Pitney Bowes.

"Our employees," reported Peck, "are a cross-section of those who work everywhere and our drug problem is no better, no worse, than any other company's." He added, however, that use of drugs has showed up "shatteringly" among young job-applicants. The firm does not knowingly employ anyone with a drug problem although a "restricted" number are accepted from such institutions as Greenwich House which places persons in process of rehabilitation. The company has had "some successes and some failures," the failures being among heroin addicts.

Pitney Bowes has a five-year-old program "still not working," according to Sasso. "It's a time-consuming, frustrating job." He suggested that management functions and techniques—observing, analyzing, and taking active steps tailored to individual company needs—apply to drug abuse as well as to other problems. The company handles drug abuse as one of three major social problems, the others being alcoholism and mental illness.

Corporate Guidelines for Employment of Ex-Drug Addicts, Ex-Convicts

"Drug usage may, at least potentially, surpass alcoholism as a problem. Apparently, an increasing number of young people are exposed to drugs of all types and are experimenting with them. Addiction easily follows experimentation. Drug addiction, just as alcoholism, has no boundaries; it affects both white-collar and blue-collar workers."

This is the sobering opinion of the personnel relations director of a textile company who participated in a survey conducted by The Conference Board among a cross-section of companies on drug abuse in business.

Nearly two-thirds of the 222 firms, whose employee roster ranges in size from 250 to 250,000, express concern about the situation. Twenty-five percent say drug usage has already become a problem in their firms; 40 percent, that it shows signs of becoming one.

Of ninety firms mentioning the most common management problems stemming from employees' drug consumption, 41 percent cite absenteeism; 30 percent, turnover; 29 percent, decreased productivity; 21 percent, theft; 13 percent, interpersonal or morale problems.

While drug abuse is more prevalent in the large cities, it is noted in virtually all sections of the country.

Among firms that have had experience with drug abuse, 35 percent cite "soft" drugs and 15 percent specify "hard" addictive drugs. The other employers mention a broad cross-section of drugs.

Generally, the executives are relatively tolerant on the use of soft drugs —so long as this doesn't interfere with the person's job performance. Three percent of the respondents report they aren't concerned about drugs unless productivity is hindered. Many others reflect a laissez-faire attitude about use of drugs away from work.

The vice-president of a steel company warns against lumping all drugs together. He explains:

"We distinguish among three types of drugs: 1) Marijuana—most use this as older people use alcohol. We do not see it as a problem although, of course, it could be if the individual continually smoked at work. 2) Barbiturates, tranquilizers, and amphetamines—most people who use these are taking them on a doctor's prescription. Unless the use is excessive and produces significant behavioral changes at work, we expect to leave the question to the personal physician. 3) Hard drugs—these are the real problem. Increasing tolerance means the need for increasing amounts of the drug, which reaches a point that no salary or wage can support. The hard drug user becomes an increasing safety and security hazard."

As to what action companies take when they discover an employee is using drugs, a department store vice-president replies: "We would prefer to refer addicts to rehabilitation agencies since the police are notoriously inept at handling such things, for addiction is an illness. But where crime has occurred, we have no choice but to refer the offender to the police."

Findings on this point from the study as a whole:

Thirty-five percent of the companies either provide treatment or counseling or refer the employee to medical authorities; 22 percent fire the employee; 4 percent notify company security or local police, and 3 percent ignore it if job productivity isn't affected. About 36 percent have not yet had direct experience with the problem.

Drug users are more likely to be discharged from nonmanufacturing companies (retail, finance, utility, transportation) than from manufacturing firms. And newer employees are more apt to be dismissed than long-standing employees with good work records.

One hundred of the companies give funds to community programs of drug education, treatment, and rehabilitation. Only sixteen of these firms, however, donate money directly to such programs. (Two companies give $40,000 and $50,000, respectively, each year.) The remainder refer to corporate contributions to United Funds, Community Chests, or similar central community fund-raising organizations, some of whose funds are distributed to treatment and rehabilitation centers.

Seventeen companies participate in community programs to educate the population on drug abuse and rehabilitation, and two others lend professional personnel to such programs.

Ex-drug addicts fall into the category of people least likely to be acceptable to business and industry as potential employees. If this is true in normal times—and it is—imagine how much more of a fact of life it is during a period of recession.

The Manhattan Community Rehabilitation Center of the New York State Drug Abuse Commission sponsors an education department, including academic and vocational classes, for the females comprising the entire population of this residential treatment facility. Sewing, power machine operation, basic electricity, beauty culture, food service, typing, stenography and bookkeeping are in the vocational program. Twelve teachers and four para-professionals, supervised by Cynthia Dodge, comprise the education department. Among other activities are creative arts and crafts.

The center has an in-house population of about 150 and a capacity of 200. About twenty of the residents are on work or study-release outside the center and return in the evening for therapy. Another three hundred are in an after-care program geared to individual needs. Sixty percent of the "clients" are blacks; 20 percent, Puerto Ricans, the remainder mainly Caucasians. Average age is twenty or twenty-one.

296   MANAGEMENT'S CHALLENGE

This is the only such downstate New York center. There is another female facility elsewhere in the state and thirteen centers for males.

The sewing department is a licensed, sheltered, transitional workshop. Contracts from the outside enable the girls to receive piece-work pay based on Department of Labor standards. Thirty-two girls are in basic or intermediate sewing, fourteen in advance sewing, and ten in the transitional workshop. The advance students learn to operate machines and make apparel for themselves. Twelve girls in a boutique setup design apparel and accessories which are sold to the staff and outsiders.

Basically, however, the workshop develops industrial, not entrepreneurial, skills.

Hale N. Alpern, who has been in the dress industry twenty years, has been involved as "a friend" in the rehab center's sewing department since May, 1974. Alpern's father Milton was a founder of Weinberg, Weinberg & Alpern, dress manufacturer, seventy-five years ago.

Looking for job and contract opportunities, Patrick Daly, the center's senior placement officer, met Hale Alpern. Soon thereafter, the socially conscious manufacturer was making regular visits to the West 41st Street center. Alpern, now employed by a dress house in a sales, styling, and production capacity, shows up at the center in the early morning and during his lunch hour. As an unpaid volunteer, he has aided the staff in setting up the transitional workshop under industrial standards. He has also helped obtain a number of contracts.

Offering the industry "a training and placement proposal for a blue-collar female labor force," Alpern quotes the center's Pat Daly: "The clients at Manhattan Rehab are among the least employable in our society and, unless programs provide them with skills and motivation necessary to break the cycle of welfare dependency, they will continue to receive public assistance throughout their lives."

A viable alternative, as Alpern sees it, is to recruit women from narcotics rehabilitation institutions, perpetrators of victimless crimes and from the welfare rolls for blue-collar labor in the apparel industry. "Fully aware" as he is of the depressed state of the economy and of the increasing unemployment rate, he nevertheless stresses "it remains critically important to recognize that the apparel industry continue to search for skilled sewing and special machine operators to fill the shrinking ranks of blue-collar workers. The exodus of New York City manufacturing plants, in part the consequence of a diminishing skilled labor pool, threatens the tax base and thereby exacerbates the social problems."

Alpern suggests that females be brought into the apparel industry's mainstream in three stages:

1. An expansion of the training program at Manhattan Rehab.
2. Funding for implementation, perhaps the most critical stage. Women

would be coming into the program from an institution or directly from welfare with little or no training in apparel production. They would be trained and paid on a piece-work basis in an environment unlike the artificial conditions of institutional life but, rather, according to the exacting conditions of industrial production. This stage understands the continuing need for ego-building—fear of failure may be the most significant cause of recidivism. Stage 2 is analogous to a ferris wheel. As new trainees enter the program, they replace those who are competent to enter stage 3.
3. The actual job market. In order to make a successful transition between stages 2 and 3, the individual must adopt the motivation and resiliency that are necessary qualities of regular employment.

Marguerite T. Saunders, Manhattan Rehab's director, says "we want to work more closely with the apparel industry in creating a semi-sheltered factory situation that would give the ex-addicts a greater sense of accomplishment. We also want to train more of our women to assume craft and machinist jobs traditionally held by men."

"An ex-addict without employment is an ex-addict without cure."
This is how Rexford Tompkins, president, Dry Dock Savings Bank, put into perspective a two-day labor-management conference, on "Drug Use Among Workers: Developing Policies and Guidelines."
William I. Spencer, president, First National City Bank, another conference speaker, echoed Tompkins' comment: "We recognized the ultimate harm of treating addicts as social lepers. If a person has been rehabilitated from the habit but is treated no differently from a current user, there is little incentive for a cure."
Dr. Henry Brill, psychiatrist and regional director of the New York State Department of Mental Hygiene, urged labor-management cooperation in bringing the model of treatment for alcoholics to bear upon building a program for dealing with the drug problem. In the case of drugs as of alcohol, the approach is through education of all concerned as to why "the man takes a drink, and then the drink takes the man."
Principal sponsors of the meeting were the New York State Drug Abuse Control Commission (DACC) and Provide Addict Care Today (PACT). The former is a state agency; the latter, a private, nonprofit organization created by business and labor in 1972 to locate jobs for rehabilitated drug addicts and give technical assistance and liaison to employers and treatment centers.
Citibank hired thirteen presumably rehabilitated addicts from 1970 to 1972. Of these, six are still with the bank. Three were released for suspected drug use. In 1973, a goal of hiring fifty rehabilitated addicts was set. Screened by PACT and others, thirty persons were hired of 142 interviewed. Twenty-three of the hirees are still employed. Of the remainder, terminations were

almost evenly divided between voluntary resignations and releases for unsatis-factory performance. No one has been dismissed for drug abuse.

These statistics, Spencer suggested, demonstrate, "addicts can be treated and rehabilitated to lead lives that are satisfying to themselves and useful to society."

Disavowing any idea that ideal solutions have been found, Spencer ob-served: "One thing we are discovering is that many people we interview are medically and emotionally equipped for work, but they lack the educational fundamentals and elementary skills needed for anything but the most menial jobs. I know rehabilitation centers would like to offer these, but they don't have experienced personnel or sufficient funding for the task. On the other hand, business and labor have long carried on significant efforts to upgrade educa-tional and occupational skills. It seems logical to me that they make their expertise and resources available to treatment centers, so that individuals can get the entire range of help they need. My company, for one, is ready to join in such a cooperative program."

Brill's advice: "There are a number of misleading stereotypes: that all drugs are heroin; that, once a drug user, always a drug user, that a drug user is a criminal by nature who has to steal to carry on his habit. We must consider how drug use interferes with productivity on the job. Remember, there are many intensities of involvement with drugs. People who have tried marijuana and other 'soft' drugs—no fewer than twenty-five to thirty million Americans have experimented with marijuana—aren't necessarily drug fiends, pushers, or potential thieves. This drug may be used daily without interfering with regular lives. Large numbers of heroin users are not physically hooked. Cocaine is probably the most addictive of all drugs.

"Drug users are found at every level of an organization. Sometimes, overdriven, sensitive people find their way into use of drugs, mostly minor tranquilizers, in an attempt to balance their lives. The social use of drugs is to be compared with the social use of alcohol. The same principles for the rehabilitation of alcoholics are applicable to drug users. However, marijuana on the job, as alcohol on the job, should not be tolerated."

Anthony Cagliostro, DACC chairman, told the gathering that the state's Civil Service Commission and his agency have instituted a set of "operating principles" that bar discrimination in state civil service jobs against ex-addicts. The New York City and federal civil service systems have similar regulations.

The Central Labor Rehabilitation Council of New York sponsors a six-week training seminar on the education and prevention of drug abuse.

Gerald R. Waters, Sr., the council's administrator, is director of the Community Services Committee, New York City Central Labor Council, which founded the rehab council in 1963. Since then, 8,500 individual cases of all social problems of members, their families and neighbors have been handled. An estimated 9 percent of these cases concern drug abuse. Waters says alcoholism has become a greater problem than drugs in the past few years.

The consensus of the conference's participants was that, in drugs as in alcohol, companies shouldn't confine their interest to the failures of "skid row" but should share positive experiences as well. Just as important, commitment of top-level executives to a liberal policy with realistic goals is vital to the success of any antidrug-abuse program.

As with alcoholics and drug addicts, the business community has begun to view ex-convicts with enlightened self-interest. Training and hiring of such rehabilitated men and women—too often condemned out of hand as outcasts —for meaningful jobs are being increasingly regarded not only as an evidence of social consciousness, but also as a forward step in reducing insurance rates, taxes, and the cost of doing business.

With these results as a goal, the New York metro division of the National Alliance of Businessmen conducted five two-hour workshops for representatives of various types of business. All were concerned with employment programs for "ex-offenders," the term used by the organization when referring to ex-convicts.

The retailing workshop was attended by a dozen personnel executives of New York-area stores and chain headquarters as well as others from industrial companies and social agencies. Views expressed by several of the retail representatives:

Retailing has "particular vulnerability with respect to exposure of ex-offender employees to money and merchandise. They should be placed in work situations most calculated to help them make the best possible job contribution. We in personnel must be concerned about the criticism to which we would be subjected in the event an employee who assaulted a customer was found by top management to have a criminal record. I think that retail security people, to a man, would be opposed to hiring ex-offenders. They would say they are already up to their ears in problems and don't want to compound them." (A hotel security head took exception to this comment. He argued he had hired twelve ex-felons and eight have worked out well.)

Another participant: "It might be better to employ them in warehousing, receiving, wrapping and packing."

A third personnel executive: "I'd be wary of choosing an ex-offender who had a rape or armed robbery record for a sales clerk. I'd employ someone who committed one murder. That's usually a once-in-a-lifetime thing."

Still another: Let's not play God. Why not employ them in any jobs for which they may be fitted, not just behind the scenes."

And yet another: "What are the true credentials, rather than preconceived notions based on education and business background, that tell us everything we should know about any job candidates, let alone ex-offenders? I wonder if we have all the information that really matters."

It was agreed that top management's support is absolutely necessary for any cooperative program with NAB and social agencies to be useful. It was further noted that "everyone has built-in prejudices and, at least, this meeting is an ice-breaker in providing food for thought toward specific action."

William M. Ellinghaus, president, New York Telephone Co., and chairman, NAB, which is a combination of business, labor, and government, urged his fellow executives "to see what you can do about placing ex-offenders in jobs." He pointed out that social agencies work with such persons until they meet standards of ability and determination, after which they are screened by businessmen on loan from their companies to NAB.

John Armore, ex-offender, program director working out of NAB's national office in Washington, another speaker, described himself as an "ex-con." He was a California lawyer, assistant city attorney, and a municipal prosecutor. While employed as a branch manager for an insurance company, he started gambling on a regular basis in close-by Reno and embezzled money from his firm to cover his losses. He finally turned himself in and served three years of a two-to-twenty-eight-year sentence in San Quentin. After he was paroled, he undertook social work.

"If ex-offenders are rejected time and again by society," he warned, "we sentence them to a life sentence on the installment plan . . . we're opening the door to bigger and better crimes. Seventy percent of ex-offenders become recidivists—return to crime—in a period of five years because they can't find a meaningful job. Nationally, crime costs over six billion a year, 3 percent of the GNP. We can't turn our backs on them."

In a message to the gathering, Senator Javits reported that NAB's ex-offender program in less than one year provided 4,620 jobs. Of these, 337 were in New York State, with New York City responsible for 223 of these jobs. Javits found this only the merest beginning when it is considered that twenty-five times more ex-offenders—over 100,000—are released from prison each year than obtain employment. He advised that, "if every third business establishment of the 3,500,000 in this country hired an ex-offender, the problem would be licked."

NAB also has job programs for disabled and other veterans, minority groups, and young people in summer internships. Companies grant six-to-twelve-month sabbaticals at full salary to executives to work at NAB on training and placement projects and as "a clearing house and catalytic agent for guidance of business firms and social and governmental agencies."

He's a black man about thirty. He's had a tenth-grade education but reads at a fifth-or sixth-grade level. He's had eight arrests and four convictions on his record. He's an ex-heroin addict, usually maintained on methadone. He has not been employed more than six months in the last two years and the jobs he has held have been menial and dead end. He has no marketable skills.

You couldn't pick a less likely potential candidate for a job. Right? Wrong!

Wildcat Service Corp., an organization that describes itself as "purposefully seeking employment opportunities for socially disadvantaged persons with the worst work records," draws this profile of the typical person on its roster.

The above profile is an average. Wildcatters come in either as ex-addicts or ex-convicts. Within the two groups, about 75 percent of the ex-addicts are ex-convicts and about 83 percent of the ex-convicts are ex-addicts. About 65 percent are black; 25 percent of Hispanic origin, 10 percent white. Ten percent are women. Less than 20 percent of the total have completed high school.

The name "Wildcat" derives from wildcatting—to prospect and drill an experimental oil or gas well in territory not known to be productive. This public service corporation is an offshoot of Vera Institute of Justice, founded about twelve years ago by Louis Schweitzer, a retired chemical engineer, as a private, nonprofit research and demonstration organization in the field of criminal justice. For years before his death in 1971, Schweitzer financed the project, which he had named for his mother, primarily from his own pocket. He willed Vera Institute a six-story midtown building for its headquarters. Vera is supported by a $1,500,000 yearly grant from the Ford Foundation plus federal and other funding.

Wildcat is funded by the Department of Labor, the New York City Department of Employment, the Law Enforcement Assistance Administration and Welfare Diversion (money from the Social Security Administration). Wildcat has units in Manhattan (also covering Staten Island), Brooklyn (also covering Queens) and The Bronx. Largest is the Manhattan unit with seven hundred employees and a staff of about seventy-five.

Over twenty-five hundred Wildcatters have been employed in all projects since the group's formation in July, 1972.

There are quite a number of agencies that, in one way or another, parallel Wildcat-Vera's work of seeking to restore ex-addicts and ex-offenders to the mainstream of the economy. However, Wildcat is the only one that puts people on its own payroll and gives them on-the-job experience to make them employable in the public or private sectors.

More than fifty projects are under way in Manhattan. The largest is at the South Street Seaport Museum. There, ninety persons at the museum's Pioneer Marine Technical School are repairing boats in training for jobs in marinas throughout the country. Three information booths, manned by Wildcatters, are at Seventh Avenue and 39th Street, Lincoln Center, and the South Street Museum. Co-sponsors of the Seventh Avenue booth are Fashion Capital of the World, the Mayor's Office of Apparel Industry Planning and Development, the Midtown Realty Owners Corp. and eight banks. Other Wildcat operations in the area are servicing one hundred trash baskets and placing stamp-registered identification numbers on movable equipment used by businesses.

More than thirty Wildcatters are employed in the mid-Manhattan branch of the public library and an additional twenty-one are with the library in "roll-over" positions—Wildcat "alumni" who have been hired by outside agencies after a period of supported work.

Wages average more than double the welfare checks which, on a voluntary, nonpunitive basis, are diverted to Wildcat. The Wildcatter starts at $95 a week and, if he remains a crew member, can go within thirty-six weeks to $115 plus bonuses up to $20 a month determined by on-time attendance and productivity requirements. Crew members can move up to deputy division chief. One ex-addict who has moved up into that capacity makes $13,673 with the potential of going to $15,000.

However, Wildcat usually discourages any movement beyond the foreman level which pays $125 to $135 a week because "we are a transitional employer and our major goal is to move our people to jobs in the private or public sectors. Our average employee is ready in nine months to move into the regular economy, but if he is doing well, we don't throw him out. Of some four hundred hired in the first nine months of Wildcat's operation, only 8 percent are still in a crew capacity."

Supported work, based on the Wildcat model, has already spread to projects in Boston and Philadelphia and is expected to be expanded to a total of nineteen municipalities all over the country. The Department of Labor will fund plans not only for work for ex-addicts and ex-offenders but also for alcoholics, welfare mothers, and youth.

Of about 250 Wildcat ex-addicts and ex-convicts placed in jobs in the private or public sector, 80 to 85 percent are still on the first job or in better positions.

Peter M. Cove, director of Wildcat's Manhattan unit, and Paul A. Strasburg, Vera's citywide director of job development, are particularly proud of this result in light of the fact that the background of these socially disadvantaged persons includes bad work records.

Strasburg reports that "most of the employees we have placed in regular business and industry are highly motivated and productive. It's very rare that a guy gets sacked for theft, violent behavior, or drug use on the job. Firing for poor attendance, poor punctuality, or poor performance follows the pattern in the general population."

On the whole, though, overall results of a concentrated effort by Wildcat and other agencies to encourage more private-sector placement have been disappointing. Employer anxiety about possible on-the-job behavior of such employees as well as the adverse turn in the economy are cited as leading reasons for continued negative reactions.

Still, a number of positive experiences indicate slow but sure progress is being made.

Two years ago, Chemical Bank hired thirteen ex-addicts, some of them ex-offenders, who had been recruited and screened by Wildcat but had not followed the usual procedure of being first employed by that agency. With the approval of a bonding company, they started in the bank's check encoding unit. In the first four weeks, one dropped out and returned to his old habits. Two were terminated for poor attendance or persistent tardiness after warnings and suggestions. Of the remaining ten, four have been promoted, one to a supervisor. The usual turnover rate in Chem Bank's check encoding area is about 30 percent, so the bank feels this particular employee group is well within limits.

Other Chem Bank employees are kept apprised of the employment of these people and the reasons for their being hired.

A similar project at Off-Track Betting Corp. offices is also reported to have worked out well.

A pre-employment job-training program for ex-addicts, ex-offenders, and other disadvantaged people at Con Ed is said to be highly successful.

IBM has helped Wildcat set up a training program for twenty-five Wildcat employees in word-processing—clerical and secretarial work. The agency pays its people while in this training, and IBM supplies the space, equipment, and staff. IBM has support from twenty other companies, in such fields as oil, banking, engineering, advertising, and media, which have agreed to hire these persons.

A vice-president of one major New York department store, insisting on anonymity, says "we are just now putting one toe in the water. After discussions with the NAB, we are taking on one or two first-time offenders for whom the job prognosis under supervision is favorable."

Wildcat plans to ask major companies through "private-sector buffer agencies" to set up a board of "friends of Wildcat" who have had good personal experiences with such employees and might be able to influence other employers "to squeeze out placements." Through this means, Wildcat hopes to come up with one hundred companies each of which might supply three positions for a total of three hundred assured placements a year.

Norborne Berkeley, Jr., Chem Bank's president and Wildcat's chairman of a board including representatives of business and labor, sums up:

"Business must become increasingly responsive to providing solutions to problems we once believed were strictly the responsibility of the public sector. If the business community fails to meet this challenge, our central cities as we know them today may well disappear.

"The business community must work with our elected representatives to bring about meaningful reform in the criminal justice system—NOW. We must cooperate with government in trying to better prepare individuals in prison for successful reentry into the job market and society. Again, working with government, we must make every effort to provide employment opportunities for ex-offenders and to make certain there is every chance for success. Beyond the fact we can materially help in employment and reduction in crime, we can demonstrate to young graduates whom we try to attract to our business that our sole objective as a member of the community is not simply profit."

14

HELP FROM
THE EXPERTS

What Can Be Done about the Parent,
Adult, Child in Us All?

Muriel James, human relations counselor and consultant, has been involved in transactional analysis (TA) for more than a dozen years. She has a doctorate from the University of California in the psychology of adult education. The "transaction" in TA means "you do or say something to me, and I do something back." Every person, the theory goes, is made up of three parts: parent, adult, and child. These are all present in varying degrees inside the same person and make themselves felt in behavioral changes in the total personality evidenced in facial expressions, word intonations, sentence structure, body movements, gestures, tics, posture and carriage. Originally, TA was a method of psychotherapy to be used in group treatment. Its principles have been extended to application on the job, in the home, in the classroom, in the neighborhood—wherever people deal with people.

The parent emerges from recordings in the brain of imposed, unquestioned, external events between birth and age five—what Mom and Dad and other significant authorities said and did. The child comes through from

recordings in the brain of internal events and emotional feelings in response
to external events between birth and age five. The adult is reflected in recordings, acquired through independent rational exploration and testing, and operating as a computer and data bank beginning at ten months of age.

Aim of TA, as taught by Thomas A. Harris, medical doctor with special
training in psychiatry and psychoanalysis, is to instill in everyone the philosophy, *I'm OK—You're OK,* the title of his book. The concept is that what makes
a person unhappy is an unbalanced relationship between the three permanent
parts constituting every human personality: parent, adult, and child. The
human brain shifts gears from one of these "ego states" to another, depending
on the way one individual reacts to another at any particular moment.

The most common of four life attitudes is, "I'm not OK, you're OK."
The others are, I'm OK, you're not OK," "I'm not OK, you're not OK," and
"I'm OK, you're OK." Even the last-named attitude—the only adult life
position—is not perpetual because unhappy relationships in one's past or
present are inescapable, but it does promise greater ability to withstand depression or despair. The theory is that, unless the rational adult dominates the
personality, the overly restrictive parent and the self-deprecating child will foul
up most "transactions" or relationships with others.

Harris endorses ideas previously propounded by the late Eric Berne, who
in 1964 wrote *Games People Play.* Berne's beliefs stem from psychiatrist Alfred
Adler's teaching of a universal "inferiority feeling." An estimated three thousand psychiatrists, psychologists, social workers, ministers, business firms, and
governmental agencies in the United States and fourteen other countries have
experimented with this method for improving personal and organizational
effectiveness and productivity. If it doesn't cure neuroses, it at least provides
a creed that might help men, women, and youngsters live with themselves.

Dr. James is director of the Oasis Education and Counseling Center and
of the Transactional Analysis Institute, Lafayette, Calif., where she lives with
her husband, Ernest Brawley, an officer of the California State Department of
Correction. She is a consultant to business firms, government agencies, and
school systems and an associate professor at California State University at
Hayward. Dr. James is a licensed marriage and family counselor, a trustee and
teaching member of the International Transactional Analysis Association and
an ordained minister and guest preacher in the United Church of Christ
(Congregational).

Dr. James stresses the words "winner" and "loser." A winner is "one
who responds authentically by being credible, trustworthy, responsive and
genuine, both as an individual and as a member of society." A loser is "one
who fails to respond authentically." As almost everyone, depending on a
particular situation, is parent, adult, or child or a mixture of each, few people
are 100 percent winners or losers.

There are nine common ways of transacting but dozens of variations.
Among other principal TA terms are:

Scripts. The life drama a person may be unaware of but feels compelled to live by.

Stroking. Recognizing, positively or negatively, other people through touch. Because society generally frowns on physical touch, a person touches another with words.

Contracts. An adult commitment to one's self or someone else to make a change in feelings, behavior, or psychosomatic problems.

Dr. James sees many salespeople in a parent-child relationship. She can't stand "some creepy saleswoman saying to me, 'Honey, that looks beautiful on you,' when I know it doesn't or the clerk who tries a child-child transaction with, 'Now, if you wear that, you'll surely attract the men.'" She doesn't encounter enough clerks who treat customers on an adult-adult basis—"This style is not as becoming as something else I want to show you." As an example of a parent-parent transaction, there is the clerk who says, "Ain't it awful the way kids dress nowadays?"

Dr. James laments the scarcity of ads that treat women as "realistic adults who might well wonder why they're being conned by pictures of tall, willowy, gorgeous models when a large part of the female population is short and round like me. I think more and more women are showing an adult ego state by refusing to buy certain apparel and shoes because they're the things to wear."

Samuel N. Park, director of TRANSACT, consulting organization, contends: "I'm so sure of TA and its proper follow-up, I'm trying to get up enough nerve to assure companies using our program that, if they don't raise sales, there will be no charge." For department and specialty stores, he suggests, "certain techniques for stroking personnel and customers should improve sales."

Donald G. Livingston, vice-president, administration, Western Union, Data Services Co., Mahwah, N.J. asserts: "People are born to win but learn to lose by their experiences in life ... Most people in industry are manipulated, only a few are rewarded" and "The thicker the rule book and the labor agreement, the thicker the management."

"Management must give TA more of a chance. Too often, they are turned off in advance by adverse experiences with other techniques that have come out of the social sciences. In this category are group dynamics, sensitivity training, laboratory training, management grid, and Management by Objectives. These all have positive elements but are misunderstood, misused and oversold, with the result that the baby is thrown out with the bath water. Instead of viewing them as panaceas, management should use them selectively, working on clear-cut objectives for specific problems."

A dozen young men and women—assistant buyers and others in comparable operating posts—gathered in a conference room at Sears, Roebuck's New York fashion-buying headquarters for their first of a weekly series of ten two-hour sessions on transactional analysis and group dynamics. This was part of a voluntary program instituted in August, 1973. Each group is composed of peers so as to minimize the possibility of domination. The course would eventually be taken by all managerial employees in the New York office in groups of up to fifteen.

Winfield Firman, Sears' personnel director in the New York fashion office, introduced this program of group dynamics—bringing the thinking of the group to bear upon a problem—to his company. He has studied TA at night under professional auspices. He serves as co-facilitator (co-leader) with Mary Sabel Girard, personnel consultant who retired in 1972 as personnel vice-president at Ohrbach's. She learned TA from the Institute for Transactional Analysis of New York and Connecticut. She attended the Post Graduate Center for Mental Health and was awarded a certificate in psychoanalytic counseling. Ms. Girard works in that field in business and industry and in social organizations.

Stressing "there's no therapy in our concept of TA," Firman says he is "seeking a means to make our managers better communicators and, through self-awareness, better able to understand themselves and deal more effectively with people over them and under them."

At the end of the ten weeks, each participant is asked to answer five questions for Ms. Girard as an evaluation of the program:

1. What parts of this series of meetings meant the most to you as a person in your personal life?
2. What part meant the most to you as an executive in Sears?
3. What did you consider the strong point?
4. What did you consider the weak point?
5. Do you have any suggestions for the program?

Ms. Girard reviews the replies and sends a summary of the critiques and her opinions to Firman, keeping specific identities of all participants anonymous. The two co-leaders emphasize that the only suggestions weighed are those for possible changes in the program, not for changes in the company. They concur that, "Any changes in the company will be the result of personal growth of the individuals."

Since 1971, 22 of 30 member companies of Associated Merchandising Corp. have adopted TA as part of their training programs for salespersons, adjusters, credit interviewers, and other customer-contact employees.

According to Janet Freeman, AMC's divisional vice-president of store personnel, the members' TA venture "grew out of dissatisfaction with traditional training for such personnel. This has tended to teach salespersons and other customer-contact people about systems and general selling principles but to neglect a vital part of the sale—the customer."

AMC believes TA is a viable addition to traditional training, that it is a useful approach in that an employee can easily identify his own experiences in TA terms and relate these to actual workaday encounters. The program was tried at one store and then at a second, and only when these tests proved successful was it introduced in the other twenty companies.

TA training is given in five three-hour sessions spread over five weeks. This permits people to try out TA on the job and feed back their experiences in subsequent training seminars. TA is also approached within a larger framework of "awareness" training, and the seminar content is only about one-third devoted to theory. The rest of the time is spent in analyzing actual on-the-job experiences of the participants, along with group discussion of the roles they play in customer contact. This program is called AURA, an acronym for "Awareness, Understanding, Responsibility, Action."

AMC has also developed a more complex, in-depth series of executive seminars. These are called TAPE, an acronym for "Transactional Analysis Program for Executives." Ms. Freeman and two outside consultants trained five representatives of as many member firms. After a year's testing period in several stores, TAPE was launched in 1973 in Filene's, Bloomingdale's, Woodward & Lothrop and the AMC office and since then has been adopted by another five members. These seminars have been designed for "cousins" groups—managers at approximately the same hierarchial level.

Both the AURA and TAPE terms were devised by Ms. Freeman and are copyrighted by AMC.

An estimated twenty thousand employees in AMC's member stores and office have had at least initial TA training.

Ms. Freeman reports, "We have seen some improvement as a result of AURA in 70 percent of the service people, some a little bit, others a lot. As to TAPE, about half of the executives who have been through the seminars have found it useful in their work, especially in supervising others. The others have failed to accept it because of a combination of store atmosphere and executive attitude. They don't feel it adds another dimension to their managerial style."

AMC has sold kits of these programs to hospitals, a telephone company, and a number of non-AMC stores. A distribution agreement has been entered upon with Reuben H. Donnelly Corp. on AURA which has been upgraded and otherwise made more sophisticated for broadened application outside retailing.

TM: Personalized Technique to Relieve Harmful Stress

Transcendental meditation is described by its adherents as neither a religion nor a philosophy but, rather, an effective method for relieving the debilitating effects of stress. "Transcendental" means "going beyond"—a term indicating that TM spontaneously takes its practitioners beyond the familiar level of their wakeful experience to a state of profound rest coupled with heightened awareness.

The technique was introduced in the United States in 1959 by Maharishi Mahesh Yogi, an Indian teacher, and has since been taught to more than a third of a million Americans. Worldwide, it is claimed, there are over 1 million meditators.

TM can be learned in a few hours and is then practiced for only 15 to 20 minutes each morning and evening. Specifically, it allows the activity of the mind to settle down while one sits with eyes closed. This mental process automatically triggers a physiological response conducive to both deep rest and increased wakefulness. Because learning to meditate does not involve cultivating a new skill but, instead, simply allows an innate ability of the nervous system to unfold, it requires no particular attitude, preparatory ritual, special setting or unusual postures. Though the technique is usually practiced at home, it may be done in any place where a person can sit comfortably without being disturbed. Meditation may be carried on in trains or buses or on planes.

After a few short training sessions with a teacher of TM (usually two evening lectures and an hour of individual instruction at a cost of $125), the student is assigned a "mantra." The mantra—a Sanskrit word for a kind of pleasant sound—is selected upon the basis of the personality of each student. Maharishi suggests that a proper, individual mantra can be prescribed just as a doctor can determine a person's blood type.

Harold H. Bloomfield, Michael Peter Cain, Dennis T. Jaffe and Robert Kory have written "TM: Discovering Inner Energy and Overcoming Stress." Bloomfield is clinical director of psychiatry, Institute of Psychophysiological Medicine, El Cajon, Calif. He is the first medical doctor to have become a trained teacher of TM. Cain is professor of art, Maharishi International University, which has residential campuses in Fairfield, Iowa, and Seelisburg, Switzerland, and programs in many other schools throughout the world. Jaffe is connected with the Department of Psychiatry, UCLA. Kory is vice-president, American Foundation for the Science of Creative Intelligence. AFSCI, which has headquarters in Los Angeles, is an official branch of the International Meditation Society, devoted to the application of TM to business. TM training programs are offered for executives, either through business schools or directly within the companies.

The authors cite scientific research that the body is in a distinctly different physiological state during meditation than during the other three states of consciousness—sleeping, waking and dreaming. The transcendental state of deep rest is said to remove many stresses, thus releasing previously blocked sources of energy, intelligence and creativity. Through the subsequent relief of fatigue, frustration, anxiety and mental and physical abnormalities that impair normal functioning of the nervous system, TM maintains, it helps people avoid or alleviate the diseases that such conditions can cause: insomnia, tension headaches, hypertension, bronchial asthma, emotional distress and overuse of cigarettes and alcohol.

Bloomfield and his co-authors report that over 30 executives at Arthur D. Little, management consulting firm, practice TM regularly and have set aside a room for meditation. Among other firms where executives practice TM are Monsanto, General Motors, Travelers Insurance, Sprague Electric, Westinghouse, Aetna Insurance, IBM, Eastman Kodak and Xerox. Still other organizations that have taken SCI courses are AT&T, Crocker National Bank in San Francisco, General Foods, the Detroit Engineering Society and Rensselaer Polytechnic Institute.

David R. Frew, director of the graduate administrative program and professor of organizational behavior, Cannon College, Erie, Pa., has written about TM as a management tool.

On the basis of interviews with about 400 practicing meditators at all corporate levels, Frew finds "a strong, positive relationship between TM and productivity. Reduction of stress, facilitated by TM, has resulted in increased job satisfaction, higher levels of output, reduced absenteeism, better relationships with people at work, improved relationships with superiors and a reduced drive to climb the executive ladder." The higher the job level, the greater the gain in creativity and productivity reported by the respondents.

Frew's investigation discloses existence of what he calls "the closet-meditator syndrome." Pressures for conformity among many upper and middle-level managers have led to a basic reluctance to admit to a practice as "weird" as meditation. As one bank president puts it: "If my board of trustees heard that we were paying for the executive staff to learn TM, they would have my head." But, in more than 30 "TM companies," the common feeling is that meditation "is both personally exciting and organizationally useful."

Bloomfield and his associates emphasize TM "is not a miracle cure or panacea. TM should never be considered a replacement for antihypertensive medication, an ulcer diet or anti-epilectic drugs. On the basis of our present knowledge, however, regular practice of TM does appear to make a significant contribution to the prevention and alleviation of psychosomatic illnesses."

Every company would do all its employees a good turn by offering a "relaxation response" as a self-cure for combating stress.

This is the advice of Dr. Herbert Benson, associate professor of medicine, Harvard Medical School, and a former consultant to the National Institute of Mental Health.

Benson defines relaxation response as "an innate integrated set of physiologic changes opposite those of the fight-or-flight response, also present in man. The practice of one well-investigated technique—transcendental meditation—results in physiological changes consistent with generalized decreased sympathetic nervous system activity. There is a simultaneous decrease in the body's metabolism, in heart rate, and in rate of breathing. Blood pressure remains unchanged." Among other techniques are Zen and yoga.

On the other hand, the flight-or-fight response is characterized by coordinated increases in oxygen consumption, blood pressure, heart rate, rate of breathing, amount of blood pumped by the heart, and amount of blood pumped to the skeletal muscles. This response is still a necessary and useful physiologic feature for survival, but its harmful effects can be counteracted.

Benson cites four basic approaches common to relaxation techniques long framed in the vocabularies of religions and cults—elements he has used in his own laboratory:

1. A quiet, calm environment with as few distractions as possible. The place could be an office desk. Sound, even background noise, may prevent elicitation of the response.
2. A mental device. The meditator employs the constant stimulus of a single-syllable sound or word. The syllable is repeated silently or in a low, gentle tone. The purpose of the repetition is to free oneself from logical, externally oriented thought by focusing solely on the stimulus. Many different words and sounds have been used in traditional practices. Because of its simplicity and neutrality, the use of the syllable "one" is suggested.
3. A passive attitude. One should not scrutinize his performance or try to force the response because this may well prevent the response from occurring. When distracting thoughts enter the mind, they should simply be disregarded.
4. A comfortable, restful position. The purpose is to reduce muscular effort to a minimum. The head may be supported, the arms should be balanced or supported as well. Shoes may be removed and feet propped up several inches, if desired. Loosen all tight-fitting clothing.

Benson then discusses the "mental, noncultic" procedure that subjects have used in his laboratory:

"Deeply relax all your muscles, beginning at your feet and progressing up to your face. Breathe through your nose. As you breathe out, say the word 'one' silently to yourself. Continue this practice for twenty minutes. You may open your eyes to check the time but do not use an alarm. When you finish, sit quietly for several minutes, at first with your eyes closed and later with your eyes open. The technique should be practiced once or twice daily and not within two hours after any meal, since the digestive processes seem to interfere with the elicitation of the expected change. Permit relaxation to occur at its own pace. With practice, the response should come with little effort. However, people undergoing psychoanalysis of at least two sessions a week experience difficulty in eliciting the response."

According to the doctor, "the great majority of people report feelings of relaxation and freedom from anxiety during the elicitation of the response and during the rest of the day as well. These feelings of well-being are akin to those often noted after physical exercise, but without the attendant physical fatigue."

Benson claims results confirming this finding from a control group of over eighty subjects who participated in a four-month study of the effects of transcendental meditation on high blood pressure.

Benson further observes 1,862 individuals in an investigation completed a questionnaire in which they reported a marked decrease in hard liquor intake, drug abuse, and cigarette smoking after they had begun the elicitation of the relaxation response through the practice of transcendental meditation.

Benson cautions "no person should treat himself for high blood pressure by regularly eliciting the relaxation response. He should use the technique only under the supervision of his physician."

Benson's prescription is posed against the somber backdrop of prevalence of emotional stress in the Western world and especially in the business community, whose members "have been forced to make certain behavioral adjustments to a faster pace and a more pressured life." The penalty for stress may be hypertension (high blood pressure) which predisposes men and women to heart attacks and strokes. These diseases are present in various degrees in from 15 to 33 percent of the adult population, affecting between twenty-three and forty-four million individuals, and account for more than 50 percent of the deaths each year in the United States. Particularly disturbing is that heart attacks and strokes now increasingly affect a younger population.

Benson assures the business community that executives, "victimized by the stressful world they have helped to create, need not accept stress as a necessary component of their existence. The regular use of the relaxation response in our daily lives may counteract the harmful effects of the fight-or-flight response and thereby mitigate these extremely prevalent and dire diseases.

"However, modern Western society has turned away from many of the traditional techniques that elicit the relaxation response, such as prayer. Our society has thus lost an important means of alleviating stress and maintaining equilibrium in a changing world. We can probably greatly benefit by the reintroduction of the relaxation response into our society.

"Because of its far-reaching influence in our society, the business sector could take the lead. For example, programs could be established in which time is made available for employees to practice the relaxation response."

Assertiveness Training: "Don't Say Yes When You Want to Say No"

Do you frequently want to say no to a request from family or friends but find yourself saying yes?

Do you sometimes or often speak up to your spouse but never to your boss?

Do you take refuge in "other people pick on me" and "I don't have the courage to try it" syndrome?

If your answers to these questions are in the affirmative, you suffer from a condition known as "lack of assertion" and need "assertiveness training."

Herbert Fensterheim, a psychologist and clinical associate professor, Cornell University Medical College, holds AT workshops throughout the country. He and his wife, free-lance writer Jean Baer, have written *Don't Say Yes When You Want to Say No.*

The authors claim that AT, a behavior therapy technique, "will help you stand up for your rights, express your feelings, cope with putdowns, lessen your fears and achieve professional goals." AT is based on the premise: "People have learned unsatisfactory forms of behavior that make them unhappy, inhibited, fearful of rejection. They can unlearn these, even if they represent a lifetime pattern."

The book takes the reader on a step-by-step explanation of AT. It suggests the difference between assertion and aggression, how to work out mutually satisfactory decisions in close relationships, how to develop many new friendships, how to control anxieties on the job, and how to improve sexual performance. Many real-life cases are included.

Some concepts advanced by the Fensterheim-Baer team:

Aggression. Do not confuse aggression with assertion. Aggression is an act against others. Assertion is appropriate standing-up for yourself. If you are basically nonassertive, you come on too weak. Because you don't stand up for yourself, you feel hurt, anxious and self-contemptuous. Conversely, you may behave aggressively and come on too strong. Because of various life experiences, you are so filled with hurts and angers that a major core of your psychological being centers around the goal of hurting others, sometimes out of vindictiveness, at other times out of a perceived need to defend yourself. While this aggressive behavior may accomplish your ends temporarily, in most cases it leads to disrupted communication with friends, calls forth counter-aggression from others and tends to make you even more aggressive. Properly assertive behavior, by contrast, leads to a good feeling about yourself even if it does not always result in the accomplishment of your desired goals.

Neurotic Job Goals. Many unassertive people become very concerned about whether or not people like them. They fear that, if they say no to a request, no matter how unreasonable, and speak up firmly, other people will not like them. Maybe they won't. But respect matters far more than liking.

Handling Put-downs. Follow these AT rules: 1) If you feel someone put you down with a remark, you must answer. 2) Take time to think of an effective answer. 3) In most situations, the first sentence of your response should not contain the words, I, me or because. Use of any of these words makes you sound apologetic or defensive.

"Feeling" Talk. Deliberately use the following three pairs of phrases as often as you can: "I like what you said"; "I don't like what you said"; "I like what you did"; "I don't like what you did"; "I want you to"; "I don't want you to." By the practice of "feeling" talk, you learn a new skill of expression of feeling. **The Neurotic Spiral.** You constantly placate others because you fear offending them. You allow others to maneuver you into situations you don't want. You can't express your legitimate wishes. You feel the rights of others are more important than your own. You are self-conscious before superior and authority figures. You are so easily hurt by what others say and do that you constantly inhibit yourself. You feel inferior because you are inferior.

The authors contend that, "of all the tests that reveal your power to be assertive, your handling of love and work reveal the most. To be assertive in either area, you must possess an active orientation and set goals that enhance your self-esteem. But, in the close relationship of love, your aim should be openness, communication and sharing of your whole emotional being. Feelings come first. In the job, the assertive emphasis reverses. Doing comes first. Feeling comes second. Relations with people at work tend to be superficial. The stress in the feelings you express there is more on appropriateness than openness."

Five basic skills are cited for assertion on the job:

1. Think through your work goals, the steps you must take to achieve them and how, in doing this, you can utilize your talents to the fullest possible extent.
2. Ability to do the job; minimizing obstacles that arise in the work situation because you have not mastered the necessary skills for your particular job.
3. Control of your anxieties and fears—inappropriate emotional reactions interfere with work performances. General tensions may produce fatigue, irritability and poor judgment.
4. Good interpersonal relations—you must be able to relate to peers, subordinates and superiors.
5. The art of negotiating the system—knowledge of the job society and the specific skills that will enable you to work within, through or against it to achieve your goals.

Is Primal Therapy Panacea for Emotional, Physical Ills?

In a world of many unresolved values and issues, it's somehow both comforting and disturbing that one man claims to have a firm grasp on the solution of the most elusive of all questions—emotional and physical well-being.

The man is Arthur Janov, Ph.D., clinical psychologist and psychiatric social worker. His contribution to the cure of human ills and to the jargon is Primal Therapy.

A native Californian, he is the director of the Primal Institute, which he founded in 1970, and research director of the Primal Research Laboratory. Both organizations are in Los Angeles near Beverly Hills. Michael Rosenbaum, physician, biochemist, and psychiatrist is associate director of the research program.

Primal Therapy, purporting to be the only cure for psychophysical illness, relates a neurosis or psychosis to the trauma of personal history of early childhood. It helps the patient relive his primal physiological and psychological pains—supposedly often going back to birth pangs—and interpret and resolve their meaning for himself so that, according to Janov, he will never again need therapy. He "discovered" Primal Therapy in 1967 and has copyrighted the term.

Janov has the tolerant air of one who has managed to survive the slings and arrows of the outraged psychiatric-psychological world. He is the author of *The Primal Revolution* and *The Anatomy of Mental Illness.*

His techniques, Janov insists, solve neurotic problems "far faster, far more effectively, far more permanently through the feelings, the actions, the words of the patient himself. Through Primal Therapy, a person can quickly gain awareness of his real feelings and his true needs, giving up the defenses and role-playing that block his capacity for a deeply feeling and satisfactory life. We have helped people overcome many different neurotic symptoms and afflictions from tensions and anxiety to such other complex problems as overweight, stuttering, alcoholism, drug addiction, arthritis, colitis, ulcers, exhibitionism, and homosexuality."

Janov's wife, Vivian, the institute's director of training, admits "only a very small minority of our patients are business executives. That doesn't mean we shouldn't have more of them, but it does mean most executives, who influence many people around them, don't admit to having such problems. They're successful, aren't they? Of course, that's not enough."

A ten-minute sound film shows a forty-five-year-old woman patient, an alcoholic, whining, whimpering, writhing, and screaming on the floor while Janov observes her. He describes the action as "reliving the trauma of being shoved into a world where she was both helpless and defenseless, redirecting memory circuits coded in the brain back to the original pain. The woman's problem is solved and her tension and alcoholism eradicated. She has felt the feeling under the craziness, and the craziness has gone away. Under and after treatment, the patient, not the therapist, is the guru."

The film also depicted the same woman, now smiling and confident, telling Janov she can no longer endure any makeup, she is no more a bleached blonde but is letting her hair go gray—"everything hangs out."

Of over six hundred patients at the institute in the past six years, Janov reports "we have had a 3 to 4 percent failure rate, rather outstanding in the field of psychotherapy."

Some of Janov's provocative contentions in his book:

"Clearly, neurotics and normals can behave exactly alike. They both may be highly efficient on a particular job when measured on a rating scale. But one is loaded with tension and the other is not. A person, who may seem well-adjusted and productive, may be functioning socially while all the time his body is disintegrating from neurotic tension. The normal doesn't pay a price for his functioning.

"Society happens to approve of heterosexual 'macho' behavior, so we tend not to see it is sickness. If he acts out the need for a parent of the opposite sex, he can be a hero—the Namath syndrome. We should be just as concerned about the rise of neurotic heterosexuality as we are about neurotic homosexuality. Both are indices of a sick society.

"Success is evidently an illusion. Like prestige and status, it is no more than someone else's idea about us. . . . Food, sex, money—all are used to quell feelings and are therefore ultimately unfulfilling.

"There are no disease entities called 'addiction' and 'alcoholism.' These are but names of the medicines for pain.

Before patients are placed in therapy, they are asked to stay in a hotel room for from twenty-four to forty-eight hours in complete isolation—no visitors, no phone calls, no books, no TV, no smoking. Inevitably, they suffer rising tension and, "when therapy begins, they are ready to expose their feelings completely and the gates of their early life experiences open little by little."

Patients undergo six months of therapy—three weeks of individual treatment succeeded by group therapy three times a week. A week of follow-up treatment is tacked on. For all this, the cost is $6,000.

The institute has trained mental health professionals as Primal Therapists, requiring them to go through the therapy program as patients before they may be enrolled in seminars, lectures, videotape demonstrations, and supervised work with patients—a regimen of at least one year. The Janovs, who served as therapists for each other, are aggrieved that some other analysts and psychiatrists, whom they have not trained, are "picking up our ideas although we have no control over them. Primal Therapy should not be practiced by any person who is not a graduate of our institute regardless of professional background."

Janov concedes "a mixed response" from the profession. For example, Anthony Storr, a British psychiatrist, says Janov "makes remarks of an unbelievably dogmatic kind—the statement that Primal Therapy is the only cure for neurosis is not only arrogant but demonstrably false." Seemingly unperturbed, Janov retorts: "It would help if he would read my book."

Harvard Class of '49 Turns to Mastering Business of Sex Partnerships

The sex partnership of husband and wife was analyzed and synthesized, deified and demolished, by and for Harvard Business School graduates of the class of '49 and their wives. The combined battlefield and playground was the twenty-fifth reunion in mid-1974.

The unrestrained dialog of the sexual research team of Dr. William H. Masters, director, Reproductive Biology Foundation, St. Louis, and his wife, Virginia E. Johnson, co-director of the twenty-year-old, nonprofit organization, captured rapt attention from the audience. The median age of the '49ers was fifty; of their wives, forty-seven. Masters, in his earlier career an obstetrician, is fifty-nine; Ms. Johnson, fifty.

Harvard B-School alumnus Frank K. Mayers, president, Bristol-Myers, cracked: "We decided we'd better have them now, while there's still hope. The next reunion could be too late."

But the tenor of the Masters-Johnson remarks on "The Next Twenty-five Years—Together" was it's never too late, and doctors who think otherwise "don't know what they're talking about." The sexual scientists pointed out they have corrected dysfunction in men and women from seventy-five to over ninety. Masters, who generally assumes a somber appearance, chuckled with the appreciative gathering when he added: "We have no knowledge of sex after one hundred, but I have every confidence." Ms. Johnson told the middle-aged men and women there is a "use it or lose it syndrome" in sex.

Gail Sheehy, contributing editor, *New York* magazine, which conducted an anonymous survey of the lives of the Harvard wives in relationship to the lives of their husbands, was moderator of a panel commenting on results of the questionnaire entitled "The Last 25 Years—Was It Worth It?" On the woman's sex lives, Ms. Sheehy said the indications were "they may be having it less but enjoying it more, or they're grateful for small favors."

The study was the brainchild of Lee Traub, wife of Bloomingdale's president Marvin S. Traub. She was a panelist together with two other wives of '49ers—Betty Greenfield and Betty Jones. The questionnaire was answered by 241 wives. One of the findings reported by Ms. Traub: 10 percent of the women have strayed from the marital bed with from one to five men, and 20 percent have considered affairs, but "the road to hell is paved with good intentions."

Only 3 percent of the wives owned up to fighting with their husbands— this drew one of the most sustained outbursts of laughter, mainly from the husbands. On average, the women are strong for the free enterprise system, "limp" on women's lib.

Masters and Johnson said that "historical openness of the subject of sexuality and sex—sex is only one of the ways in which to express sexuality —started only twenty years ago. Even fifteen or less years ago, a woman knew sex only as an acceptor—what was done to her. Since then, there has been more understanding among men as to what to do for her. This is leading to greater communication—mutual knowledge and desire on what to do for each other."

Sex, Masters pointed out, "is not just 'go to it.' Somewhere around the age of fifty, sex becomes thought of as you've probably had it, or are beginning to have had it, and it's dirty. But there must be changes in sexual functioning, from the mid-forties on, as there are in breathing, in the function of the bladder, and in your ability to run around the block fast."

Getting up steam, he said that, about midlife, "it takes longer to have sex. What's wrong with that except that the culture thinks there's something wrong with lack of potency? If the man is fearful he will not perform, he's on his way to impotence."

Masters said he always asks the wife who becomes his patient how often she and her husband have intercourse. He never asks the man "because I would get an incredible amount of misinformation." (Much laughter.)

Taking up the woman's role in the partnership, Ms. Johnson reported "the wife's concern is 'What's wrong with me? Am I less attractive, less giving? Am I a reason for the diminution in our sexual activity'?"

Masters looked askance at the wife who says to her husband who's not functioning up to par, " 'It's perfectly all right, but why don't you see a doctor?' (A burst of self-conscious laughter through the room.) And, when the doctor asks the man, 'How old are you?,' that takes care of it."

Masters knows of many couples who have wondered how soon after the husband has had a heart attack they could safely return to normal sexual activities. He derided doctors who have automatically advised such couples: "All right, go ahead, but take it easy."

Ms. Johnson counseled that a hysterectomy need have "very little effect on effectiveness as a woman." About male prostectomy, Masters declared that only one of three surgical procedures—and that the least common—interferes with sexual functioning. This is perineal prostectomy—the surgical incision in the area between the rectum and the scrotum. However, there are a great many more of the first two operations than of the third that leads to impotence.

He deplored the fact that 98 percent of sex manuals are written by men. As he sees it, "how to do it" books and pornography are "two great sources of sex misdirection, misconception, and misinformation." About X-rated movies, Ms. Johnson held that "We do not set ourselves up as judges. Conceivably, there is no special harm in such entertainment or titillation, but most sexual acts depicted are exploitative of each other."

Masters and Johnson are conducting research on homosexuality but are not yet prepared to discuss scientific findings. Nor have they had an opportunity to evaluate, post-surgically, people who have undergone a transsexual change.

Answering questions from the floor, Masters said, "The greatest sex education is Pop coming home from work, patting Mom on the fanny, and having the kids watching and saying to themselves: 'Boy, that's for me some day.' "

Effect of Sex, Marriage Problems on Job Performance

The business executive "who presents a facade of being in full control of every situation" is prey, more than anyone else, to bottled-up sex and marriage problems. The way a man acts in the boardroom may well be an extension of the way he operates in the bedroom.

This is not to minimize the effect of such problems on rank-and-file workers: absenteeism and job performance and productivity often reflect these home difficulties. A conservative estimate is that more than 50 percent of American couples suffer from serious sexual dysfunction exacerbated by inhibitions and taboos that place the entire subject in largely uncharted waters.

This was the message brought by professional counselors who spoke at an all-day conference on "Sex, Marriage, Job Problems: An Exploration," at C.W. Post Center of Long Island University.

A key speaker at the seminar was Kathleen Vernam, representative counselor for the Family Service Program at Xerox Corp., Rochester, N.Y. Ms. Vernam, who has a master's degree in social work, joined the organization, a unit of the Family Service Association of America, in 1973. The association is a private agency primarily funded by the United Way campaign (the Community Chest in Rochester).

Xerox began its counseling program under contract to Family Service in 1970. Ms. Vernam's work at Xerox is confined to all levels of employees of the Information Technology Group. In seeking to maximize communication and minimize job pressures, Family Service conducts counseling as part of the training of incoming Xerox employees and also engages in marriage and family counseling. It advises employees under severe emotional stress where to go for psychiatric and psychological help. Family Service participates in week-long seminars for new and incumbent foremen to help them put their people at ease in discussing personal problems.

Employees are seen at the Xerox medical department or at the Family Service facilities. The service is voluntary, confidential and free.

Principal speakers were Dr. Leon Zussman, gynecologist, and Dr. Shirley Zussman, psychologist. They are a husband-and-wife team who are, respectively, director and co-director of the Human Sexuality Center at the Long Island Jewish-Hillside Medical Center in New Hyde Park and are also in the private practice of sex therapy in Manhattan. Leon Zussman teaches at Mount

Sinai School of Medicine and Shirley Zussman is professor of human sexuality and marriage relations at Finch College.

Leon Zussman said in part:

- An executive has to maintain a facade of confidence, pleasantness and control and, therefore, can't readily get rid of his tensions. He has the idea he's under pressure to score in bed as he does in golf, bridge and his balance sheet.
- The man on the assembly line may be able to get rid of his aggression on the job but only for the moment; this doesn't solve his sexual problem.
- Sexual or marital problems are concealed because of embarrassment, guilt or fear. It's the preoccupation with sexual performance that's bad. Every man should have an occasional, normal episode of impotency. It's only when impotency is chronic that the man and his wife have a real problem.
- Proof that sex is a healthy birthright that should be enjoyed by men and women throughout their lives is the fact that a male baby may be born with an erection; a female baby, with a lubricated vagina.
- The trouble is that sex problems are hidden, not frankly discussed with a professional consultant or, alternatively, a personnel manager or other company employee trained to draw out the truth about the most personal problems of associates.

Shirley Zussman's advice:

- Sexuality is the way we feel about ourselves in all ways. Good sex lives have a ripple effect on the way we deal with our children and business and social friends and acquaintances as well as with our spouses.
- Probably more than anything else, a sex problem will be solved if men and women touch, caress, hold hands—all part of sexuality—and otherwise communicate with each other, not necessarily toward culmination in intercourse. They should not allow the pressures of society to work out in anger or withdrawal on their part—actions and attitudes that interfere with best performance, whether in the home or on the job.

The New Hyde Park center's program was started four years ago with a $1 million grant from an anonymous businessman. This was the first hospital-and-community-based project for the treatment of sexual difficulties in the country. The Zussmans view Greater New York as the community they serve.

Other hospital-based sex therapy clinics are Cornell at New York Hospital, New York Medical College at Flower and Fifth Avenue Hospitals, Johns Hopkins Medical School in Baltimore, University of Minnesota Medical School in Minneapolis and University of California in San Francisco. Zussman quotes Masters' charge that only 50 of the estimated 5,000 sex therapy clinics in the United States are "reputable."

Giving full credit to Masters and Johnson for their pioneering roles, Zussman says a major difference between his program and Masters' is the Human Sexuality Center's concentration on the New York area whereas the

St. Louis institution draws from the world at large. People, who come to the Zussmans in daytime or evening sessions on a weekly basis for three months, ordinarily come from home. The Zussmans feel that patients should live within the framework of their everyday business, family and social lives "with the usual pressures, frustrations and gratifications from many sources." Masters and Johnson, they point out, believe that patients should remove themselves from their home environments, which are generally some distance from St. Louis, for the duration of treatment on a daily basis for about two weeks.

The Zussmans insist on both husband and wife at the sessions because of their conviction "there is no way to treat a person with a sexual dysfunction unless the partner is directly involved in the therapy." Ms. Zussman observes that "It's usually the female who originates the idea of going to the center. This may be because the woman traditionally admits weaknesses, but men are supposed to be strong."

Simultaneous treatment of a married couple by a dual sex therapy team —the four-way approach—was made popular by Masters and Johnson. It is based on the assumptions that 1) treatment of a sexual dysfunction requires the involvement of both partners and 2) a female is more likely to understand female sexual arousal and response, while a male is more likely to understand male sexual functioning. Conjoint therapy, as it is called, serves to reduce conscious and unconscious distortions that each person tends to present. Each patient has "a friend at court."

Initial physical examinations are given each patient after which the therapy is all verbal. The examination is carried on in the presence of the other member of the marital unit as well as of the therapy team. The role of the non-examining therapist is that of encouraging communication, reducing anxiety, and dispelling myths and misconceptions about anatomy, physiology and sexual functioning.

"In perhaps 99 percent of our cases, the dysfunction is psychologically based," says Zussman.

"We find that couples often make love only after they are exhausted from the day's routine and after the late night news. This is the most anti-erotic mood in which they could put themselves. They should, instead, try for more love in the afternoon.

"The notion that older people are not supposed to enjoy a sex life is foolish and naive. A recent study at Duke University concluded that 65 percent of men between the ages of 65 and 70 participate in regular and enjoyable intercourse and that between 10 and 20 percent of men past 80 still have sexual relations on a regular basis.

"Of course, if one partner wants to make love once a year, and the other once a night—that's a problem.

"Even if a couple should separate after therapy, the time is not necessarily wasted. They part on a mature level rather than in the throes of anger. Maybe they have gained some self-knowledge that they can bring to another relationship."

The prime job of the sex therapist, "the giant step forward," Ms. Zussman adds, "is to get couples to open up to each other in communication about their common problems. There has to be a give-and-take in listening and understanding the other's needs and desires so that inhibitions may be broken down, marital conflicts reduced, closer relationships established and more marriages saved. An excited partner is the best aphrodisiac."

Of 200 couples, ranging in age from 19 to 77, who have come to the Human Sexuality Center, according to Ms. Zussman, 77 percent improved both their marriage and sexual relations and 82 percent improved one or the other in the 15 sessions the Zussmans consider necessary for most people. Follow-ups of results indicate some retrogression to an average improvement of 68 percent. The Zussmans see some couples who have relationships although not married to each other. Fees are set on a sliding scale dependent on individual or family income.

The Zussmans don't claim they can help all patients. For example, a man with diabetes will be impotent 50 percent of the time and nothing can be done about it. High blood pressure, anemia and thyroid and metabolic changes may be reflected in sex problems. On the other hand, the man who has had a prostate operation "has not necessarily reached the end of sexuality. Almost everybody can be helped, even paraplegics and the mentally retarded."

This sex therapy team also offers a sexual enrichment program for individual couples and small groups without particular problems in this area.

The center held eight seminars for professionals. In 1975, the Zussmans gave a seminar on human sexuality at the Columbia University School of Social Work. The program may be expanded into a year-round course as the first of its kind in a school of social work.

Forty French doctors visited the center to learn about sex therapy. This leads Zussman to observe that "50 million Frenchmen could be wrong." The center has also drawn medical groups from Italy, Switzerland, the Philippines, Canada, Denmark and Holland.

"Shared Participation": Key to Riddle of Human Behavior?

People in general want a greater share of participation in what goes on in their companies, organizations, and in other things that affect their working and private lives. However, more often than not, this is denied them except in token form.

Ego, self-interest, inferiority complex, and prejudice are principal obstacles to communication between one person and another and among groups of all kinds. These human feelings minimize sensitivity to others' needs and feelings and serve to shatter bars to mutual understanding.

Warren E. Avis, founder and former owner of the Avis Rent-A-Car system, offers his plan of "Shared Participation" as a key to the riddle of human behavior.

In Shared Participation, men and women, who may or may not know one another, are brought together in a workshop to discuss the challenges they face from a fresh perspective of ideas they have previously submitted anonymously. A group might include a businessman, a housewife, a policeman, and so on. Cary Grant, a friend of Avis, was a participant in one of these sessions. If the members do not have sufficient experience or knowledge about a particular problem to be solved, outside experts are brought in. Shared Participation, Avis emphasizes, has nothing to do with group therapy but is solely a problem-solving device that stimulates creativity and results in decision by consensus. However, he points out, the effect is therapeutical because participants experience "a feeling of elation, camaraderie, and enhanced self- and group-respect."

Avis further explains the process:

"Everybody in this world is 'them' to somebody else. If you're a corporate executive, you're 'them' to the union people in your company; if you're a blue-collar worker, or even a low-echelon white-collar worker, you're 'them' to the guys in the executive suites; parents are 'them' to children and vice versa. We'd be well on our way to better lives and a better society if we could band together to turn all our 'thems' into one big 'we.'

"Shared Participation is just what the name implies—a system of pulling all the 'thems' together into a multi-experienced group that can operate as a cohesive, comprehensive decision-making task force. If two heads working together under a proper structure are better than one, why not put ten, twenty, or fifty together?

"Members of a group contribute information and suggest solutions to a specific problem. The solutions are submitted in 'secret ballots.' Solutions from persons untrained in a field are discussed as fully as those put forth by experts. The solution reached—a voluntary consensus of the group—often is not one of the original suggestions at all but a new one or an amalgam that evolves out of the ensuing discussions.

"But it is always one in which all the members are involved, one they are committed to. It owes its success to the fact that nobody in the group knows who suggested what. The reasoning is that a genuinely good idea is often lost when members of an organization are playing power politics, taking ego trips, performing roles, or seeking status. If you know you can get fired for criticizing your boss' idea, you'll think twice. But, if you didn't know it's his, you will give your criticism freely. And if you are a boss, you will be much more inclined to accept suggestions whose origins you're not sure of, because your status weapons will have been taken away from you."

Avis views this interacting process as a positive program for handling executive-employee, male-female, racial, religious, husband-wife and generation-gap conflicts. He extends the philosophy to government, school, and church problems.